Praise for *Vanilla Beans & Brodo*

'The subtitle of *Vanilla Beans & Brodo* is "Real Life in the Hills of Tuscany" – and it jolly well is. She actually describes the village in magnificent terms and it makes me want to go there' Simon Calder, *Independent*

'Another tale of outsiders making a new life in Italy would need to be something special. Luckily, Isabella Dusi's account of her acceptance of the proud, warm-hearted natives . . . is absolutely captivating' *Irish Times*

'Full of the passions and pleasures of life in the midst of a warm-hearted and proudly independent community in the Tuscan hills' *Daily Express*

'Enticing' *The Times*

'Communicates well the rhythm of time-honoured activities in a close-knit community, which, over the centuries, has defended itself against the Florentines, Sienese, Spanish and French' *Sunday Times*

'Dusi's account of her assimilation into the customs, people and food of her new home in Tuscany is the stuff of daydreams' *Woman & Home*

'Dusi does far more for Tuscany than Peter Mayle did for Provence in her fascinating look at day-to-day life in the Italian hills' *Lancashire Evening Post*

'Deeply satisfying' *Doncaster Star*

'Dusi tells the story of twelve months in this remarkable world, and does so with such evocative and glowing prose that she transports the reader to her new found home' *Wigan Evening Post*

'It is, without doubt, a joy' *Dorset Echo*

About the Author

After many years working in Australia in interior design, Isabella Dusi decided to move to Italy with her husband Luigi. Living permanently in Montalcino, they now work in the travel business. She is also the author of *Vanilla Beans & Brodo*.

Bel Vino

A Year of Sundrenched Pleasure
Among the Vines of Tuscany

Isabella Dusi

POCKET
BOOKS

LONDON • SYDNEY • NEW YORK • TORONTO

First published in Great Britain by Pocket, 2004
An imprint of Simon & Schuster UK Ltd
A CBS COMPANY

Copyright © Isabella Dusi, 2004

Illustrations copyright © Barbara Horne, 2004

This book is copyright under the Berne Convention
No reproduction without permission
® and © 2000 Simon & Schuster Inc. All rights reserved
Pocket & Design is a registered trademark of Simon & Schuster Inc

The right of Isabella Dusi to be identified as author of this work
has been asserted in accordance with sections 77 and 78 of the
Copyright, Designs and Patents Act, 1988.

3 5 7 9 10 8 6 4

Simon & Schuster UK Ltd
1st Floor
222 Gray's Inn Road
London WC1X 8HB

www.simonandschuster.co.uk

Simon & Schuster Australia
Sydney

A CIP catalogue record for this book is available from the British Library

ISBN 978-0-7434-7844-1

Typeset by SX Composing DTP, Rayleigh, Essex
Printed in Great Britain by
CPI Cox & Wyman, Reading, RG1 8EX

To my grandchildren
Brodie John and Breanna Jade

Contents

Illustrations

Acknowledgements and Sources

The Ingegnere, Signor Guido Padelletti
Signora Francesca Colombini Cinelli
Signor Andrea Costanti
Signor John and Signora Pamela Mariani
Mayor Massimo Ferretti

Anderson, Burton, *Biondi Santi*, Union Design
Biondi Santi, Franco, *Il Brunello di Montalcino, il Passato ed il Futuro*, F. Biondi Santi
Bonucci, Bruno, *Montalcino Pietre e Storia*, Editrice Donchisciotte
— *Il Sammichele di Castiglione del Bosco*, La Piazza
The Brothers of the Abbey of Sant' Antimo, *A Stone That Sings*, Edizioni Cantagalli
Caprioli, Ivo, *Diecimila Anni di Vita*, Grafica La Proposta, Montalcino
Caprioli, Ivo and Francesco Pescatori, *Artigianato: Commercio e Attività Diverse nel Borghetto*, Grafica La Proposta, Montalcino
Carle, Lucia, *La Patria Locale*, Regione Toscana, Giunta Regionale
Christie, Neil, *The Lombards*, Blackwell Publishers
Mantaut, Elena, *Citta Murate del Veneto*, Bell'Italia
Raffaelli, Ilio, *Montalcino . . . Collina d'Italia*, Type Service Editore, Massa
— *Creatività Popolare Montalcinesi*, Nencini Editore

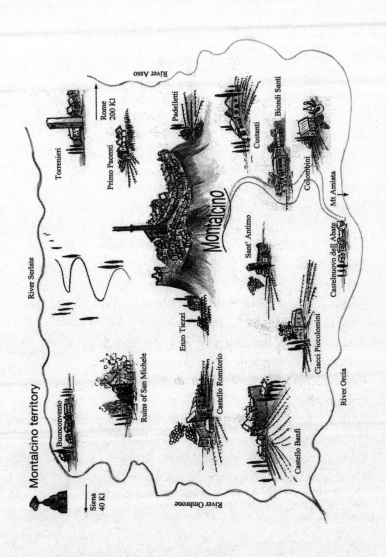

CHAPTER ONE

The Monks' Sandals

Following the contours of the wooded crag the pebbly track curves downwards, then climbs steadily into oak woods. An hour crossing from hill to hill drifts into two. My knees adjust to the hilly terrain, and my mind is soothed by the silence in this shadowy oak coppice. For the first kilometre or two I have skirted ranks of vines surrounding stone farmhouses and stepped stealthily along a rocky track, hoping not to rouse sleeping dogs. Then a pack of three, sensing my intrusion, erupts from a barn and races towards me, baying in a frenzy at my boldness as I hurry along the flanks of their vineyard. Nothing stirs in the farmhouse. Nor from the shuttered windows further on where other dogs, alerted by the barking back along the track, lie in wait, heads raised and ears at full cock. Beside a paddock of grazing horses the track dog-legs into a thicket before sinking into a dark glade, giving me a last glimpse of the bell towers above a walled Tuscan village strung along the ridge. Montalcino, my home.

My eyes at last accustomed to the dappled light, I pick my way along the eroded bed of a ditch where a trickle of water ripples over stones and mossy logs. I suspect I have hastened to follow this remote track too early in the season. Stooping to inspect fresh droppings beside the water, I gaze at animal tracks in the mud – the hoofs of a wild boar that has still to retreat into the dense underbrush for the mating season. Hoping this Tuscan cinghiale is as reluctant to show itself as I am to confront it, I quicken my pace and do not look back until the track rises abruptly from the glade and takes me into an oak coppice where small birds swoop skittishly about, diving among the branches, twittering one to the other, confidence sky high.

I work my way through scree and up to a rounded hill crowned with tall pines. At last the underbrush thins and I breathe in the evocative smell of damp earth and pine needles. Bursting suddenly into view, an abbey sits in a gloomy valley where woods and undergrowth give way to green meadows. The sun has not yet touched the abbey, which pleases me, because my arrival before the sun promises that my lonely dawn start will not be unrewarded. I follow the downward path and plough into the woods, shut in close by hills once more; shadows deepen as the track descends.

After a couple of silent hours trekking through the Tuscan hills with little but encounters of this nature and my thoughts for company, I'm almost sorry that in a few hundred metres the track peters out. Walking between ear-flicking and unfettered cattle, their breath steaming in the morning air, I hurry across the meadow towards the Abbey of Sant' Antimo, nestled pale in the Valley of Starcia.

Certain that the abbey doors will be open at first light, I don't intend to delay my entry, but I halt mid-stride to capture an overwhelming moment. Reaching into the sky, the abbey is a visible layering of architectural signatures through the centuries, yet there is a harmony to the whole that unites the hand of the architect to the wilderness of the valley.

I scan the abbey grounds, straining to hear the human sounds penetrating the stillness. Where the glory of God is sanctified, his Tuscan servants thought to plant an olive grove. Four wooden ladders are wedged in the branches of an olive tree. Chatting monks are visible from the knees down; white gowns flap around their ankles but their shapes are immersed in foliage. It is a quick exchange; words cease and work resumes. Strapped sandals, the sight of which make me smile, offer their feet no purchase on worn rungs. The monk nearest me rocks back and forth as he saws, causing his heels to drop over the back of the rung and then push forward, sinking his toes into hollows in the leather as his sandals buckle and bend under the strain. A cloaked arm pushes a cut branch into the air and it thumps to the ground. Four monks in one olive tree; one slices with a machete, one supports a doomed branch, one saws at the heart of the tree and the fourth reaches out and drops the pruned branch to the

3

grass. Hessian sacks, bulging with twigs and leaves and knotted roughly at the neck with a length of rope, lean against a tree which has been pruned this morning. In orderly groves the trees follow one another in lines over the hill, each tree a precisely calculated distance from its neighbour. But these olive trees were planted across the abbey grounds at random centuries ago, their purpose as much to provide tethering points for vines as to pick and crush olives for the abbey's oil-burning lamps. Gnarled trunks contort and twist; it is as if each tree has agonized about the direction in which to grow. High among the branches where the monks are at work spring growth is at a spurt and wispy tendrils bear double-fronted grey-green leaves. More than one of these olive trees has stood here for a thousand years.

Lying beside the hessian sacks, three unlabelled bottles of wine rest one against the other, probably wine made at the abbey. Monks have a measure of winemaking experience, judging from historical frescoes in which they discard sandals and stomp purple grapes in open vats. They are the first documented winemakers of Montalcino, producing a necessity for life that centuries into the future would bring fame and wealth to this corner of Tuscany. The wine they made hundreds of years ago was sweet white Moscadello, not the red Brunello di Montalcino that has carried the name of the village to wine lovers all over the world. Medieval monks preferred the newly fermented juice of grapes, whether white or red. And it was safer for them to drink new wine than old, which was a health risk, and sold cheaply . . . although nowadays we call it *aged* and the pricing structure is reversed. Even rainwater channelled into a well, or worse, a mountain stream made doubtful by the distasteful work of peasant farmers and wandering boar, could not guarantee an uncontaminated beverage. I cannot tell if the

4

bottles contained white or red wine, but I can see that they are empty.

The monks are stirring. I watch them climb down the ladders, each descending foot groping unsteadily for the lower rung below. On the grass at last, white hoods hide their faces; only by studying the sandals of each monk do I know them. Leaving the chopped twigs and sawn branches where they fell, the four monks unsettle the tapered ladders and hurry across the grass, carrying their tools in the direction of the next tree.

The bronze bells in the tower begin to peal, and a moment later the bell in the village above the abbey announces the hour with a clear and gentle chime. The two bells in the tower draw my eyes back to the abbey as the first beam of the rising sun climbs over the hill in search of the Valley of Starcia. Washing buttery gold over the topmost edge of the bell tower, a diaphanous light, like a delicate shawl, creeps down the tower and traces a warm pinkish bronze across the travertine walls. A tangential flush dances across the travertine and onyx as if the abbey were hung with sparkling jewels. The bells swing across the tower, a warning chime rings solid, and in the fleeting passage of a moment, before the bells swing back, a powerful sun pierces the pale dawn light, breaks the spell, and sunshine floods unchecked over the Abbey of Sant' Antimo, reaching into the woods that brought me here.

Turning to see if the monks shared this divine moment, I am surprised to see they have not begun work on another olive tree. The ladders lie upon the grass. The monks have vanished. Clamouring bells command from the tower, calling them to Lauds.

A brotherhood of monks has inhabited the Abbey of Sant' Antimo since the eighth century. Not continuously, indeed there have been grave moments, some lasting centuries, when the temptation of worldly sin overtook the spiritual calling of monks to a life in seclusion. The Starcia Valley, close to a Roman road and nine kilometres from the village of Montalcino, was chosen thirteen centuries ago to raise an abbey to the glory of God, and to house meditating monks. By medieval times the abbey's coffers were filled with the tributes of pilgrims on their journey to the city of Rome. These pious travellers stumbled along the old Via Clodia, the mountain track that brought me to this enchanting valley to witness the rising of the sun. White-hooded monks, or brothers, through the centuries, have chosen to nourish the spirit and renounce the world at this abbey, but it is apparent that the world, at least the nearby world in which Luigi and I dwell among winegrowers and village folk in Montalcino, is not compliantly willing to acquit the monks of a lingering temporal hurt. A curious, provocative rhyme is often recited within the walls of Montalcino, hinting at bitter dealings in the past not yet forgotten or pardoned, and most assuredly, unforgivable: 'What Siena could not do in a decade, the monks of Sant' Antimo did in half a morning.'

On the carved portal, as I step across stone flags worn smooth by the passing feet of pilgrims, geometric foliage entwines and loops across the monolithic lintel above my head. A stone rabbit turns his back, crouching on his haunches, but a menacing lion bares his teeth and jeers, blinking in the sunlight. Moving inside, I glide down the aisle under the gaze of almond shaped eyes and too large ears protruding from heads glaring from friezes and roundels on travertine and onyx pillars.

I sink on to a polished pew and watch a lone monk in white hood and cape, hands and wrists tucked cosily into flowing sleeves, enter and begin preparations for the coming of the brothers. He places a chalice covered with a square of white lace on the altar. Backing and bowing down the altar steps, he turns and deposits a song book on each rostrum behind which two rows of monks will stand. The silence is broken by the dull slap of sandals padding across stone flags as his brothers, heads bowed, file one behind each other into the abbey, momentarily bending a knee to genuflect at the altar. With a swish of his gown, each takes his place, head lowered. Moments of stillness pass; they turn to face each other, bowing deeply from the waist. The brothers are ready to begin.

Two voices, one from each row, split the silence, rising up to lead the first chant of the new day. In sombre harmony they gather strength in numbers as one by one the brothers join the melody until all have raised their voices. The resounding notes, magnifying in the emptiness of the abbey, affirm the primacy of God. For the second time on this new morning I am the sole witness to a moment of divine beauty. Sunbeams which penetrated the valley minutes ago shaft through a window assigned its arched perfection by a medieval mason. The sunlight slants around the apse, dappling lightly on the hoods and capes of chanting brothers. The crystalline notes of praise chase one another in the faultless medieval acoustics. The soaring walls of chiselled stone become hollow vessels filled to the brim with song and, unable to absorb any more ringing praise, seem to return each note to its white-hooded sender. I sit motionless on the pew, gazing into a veil of dancing sunbeams, listening to melodious plainsong reverberate from the singing stones.

A handful of monks have found their spiritual home at the abbey. Among them are Fra Domenico, Fra Andrea and Fra Giancarlo, but this is not now a closed order, rather, it is a brotherhood that is restoring the once abandoned monastery and its cell-like rooms, as well as ministering to the spiritual needs of those in search of God. Although it stands alone in the hollow of the valley, Sant' Antimo is no longer isolated from the world. For pilgrims who foolishly forgo the rising of the sun in the Valley of Starcia, blissful moments in solitude are impossible to capture.

Blinking my way out into the blinding sunlight, my feet sound like those of a buffalo as they crush the gravel. I peep over the fence enclosing the monastery to watch for the first monk to emerge through the arch nearest the Chapter House. One by one they spill into the courtyard, sandals scattering pebbles.

Had there been continuous habitation of the abbey through the centuries it is plausible the abbot would now be the wealthy proprietor of the rows of vineyards that encroach ever closer to the abbey grounds. The abbots of ages past grew rich from *Crocus sativus*, the pretty lilac flower from which saffron threads are harvested. Densely planted in the courtyard, it required dedicated labour – something meditating monks did not lack – because the crocus flowers for only twenty days. With nimble fingers, from each tiny flower thin threads were lightly plucked early in the morning, as soon as the petals opened, then quickly toasted to a burnt sienna hue. Saffron was a form of monetary exchange, one of the commodities that brought fabulous wealth to Venetian merchants who sailed in galleys to the east to trade in exotic spices. Venetian importation of saffron from the orient inadvertently contributed to the abandonment of cultivation at abbeys like Sant' Antimo. There is no saffron in the courtyard now. Youngish bespectacled Fra Giancarlo, who is from France, decided to switch to lavender perhaps as a sentimental reminder of his homeland. Fragrant blue-mauve lavender is growing into a sprawling hedge.

Living communally at the abbey, chanting Gregorian praise and cultivating lavender is not the extent of the temporal and spiritual vocation of the brothers. In the 1200s monks tended to pray and work in isolation, withdrawing from the wickedness of the world, but today they have chosen pastoral care, not only for those who pass in pilgrimage, or on a less holy mission, but also at parish churches, including those at Montalcino. On Sunday morning Fra Giancarlo or Fra Domenico find a faithful congregation awaiting Mass in our village. Two or three brothers always come to Montalcino on Friday morning, because that is market day, when outlying parishioners are in the village, eager to commune. I have come to recognize three or four of the brothers because market day seems to be a weekly diversion they relish. Every Friday their sandals are a source of fascination for me, and, knowing the monks' faces, if not all their names, I cannot resist surreptitiously glancing at their feet to see if I can identify the hooded brother by his sandals. Fra Andrea's sandals are so moulded around his bony feet that his toes are embedded in hollows, which is why I smiled knowingly when I recognized him by his feet as he rocked back and forth on the ladder in the olive tree. The constant mending of the pair worn by Fra Domenico has necessitated the improvising of thick brown thread with which the ankle strap is crudely bound to his right sandal, with stitching resembling coarse rope chain.

The brothers are not returning to the olive trees. I think they are heading into the refectory for breakfast. A brother sets his heel at an angle in the gravel and bends down, poking his fingers below the straps. I am too far away to identify his sandals, but now his hood is down. Fra Domenico lifts his foot and shakes away annoying stones. The workshop where the brothers have their sandals mended, if the need is beyond that of tinkering with a hammer and a few tacks after vespers, is in Montalcino. In all probability, Montalcino is where the first pair of monkish, sensibly strapped, sturdy brown leather sandals was crafted because the village has a cobbling history going back centuries. Luciano is our last artisan shoemaker, a diligent calzolaio with a tiny workshop, nothing more than a wooden bench resting unsteadily in front of a cut-down chair, above which swings a bare lightbulb from the end of a length of wire tacked along a chestnut beam. Both bench and chair are concealed behind a narrow pane of glass hung with a tattered yellow curtain, which you would never suspect you were passing as you wandered the main thoroughfare or sat outside with your caffè. A calzolaio like Luciano does not only repair sandals and shoes, he once also fashioned new ones from tanned hides. 'I began to learn my trade in 1961,' he told me, 'and a decade earlier, when I was a boy, there were sixty Montalcinesi making and mending shoes. The hides were traded from the Tuscan Maremma and tanners cured leather down at the springs . . . there was plenty of work for all of us. One of our shoemakers even went to Rome and designed shoes for the Queen of England.'

When I require a quick repair to the heel of a shoe or the shortening of a handbag strap, Luciano invites me to wait while he punches and taps. I sit uncomfortably beside his bench on a chair that rocks uncontrollably because Luciano, at some moment of frustration, has sawn the legs so that customers must balance at a lower height than his cut-down chair, which means I am so near the floor that my knees poke inelegantly towards my nose. While he taps away I marvel at the ornamented folly he has created through the decades. Crammed into overflowing shelves, deposited around the floor, and spilling from cardboard boxes are scraps from leather hides, steel heels and leather soles, sharp tacks and blunt studs in collapsing boxes, a bronze cow bell waiting for a new strap, jam jars of glue, and on the floor a heap of wooden forms for shaping farmers' boots and delicate slippers for a grand signora. Black and brown laces drape over a nail and dangle on the bench, bits of wire and crooked extracted tacks lie scattered over unopened letters. There is not a square inch on his bench which is not littered with the evidence of his trade ... with a few weird additions, like balls of string, electrical plugs, and a couple of deer horns. The unmended shoes from the feet of the Montalcinesi lie anywhere he can find a space for them; every imaginable size and shape including bulky farm boots, shiny black shoes for priests, and sensible low-heeled village shoes for the women. His tools are the same he began with forty years ago. A lesina, a wooden-handled tool with a long hook for pulling threads, a fornellino, which is a tiny oven for heating a block of wax for polishing leather, nimble pliers and dainty steel-headed hammers.

Luciano, in his Aladdin's cave, has been concealed by the tattered curtain for more than four decades, ensuring the feet of the Montalcinesi are well shod. In this absorbing atmosphere I always come away with some interesting anecdote about his life behind this wooden bench. 'Luciano,' I asked incredulously, not able to withhold my curiosity while precariously balanced as he tacked a new heel on my shoe. 'What is this for? Are you making a scrubbing brush?' Sitting on his bench was a bundle of black bristles tied with a piece of string. 'I'll show you,' was his curt reply. Withdrawing a bristle about as long as his hand from the bundle and holding it in one hand while running the fingers of his other across the tip, he sensed rather than saw where to apply faint pressure, and, before my eyes, the bristle split in two. Taking a length of string a hair's breadth fine, he then proceeded to weave the string and split bristles. 'Now watch,' he instructed, but I was already mesmerized. He slid a new sole out of a stack at his elbow, an upper from another, and said: 'A needle is too solid, too inflexible for this work, so I use woven bristles.' Pushing a tiny hole through the leather, he deftly pulled the bristle through, over and under, gradually sewing the upper to the sole in rhythmic loops. 'Where do you get the bristles from?' Immediately I wished I hadn't asked for the answer is obvious. 'From a hunter. A friend pulls the bristles from the neck of a cinghiale, because that is where the hairs are stiff and strong. This bundle is from yesterday's hunt.' The sandals Luciano repairs so frequently for Fra Domenico are crudely sewn with wild boar bristles.

Our birth dates are no more than a week apart, yet Luciano belongs to a world gone long ago. Flashing images of the fashioning of my life, youthful adventures travelling the world, an interior design career dashing around in aeroplanes, fitting out sky-scraper towers and luxury resorts, I pictured myself rushing through one commission after another in a frenzy to be successful enough to be able to afford the finest Italian handmade leather shoes. Luciano is not dissatisfied with his life spent hammering away on his last at his bench in the village where he was born, surrounded by the clutter of his trade. Content to be mending shoes for his friends and sewing straps back on bedraggled sandals for Fra Domenico and the other brothers of Sant' Antimo, he had no need to search for anything else. I was driving myself half crazy, propelled into an ambitious world, super girl, super mum and super woman, and all the while Luciano was sitting at his bench crafting my coveted leather shoes in a walled village in the hills of Tuscany.

CHAPTER TWO

Four Cats on a Terracotta Roof

At ten minutes to seven a ripple of anxiety courses through the groups gathered in the garden opposite the wall where the bus is stationary. Twenty youngsters who live in the village are understandably anguished. Tension heightens when they are joined by another ten as mothers, tugging collars round their necks to camouflage frilly nightwear, career to a halt and the young who live on the farms and out among the vineyards leap from cars. Thirty youngsters, some from my neighbourhood of the village, dart back and forth, prowling around the locked blue bus that should be on its way round the medieval walls right this minute, carrying them away from the hill on which Montalcino rises. They are at the start of their morning journey to college or university in Siena and Florence, but if the bus does not carry them down the valley to Buonconvento on time they will miss the morning train. It seems that the bus driver is nowhere to be found.

Even at this early hour the locked blue one is not the only bus beside the garden wall. The bus from Mount Amiata has brought those that live in the hamlets on the slopes of the mountain down to the village, and the smaller yellow bus which fetches the little ones who go to school in Montalcino from nearby farms and the village of Castelnuovo del Abate is here as well; later it will set off on the first school pick-up for the morning. Two uniformed drivers languidly puff on cigarettes behind trees opposite Bar Prato. I watch a group of youngsters, among whom I recognize Samuele and Filippo, race over and alert them to the locked bus that should have left minutes ago. Uninterested, the drivers wave their arms imprecisely towards Bar Prato, but the youngsters insist the bar doesn't open until seven o'clock, so they are certain the driver cannot be tossing down espresso and munching brioche. Running to the police office, Samuele tackles Andrea, but the yawning policeman, cap tilted back, shakes his head; he has not seen anybody. Mario the sweeper has been labouring in Via Mazzini since six o'clock, swishing at butts in the cracks between stone slabs with his twig and brush broom, but he, too, indicates that nobody has passed up this cobbled road in half an hour. 'Where the hell is he?'

questions Samuele in despair. Samanta has a bright idea. She lives in my neighbourhood, too. I recognize the faces of almost all the youngsters who live in the village, but some are members of other neighbourhoods so I do not know all of their names. 'Do you know his mobile number?' Samanta bristles frostily at one of the smoking drivers who at last exhibits interest. 'Si, si, good idea!' He pulls out his phone, quickly punching in the numbers. 'It's ringing . . . I can hear it ringing! He's somewhere near, listen!' Samanta gestures towards the bus and in a flash ten fists are hammering on the door. 'Filippo! Come over here, let me stand on your shoulders, hoist me up so I can see in the window.' Filippo bends and Samuele clambers on his shoulders, then Filippo straightens and, wobbling unsteadily, Samuele rises. Cupping his hands around his eyes he leans forward and peers inside the dusty rear window of the bus. He drums his fists on the glass and screams: 'Cretino, you cretin . . . svegliati . . . wake up!' A few seconds pass. Half a dozen others are soon hoisted on to shoulders and with all the thumping and rattling on the glass, and a plethora of wicked abuse, the driver, stretched along the rear seat, sound asleep, opens his eyes which meet a host of furious faces. 'Cretino!' they screech at him. 'We're going to miss the train. For this you can drive us all the way to Florence. What a stronzo! Wake up, you moron!'

Grabbing jackets they had tossed aside while they hunted for the driver, the students race to the wall to fetch school bags and, dragging them towards the bus, fiery eyes follow the driver as he stumbles up the aisle and slouches behind the wheel. At last the creaking door unfolds but the menacing students are gearing up for retribution. He starts the engine, defending himself from a barrage of insults by raising an open hand in a pleading gesture, while rolling back his eyes and scowling sheepishly. Each student hurls abuse at him as they struggle aboard and, one after another, sling bags of books along the aisle and collapse into a seat. This bus is not going to reach Buonconvento before the train unless this guilt-ridden driver knows a shortcut down the mountain. Perhaps he will drive them all the way to Siena and then on to Florence.

From a bench in the garden I watch the bus chugging up the hill on its way round the walls. Volatile exchanges such as this are not unusual among Tuscans who live in close-knit communities like Montalcino. The driver lives on the hill, and all the students know him personally, and his mother and father, they know all his aunts and uncles, even his grandparents. To unaccustomed ears and eyes wild accusations and ugly threats almost warrant the summoning of the law, but in Montalcino histrionic displays seem to form part of each day. Witnessing this early morning theatre on the heels of drama at midnight last night at Pianello headquarters, experience is teaching me to maintain a generous measure of perspective when volatile voices rise into verbal abuse.

Each of the four quartieri, or neighbourhoods, namely Travaglio, Ruga, Borghetto and Pianello (of which Luigi and I are members), holds functions in their sede, or headquarters, throughout the year. Occasionally, but admittedly not frequently, the four neighbourhoods join together for a special event. It is more likely that the event will be one of two passionately contested archery tournaments staged each year on the campo between the four quartieri. Archery brings the four quartieri together, not in friendship but rather with loyal territorial pride. This should not be looked upon as a day of fun-filled competition. The emotion-packed tournament day is filled with a fierce passion to triumph. But as well as fulfilling an emotional need, supporting our archers and trainer, each of the quartiere headquarters is a gathering place, where the very young and the young, the not so young and the elderly, come together in a kind of territorial or neighbourhood kinship. It is a social organization that goes back many centuries, established in Montalcino before the year 1300. For instance, if you were born in Borghetto, that becomes your quartiere, by territorial possession.

Last night Luigi and I were at our quartiere, Pianello, not because we were born here, but because a decade ago we were invited to take up membership. We were summoned to an assembly and planning dinner because members are required to support our quartiere cooks in preparing and serving lunch for several hundred strangers, experts in the world of wine, who are coming to Montalcino next week. Signora Luciana is head cook at Pianello, a role she has enacted for many years, ever since Luigi and I melted into another way of life and set up home here. The role of head cook carries burdensome responsibility considering the sacred importance of anything to do with planting, harvesting, preparing, cooking and consuming food in Montalcino – even more so when quartiere pride is at stake and visiting strangers are expected for lunch. Luciana is a buxom and boisterous woman with a booming voice that resonates an octave or three louder than anyone else's. She is indomitably in command of the Pianello kitchen and even after ten years I quail in awe of her undisputed potency when she dons her flowery pinafore and brandishes her wooden spoon at we kitchen minions, galvanizing us into our kitchen chores.

For the last year or two I have been endeavouring to wheedle my way into her good books, obeying her sharp and always succinct commands with a seraphic smile, praying that one day, or one year, she will allow me to do more than peel garlic. Once, when my childish impulsiveness compelled me to grab the wooden paddle, determined to stir savage circles in a cauldron of ragù sauce which she had set simmering for the pasta, Luciana materialized beside that pot like a wand-wielding sorceress. 'Ninni!' she howled churlishly into my ear before I had grasped the paddle long enough to complete the first vindictive stir, causing me to jump and splash the paddle into the bubbling sauce. With a great sense of the dramatic Luciana delivered one of her quelling looks that cut to the bone, bossily reproving my daring. 'Leave the ragù to Maria-Rosa, she knows exactly how to stir it.' Obviously there is some skilful ritual I have not yet learned about stirring ragù sauce. Luciana loves to call me ninni, which is the pet name Tuscans use as a term of endearment for grandchildren. Looking mightily dour, as if to reprimand me for my child-like naivety, she groped in a drawer and snatched a sharp knife. With an extended lunge and a rhythmic movement of her wrist she slit a whole bulb of garlic from a plait dangling from the rafter, waggled her finger at a chopping board and, wordlessly, dumped the garlic and knife in my quivering hand. I am certain I have peeled a million garlic cloves in the Pianello kitchen over the years, petrified under the flashing eyes of the bewitcher. I patiently wait for the day, or even the year, when Luciana is satisfied that my loyalty and kitchen ability warrant promotion to a higher duty. But an angelic smile is plastered to my face and I exude calm enrapture because being in the kitchen with Pianello ladies when they are chopping and rolling and stirring initiates me to new and vital rituals concerning the preparation of a delicious Tuscan meal . . . and succinct lessons in the way things are done. Thankfully, last night's dinner assembly did not call upon my decade of profound expertise in peeling garlic because Luciana, in her unchallenged wisdom, had layered deep iron trays with spinach and ricotta lasagna earlier in the day. A tantalizing aroma of fresh sheep's milk ricotta wafted around the sede as we filed through the door, greeting fellow members with a kiss on each cheek and warm hand clasps.

Maurelia, who has been President of Quartiere Pianello for as long as Luciana has been head cook, alerted members to a late start because she wanted everyone to have time to return home to Montalcino in time for the assembly. Most of our members live and work in the village, but many workers and students travel daily to Siena or beyond, and some go to university. (That is, if the driver, Marco, is not asleep and the bus takes the young people down the valley in time to board the passing train.) Our meeting was scheduled to begin at nine-thirty, which really means ten o'clock. Such late-night appointments are not out of the ordinary in Montalcino, but forsaking a warm living room to attend a meeting at that hour is one of those awkward adjustments to our up-turned life that Luigi and I struggle to get used to. At nine o'clock on a cold dark night I'm thinking about preparations for bed. But by ten o'clock last night we were cosily chatting and laughing with our friends seated at wooden trestle tables spread around the dinner room in Pianello, warmed by a crackling fire that Vittorio arrives early enough to light and take the chill from the room before every winter meeting. Massimo, our most senior archer, and his wife Ofelia, who, over the years, has become one of my closest friends, joined my table, but Luigi sat with Ercole and Lola, our elderly landlords, who have become our unofficial grandparents, at a table on the other side of the room, closer to the hooded fireplace adorned with the blue and white emblem of Pianello.

Fiorella and Maria-Rosa are Luciana's left and right hand in the kitchen, so to speak, and as soon as we were seated they climbed the stairs, bearing salvers of toasted crostini topped with liver pâté, chopped mushroom and my most adored parsley and basil sauce, which we launched into while aromatic lasagna was warming in the industrial sized ovens in the restaurant-like kitchen.

Maurelia, never hidebound by formality, explained the number of volunteer helpers who were needed for the lunch next week, and for which jobs, and we proposed ourselves according to our availability and talents. Emotions warmed by red wine, I threw up my hand striving to be accepted to wait at tables, but Fiorella objected, snatching me back to sober reality with an indignant wail. 'Isabella! No! You will be needed in the kitchen with the cooks. You cannot serve as well!' I gulped, shrank back on my bench, and with an inclination of my head submitted to her sensible declaration. Oh, bother. The annual dinner for three hundred strangers who are invited to Montalcino to taste wine produced by a couple of hundred growers will demand a thousand slippery garlic cloves. From the corner of my eye I am certain statuesque Luciana nodded her head in confirmation of my destiny. Maurelia cast about from table to table, issuing instructions and jotting notations on her presidential clip board, using one after the other her most favourite words, which are *però*, which means 'however', and *comunque*, which is similar to 'in any event', or 'anyhow'. But she frowned, glancing around confusedly when Michele and Cecilia hissed in lowered tones and gestured to Gloria and Francesco and the young archers to join them at their table. '*Allora!*' said Maurelia, using her third favourite word to rein in control. She summonsed the young to attention because they had switched tables and were bent low in muffled chatter. 'Well now, which of you girls are available to serve at the tables, and which boys have volunteered to be wine waiters?' Satisfied with their responses, she reminded the boys that they are expected to be in black dinner jackets, formal and correct attire, just like the sommelier who will oversee the ritual decanting of Brunello. This stipulation brought guffaws and taunts from young friends who took delight in good naturedly counselling the boys that Brunello will be the red liquid in the dark bottles! 'Dai, dai, you don't say,' retorted young Francesco, 'I've been putting that red stuff in bottles for the last month and sending it all over the world . . . what would you know about it?' Perfectly true – Francesco is the grandson of a contadino wine grower who is a personal friend of ours, Signor Primo Pacenti, from whom Luigi and I have learned much about the wine of Montalcino, and, along with that, the story of contadini winemakers who are but one fascinating piece in a confusing riddle about the families who make superb wine on these hills.

We have passed many such evenings with our friends in Pianello, supping delicious food and sipping red wine in our sede which is as familiar as our own cosy living rooms which lie just a twisting lane or two from the door. By the time Maurelia was satisfied she had rounded up the helpers needed to fulfil quartiere commitments, and we had devoured every single crostini and scraped the crust from Luciana's scrumptious lasagna in the iron trays, the strokes of midnight were echoing from the village bell tower. Our plates were stacked by Fiorella and Luciana began noisily bashing about in the kitchen. No one took notice of a bitter debate under way at the table where the younger people hovered. I thought their unsmiling faces were a glum reflection on the midnight hour. We gathered ourselves up and Luigi and I were bidding goodnight to Ercole and Lola, and arranging a time to meet Fiorella and Vittorio next week to assemble for our respective duties peeling garlic and delivering wine for the lunch. Everyone was staggered when a dozen youngsters erupted from a table and blustered their way down the stairs two by two, blocking our descent, intent on way-laying President Maurelia and Dottore Luciano, who trains our archers. That was when the unpleasant exchange that was still fresh in my mind this morning at the bus stop broke into a verbal battle.

The young archers contributed not a word to the dissenting voices, but it was evident that they concurred with the argument put forward by senior friends. The reason Michele and Cecilia called in muffled tones for Gloria and Francesco, as well as the young archers and Samanta, to join them at their table was because they intended to vent their anger. They must have anguished about how to raise a contentious subject. Farewelling Ofelia and Maria-Rosa, I draped my coat around my shoulders and Luigi and I were heading towards the stairs, arms linked with Ercole and Lola, when we could not help but be stunned into listening.

Our President, Maurelia, cheerful after an efficient execution of her task for the evening, and employing her oft resorted to diplomatic skills, immediately sought to dampen the flame. 'Oh, ragazzi,' she pleaded, digesting the implications, 'it serves no purpose to blame an archer, or the rules, or another quartiere. Per favore, please, we are four cats on a terracotta roof . . . we have to make the most of what we have, how things stand, without finding fault with anybody else.'

'But Maurelia,' objected Cecilia. In her final year at university and something of a spokeswoman for her generation, she was unwilling to let this opportunity pass now that every member present was riveted to the spot. 'The rules need to be updated. They haven't been considered for more than fifty years. It isn't right because the skill of an archer is not the criterion for winning a tournament. There is an unjust gap between an archer who, time after time, sinks his arrows into the heart of the boar and an archer whose arrows are scattered all around the target.' Young Doctor Francesco, deciding this was the moment to offer substance to Cecilia's words, broke in. 'She's right, an archer can shoot an arrow that hangs on to the tail or nose of the boar by a thread, and at the end of the shoot the target looks like it has been dissected by my anatomy class. Then you have someone like Massimo who shoots nineteen perfect arrows one after the other. The arrows practically split each other down the shaft they are so tightly packed into the heart of the boar. But if he misses one arrow because of the wind, or a distraction, then he loses the shoot and the archer whose arrows are all over the target takes the victory. But how can his quartiere claim he is the best archer?'

Maurelia glanced anxiously at the elders grouped at the bottom of the stairs, willing someone to offer a convincing response in the face of this reasoned argument. She turned to the stairs where the rest of us were poised halfway down, but we were tight-lipped, not daring to inflame the young or wanting to be dragged into hostile crossfire. Dottore Luciano, who has been training the Pianello archery squad for years and has experienced dozens of tournaments, and probably dozens of conflagrations in Pianello, saw this as a grievance that was not going to be placated with platitudes.

'Ragazzi,' he implored, 'we have talked this over within the junior and senior archery squads, even with one of the other quartieri, but the truth is that not everyone agrees with your point of view. Not even our own archers are in agreement. Some archers argue that you cannot expect that Pianello will win a tournament just because of a change in the rules. Your accusations are getting us nowhere! All archers from the four quartieri are compelled to fire their arrows under the same rules, whether we like them or not. Your dissension and grumbling is causing our archers to lose hope, they sense defeat before the tournament is even here. You are damaging our young archers, because they are losing the will to become great archers for Pianello.'

'But Dottore!' Michele and Cecilia, sullen faced, clamoured to be listened to, ignoring the expectation of finality in the Dottore's tone. Michele reacted fast. 'That's the whole point! Exactly why we are angry and we *demand* that something be done. *If* there is no advantage in being the best archer, *if* there is no regulation about shooting every arrow with precision into the heart of the boar – which we all agree requires tremendous skill and months of sacrifice and dedication – then, not just Pianello's but *all* the young archers, at least in their minds, are tempted to settle for being able to hit the target anywhere at all. Why should Samuele, Filippo and Francesco train day after day on the practice range, missing out on other things, if, when it comes to tournament time, all they have to do is get as many arrows as possible to sink somewhere, anywhere, into the boar!' The three young archers stood at the top of the stairs, but as their eyes shifted I recall the slightest flicker of emotion passing between them, and when Samanta bent forward to see their reaction, almost imperceptibly, their heads inclined, supporting Cecilia and Michele. A few of the elders folded their arms across their chests, demonstrating, by this defensive pose, solidarity with

Dottore Luciano and Maurelia. The rest of us stood frozen, lips tightly clenched.

Cecilia seized the moment to drive home her point. 'How can you not agree? We want to see archers of the highest calibre on the campo, bravissimi archers who win the tournament with dedication, sacrifice and skill, not by a margin of luck. Anyway –' she lowered the tone of her voice to a petulant growl – 'it isn't the arguments which are damaging our young archers, it is because the tournament elders will not admit that the rules have become inadequate. Fifty years ago it probably was different. But we are in a new era. The bows and arrows we purchase these days are of a standard that technically assists archers, provided they train consistently, and provided their goal is not just to hit the target, because that's not difficult, especially in the early rounds.' Throwing down the challenge, she released her final volley justifying her accusation. 'For heavens sake, Dottore, you've even seen *me* hit the target on the practice range from twenty-five metres! If an archer knows he has to sink twenty arrows, one after the other, into the precise heart of the boar, and if points are awarded according to the accuracy of every single arrow, then we would witness a tournament that is won by the quartiere with the bravest archers of Montalcino. That would be a true victory.'

Dottore Luciano nodded his head in tacit agreement, accompanied by an expressive hand movement that confirmed his words as his outstretched hand cut vertically through the air. 'Magari, perhaps you may be right, but it is not as easy as it may seem to you to change the rules whenever someone is not happy. I know you are deluded, but how do you think Massimo and Alessandro and our other senior archers feel? They carry this tremendous responsibility on their shoulders, everyone's expectations and the honour of our quartiere, all through the year. I have been training our archery squad for twenty years, and before that I was an archer myself. I know a thing or two! How do you think I feel? If there are those among you who want someone to blame, well, you can blame me if it means we can restore harmony in our quartiere. For the sake of our archers, I will offer my resignation right now!' Dumbfounded by this frightful threat, we all held our breath, and the young were speechless, so he switched tactics. 'We have been close to victory at so many tournaments, but you must be patient. All this resentment, this bitterness which is causing divisions in our quartiere, and moaning about changing the rules, will be wiped away in an instant because I promise each of you that one victory is all it will take to release us from this pain and anguish.'

A trodden dirt path takes me up the hill above the medieval wall that girdles Montalcino, capturing huddled stone houses within a stone belt, and overlooking an endless valley rolling away to the mountains. Leaning over the wall, embracing the wide-flung landscape stretching to a crown of purple mountains, I raise my eyes and let them sweep across these hills all flushed with light and shadow, down to valleys patterned with vines, olive groves and fields of wheat punctuated with thousand-year-old castles. I shake my head in disbelief that this dream is real. Sometimes, in the nearest valley running steeply from the village, I see a hunter with a gun propped over a shoulder striding along with his snuffling dog, or curls of smoke rising from a chimney. Often I gaze at a worker clipping vines or picking fat plums, or at billowing white-as-snow sheets, incongruously flapping from the sill of a turreted castle defending a clearing in the woods. The merest alteration offers a rhythmic rearrangement of all its unique credentials. This morning, with spring on its way towards us, the horizon is acutely limpid. Not all traces of winter have vanished. Below this wall the hill falls into a wood where chestnuts rustle in a light breeze, wanting to shake off a winter mantle of crinkled leaves and barren casings. The chestnut trees are awakening, reaching for the morning sun, eager to begin again. Bare hills rise and fall in gentle waves, not yet yielding up their secret; the seeds the farmer sowed last November are germinating, readying to burst through the softening earth. Through months of freezing winter the land lay in the rough; clods of earth that were rendered down into grey clumps became as hard as granite, compounded by occasional frosty mornings and frequent falls of snow. '*Sotto ghiaccio c'è fame,*' below ice there is hunger, the farmer says, '*ma sotto neve c'è pane*': but below snow there is bread. The snow has melted, sending life-giving water seeping slowly underground. Green rising grain will transform these barren Tuscan hills, sweeping away the winter cloak that protected the farmer's bread, heralding another rearrangement of this never finished picture.

A decade has passed since Luigi and I packed our bags and bade farewell to family and a commodious life in Australia. At the time it did not seem courageous, but in me there were wounds to be healed and a hunger to step away from who I was, from the spurious world I had constructed. Luigi, in utter contrast, is a man who refuses to recognize any complications in life. Anything is possible to Luigi and, living here for a decade, among Tuscans who understand precisely what the important things in life are, has simplified his already uncomplicated philosophy. We watched and listened from a discreet distance, learned patience, recognizing our lack of familiarity with the way things are done in Montalcino. This is an insular community and there are rituals to be observed. Over time we familiarized ourselves with daily habits, joining the passeggiata each evening, participating in the rhythm of the festivals and pageants that punctuate the sacred and secular Montalcino calendar. We were offered and accepted responsibility in our quartiere, Pianello, which requires unquestioned service and we have witnessed as many tournaments as the young archers, although a number of years slid by before we understood the depth of loyalty we must harbour towards Pianello, and the centuries of passion behind the archery tournaments themselves; perhaps that is something we can never possess.

The citizens we share our lives with are not just Tuscans, they identify themselves as *Montalcinesi*, while those whose ancestors were born on the hill, whose unbroken genealogy goes back many centuries, can claim to be and are referred to as *Ilcinesi*, an ancient label that harks back to the 1200s, or even earlier. All of them carry the hopes and aspirations of a community that considers itself defiantly unique. We have occasionally been snared in unexpected pitfalls because it has taken us a whole decade to fathom some of the mysterious ways of the Montalcinesi with whom we mingle daily. Only now are we beginning to grasp the complex network linking one family to another in intersecting horizontal and vertical branches, and all of them to the village as if all two thousand souls living on this hill stem from one single oak tree, which was fought over with the blood of their ancestors who defended their right to dwell here. As the first five years slid away we sensed a measure of acceptance, but the citizens who live inside these medieval walls jealously guard an individuality, an identity that is difficult to penetrate. Determined that Montalcino will be our home, and wary always of falling into the trap of comparing our evolving life, upside down and inside out though it may be from time to time, with our organized life in the past, we have remained persistent. Yet sometimes we are forced to recede silently into the background, wait another year, or two, and keep a low profile while the Montalcinesi, by their actions and cautioning words, subconsciously enlighten us about the way things are done in their hilltop village atop a sea of vineyards. It is a world we never imagined existed when we waltzed through the walls and into their inward looking lives. In truth, we are intruders, and they do not *need* us to be here.

We have absorbed much about the history of Montalcino, listened to stories from the descendants of village families, and pieced together intriguing parts of the Montalcino puzzle, but there is much still to be learned. To a stranger, hearing an Ilcinese, someone whose ancestors were born on the hill of Montalcino, conversing with Luigi in the piazza about the football team, or exchanging news about the harvest, or overhearing a Signora confiding in me about some minor family crisis, even inviting us to their homes in the village or in the vineyards outside the walls, it could mistakenly appear that we have gained acceptance. Perhaps some strangers who come to find a new life in Italy are satisfied with those important milestones, perhaps they should be, because we understand the patience and perseverance required to reach that point. But *we* are not. To become an integral part of the life we have discovered here, a life we value, and assimilate ourselves into the cultural quality and rhythm of the lives of our friends, with a part to play in the living history of Montalcino, requires a sagacious mind and longer vision. In our tenth year, drawn into their lives though we may be, we are more than ever aware that we risk much if we display an outwardly bold attitude, or if we assume, simply from prior experience of the wider world, to know more, or better, than an Ilcinese. But, at the same time, after a decade, we occasionally step into exposed terrain and trust that the patient foundation we are laying, year by year, is becoming firm enough for us to leave our comfort zone and, searching for long-term integration, find and be entrusted with a role to play in the future of Montalcino. We are adjusting to unspoken rules that adopting and living in a new culture demands if you sincerely want that culture to become your own.

Movement to the west draws my eye; the train that left Grosseto an hour ago hurtles out of the woods below Castello Romitorio. Directly ahead, easily distinguishable, lies the village of Buonconvento. Already the train is roaring through the valley and in a couple of minutes will clatter into the station, but there is no sign of a blue bus along the road between the hills. Samuele, Filippo and friends will not reach Florence in time for morning lectures.

My mind returns to last night's assembly because young Pianello members who witnessed that ugly confrontation are among those who departed on the late bus. When Luigi and I were invited to join Quartiere Pianello, Samuele and Francesco were little boys at elementary school. Filippo is older by a couple of years, but the three of them would race around Pianello headquarters playing tag, or shooting at each other with imaginary arrows until Massimo, our veteran archer, would hoist one or other of them on his broad shoulders and quieten them so members could concentrate on the news our President needed to impart. They have grown from rowdy children to young adults anxious about missing a university lecture. On weekends we watch them, smart young men walking hand in hand with girlfriends, greeting us on the evening passeggiata around the village. And we have watched them grow in confidence and skill, training with Dottore Luciano, proud to become archers for Quartiere Pianello.

Dissension has surfaced because the archery tournaments between the four neighbourhoods have been won year after year by each of the other three quartieri. Pianello has not been victorious at an archery tournament in nearly a decade; understandably, the young are dejected. None of those Pianello youngsters on the bus has ever seen a victory in our quartiere. A whole generation of Pianello has never heard the bells of the Church of San Pietro, our own quartiere church, peal the news of victory. They have never marched through the village behind the quartiere banner, claiming glory and honour for Pianello. And precisely when things are at their lowest there is friction within the ranks of our archers and frustration and grumbling about inadequate rules among the young adding pressure to the delicate work in the months to come as our archers sacrifice their time on the practice range. And now our trainer is threatening to resign. We desperately need a victory in Pianello.

Leaning over the northern wall I sense footsteps as I muse over how I must accept my share of the responsibility for the despair of Pianello young, and help to find a way to raise their morale. A familiar voice greets me. 'Buongiorno, Signora.' Bruno offers a respectful salutation. No matter how many invitations I put forward Bruno cannot bring himself to call me by my first name. Most of my friends do, and Bruno and his wife Amelia are among the most loved and special of elderly friends, but Bruno cannot let go of this deferential expression of respect even though our paths cross two or three times a day. This morning, automatically, he reaches a hand to his battered cap.

He has spent his life doffing his cap to one padrone, master, or another and he feels discourteous if he does not acknowledge me in this way. Well into his nineties, he carries a serrated curved blade and a length of rope is wound from elbow to bony shoulder, for he is a thin man. 'Buongiorno, Bruno.' I smile warmly. 'Where are you going?' He points towards low scrub in the wood from where I watched the hurtling train gather speed below Castello Romitorio. 'I left some branches near the castle yesterday because I couldn't carry them. I'm going back to fetch them.' Bruno is a boscaiolo, a woodcutter, a lingering trace of a way of life that offered little more than survival for many Montalcinesi families not so many decades ago. He chooses to occupy his old age doing what he once had little choice in life about. He walks kilometres into the woods and saws and gathers branches for the fire, because his wife Amelia cooks their meals over a fuel stove. By the time he returns home around midday Amelia has handmade pasta rolled and ready, and while he stacks the wood and hangs up his blade, she sets the water to simmering and, giving Bruno a minute to strip to the waist and wash at the scullery sink, she drops the pasta into a pot and the very second he steps through the door, pulling on a clean shirt, she lays a mound of macaroni and his favourite tomato and garlic sauce at his place at the table.

'Buon passeggiata, Signora,' he farewells me warmly. He knows I am on my morning walk around the walls of the village. When he returns for lunch Amelia will ask if he met me this morning, as usual.

Turning towards the hunting woods the stone wall curves sharply on the crest of the hill behind a white stone church known affectionately as the Madonna. The morning air has liquefied a white frost but the sun has not warmed the grass, which is heavy with dew and lies inert beneath the trees. Not yet in bloom, miniature stems droop under the weight of elongated buds hanging low, each with a violet membrane defining closed petals. Crocuses burst from the earth in unison, but these aspiring blooms cannot raise their delicate heads among pearly dew drops clinging to blades of grass.

Soon I am on a stony track above the farms facing the hunting woods. There is always early morning activity here, but as spring looms there is a sense of renewal of energy in man as well as nature. A farmer plunges his axe into a log, draws it out and raises it above his head, rhythmically swinging his body as he prepares for the next blow. Unaware that I am standing above, he labours on, adding to a pile of chopped wood beside which his peaked black cap is resting. He wears an odd uniform for chopping wood. No jeans and T-shirt for this Tuscan farmer; he is habitually dressed for wood chopping in baggy trousers, a collarless white shirt with the neck button fastened, waistcoat and black jacket. Shabbily comfortable, it was once a part of his best Sunday suit. Wood chopping is not his first chore for the morning; a plot has been turned and narrow troughs scooped out, ready for planting. His sturdy wife, peasant scarf knotted under her chin, draws wooden pegs from the pocket of her floral apron and secures a row of tea towels along a wire strung from tree to tree. So ordered, so predictable is their day that they are insulated by their own uncomplicated existence. Yet they rise early each morning with purpose. They seem to me to love their simple life. Besides chopping wood and growing artichokes and lettuces, they are live-in caretakers for the church of the Madonna. Often, clutching his cap to his side, the man dresses in his best black when he carries the cloth bag round the Madonna to receive offerings from the faithful.

*

A tractor crackles and splutters then settles into an angry purr as I reach the cypress pine guarding the boundary with the next farm. Years ago an abandoned farmhouse near where I stand was surrounded by fruit trees alternating with olives, but the farm around the stone house had not been worked for years and had degenerated into a tangle of golden ginestra and domestic plants gone wild. Olive oil cannot keep pace with the returns for planting vines and producing the wines of Montalcino, especially if the farm lies within the zone authorizing production of Brunello, as this farm does. Wine lovers all over the world covet Brunello di Montalcino and pay handsomely for even one bottle; this handkerchief-sized plot produces a few thousand bottles. Once the hillside, which slopes away from the wall at a steep angle, had been lightly cleared of tangled vegetation, and after massive boulders had been trucked away, the terraces that peasant farmers had cut by hand into the hillside long ago to plant the olive grove were revealed. But the changes were not violent. Cherry and plum trees, a huge almond, several chest-nuts, as well as a few olive and cedar and, where possible, even wild rose bushes, were intentionally spared from destruction. This brought me relief because I pictured farmland in the new world cleared of everything that resembled life or growth, or that stood in the way of a concrete dream engineered on a planning desk far from the countryside. But as the clearing plan unfolded I wondered how the grower was intending to sink soldierly lines of wooden staves, which march in resolute rows in most vineyards, if he had to weave a circuitous path to avoid plum and cherry trees, as well as the spread of a gigantic almond. My curiosity walking past this farm each morning, pausing to scan evidence of the previous day's labour, led to an exchange of polite smiles with workers, then frequent greetings by way of waving hands followed by mouthing friendly buongiornos until the day I encountered the grower, Enzo, on the path, on his way down to the farmhouse. Our friendly exchange of passing gestures blossomed.

Enzo became the fortunate owner of this farm only a few years ago, acquiring a hectare and a half and an abandoned farmhouse from the descendants of the Paccagnini, an ancestral Montalcino family. An outsider would not have had a semblance of flickering hope of even finding out that it might have been on the market because a treasure like this handkerchief of farmland with a stone house to boot on the doorstep of Montalcino, a few minutes' walk from the heart of the village, is the stuff Italofiles from afar daydream about. But for many years Enzo has reaped no financial return as a result of ripping out olive trees and planting a vineyard with the clone of sangiovese grosso, the grape from which Brunello di Montalcino is produced. Enzo, like all Montalcinesi, thinks in the long term; life has been unfolding on this hill for a couple of millennia. This morning he is sitting behind the wheel of his tractor bumping along at an even pace between the rows. Enzo is not a contadino, the descendant of a peasant farmer, but a cittadino, a village dweller, and a respected Doctor of Oenology. He proffered unexpected answers to my questions about unconventional logic in this vineyard.

'But Enzo, what about the sun?' I cleverly interrogated him because sangiovese grosso needs sun, as hot and as bright and constant as nature will bestow. The shadow cast by the leafy almond from April to October consumes a stretch of land of a monetary value that made no sense to me. 'It is part of my ecological plan,' Enzo assured me. 'For years I have monitored the shadow and thought about how to use it to advantage. Every vineyard needs a cantina where huge oak barrels can rest in silence, but I'm going to make this one invisible! It will be concealed under the slope of the hill where the almond tree shadow falls. The shade will help keep the temperature under control in the cantina.' Enzo is an environmentally conscious grower. He anticipated what he thought my next question might be, because he chatted on, testing to see if I knew the answer. 'That is only half of the equation, Signora. What about rain?' The regulations the Brunello growers are bound to adhere to, if they apply to call their wine Brunello, stipulates that no artificial watering, no irrigation, is permissible. 'I was wondering about that,' was my guarded response, but it was really a pretence to encourage him. I want to learn more about growing this great wine because, curiously, there are occasions when my ears prick up. I sense, scrutinizing barely perceptible glances to the side, or raised eyebrows replacing unspoken words, ambiguous hints of an unpleasant nature. Obscurely gathering clouds in my mind bother me. I fear something is not quite right between the families of growers who live in the hills surrounding Montalcino.

'Wouldn't you think the roots of the chestnut, cherry and plum trees would steal the moisture the vines will be searching for when the sun beats relentlessly down from a cloudless summer sky?' Silence was the wisest option when Enzo's shaking head told me this was the wrong question.

'Does it look to you as if the vines have died of thirst? Come with me, if you don't mind dirt on your shoes.' Was that another trick question? Enzo led the way down the hill, then turned into a row of vines and stepped guardedly between clumps of earth, although I did not understand the implication of his gingerly placed boots because I could see they were already clogged with dirt. Just the same, I mimicked him, not wanting to appear ungrateful for his concern about my footwear. He stopped in front of a twisted trunk branching horizontally seventy centimetres above the ground. To my eyes it looked lifeless, or at least dormant. Enzo lowered his voice and in a hushed tone so as to unite us in this moment of truth, took on a conspiratorial expression and said: 'If you can imagine, Signora, below the ground, as deeply as the soil allows and probably at the level where it meets coarse shale, curly rootlets are right this moment wriggling beneath our feet. A rudimentary form of life is sending hair like feelers writhing through the darkness searching for moisture and minerals in the soil with which to feed embryonic shoots.' I found it difficult to respond to this science fiction image described with barely controlled emotion, but I was instantly pleased I had placed my feet precisely in his footprints. My eyes were riveted upon the hillocks and craters in the crusty earth at our feet as a smile of knowing satisfaction crossed his face. 'This is really the very first stage in the making of Brunello di Montalcino, but it is a step for which man can claim no credit.'

'Because the shale table is lower down on this farm the soil is deep. The roots of these ancient fruit trees that have been wandering in silent darkness deep underground for years are nature's repositories for scarce moisture from which the roots of the vine feed during the hot days of summer. The cherry, plum and chestnut trees are watering invisible stirring rootlets.'

This morning Enzo is travelling slowly, his head and shoulders turned towards the hoe at the rear of the tractor, preparing for the dawn when a subterranean scramble of wriggling rootlets manifests itself in the first green shoot. He is letting the hoe gently drag the earth open, turning and aerating fat clumps of soil, but not causing it to fragment violently.

Instead of turning for home at the guard's tower halfway along the track, I walk on to a rampart rising to the fortress and pass through a pointed archway in front of wooden doors to this medieval stronghold. Once around the fortress a path cobbled with uneven round stones brought from a riverbed will take me into the quartiere of Travaglio. This will lead me, by and by, to one of my secret places in Montalcino to which I retreat when turbulent events, such as my angst with a bus driver with whom I have no justifiable reason to feel personal annoyance, and horrible divisions in Pianello dump a load of disappointment on my mind. I need to be with myself.

A drystone wall is thoughtfully furnished with rough-hewn steps cut into the rocks. From the lowest step, breathing in the scented air of wild rosemary growing over the wall, I am high enough to see into the garden. The drooping bowers of golden wattle from a flowering acacia almost touch the earth where daffodils turn up their sunny petticoats. Dancing around the daffodils miniature bluebells and violets creep into the light, struggling for their share of warmth from the sun. Potted primula sit along a dirt path trodden smooth, while terracotta tubs seem only to harbour damp earth; tulip bulbs prepare for their moment of entry. A patch of green stems twenty centimetres tall and standing straight is unfamiliar. The stems have risen amongst the flattened leaves of last winter's cabbages and meander between acacia and olive trunks. Rising to a higher step, edging my body along the wall I regret, for the umpteenth time, that botany is not something in which I excel. One of the reasons I derive so much happiness from visiting these gardens daily is because I see the blossoming of seasonal flowers and vegetables familiar to me. Luigi and I never harboured rustic notions of living on a farm. We are content to leave the dirty hands, shovels and manure to others while we take morning caffè at a civilized hour, socializing with friends in the village. Visiting the gardens inside the walls has taught me when, and how, but I am satisfied to observe nature from this side of the wall. There is a furriness about these rigid stems; each trifoliate leaf is curling downwards, as if an invisible force is pulling it towards the soil. With my feet embedded firmly in the stone wall and toes wedged beneath the protruding rock ledge I bend over at the waist and reach down, managing to keep myself from toppling long enough to run my fingers along a furry stem. Returning upright, I raise my fingers to my nose, close my eyes and inhale. Recognizing the sweet scent I glance back at temporarily upright patches of wild strawberry.

Leaving the perfumed garden and continuing down the pebbly path and through a ruined gate there are no more gardens to peep into now that I am outside the wall. Instead, wild growth confronts me. Not far from here, a little way outside the walls and down an isolated track, is my secret place of meditation. Turning from the gate as the track slopes down I am startled by agitated twittering and the flurry of wings. I have disturbed the morning song of a hundred birds. Understandably terrified, they swoop from a thicket and tear around in a scolding frenzy, alarming mates further down the track who whirl into the air chittering warnings. Waiting until the timid creatures find a safe place to settle I set off down the track, but soon it is apparent that I am not the only interloper on this peaceful sunny morning. My predicament calls for prudence. Should I turn back? Instinctively seeking not to betray my presence I crouch below the crumbling wall. Back bent and head down, I creep along the track. In the silence it is impossible not to overhear the rebounding voices of Carlo and Pierluigi, two Travaglio archers comparing firing technique on their practice range. Concealed behind leggy thistles, my covert shelter incriminates me of archery espionage more harmful than if I had strolled boldly past and waved a greeting . . . but it is too late. Halted by the recognizable whir of blurred arrows flying down the range and sinking into the target with a thud, my thoughts turn yet again to the reason I am following this track. Carlo carried on his shoulders the weight of quartiere honour for loss after loss at tournaments for every one of the eighteen years in which Travaglio never had a victory. When he fired the winning round at the annual Sagra tournament a few years ago it broke a heartbreaking drought. Entire generations of Travaglio members had never seen a victory; for the older members it was a leap into the modern era. Now it is our turn. Dejected Pianello members may be called upon to endure the pain of defeat this year as well. Except for the happy twittering of finches satisfied that they are not under threat and thus unconcerned at my crouching, there is no sign of movement along the deserted track. Carlo's voice becomes muffled, then inaudible as silence descends and, with a few more bent-double stilted steps, I reach my destination.

When I come to my secret place, never quite knowing what I will find, I am overcome by an inner calm that sweeps through me as soon as I see Her face. An ivory ring of spent wax from a candle lies in a heap on the stone step; wax has dribbled into the cracks leaving a trail of white veins across the shrine. Someone must have visited the Madonina, the little Madonna, last evening, leaving this flickering candle as a votive offering. Embraced in this peasant shrine are intoned prayers of supplication of the Montalcinesi going back hundreds of years. Tawdry plastic flowers ornament the shrine, and a straw wreath festooned round about with ribbons is lassoed to the wire grille. Naively worked in terracotta by the hand of a peasant, not artistically rich and undoubtedly worth nothing at all except to those who seek the answer to their prayer, my sweet Madonna of benign simplicity smiles into eternal silence. She is cloaked in a blue mantle, often depicted to accentuate majesty. But it is Her serene smile, untroubled by the weight of burdens of all who come to seek Her mercy, that brings me here from time to time. A few white daisies have been poked through the wire no more than an hour ago; proof that this Madonna is part of the daily life of many who trust in Her benevolence. A narrow slit in the wire grille invites the deposition of coins which rattle down a crudely fashioned metal tube and land with a clang in a rusty tin. My reservedly Protestant upbringing prohibits me from seeking Her direct mediation in restoring harmony at Pianello. But I am unable to resist feeling the exaltation when I slip a coin through the slot and it rattles about in the tube and races with a spurt, twirling before dropping into the tin, leaving me with a sensation of triumph over that which afflicts my mind. Perhaps it is the finality of the action; the die is cast, the request made, my coin irretrievable.

The first time I discovered this serene Madonna was in my twentieth year. Wed to my handsome man we were dashing around Italy without a care in the world. But that was more than thirty years ago, and, my unknown destiny mapped out, I dragged my daughter, Rebecca, down this track when she was eighteen, but she did not understand the significance of visiting the Madonna because I did not tell her. In happy early years, which all too soon became traumatic survival ones, followed by the wilderness of the middle years, I did not imagine that one day, having met Luigi, I would run away to Italy, seek and find my home in Montalcino with liberty to visit my Madonna whenever I wish, and whenever I need. It pleases me that rarely do I meet anyone else at Her shrine. Selfishly, I want Her for myself because this is a secret place in my heart. Sitting on the steps at Her feet are treasured moments with fragments of a broken life that needed to be left behind, and of precious times that are not recoverable. Luigi has never been here, he has never seen my sweet Madonna because he is my now.

Calm of heart, carrying Her benign smile with me on my homeward path, I loop through a chestnut wood and follow the drystone walls to the east of Montalcino. Sleeping drivers, missed lectures and Pianello dramas, serious though they are, recede into perspective. Reflecting on my responsibility as changes flow through Pianello, I can see that as one generation completes university and enters the workforce, their careers force frequent absence from Montalcino. Today's youngsters, Samuele, Filippo, Francesco and Samanta are unconsciously stepping into the shoes of the presently voluble generation above, forming a strong nucleus around whom their own generation of the quartiere will group. Nurturing the young within the protection of the quartiere provides training, which reaches them through the generation above their own. Samuele, Filippo, Francesco and Samanta will soon be called upon to play a prominent role in our quartiere. Last night they stayed silent during the angry exchange, but they are learning, and so am I. Maybe this year, along with them, I will experience my first victory in Pianello. Maybe we will ring the victory bells together.

The dank track crosses a valley where I hear a torrent from a hidden spring drop into a gully and rush down the side of the mountain. The lively torrent stays with me until I reach the communal washing fountains marking the boundary between Travaglio and Pianello, close to home. Along the cobbled road in the heart of Pianello the delicious aroma of simmering wild boar sauce, then the scented tangle of chopped basil and parsley, waft into my nostrils, rousing my hunger. From a shuttered window a head pops out and glances along the road just as a blue uniform rounds the corner ahead of me. 'Buongiorno e buon appetito, Marco,' is all I can think of to say, disguising the angst in my voice, and trying not to smile too widely. 'Altrettanto, Signora, the same to you,' the yawning driver responds. The bus did not go all the way to Florence.

CHAPTER THREE

Like Salt in Water

'My life has been one long struggle to preserve something. Almost everything has been stolen, indiscriminately frittered away, or squandered. The world is full of thieves, and I am unfortunate enough to have most of them living close to me. It seems as if it is my destiny that there should be nothing left when I die; I am eighty-six years old, so it will not be long. An enormous patrimony which began with my family a thousand years ago has all but vanished, and fate has chosen me to be the one to witness the closing of the drama. The last stroke of misfortune in a long and luckless life . . . and then it will dissolve into nothing, like salt in water.'

Tension fuses our two minds. He, face charged with memories, struggles with the bitter irony of his misfortune, and I hastily reflect on the questions I had planned to ask when I arranged an appointment to meet the Ingegnere, the Engineer. I didn't know how to respond, fearful of clumsy words in the protracted silence, so I left him to begin again. 'It is difficult to know where to start . . . there are many fascinating things . . . it will take hours and you may need to come back another time; even that may not be long enough.' I nod as he cautions me about hours of commitment that could be expended in plotting this protracted conspiracy. I sense that his family leave him alone with his memories in this biblioteca and the dusty archives. Probably they are weary of listening to the anguish in his voice, the pained hurt, harping at them time after time. A flicker lights his eyes when he catches my smile and I murmur that I will dedicate as much time as we require, assuring him that I can return tomorrow, if he is feeling up to it. I am persuaded we stand on mutual territory; he is hungering to tell me, and the sparkle in his eyes convinces me he believes he has found someone who genuinely wants to listen. Grasping his next gambit accentuates my apprehension that my questions are not the appropriate ones for this encounter. 'At the end, when I tell you about my father,' he warns, 'you will understand why I believe a monument should be raised to him in Montalcino. My father possessed immense wealth and he consumed it trying to create great things for these people. His one great wrong was that he was in love with Montalcino; he wanted only to be loved in return. But he was not; they wanted to kill him.'

This dramatic declaration, tinged with bitterness, is not what I expected to hear, nor even the subject I anticipated when I arrived this morning to meet Ingegnere Padelletti. An appointment which, fortuitously, transpired through his grandson who I discovered is a fellow member of Pianello, and because Brunello di Montalcino inadvertently rescued me from peeling a thousand garlic cloves. Barely able to conceal my ill grace I telephoned Luciana the morning after our Pianello planning dinner. Begging her forgiveness, lamenting quartiere misfortune and feigning sufferance all in one wicked breath, I declared that, unexpectedly, I was holding in my hand an invitation that had arrived that very morning from our friend Primo Pacenti who grows Brunello down in the valley. I intoned regretful resignation to be Primo's guest, among three hundred others invited by Montalcino's winegrowers, to a lunch staged by the Consorzio del Vino Brunello di Montalcino. It would hardly do to be in the kitchen peeling my own garlic cloves, would it?

Before subterranean rootlets stirring underground convey their message to the earth's surface, and while passive grey trunks stand inert, waiting for spring to advance, the Consorzio del Vino Brunello, which is the official body to which the majority of Montalcino's renowned winegrowers belong, stages a three-day spectacular inviting national and international judges, sommeliers, writers and an assortment of dignitaries and gurus in the world of wine to Montalcino. The double climax of the weekend, aside from hundreds of tastings throughout the three days, and aside from the lunch for guests of growers and other VIPs, to which I am invited, cooked and served by the four quartieri, is, first, to assess the quality of the harvest brought in last autumn. Reposing, calm at last, the fermented juice in huge oak vats is stable enough for winemakers to study its evolution into wine and to forecast with a high degree of accuracy the transpiring organoleptic progress. In four years' time the maturing wine in the vats will be released and shipped, but, as a consequence of the weekend spectacular in Montalcino, the world receives advance warning of the characteristics and star rating of the ageing wine. The second motive, after which the event, Benvenuto Brunello, Welcome Brunello, is named and justifying all this theatrical extravagance, is the ceremonial surrender of the Brunello to an eager market, awaited by those who may have purchased the wine years in advance – before it was ready to drink.

With not a sliver of garlic under my fingernails I sat down to an Ilcinese lunch prepared by the four quartieri accompanied by superb Brunello, my first emotional sip almost five years after the grapes were harvested to make this wine. I was among familiar faces, but, as we devoured plate after plate of garlicky crostini and mounds of tagliatelle with tomato and masses of whole garlic cloves, I became increasingly conscious of less familiar faces. My thoughts turned from wine to growers and my oft sensed foreboding that something is not right. Glancing around, it was not difficult to isolate contadini growers like Primo Pacenti, because many are our friends, and cittadini growers, too, like Enzo, who farm smallholdings. I recognize them because they live in the village, rather than out on the farms. Invading Italian investors from far-away cities were conspicuous; Milanese, Torinese and Romans who descended, or rather ascended, flapping millions, hoping they were not too late to benefit from the prestige of growing Brunello. There were a handful of wealthy Germans, Swiss and Americans, as well. But there were other growers that I did not recognize, lordly persons who posed rather than sat, and with excessively puffed out chests strutted to the President's table to secure personal introductions for their guests. I should not jump to conclusions, but could these be the growers about whom I have sensed something is not quite right? A confusing tangle of ambiguous and at times vaguely unpleasant taunts bothers me.

The concept of a noble class, or, conversely, a peasant class such as the contadini of Montalcino, is troublesome. Migrant children taken to the other side of the world never learned about their birth land because parents sought to obliterate from our lives the trauma of exhausted nations facing postwar hardship. Children from all corners of the war-torn world were in my school in Australia, among them German, Irish, Greek, Italian, Yugoslav and Polish, as well as children from other British families. We were equals, possessing no more than each other, hence less aware of class structure. A sense of social inferiority, or superiority, does not spontaneously register and it does not occur to me that someone belongs to a class above my own. Making Montalcino my home I need to come to grips with a centuries-old social structure so that I can understand the legacy of class rankings that prevails in the village. But parallel with these social deliberations a troublesome riddle has arisen, shrouded in mystery and unspeakably taboo. Grasping at unverifiable allegations, my curiosity has been roused to an obsession. Sitting alongside my friends at the Benvenuto Brunello lunch, observing superficial interaction flowing between those whom I do not know brought back to mind the reasons why I am bent on unravelling the social structure. But first I need to figure out if these unknown growers are descendants of a noble class of Montalcino.

Eavesdropping, not deliberately, but unavoidably, on private conversation around the bars, I sense jealousy and the sour aroma of poor-cousin relationships, family names that no one will audibly denounce. Perhaps this rumbling undercurrent has been worsening in recent years. Reports couched in doublespeak seem loaded with barbs which, by omission rather than inclusion, denote disharmony. Because social position and class structure are alien concepts to me, and because shadowy secrets hover in the background between some growers, I cannot resist investigating the root of the angst. I learned much about the contadini on the farms, and am studying the cittadini, seeking to work out the class structure of those who live in the village. But what of the elite class?

Snooping along this trail at the Benvenuto Brunello lunch I probed for clues about a family I had been informed is one of the most ancient in Montalcino. As he poured ruby Brunello into my glass I chatted with a smartly dinner-suited youth, Silvano Padelletti, who I was taken aback to learn belongs to Pianello. He lives in Siena to attend college and if he had not been wearing a name tag I should not have established his family identity. His grandfather, Signor Padelletti, produces Brunello, is a member of the Consorzio, and, from time to time – though less in recent months – I have identified him as an elderly gent with a wooden cane, addressed as the Ingegnere, a mark of respect, at the post office or the bank. The Padelletti family might be part of the nobility or, alternatively, Ingegnere Padelletti could be just the person to explain to me if there is an elite, a noble class of Montalcino. Silvano offered to arrange my appointment.

*

Watching attentively as Ingegnere Padelletti drags his memories to the surface, forcing his mind back through the centuries to recount the story of his family, warning me that he may need more time, I am less persuaded that, after all, I am on the right trail. Nevertheless, I am athirst to begin. The Ingegnere, I suspect, has a story to tell me of which I know nothing. Lifting my scribbles from the table, I fold the pages and slide interlocutory notes into my bag. This is an occasion when I am not the talker; I am here to listen.

'Signora,' he began, softly, staring deep into my eyes, imploring patience, 'I may wander about a bit, there are so many issues to become sidetracked with. I have spent years finding out about my family and many things I know because my great-grandfather, Pierfrancesco Padelletti, was a friend of the Grand Duke of Tuscany, so it has all come down to me through my grandfather and father.' A weary sigh and a long pause, then, having released his memories, the words spilled out. 'This is a tale of legends and truths, a story of death by poisoning, of Napoleonic generals and Huguenots, of Engels and Marx, of royal castles, petroleum corporations and communists, of emperors and heretics, of Wittenberg Cathedral and flight into exile, of the genius of my family, and a man who was a saint, but also an economic criminal. I believe I can claim that the whole intricate plot is gathered here, in my biblioteca, in this medieval palazzo in Montalcino. This is the past, and it is my heritage. The only hope I have for the future is with my grandson, and I will work till I die in the hope that there will be something to leave Silvano, even if it is only my home and the vineyard on the hills outside that window. But in Montalcino there is a saddening tendency to destroy everything, a suicidal undercurrent, as if they need to go on and on sacrificing, defying, killing history. I believe this inclination began in 1559 when the Montalcinesi suffered that great trauma; after four years of fighting someone else's war, the suffering populace was forced to surrender to the Spanish . . . *that* is when they were fallen upon by unscrupulous carpetbaggers.'

It was not difficult to locate the Ingegnere's home. Everyone knows Casa Padelletti, and, after a false start hammering on wooden gates which I mistook to be his front door, I was put right by a grey head behind a slatted shutter and stood high on the adjacent threshold to press a brass buzzer. A few minutes passed as I waited for the Ingegnere to release the door, whereupon, leaning unsteadily on a wooden cane, with a formal handshake and exchange of courtesies, he invited me in. Closing the door, he enveloped us both in a gloomy ante-room, austere and military; a vague sensation of damp, or cold disuse, descended. Without uttering another word, because he was inhaling and exhaling deeply, fighting to restore his breath, he dragged his legs in inching steps and steadied himself by gripping dressers and cupboards along the wall. His shuffling gait is painfully slow, and I followed him through a door from which dangled a loop of rope which he yanked to make the door swing. We were then in a hall cast in shadow, which seemed to run the length of the rambling home, but it was too dim for me to be certain. Persian rugs and tapestries worn thin, or even threadbare, are positioned along the walls to halt draughts. He stooped to negotiate a step and manoeuvred through a low opening in the wall. Suddenly aware that I was slipping backwards in time, at least a hundred and fifty years, I gasped faintly. He exhaled and whispered: 'Let us sit here, we can move into the biblioteca later.'

His legs were trembling after the energy exerted permitting

me entry, but I had already given myself up in vapid enchantment to the first glorious moment on our journey. This salon has gathered unto its bones a patina, a harmony and regal dignity that could never be achieved in a single lifetime. Everything in it seems kissed with the breath of ages. The Ingegnere croaked that he required a couple of minutes to recover his strength. He lowered himself on to a French chair, and pointed to another for me. Forced to sit upright, the seat sags and threads of raw silk upholstery are beginning to shred, but I was glad of precious time to think of the many beautiful things in this room. A graceful Gothic arch frames a mullioned window, softened by weary yet elegant brocades and folds of crimson silk; a similar arch I have seen in the wall of another home in Pianello, but I have admired it only from the roadway. A slim grey column divides the dimpled glazed panes. Through the window, unfurling leaves from the branch of an elm tree wave in a gentle wind. The whole is like a framed painting, but when I straightened my back and raised my head higher than the window sill, I gazed way into the far beyond, into an apricot glow stretching across a valley, a divinely framed picture of the hills and farms of Tuscany in a patchwork palette of vines, fallow fields, olive groves and farmhouses.

Dragging my eyes from the window, I had a moment or two more while the Ingegnere closed a book he must have been reading, and which for some reason he was determined to replace on a bookshelf, an awkward arm's length from his chair. This gave me more moments to cast my eyes around the salon, eyeing lamps with lop-sided shades, carved and gilded mirrors from which the gilt has faded, even the silvery coating on the mirror glass is all but lost. Wallpaper is Gothic in style, an involved design, and the ceiling is sponged earthy Tuscan red, proof that nothing has changed in this room for a hundred years. This unexpected retreat into the last century is bewitching. Pretty spring flowers, arranged in a crystal bowl, sit on a table; there must be somebody else at home. I visualize a Signora rustling from the room in stiff-necked emerald taffeta, fluttering an ivory fan, upswept hair tumbling from pins of mother-of-pearl. But perhaps it is the daily help.

Once we felt ourselves settled, the Ingegnere told me of his life's work to preserve something from the patrimony of his family, and of his sad destiny, his disgrazia, or bad fortune. Preparing me for what is to come, he warned that I may not believe his story. Facing him across the room I make myself as comfortable as this straight-backed French chair allows. This is a story I want to believe. He is ready to begin.

'I will start in the second half of the eleventh century,' he opens, amused that he has immediately dealt an unexpected hand, 'because that is when the story of my family begins. A thousand years ago the superpower in Europe was a king of Germany, who invaded Italy and, cleverly coming to the aid of a pope, when summonsed, found himself rewarded with the imperial crown on his head. But German emperors meddled in the affairs of Rome. From that moment you could say great friction between potent emperors and the papacy began.'

The Ingegnere speaks with slow deliberation because his diction is slightly muffled, and there is a quaver in his voice; he gathers his thoughts.

'We will move on a hundred years to the late eleven hundreds, when the family Hohenstaufen took power through German imperial bloodlines because from that point, this friction, a bitter power struggle, would not end until one power was eliminated. You see, German emperors had a dynastic claim to the imperial crown, but the great strength, and by paradox, the great weakness, of the pope, is that the successor of Saint Peter is mortal. At loggerheads with the papacy were emperors like Frederick I, an impressive personality known as Barbarossa, or Red Beard, and Frederick II, who was one of the most remarkable emperors in Italian history. But that is another story . . . I had better not get sidetracked. This was not the only battle waged by the papacy, because we are in the epoch of the great crusades. Kings and rulers from all of Europe heeded the ordinance of the pope, leading armies of pilgrim warriors on religious quests to wrest from the grasp of the infidel the holy relics of Christ. German emperors, too, for more than a hundred years, led crusading knights to the east. We have to remember that at this time Franciscan fervour had risen; they were grappling with dreadful poverty among the masses, and also with heresy. I will come back to that in a minute. The Castello Reale of the German emperors of the House of Hohenstaufen was at Stuttgart. I know the Castello Reale, because I have been there, and I have studied a series of frescoes on the walls of one state room leading into another. My curiosity was more than scholarly because when I studied these frescoes, as well as ancient manuscripts and archives, I found indications proving that my ancestors took flight to the Castello Reale at Stuttgart with German emperors. And I also discovered that when the emperors journeyed to Rome they travelled through Tuscany, and – listen carefully, this is significant – the emperors rarely stopped at Siena because the Sienese were hostile to them. Instead, because this was a città that was consistently battling for its liberty, the German emperor and his entourage halted here, at Montalcino! My ancestors who dwelled in the Castello Reale in Stuttgart were doctors, and an emperor never travelled without his doctors. This is the legend that has come down to me; the doctors who accompanied the German emperors during that hundred years are the earliest record of my family. You may not have known, Signora, but I am of German descent, and up until the year 1250, my ancestors, resting here with emperors, set down family roots in Montalcino.'

Astounded by the revelation that the Padelletti are not Italian but German, I am unable to repress the urge to ask a question when he pauses. 'What do you mean, until 1250, what happened then?' He smiles, harbinger of the second half of the first arresting story of the morning.

'Now we must return to heretics. As well as rebellious emperors accompanied by a royal court and shielded by an army, the Pope had other problems on his hands. The crusading poor who trudged on foot to the east on pilgrimages, at least the miserable few that survived, saw the virtuous life of Christians in the east and, disgusted at the corruption of the clergy here, decided things needed to change. A heretical sect began to blossom; the Cathars, or Albigensians – it is the same thing – who took on a dualist religion: Christianity and Zoroastrianism, which came from the east and went back a thousand years to the Romans. Living among the impoverished masses their purity of life was in astonishing contrast to orthodox priests, and they became known as the *puri*, the purists. This sect, spreading alarmingly, was a threat to the papacy and had to be extinguished, but the only way the Pope could curtail the puri was with violence. Frederick II was Holy Roman Emperor and, although he had taken the cross, he dillydallied when the Pope decreed that he ought to be crusading and the Pope excommunicated him. Frederick did not feel this was altogether just, so he declared a state of war against the papacy; subsequent reactions lent the papacy a hysterical bent and the panicking Pope launched a crusade of death, which endured for twenty years, upon heretics. They were murdered, not by the thousand, but by the tens of thousands, all over Europe. The papacy managed to be rid of the puri, but countless faithful souls were caught in the killing, or were forced to flee, and some fled to Germany. The Cathari sect was extinguished, but the Pope was still facing his other formidable opponent. Frederick II was a powerful emperor, and he was *stupor mundi*, the wonder of the world.

'The Pope was terrified of facing Frederick in battle, but recalling his success against the puri he cunningly fired up religious fervour, enacting a decree for a crusade, naming Frederick and his followers as heretics. Within two years Frederick II was dead and his court and followers were fleeing for their lives, seeking refuge in the Castello Reale at Stuttgart. Many of my ancestors escaped into exile in Germany, where they stayed for three hundred years, waiting for the moment to return. The last surviving Hohenstaufen, a sixteen-year-old boy, was beheaded and the royal blood line of the German house of Hohenstaufen was extirpated. I cannot trace, with certainty, those of my family who put down roots in Montalcino around 1250, but I know many stayed, as you will find out soon. Persecution of heretics was lighter here because the Montalcinesi never accepted absolute rule by the Pope. But for their own safety they were forced to disguise names, separate themselves from heretics, and also from the court of the German emperor.'

He pauses, watching me, waiting to see if I understand, but my head is reeling. 'So all you know for certain is that in the 1100s some of your ancestors put down roots here in Montalcino, and in 1250 some fled back to Germany?' He nods his head, adding, 'It is important that you know about my German ancestors, and about heretics. My story must leap three hundred years, but Germany and heretics remain a part of it. I am sure you are aware we have no surviving archives in Montalcino before 1460 – everything was destroyed in a fire – so we can glean nothing. At the Castello in Stuttgart the archives expose scarce detail but I am convinced that my ancestors who escaped back to Germany did well enough, and I am just as sure that when the first one returned, three hundred years later, he was openly welcomed in Montalcino.'

There is no time to question why because with a sudden spurt the wooden cane, which has not left his hand, is repositioned as a vaulting pole and he is edging unsteadily upwards from the chair. His knees have stiffened, sitting so long. It is a supreme effort of will to keep his weary bones flexing; he is a proud man, infirmity in his elderly years frustrates him. I fancy a firm refusal were I to offer my arm. A minute passes and, once his legs stop trembling, seeming to groan as he transfers his weight, he unbends his back and swaps the cane to his right hand, wheezing with the effort. 'Signora –' his chest makes a whistling sound as he breathes out the words – 'I need to stretch these useless legs which let me down more every day . . . we will adjourn to my biblioteca.'

We turn out into the hall. The rugs and tapestries form a barrier dividing the sunny salon from the gloom. Now I see they are not worn thin, but the work is delicate, the tracings are fine. Perhaps they are hand-worked silk tapestries from the east? Passing room to room, at a discreet few paces behind the Ingegnere, stronger traits of Gothic style surround me: above my head the vaulting interlaces like a fan, and every doorway we squeeze through is a pointed arch. On the floor chequered mosaics form a geometric path, sunk to unevenness, and on the walls stylized florals mingle in stencilled decoration within circles and squares and diamonds. I have never been inside a home like this, and never marvelled more. It is clear that the Germanic ancestors of Ingegnere Padelletti continue to influence the lives as well as the minds of his family. From the roadway only the mullioned windows are visible, but inside, the love of Gothic is everywhere repeated.

Books secreting millions of words are shelved along the four walls of the library. Manuscripts, maps, prints, handwritten notes and tattered unbound folios lie scattered across tables, balance on chairs, gather dust on windowsills and protrude from glass-fronted cabinets. Layers of dust and peeling paint, together with the smell of mould, or mice, or worse, add to the urgent need to search for words written by another's hand. There is a wondrous richness in this library, an accumulated hoard in pursuit of truth or a marginal scribble that might allude to the comings and goings of the family Padelletti. The Ingegnere is an assiduous bibliophile, and this is his lair.

He lowers himself into a chair. A red satin cushion pads the wood; he seems to fit well into the wide seat and rhythmically bending his arm backwards at the elbow, as if he carries out this simple manoeuvre several times a day, he hooks the crook of his cane over the chair back. But he is red-faced and his chest rises and falls with appalling gasps. I am thinking that perhaps I ought to offer to return another day, but he waves an arm towards the shelves and puffs: 'This is what has befallen me, what I am reduced to, but it is also my life.'

A half tender and half caustic smile crosses his face; there is self-mockery in the words, but there is humorous irony in his eyes and in his croaky voice. He is glad that I am here to listen,

but he needs recovery time. His blue eyes captured my attention
the moment we faced each other in the Gothic salon. Blue eyes
are uncommon in Tuscany and his are so like my own, and my
father's. In subtle ways the Ingegnere bears an uncanny likeness
to my father. He is not tall and a formerly robust body has settled
into a thick waist; he is round faced and fair skinned with a
ruddiness about the cheeks. A quiff of hair strays about his brow
but I cannot tell if his wispy hair was once Nordic blond, like my
father's, whose ancestors arrived in Scotland by way of Gaul. It
all fits together, now that I know about Padelletti Teutonic
ancestry.

'I cannot tell you a lot about the Padelletti in Germany during
those three hundred years because I would need that long to go
and dig it all up. The story is somewhere there, in the archives of
monasteries and royal vaults, but I know not where, and it is too
late. Anyway, I am running out of time to search for all the
details of the story I will tell you next, about the Padelletti in
Montalcino. But in Germany I *did* uncover a most amusing tale
about a certain Giovanni Padelletti who, doing well for himself,
living and working among the higher social class, found he
needed to vanish swiftly otherwise his head would roll.
Giovanni, it seems, was attracted to beautiful women, especially
upper class women of noble blood and it was in the matrimonial
bed of one such noble woman that he was undone. Giovanni was
in the wrong bed at the wrong time and taking flight from
Germany, because he had knowledge of ancestors here, he
arrived in Montalcino in 1529. This is the first mention of a
Padelletti in surviving archives of Montalcino and it is
provoking to reflect that the recording of his name in
handwritten documents tells us he was an architect, given no less
vital a commission than to strengthen fortification of the fortress

during a decade when Montalcino was frequently under siege. Do you believe that a German appearing out of nowhere would be awarded this vital commission, paramount to the very survival of the village, if there was not some link, some knowledge of his background?' There is nothing for it but to shake my head for within a second he resumes. 'But there is another clue that Giovanni had Padelletti family here, which can be found in an extract, testifying that he submitted to the Comune an application to be admitted as a cittadino of the first class in Montalcino!'

Embarrassed that I cannot conceal doubting eyes, I smile, but he sees I have not grasped the significance. Perhaps this thread might be helpful in my quest to untangle the social classes of Montalcino. I had not expected the tale of Giovanni's love exploits to end in a riddle about cittadini.

'Signora, not just a cittadino, but a cittadino of the *first class*!' He has not finished with my ignorance and is rightly suspicious that he needs to broaden my perspective. 'The cittadini of Montalcino divided into classes depending on their skills. At the lower end of the scale were those who laboured for someone else, people who worked the bellows at the forge, or carted water for the tinters; they were fourth in the rankings. Then those who had a kind of independence, who worked a business, like butchers and merchants, were ranked third. Higher up the order, at second position, were artisans, the shoe and slipper makers, leatherworkers, maybe even tailors and the like who were skilled as well as independent. But at the top of the pile, as in any society, were jurists, doctors and other professionals, like architects and school masters. Those with a privileged education, notably jurists and doctors with a laureate, are still hallowed in Montalcino. It is one of the things that sets this village apart and one of the reasons for the iron-clad link between us and Siena . . . but that is yet another story. I had better return to Giovanni because you might think it was normal that Giovanni would be in the upper social class of cittadini just because he was an architect. No, it was not as straightforward as that. In the first place, Giovanni had to be voted in by someone else, which means he had to have friends, and the law stipulated that he must have lived *inside* the walls for no less than ten *consecutive* years carrying out his profession and constructing a reliable reputation. He had to pay twenty-five scudi, which accompanied his application and ended up in the pocket of the Grand Duke of Tuscany, and it was ultimately the Grand Duke who sanctioned his acceptance as a cittadino of the first class in Montalcino. Social status was granted, with voting rights, and he was eligible to stand for office, taking part in the social, cultural and economic life of the village.'

In one explanatory burst I have been offered a lesson clarifying the complex social class of the cittadini. Four clearly defined ranks within the walls. I file this knowledge safely in the back of my mind. Coupled with what I have derived from conversations with others, I am at last going to be able to sort that one out. Already it is making sense – I only have to think about Luciano the shoemaker, Enzo the winemaker and Fabio in Pianello! What a fuss they made at the time of his laureate from the University of Siena. It was written up in all the papers and weekly newsletters as if it was honours to Montalcino, as well as Fabio. Vaguely aware of church bells pealing, I sigh because I am going to have to offer to leave. The Ingegnere will be hungry; the hour of pranzo, lunch, is near. As if to check the validity of the warning peals, he draws out his pocket watch. We both know it is time to close our ponderings.

61

'Well, you now know that the German Padelletti returned thirty years before Montalcino faced her most horrific war against the carpetbaggers, and twenty before she withstood the vicious siege by the Viceroy of Naples ... but I promise to refrain from diverting into a story of sieges, wars and death. Instead, when next you come, we will take up the story that establishes the amorous exploits of Giovanni Padelletti. Exponential growth through marriage came quickly, and it was not long before the archives record fifty Padelletti families living in Montalcino. Through that part of the story you can follow the bloodline of my German ancestry which brought greatness to Montalcino, but so much sadness to my family.'

I dismiss thoughts of finding my own way to the door; as a gentleman of the old world he would find that discourteous. Slowly I follow his dragging footsteps back to the shadowy hall where he deftly tugs on the length of rope to swing the door to the ante-room. A formal handshake, and I agree that I will telephone to be sure he is feeling well enough for our next appointment. Buon appetito and a formal arrivederla is all I can proffer in return for a morning too marvellous ever to forget. As soon as I am over the stone step, the door closes. Not willing to relinquish so abruptly the world behind that door, I giggle with pleasure that I have uncovered, without a single question from my list, four distinct ranks of social classes among the cittadini. Speculation encourages my mind to think about the likelihood of similar ranks persisting among others. I cannot imagine it would have been possible for the contadini, the peasant class, to have had a hierarchy among themselves. Many of the contadini are today among the wealthy of Montalcino, having risen from a life of perpetual debt to undreamed of riches. Like our friend Primo Pacenti and his family.

The peasant class laboured on the farms for rich landowners under the system of mezzadria, so they could also be referred to as mezzadri, but the common label is a contadino. The mezzadria was not feudal, where a vassal lived off the land belonging to a noble in exchange for his allegiance when called upon in battle for his noble lord. Nor was it comparable to sharecropping, where a tenant farmer on land belonging to a noble handed over part of his crop in satisfaction of rent. In Tuscany the mezzadria was an ugly battle for survival. The landowner, called the padrone, could not always count on liquid wealth but he possessed enormous tracts of land. Unless he was able to convert his land holding into wealth he could not live in accordance with the expectation of his socially superior friends. A peasant had no land, no money and nowhere for his family to live. One of the earliest surviving documents attesting to the birth of the mezzadria in Tuscany recounts a plea from a peasant to a landowner, made in the year 821: Give me your two oxen and I will give you my arms. The ground was barren, laid waste by war and a solution was found whereby the peasant offered to work the land, sowing and reaping, and in return he pledged half the fruits of his labour to the padrone, who was bound to be the provider of whatever the peasant required in order to make the land produce. The crucial difference between the mezzadria and other medieval farming practices was that the contract written at law between peasant farmer and padrone imposed that the contadino's financial reward be reckoned according to the *profits* of his labour. As the centuries passed, the reckoning of the mezzadria split became a cruel battle of wits because many padrone believed superior social class gave them the right to reduce the contadini to servility. He exploited the ignorance of the contadino, which was effortless, because mostly the contadino was a simple peasant and could not read, write or add up. The contadino had one card to play. He was driven, or he resorted, to skulduggery, concealment and cunning. The padrone fought these subversive weapons with lies, fraud and harsh tactics from an iron fist.

We were not aware of the significance of the term contadino, or the humiliation and unjust cruelty it signifies, until our friend Primo told us about the life of his family, tied to the land. Primo is the firstborn son of a peasant family that had laboured under the mezzadria for centuries, bound by a contract to work the land for one padrone after another. His earliest recollection of his toddling years is when his parents, grandparents, who were already in their seventies, aunts and uncles and all the children lived in grinding poverty in a humble farmhouse above an animal byre. He grew from a child into manhood, working from morning till night beside his father in unbelievable misery because no matter how hard the family worked they could never get ahead, only further and further behind. The deadliest weapon possessed by the padrone was his ability to keep the contadini in debt because only he wrote up the ledger of the farm; the contadino did not even see the ledger and because he could not read or write he could not tally the value of his work. Even when the Pacenti family went from one mezzadria contract to another Primo says that for his family it was like going from purgatory to the inferno because the padrone claimed that the contadini were dishonest, cheated whenever they could, were lazy and would prefer to ruin the farm than make it produce. Primo once showed me the books of the family going back decades and in all of them, at the end of each farming year, the padrone wrote in the book that the family had made no profit . . . but instead he added to their growing indebtedness to him. During the Second World War many contadini were conscripted into Mussolini's army, so the farms, deprived of labour, could not produce and by the time the war was over many of the old padrone had walked off the land, abandoning it. The contadini were offered small parcels of land by the post-war government at a very low interest rate and some of them, including Primo, sensing social changes looming, were courageous enough to borrow money and settle on the hill of Montalcino. Primo and his family bought a few hectares at the hamlet of Canalicchio, just outside the walls. But when contadini like Primo began to plant vines instead of beans the old padrone, who still owned large tracts of land, called upon their friends in high places to stop them, claiming that uneducated peasant contadini had no knowledge about making wine. This was true. Most of them had never even heard of the word Brunello, but they could see a glimmer of hope for a less degrading future in wine than beans, and although it took decades of struggle and humiliation, when the Consorzio del Vino Brunello was founded in the late 1960s, their tiny parcels of land were included in the boundaries permitting growth of the sangiovese vine for making Brunello di Montalcino.

Primo's story highlights the past degradation and struggle of the contadini for social justice, but I have uncovered mezzadria social humiliation with wider and longer lasting repercussions. When he lived on the padrone's farm, the contadino carried to Montalcino the farm goods to be traded, always on Friday, which has been market day for more than six hundred years. At the market he was able to barter his share of eggs, or a chicken that had hatched unseen, or a bag of corn in exchange for repairs to his boots or a length of cloth for his wife. The contadino had food to eat, because he grew it himself, but he never had cash money in his hands. But I was shocked to discover that no contadino could ever hope to become a cittadino because the law forbade it. The huge wooden gates in the walls encircling the village swung closed at dusk and the law stipulated that every contadino had to be through those gates and gone, back on the farm with the animals by dusk – and if he was tardy, he would suffer a bashing at the hands of indignant cittadini. He was excluded by his lowly class from all functions of village life enjoyed by the cittadini, and even when he was allowed entry into the village at dawn he was segregated, because no contadino would dare use the main thoroughfares leading to the piazza. Rather, he was forced to use the dietri, the narrow roads behind, so that the cittadini did not have to look upon his lowly bearing. This practice, using the dietri, persisted in Montalcino and did not cease until 1970, and even today it is not difficult to pinpoint elderly contadini who come to the village on market day. They scurry, heads down, eyes diverted, as if they are stigmatized by their sad past. And it is not common, but sadly, neither is it rare, to overhear disparaging words, insulting comments, such as the cynically mocking: 'It takes seven generations for a contadino to change his ways' – a scornful reference to education, hygiene and wiliness. Well into the late 1960s hundreds of farmhouses that are now picturesque crumbling ruins were allocated by the padrone in which the contadino and his family could live. These farms had neither bathrooms nor toilets, or electricity; water was drawn by hand from a well outside the door. Most cooked on an open fireplace, possessed little more than a wooden table and in two or three small rooms slept a family of ten. At the bottom of the steps the pigs were penned, as well as fowl, and under the house was an animal byre. Working dawn to dusk and living in a house smelling of cow dung and damp stone offers extenuating reasons for body odour and dirt. Education was not open to contadini, and with no plumbing, it is easy to understand why they could not wash as often as cittadini. It is little wonder they acquired wily traits, cannily circling their way around rough justice. But in only a generation or two the contadini have turned the tables on the cittadini because now they are educated, they produce world-class Brunello, their farmhouses are restored to splendour, the envy of the cittadini, with every convenience of a comfortable home in the beautiful hills of Tuscany. But the once subservient peasant class have not yet shaken off the humiliation of the past, even if they are among the richest land holders in all of Italy; a contadino is always a contadino.

The piazza, echoing with the chime of church bells, is a tableau vivant; cittadini hurry from store to store, subconsciously digesting the nearness of mezzogiorno and family obligations the bells announce. As I watch, the bronze bell in the tower flounders towards an unmusical jangle, until, heaving under the strain of lolling its own weight, it swings across the belfry in its perch above my head. Hesitant strokes clang and clap while the bell widens its swing in readiness for the clapper, which, intensifying at the halfway mark, strikes the lip of this upturned cup the first of one hundred times. The one hundred bongs of mezzogiorno warn that pranzo should be cooking and sensible souls planning a route towards home. Thunderous mezzogiorno bongs subdue the musical chimes from the other churches; only the celebration from the church of the Madonna, furthest from the piazza, refuses to be relegated by the bellowing bell. The bells of Sant' Egidio, those I heard from the Ingegnere's biblioteca, ring out their bulletin early; if you do not heed the Angelus, then it is too late, you will miss morning Mass. On feast days, or saint's days, all the church bells ring, spilling a crescendo of musical chimes over roofs and into our homes. When the bells of Sant' Agostino, San Salvatore, the twin bells of San Pietro, which is our quartiere church in Pianello, and the bells of the fire station at Osservanza ring on patron saint's day, everybody in the whole village is linked by joyful chimes, held captive, united in the celebration of a day of reverberating joy. Modern worlds have curtailed tolling bells, but not Montalcino; the rhythm of daily life cannot sensibly unravel without our bonging bell. The stone tower, and the tolling bronze bell, is symbolic, a rallying call written with ancestral blood into the pages of their history on this hill. A tiny bell at the very peak of the belfry once tingled only to announce the death of a cittadino, but it is now motionless and noiseless. Instead, a solemn death bell tolls from the tower of San Francesco. Funeral bells cast me into gloom; single, mournful strokes count away dragging seconds until the defunct is borne from the church. Wedding bells, funeral bells, daily saint's and patron saint's day bells, Angelus bells, death bells, fire brigade bells, school bells, Communion bells, victory bells, mezzogiorno bells as well as on the hour and half hour the great bronze bell in the tower bongs the time of day, not once, but twice, with a margin of inaccuracy that affirms that Italians make their bells and clocks tell lies, for our happiness. What a cacophony must have flooded over the terracotta roofs when all of our thirteen churches summonsed the faithful. Living here, Luigi and I have grown accustomed to sleeping or working through tolling, ringing, bonging, mourning, chiming, timing, warning, pleading and celebratory village bells.

This morning's bonging in my ears is simultaneously a warning and heralds joyous news. Mary has received the message of our coming Redeemer, but the caution about pranzo

I am not disposed to heed. After a morning in Gothic glory I need to passeggiata along with the cittadini of Montalcino. Piazza del Popolo, the heart of Montalcino, at first appears not to be as grand as those found in some Tuscan villages, but the stone dwellings overlooking the triangular piazza, and those along cobbled roads leading to it, strike a harmonious chord. Pleasingly persistent, this is a concordant medieval village, one that has not suffered from the impetuous and discordant whims of post-war modernization. The tower which houses the mezzogiorno bell looks none the worse after seven or eight centuries standing there, slashing the piazza in two. Caffè alle Logge is adjacent to a gallery and looks on to the tower, whereas Caffè Fiaschetteria, a famed historic caffè of Italy unchanged since 1888, frequented by European royalty and socialites of past and present epochs, is on the opposite side of the piazza and tower. Sitting nonchalantly on a velvet banquette last week I found myself sipping caffè next to Principessa Maria Beatrice, the last king of Italy's sister. Village life radiates around the piazza; the symbolic bonging bell in the tower and daily greetings are habitual accompaniments to morning espresso in the Caffè.

Picturing the daily life of cittadini within the social classes illustrated by the Ingegnere, hurrying about their business wrapped in cloaks and shawls when shops were filled with artisans and merchants, the thronging piazza must have been a swell of boisterous bustle. The fragrance of baking bread would waft around, just as it does today when Giovanna crashes the oven doors at the bakery, flipping out steaming loaves of Tuscan bread. True to the past to which she belongs, Giovanna pulls a cotton kerchief around her head and with the corners knotted together, ties little peaks on her crown. The acrid odour of mashed chestnuts and the stink of skins from the leatherworker once mingled with her baking bread and wood shavings from the workshop of Beppe Sordo, deaf Beppe, who built wooden sledges for the children. Everyone of advanced age remembers where Mamma Pampillona cooked for her Osteria, a wine house which opened its door hundreds of years ago to serve soldiers guarding the fortress. Within living memory, to those approaching life on this hill for a century, Mamma Pampillona's marinated eel, sardines under pesto and tripe with saffron must have created tantalizing aromas, mingling with those less appetizing. I can well imagine the popularity of Emporio Megalli where, till recent times, cittadini ordered tordi, thrush from the woods, a delicacy of a faded era. Nearby is the hole in the wall from which Momo sold his ropes, thick coiled ones that he delivered on a cart to Siena, ordered by the Sienese as the start-rope for the Palio. Momo wove his hemp and flax below the church of Madonna, turning the coil by hand and walking backwards along the same stony track on which I walk every morning.

Sounds, smells and memories; they are a part of the past and Montalcino is a part of them. Musty barrels from a dozen wine shops would be rolled on to the cobbles to dry, the vinous fumes cut through by odorous dung dropped by horses and oxen. Cassocked priests ringing handbells on their way to give Mass would enter the fray as vendors vied and cittadini leaped over the rushing slush of waste in the gutters to the sound of artisans hammering, sawing, forging and tapping. This mezzogiorno, as I exchange courteous greetings, I imagine knots of people gossiping amid a bevy of passing carts pulled by shackled white oxen, baying donkeys with skinny legs loaded with panniers of chestnuts and barking dogs snapping at the hoofs of neighing horses and swarms of shrieking barefoot children. Flashing to mind is a childhood memory from a friend, a respectable cittadino, whose identity I am forbidden to disclose. He told me that not many years ago near Caffè alle Logge was a shop that sold salted anchovies in wooden crates stacked on the roadway. 'Walking past on our way to school, we wandered along, swinging our books which were tied up with a bit of string, and when the moment was right we grabbed a wandering dog and with a bit of playful taunting would persuade the mongrel to cock his leg ... right into the anchovy crate! We bolted off to school laughing our heads off. *Our* mothers could never afford to buy anchovies, anyway.'

The sounds and smells of noon have changed. Entering Caffè Fiaschetteria, emptying my mind of leather-aproned blacksmiths banging on anvils and my nostrils of the uric smell of adulterated anchovies, I greet Luca and Gianfranco. Luca moves to the caffè machine. He creates the creamiest macchiato; it is proprietorially elevating not to have to order. As a matter of pride a barista, barman, memorizes the daily habits of everyone who comes into the bar. A warm soporific aroma rises into my nostrils, displacing anchovies. Reposing on the banquette behind a marble table clustered on cast iron legs, my favourite seat, I tell Gianfranco that I have passed the morning talking with the Ingegnere. 'Ah, how is he?' he enquires, then adds, 'He never came here often because he was always away, but his Signora came to Fiaschetteria every day.' Raising the tiny cup to my lips I remain expectantly silent, and he continues: 'She was a bella donna, even in her elderly years, elegantly dressed with her hair ... you know ... up like this.' He swirls a hand and pokes his head to indicate coiled hair pinned at the nape of the neck. 'She always ordered caffè macchiato, and never sat anywhere except at this table, exactly as you do.' This is spooky. She is my rustling emerald silk Signora! His thoughts run on, so I offer not an inkling of reaction. 'When she was here, maybe with a woman friend, she would chat and laugh along with us, but if she came with a stranger it was more like: Cameriere, do this! Or, waiter, come here! She would put on exaggerated airs, and we had to bow to her signorile commands. But she always left a generous tip . . . there was plenty of money.'

My macchiato is perfection; did this delectable aroma rise into the nostrils of yesterday's artisans and merchants when they bustled around the piazza? Gianfranco clears cups from a table and Luca sets the spitting monster hissing steam for the next order. More like brothers, it was years before I knew they are father and son. My mind will not let go of images of cittadini, matching people I know and their roles, the mode of life in the village and the prevalence, even today, of class, social appearances and salutations, rituals that, if not observed and learned, can hold an unknowing stranger beyond an impenetrable wall decade after decade. I grin and grimace, remembering the drama when I told Luigi I had met my friend Ofelia at the bar and that we had indulged in a second campari soda. He was horrified. 'What!' he exploded. 'Isabella, you have to learn, no self-respecting signora would order *two* drinks at the bar.' I lost hard-earned brownie points for such lower class behaviour! In an inward looking mountain community like Montalcino there are rules about etiquette that, although unspoken, one needs to learn. But there are compensations for living in the way of the Montalcinesi. Like the time Luigi could not remember his pin number and, fretful about attempting a withdrawal perforce the cash machine might gobble up his card, he rang our bank. 'Oh, caro Luigi,' came reassurance, 'non preoccuparti, don't worry, keep punching numbers, maybe you will get it right, but if you don't, come past in the morning and I'll empty the machine and give you back your card. You can try again.' I suppose a cittadino bank manager, by virtue of his first-class status, can authorize such conveniences.

Outside Caffè Fiaschetteria, during cold months, two marble-topped tables are permanently wedged along the wall. These tables are for the orators. Every morning and evening wise men on pensions come to sit in the piazza and debate. They do not drink, having earlier swallowed a habitual espresso, but they come to discuss local politics, or football, or reminisce about the past. They are the unchallenged possessors of the hallowed talk tables. Peering through the glass door I spy Ilio Raffaelli laying a book wrapped in a newspaper on one of the orator's tables and raising his arms with explicit gestures. He pushes out his chin and enters into dialogue with I do not know whom, because I cannot see round the door jamb. Ilio was a left-leaning Mayor of Montalcino during the years before Brunello changed the fortunes of the village and, together with another friend, Ivo Caprioli, has recounted many stories about the artisans and merchants that I have been picturing since I left the Ingegnere. From Ilio I also learned about boscaioli, woodcutters, like Bruno, who I thought were cittadini, but they were not included in Ingegnere Padelletti's social rankings, so I am not sure where they fit. A woodcutter's life was miserable because from autumn to spring he and his family lived in the freezing woods suffering from more than lack of electricity and plumbing; they suffered from hunger as well. A few boscaioli chop wood for fuel stoves and open fires which persist among the cittadini in Montalcino, but strangely, even if they have not worked as boscaioli for decades, they vehemently claim they *were* boscaioli. They do not seem keen to shake off the stigma living as an impoverished woodcutter in the bosco awarded them. Ilio flails his arms dramatically, bringing home his argument with an oration adequately eloquent for a senator in the Roman Forum, triggering release of my memory that before too long I must find a way to concentrate his mind on the woods. Ilio chopped wood from childhood to his adult years before he became Mayor, so I am guessing he will help me dig up the story of reclusive carbonai, the charcoal burners.

Hierarchical divisions in Montalcino do not end with the once fettered but now wealthy contadini, nor with my discovery of the four social ranks within cittadini. It is a complex puzzle. I do not know if woodcutting boscaioli and reclusive carbonai will eventually slide neatly into my deliberations, but I hypothesize that Ingegnere Padelletti, as the story of his family unfolds, will shed light on the noble class, the aristocrats. If I am to resolve conjectures of jealousy and enmity between growers then I must untangle the web that links an as yet invisible elite, the noble class, to the hill of Montalcino. The Ingegnere made no reference to nobles among cittadini; perhaps no nobles live in the village.

The bonging bells have given up to silence; my cup is empty, and so is the piazza. Cittadini have melted away and wise senators have vanished to contemplate the merit of Ilio's discourse. Shutters are dropping with a rattle and crash – merchants in Montalcino refuse to relinquish their right to a sensible pause of three hours for lunch, followed by a nap and an hour hoeing onions or artichokes. By six o'clock the piazza will be crowded with cittadini, of every class, parading on the evening passeggiata.

CHAPTER FOUR

Raise the Dreaded Ladle

Two festival marquees have risen inside the keep of the medieval fortress of Montalcino. The fortress could not be mistaken for a castle: it was constructed in the 1300s as a vigilant look-out for a garrison of troops and has always had a defensive role. Not only the defence of the village, but also the protection of trade routes visible from the towers where archers and soldiers watched for an enemy army bivouacking between the hills. The Montalcinesi are tied emotionally, and with blood, to this austere stronghold because from the towers and battlements bellicose citizens have incontrovertibly proved their loyalty to each other, spilled their blood, sacrificed their sons, suffered fearful atrocities and striven for their liberty from the day they chose to live beneath the oak trees on the hill of Montalcino. Guarded by the sanguinary towers, the marquees in the keep are dwarfed by soaring stone walls. Narrow, splayed embrasures open in the walls at angles useful to archers and soldiers, but once secure within, the only trace of a world outside is the scattering of clouds across the shifting sky. Each spring, the raising of the tents signifies a link to an age of bravery, a return to ancestral defiance. For several years Luigi and I came to dinner at the festival as loyal supporters of Montalcino's football team because the object of the festival is fundraising for the club. When Angelino and Massimo, both committee members responsible for administration and fundraising, approached us a few days ago, appealing for assistance, with charitable nods we eagerly volunteered to work ourselves – unknowingly at the time – steadfastly into the ground. Suave (and noticeably tanned) Angelino intoned: 'Listen, what upsets me is that people from all over the world come to our spring festival, but we are a group of friends without experience of the wider world – can you help us? Last year stranieri, strangers, walked out confused because they did not understand how things work. You will be able to explain our system, and we will not lose their business.'

The largest marquee is for volunteer workers. At one end we have a kitchen; it *became* the kitchen when Massimo hauled in two fuel stoves, which are not difficult to source in Montalcino because many cittadini adore to cook on steel plates over smoking wood fires. Truckloads of chopped logs are stacked up to the roof and gunny-sacks of jute bulge with brittle kindling. Close to the wood pile three open-flame gas burners precariously balance on wooden platforms. A wide makeshift table on hinged trestles straddles the heart of the tent, and from this wobbly frame Olga, who is capocuoco, head cook, together with a friend of mine from Pianello, Onelia, keep watchful eyes on burning fires and sizzling hotplates while engineering vital rituals to do with food. Luigi adroitly enquired of Angelino at what hour we should be present. Angelino, using a predictable Montalcinesi escape clause, an artful skill we have not yet mastered, replied, 'Ah, Luigi, come whenever it suits, we would not want to cause inconvenience, the stranieri turn up all day long so whenever you can spare the time will do fine.' Reflecting on this exchange our eyes glazed, we both sighed deep and long, our benevolent spirit severely dampened, because, in Montalcino speak, such a double-edged open-ended invitation means we will be required all day, every day, for eight consecutive days. I knew with a terrible certainty that we had crossed the Rubicon.

Olga and Onelia are not the only women slaving in the camp kitchen. Lucia, who is Massimo's wife, and Marisa have a work bench all to themselves. They are preparing toasted crostini, the first never tiresome mouthful of every Tuscan meal. Each morning Olga twists newspaper into spiral wands and curls it under wispy kindling to light the stoves, while Onelia upturns sacks of flour on to the trestle table and with accustomed shoulder and elbow power kneads and rolls the pasta. They then chop fennel, celery and a mountain of onions for zuppa and heave boarding-school sized cauldrons over to the gas burners ready for wild boar and tomato sauces, which will simmer for hours. Lucia and Marisa stuff pork sausages down the narrow spout of an archaic hand-cranked mincer, slice slippery chicken livers, chop basil and parsley picked each morning, all at the speed of light, and grind pine nuts with a stone pestle. This kitchen energy is exerted in preparation of antipasti and primi piatti, first plates. Outside the rear door of the marquee, with only a floppy canopy with a roped fringe for protection, Giancarlo, with his beautifully tended moustache, and leathery Franco light fires which they leave to crackle down to glowing embers. The secondo piatto, second plate, is an unfailing smash hit with village-festival-roving Italians; and it is not difficult to visualize strangers salivating at the sight and aroma of grigliata mista, a nose-twitching wood-smoke-wafting aromatic bistecca from an outside grill. Giancarlo, standing over a grooved chopping block with a machete in one hand, balances half a side of pork over one shoulder while he slashes and hacks at a carcass of ribs. Tuscans dwelling in medieval villages suffer limitations when it comes to a barbecue, hence this fortress festa with gigantic iron grills to barbecue pork steaks, spare ribs and sausages is a temptation loaded tradition. The meat is fresh because Angelino is dispatched to the farm before each festa to supervise the slaughter of the pigs. Tuscans distrust any food, particularly meat, if they are not intimately connected with its origin; Angelino pledges provenance and quality.

Beppe, whose pigs they are, is president of the football club. His real name is Giuseppe, but he is affectionately coddled with this soubriquet. There is another bench laden with Tuscan salami, prosciutto crudo and a hundred rounds of black-skinned pecorino sheep milk cheese, all produced by artisans a handful of kilometres from the tent. Affettati, cold cuts, an unjust description of these delicacies, are the domain of Gigi, Marisa's husband, and behind him, from iron butcher's hooks, dangle ropes of pork sausages looped together from which, whenever Giancarlo signals, Gigi unravels an armful and roping them literally over his arm tosses them through the door to the barbecue. I do not understand the control of, or lack of, biological organisms. Roped pork sausages hang in the open air for days on end in Tuscany. Yet where are the flies? Should one sausage be carelessly deposited on a picnic table in Australia, by the time the bread is sliced a trillion ants and creepy crawlies, buzzing green flies, many legged biting bugs and screeching birds have fought a crazy war to dissect its parts and carry it away. It is an Italian mystery.

A mountain of canvas flour bags stuffed with loaves of unsalted bread is delivered from the bakery to the door of the tent at dawn for no Tuscan table is complete without door stopper wedges to sup up sauce. At the opposite end of the tent to the kitchen is Roberto. I am relieved he is a long way from me. Roberto, an Ilcinese to the bone, mutters in a dialect as old as Montalcino and thus is excused from full pronunciation of any word of more than four letters. Fortunately there is no call for Roberto to open his mouth all morning because on his broad back he carts wicker demijohns of red wine into the tent and, pouring from the nozzle poking over his shoulder, upturns the wine into a stainless steel vat. Later it will be syphoned into unlabelled wine bottles. We sell a discreet drop of red at a reasonable cost, but visitors who come to this festa are not content to drink only the *red* wine grown around Montalcino, they come year after year because it offers a scarce opportunity to taste the *stupendous* red wine, Brunello di Montalcino. Bottles of Brunello are donated by generous growers – but not all can be included in this praiseworthy category. Angelino stands bottles on the counter to enable identifying vineyard labels to be read and customers taste whichever vintage by whichever grower of Brunello is on sale that day. We sell Brunello by the glass, measured by the milligram. The economic wizard behind this banquet is burly Massimo, Lucia of the crostini bench's husband. Blustering commands disguise his cuddly warmth, and his frequent bearish growls end always with: 'Hai capito?' Have you understood?

Living inside the girdle of walls Luigi and I know almost everybody who comes and goes. We share the village and the piazza with around two thousand cittadini, although a few more than that live out on the farms, vineyards and hamlets within Montalcino territory, which covers about twenty-four thousand hectares. Many of these country folk are in the village regularly, bringing children to school, or visiting the bank, and we often share caffè or exchange a few words in the piazza. But it has penetrated my mind that Luigi and I are not friends with, nor have we fraternized, even at arm's length, with an elite class in Montalcino. Friends like the Dottore at the pharmacy, the school professors and a number of auspicious academic achievers (intellectual honours awarded by laureate are not lacking here) should be categorized as cittadini of the first order, an upper middle class, but why have we received no invitations to attend community functions where we encounter an elite?

It is a broad leap from being president of the football club to belonging to the nobility, but confusingly the label on the bottles of Brunello that Beppe propels all around the world claims his wine is the prodigy of the Azienda Ciacci Piccolomini d'Aragona. Piccolomini is a nomenclature not to be wrongfully claimed or unwittingly glossed over, because the Piccolomini forged European links and married into noble bloodlines, wielding power through immense wealth and ecclesiastical concordances.

In the enlightened 1400s a Piccolomini broadened his education with Montalcino's intellectual scholars, destined to become the humanist Pope Pius II. With my inquisitive mind focused on growers, generous and less so, socially recognizable or not, I wonder why it is that Beppe, whose name is Giuseppe Bianchini, grows, bottles and markets Brunello di Montalcino with the unchallenged authenticity of an aristocrat? Perhaps Beppe is a noble in disguise. Over eight days there will surely be a moment to pose one or two cannily worded questions. But why do tongues stop wagging and eyes roll back the instant I open any discourse attempting to root out clues about aristocrats? What is eating away at an elusive elite, if indeed there is one? Could it be apprehension that fear mongering will damage the hallowed name of the wine, and the village?

This acclaimed wine has a complexity connoisseurs swoon over, an ethereal bouquet that confounds the most dedicated sommelier. In optimum cellar conditions it has been proven to age for one hundred years. A century-old Brunello is a living, harmonious wine, its nebulous characteristics subtly refined in the bottle. Over and over I listen to speeches and read the words in the newspaper. This brilliant wine was not an accident, it was a creation. Often a tantalizing amplification is offered, and because of this I find myself lured into double-barrelled curiosity. Sometimes I hear that this wine was a creation by noble Montalcinesi – it is a noble wine. Who and where, I keep demanding, are these nobles? And if, perchance, they are here, why will no one tell me, or can they not tell me, which noble is responsible?

The contadini cannot enter into this equation. In the 1960s it was powerful people who influenced authorities in high places, seeking to prevent grindingly poor peasant farmers like Primo from eligibility to grow Brunello. It cannot have been anyone among village dwellers because their tiny parcels of land outside the walls were not vineyards thirty years ago. I shouldn't wonder if blatant one-upmanship and barely disguised jealousy between growers, who perhaps form some kind of class of their own, and barbs that occasionally find their way into the press, are tactical manoeuvres in some Hannibalic struggle. Could it be unmentionable class warfare between nobles? Is it rooted in the unspoken avoidance of the question which nobody is prepared to ask? Who created Brunello di Montalcino? And who is afraid of the answer?

'Angelino!' proposed Luigi with reckless abandon at nine-thirty on the morning of day one. 'We cannot stand about waiting to translate for stranieri, can we not help with other work?' Angelino, who is capo or boss of the whole festa, did not hesitate to gratefully accept. 'It's going to be a good day,' Massimo warned gleefully, 'the weather is perfect, sunny and warm, and today is a public holiday so it is a ponte, a bridge, to the weekend. Italians are on the move and thousands of them are coming to Montalcino.' Those prophetic words sent a chill through my heart and soul.

Dragging weary bones from bed this morning, Luigi and I looked dispiritedly at each other. 'How did we get into this?' he groaned, struggling to balance on trembling legs. 'How do we get *out* of it?' was my wry response, shoving a packet of gauze sticking plaster in my basket. Steadfast allegiance is everything in Montalcino. Today is day five, but I cannot ignore a premonition of next year's festival, and the year after that, drifting through my mind. This festa is one of those trials of fealty we must withstand, and outlive. Are we totally loyal to our football club, or are we seasonal match-takers but not givers?

Sifting through four days now ended I ask myself: how deep is my desire for integration in this mountain community?

Twenty cheerful souls are wandering aimlessly in the tent when we arrive at half past nine, a couple of hours before Angelino unhinges the customer counter and we open for lunch, or, putting it succinctly, we have a couple of hours in which to *make* lunch. As the days have passed we have become conscious of what has to be actioned to ensure this happens. But we seem to be the only workers who have grasped the essence of any objective, because everybody else, with non-conformist Italian insurrectionary spirit, practises no apparent principle of time and motion. Italians are born with an immunity to be influenced by order, preferring confusion. Cunningly, they do not respond favourably to being told what they must do, or when they should do it, nor how it should be done. The President of the Republic may pass laws and the Pope may pontificate, but unless a law or commandment suits their personal philosophy, Italians will not bow to secular or spiritual liberty stealing manipulators. Angelino perceives this endemic national trait, because he shares it. He is capo of the festa, but utters not a word of practical instruction or managerial control to help achieve orderliness or any ambitious objective. Hence, the choreography, latent but theatrically evolving inside the marquee, hints at nothing short of chaotic scene-shifting.

This battle-scarred stone fortress is not wired for electricity or piped for gas, and we have no clear mountain water trickling from an aqueduct. Nothing more than wobbling duckboards keep our feet higher than a dirt floor and rising puddles, but Massimo has thoughtfully driven ten-inch nails into the ancient stone wall so there is a row of shiny heads on which to hook jackets. Mysterious tradesmen, whose names I know not, but whose familiar faces contort and twist at football games, appear and disappear, dictated by the daily panic. Thus, we are wired for electricity which provides a live current most of the time, and some of the time spurting water blasts from a crude pipe, drenching near and wide. We are overlooked by exposed electrical cables trailing across walls and looping from the canvas roof. Ten-point multiple sockets dangle in mid air, into which a battalion of slicers, choppers, blenders and mincers are plugged by the cooks whenever they feel the inclination to slice, chop, blend and mince. Numerous fat rubber hoses and steel pails are positioned to trip over and run around all day; the safety precautions and stage management for the actors in this play is horrifying.

Things look up momentarily when I coerce myself into action on my first chore of the morning. Onelia, sweetness itself, has not betrayed my years of intensive garlic peeling training in Pianello. Lucia and Marisa rub each crostini destined to be lathered with diced tomato with an open garlic clove; above the bench swing plaits of garlic waiting to be peeled. I think Onelia, too, is in awe of the power wielded by head cook Luciana at Pianello, because, conspiratorially, she turns the blunt end of a knife at me and mouths a single word, couched as a question: 'Insalata?' Five wooden crates of lettuce, ten lettuce to a crate, to be deconstructed and rinsed in as little of the precious spurting water as can be resourcefully contrived. In two minutes I am wetter than the insalata. The accompanying side plates on the Ilcinese menu are mine alone to construct. Insalata, or, alternatively, white cannellini beans concealed in silvery vessels big enough to stick my head in. An electric tin-opener is a state-of-the-art modern convenience we do not run to, so I squeak and creak my way around these iron-plated monsters and upend tins, slithering beans into a bucket. The morning expires by the time I consign fifty dripping lettuces and an inestimable quantity of beans into the orbit of the master cooks. Dressing washed insalata with salt, balsamic vinegar and extra virgin olive oil, or glistening beans with black pepper and more olive oil, is entrusted only to Olga or Onelia who boast decades of training to accomplish this ritual with senior citizenship finesse. Glancing towards Luigi, my heart tremors; he is apron-clad bread man. The gleaming saw for splitting hard, unsalted Tuscan bread is fixed permanently to a swaying bench. A pine tree would not shudder should the trunk be sawn through by that shark-toothed blade. Luigi is on automatic pilot: extract crusty loaf from sack, turn on its head, saw down middle, let one half fall into right hand and saw horizontally into slices, scoop up second half and repeat. Slices free fall from the saw-toothed blade into a canvas bread bag held upright between his legs; reason enough for my anxiety.

As the hour for pranzo draws nigh we take up secondary duties. Luigi stacks plastic knives and forks on the bench, and, sliding a sheet of white paper between each one to form a tray-mat, piles the counter with cardboard trays. Nicking my fingers disengaging razor-edged plastic plates one from each other, I stack them ungraciously on the table, ready for Olga's soup and Onelia's pasta. Fingernails, together with the flesh of thumb and forefinger, were cut to shreds on day one; gauze sticking plaster stems the flow of blood and cushions the deepest wounds.

As the morning unfolds, Angelino, standing guard over full bottles of Brunello on the counter, calls: 'Isabella, come over here and talk to these strangers', or, 'Isabella, come and explain to these stranieri how to order lunch.' Smugly pleasing to Angelino and Massimo, the bother is that these strangers are German,

Swiss and Dutch. To Angelino it is all the same foreign language, and he assumes that I speak all their languages. Most Europeans speak some English, so I stumble through communication, but this is laying a dangerous premise.

Heralding a ponderous warning that nobody can ignore, with glinting eyes the kitchen Goddess Olga raises a giant iron ladle and waves it through the air, as if waving a magic wand, and screeches across the tent: 'Siamo pronti!' We are ready! Giancarlo launches his ash-smeared forehead through the door brandishing a barbecue fork: 'Anche noi!' he boasts, so are we! The rehearsal is over, the curtain is up, and the drama opens.

At the counter, salivating Italians and stranieri who have paid for their lunch are standing ten deep, waiting impatiently for its delivery on to cardboard trays, which they will then manoeuvre skyward above a sea of heads to the second marquee set with tables and backless benches. Italians will not be bound by the regularity brought fairly upon the masses by forming queues. It is another of those distinguishing Italian traits; which is to say everyone in this gabbling mass sincerely believes that they ought be the first one served; a forest of raised arms push across the counter, thrusting sheets of stamped white menus, food choices marked with a squiggle, under our noses. I glance through the menu. Ah, two customers have ordered two crostini, one zuppa, one pappardelle al cinghiale, two grigliate miste, two insalata and one plate of pecorino cheese. But sequential order is paramount, otherwise customers grizzle about cold pasta and hot cheese. Snatch a tray from the pile, throw upon it plastic knives and forks and a bowl of bread and dive towards the cooks. 'Una zuppa, e una pappardelle,' I call out, but seven others clamour at my elbows, shoving and yelling orders which roll rapidly from their mother tongues more easily than mine.

Olga screws up her face at me. 'Quanti?' I holler one of each as loudly as my voice box allows. Next, out the door to the grill. 'Giancarlo, two grigliate miste, please.' I aim to address Giancarlo because Franco of the leathery face terrifies me. 'Spare ribs are not quite ready,' Giancarlo recommends, 'come back in three minutes.' Back inside the tent I race to the far end: 'Gigi, one serve of pecorino, per favore.' Gigi is uncommonly courteous among our barbarian troops. 'Si, Isabella, subito, immediately.' Now for the crostini. Over to Lucia and Marisa. The women drip parsley and basil sauce from knuckles, their cheeks are splattered with diced tomato and they smell nauseatingly of straw coils in an oil mill. Frantically, they try to keep pace with orders. Marisa plonks two serves of crostini on my tray, which I guard with an arm so that no one can steal them on to their tray. Back to the kitchen. 'Olga, where's my zuppa and pappardelle?' She again queries how many I ordered. 'One zuppa and one pappardelle,' I sigh. She says, with deadpan face: 'Why didn't you say so earlier?' She is admonishing me, but I ignore her scolding because I am on my way through the swinging door to the grill. Two mixed grills are pronto – on to the tray with the crostini and back to Olga. Balancing a zuppa and a pappardelle along one arm . . . needing a second tray . . . not daring to let the first away from the crook of my other arm or someone will snaffle the grills . . . back to Gigi. 'Here you are, Isabella, is that all you want?' Bless you, Gigi. To the counter, push away flailing arms, lay down trays, try to find the eye of whomever I am serving. 'Signora! It's mine, over here,' a black jacket claims, 'but you've forgotten two insalata.' Damn, back to the kitchen. Criss-crossing, backtracking, combative elbowing and shoving, racing in and out of the swinging door, rushing up and down the duckboards, dodging leaking hoses and dipping under cables, yelling to be heard and guarding each plate on a tray, eight of us compete against each other; anyone with an empty tray or a half-turned eye is a victim, ripe for robbing.

'Isabella!' It is Angelino. 'Stranieri! Quick, before they leave!' Startling urgency makes it sound as if they are some rare breed in danger of extinction. 'I'm halfway through an order,' I implore. 'Go! Go!' he begs. 'Or we'll lose them.' Racing to the cash desk, for the first time it registers that the milling multitude stretches out through the fortress gates. To the chagrin of hundreds, progress is temporarily halted because of these stranieri. Oh Dio, they are not speaking English . . . they are Russian! What do I know of Russian? Are there no ordinary English tongues out there? Angelino, in self-congratulatory smugness, informs Massimo that I can speak Russian . . . as well! Back to my bristling Italian client, waiting for insalata and beverages, the other half of his order. Two bottles of water, una con gas, una senza gas, two different benches, as I should expect. One glass of rosso sfuso, our bulk red wine, and, damn, one glass of Brunello. 'Angelino,' I plead, 'will you pour me a Brunello?' 'No!' he snaps. 'Haven't got time, I've got to sweet-talk the grill, a group are coming in and Franco must have fifteen grigliate miste pronto in ten minutes.' I would rather explain about Brunello than face the barbecue with that news. Franco spends eight cranky days cursing the smoking grill, swearing at we lowly servants and dispatching us to go to *that* place because we rush in and out demanding steaks that he claims are blood raw in the middle. Burning his fingers, he seizes sizzling sausages and drops them on to plates, pouring forth a volley of abuse, declaring that the grill is closing that very minute. He and Giancarlo, day by day, take on the likeness of charred spare ribs themselves; red eyed and smoky, their creased faces are reddish brown and covered in soot; greasy, smelly barbecue kings. Woe betide any American who dares ask for ketchup; Franco brandishes the machete.

Above the babble I shout to my impatient black jacket that the rosso sfuso I will serve in a plastic cup, but that Brunello should be served in a crystal glass. He murmurs cautious agreement. 'Allora,' well then, I go on, 'you have to pay me five euro as a security for the glass.' He nods. The rosso sfuso sloshes with a rush into plastic, and I reach for . . . no glasses! Over to the spurting tap where Luigi is drenching himself and washing glasses. Back to the counter. The balloon glass is etched at the precise point to be reached with Brunello. I pick up a bottle of Ciacci Piccolomini d'Aragona Brunello . . . but I don't care *whose* it is! Beppe, like a silver shadow, floats ephemerally past, but other than a glance at his retreating form there has not been a solitary nanosecond to put my mind to any other cause. Forcing my shoulders to relax, with due reverence, I pour the Brunello, and, with classy execution, swill the wine in a wrist flicking counterclockwise swirl. Unappreciative of my dedicated gusto, black jacket turns away, exasperated. A white menu pokes up my left nostril. This tragicomic drama unfolds uninterrupted for three hours until, miraculously, the counter is empty.

Tired, dizzy and dirty, I sup a bowl of zuppa and gulp rosso sfuso. Luigi, eyes glazed, shovels pappardelle in the vague direction of his mouth. 'I'm okay,' he giggles incriminatingly, noting my quizzical eyes, 'I snuck a nip of grappa after I dispatched every tray!' Forty-five would be a rough numerical estimation of his trays.

Through gritty eyes I am mesmerized by cooks flapping flour bags at the table. Between lunch and dinner battle-hardened Olga, Onelia, Lucia and Marisa pound and batter dough into the shape of flying saucers. A continuous stream of Ilcinesi wander up in the afternoon to munch on pasta fritta, a treat with a colloquial name in every Tuscan village, until omnipotent Olga, Goddess with the glinting eyes, raises the dreaded ladle, and screams: 'Siamo pronti!' Off we go again. By ten o'clock beaming Angelino yells: 'What supplies do we need tomorrow?' He scribbles on a paper serviette as colourful responses reach his burning ears. Wordless Roberto flings empty bottles on to the open tray of a three-wheeler work truck. Licking his thumb, hibernating behind the wood pile, chortling Massimo counts the cash. At last the fortress gates slam shut. We lurch unsteadily towards home and crash into bed contemplating the prospect of living through three more days. Sleep overcomes us before we are even aware of it.

Years ago, initially reluctant, I fell into step with Luigi in his unwavering loyalty to our football team. Curious, and wanting to spend time in the company of the Montalcinesi because I had much to learn, I quickly found myself caught up in the emotional thrall, tearfully embracing our team when they won a championship. Following the team to away games means Sundays with Ilcinesi fans in all manner of hazardous situations, and sometimes ponderous fare at lunch, but every second Sunday when the game is played here in Montalcino, at our campo sportivo, we gather for a pizza, sharing euphoria, or grief, depending on the day's result. Beppe has been club president for years and it seems he cannot quit. Every year is his last, but then the team is victorious in yet another championship; ambitiously he targets a higher league the ensuing year. But football has reached dizzying heights. Our team has only one rung in the amateur league left to climb and should they succeed, reaching

Eccellenza, the leap into history for Beppe and the football committee will launch our team and the village of Montalcino into the realms of glory . . . and the first rung of professional Italian football. The bottom of the top league!

But the way ahead calls for sacrifice and each season is punctuated with scintillating highs and mournful lows, and is fraught with danger. How I survived the low when our team played at Tegoleto I cannot mentally comprehend. Most tifosi, fans, remained sensibly cosseted on our own snug hill, but we trudged over frozen Casentino mountains to a football field angled to entrap every blast from a raging wind that carried snow and sleet through a funnel of forest trees and into the stand. Olga and I were unidentifiably enveloped in layers of jumpers and jackets, fur hats and boots. A woollen blanket draped our knees and ankles, another hooded our hatted heads and yet another encircled our already triple-layered bodies. We huddled, a shapeless woolly bundle, dying of cold as minuscule particles of ice floated in thin air; only chador-like slits allowed our eyes to squint towards blurry figures crunching on granite, because there was not a blade of grass to play on. The wind was so unbelievably penetrating that our eyes watered and teeth chattered; when Luigi recommended grappa, in unison we croaked an unexpected favourable reply. The initial moments were, on reflection, amusing. Upholding the unspoken national tradition that all Italian football teams factor in a ratio of devastatingly handsome players, Michele skidded on to the skating rink marked out for a football game and executed his warm-up laps naked from the waist up. It was a handsomely muscled chest, which gorgeous Michele flaunted, but Olga and I were wretchedly alone in the stand; instead of sinking into a state of feminine enrapture we were unromantically aghast. Our blinking eyes boggled not at Michele's rippling chest, but at hardening icicles. Maybe our team won, maybe not. By the time Olga and I disentangled ourselves from our sub-zero igloo ninety minutes later the score was an incidental by-product of our sacrifice to be there.

One Sunday the game was on Isola d'Elba, an island Luigi and I had never visited. Calculating the distance and unpredictable sea crossing our team planned to depart the day before, which meant that, with clever advance planning, we had half of Sunday to explore Elba before the match. Luigi enthusiastically signed the disclaimer, eager that we would travel to the coast with the team, board the ferry with the team, eat with the team, sleep in the same hotel as the team, watch the team play and then we would travel victoriously home together. Faced with this stunningly zealous plot who was I to cast doubt that his judgement might not be altogether faultless?

The bus departed, late, from the fortress wall next to our campo sportivo. Not many of our friends were with us, an anomaly that heightened wavering doubts, but Illiano and Zampa, two older football friends whom we have known for years were aboard. Maurizio, team driver, was in a fiery temper. The engine would not start. Luigi is proud of a worthy bunch of lads on our team, but when Maurizio ordered them to alight, march to the rear of this twelve-metre fifty-two-seater and push it so he might kick-start the motor, worthy sentiments did not present themselves. 'We are the football team,' Vito howled indignantly, 'and you want us to push-start this ***** bus?' Maurizio has a temperament that sees only black and white and brooks no contradiction of his seldom wrong decisions. 'If you want to play football tomorrow,' he snapped caustically, 'you've got no ***** choice. Get out and push!' When the engine turned over, clouds of black diesel billowed from the exhaust; the language billowing towards Maurizio from coughing, spitting, bilious footballers who inhaled the filth is not to be laid bare in print. An ill omen for a two-day excursion.

The bus was a kind gift from a sponsor. What he demanded and received in return is lost in the folds of history, but it is an old bus, a very old, dented, peeling, hysterically pink bus, stencilled on its flanks with the emblem of Montalcino's football team. The interior is rosy pink as well, and drab, as are the sun-bleached velour seats and hideous faded curtains. When we passed through villages people halted in their tracks and stared, mouths open, then they laughed. Perplexed motorists braked and offered us right of way as if we were a gang of terrorists. Some tooted, reaching the conclusion that we were spaced out hippies. Our players detest this bus; it is hardly a fitting tribute to their sporting achievements, but the committee cannot afford a new bus. Players stuck up their fingers at honking motorists and I stuck up my nose at smirking pedestrians.

Along the way Maurizio bumped and rollicked into a service station. Only when I focused on him topping up the tank did I contemplate the peril to which we were exposed. It was not the petrol tank. He poured gallons of black oil into the engine. Back in the driver's seat, I listened as, grimly jocular, he assured Illiano that he had tightened the wheel nuts. Illiano and Zampa grimaced, recounting distressingly graphic descriptions of the quivering bus the Sunday one of the wheels vibrated loose. Rattling and creaking and lurching we reached the coast and spilled on to the dock; Maurizio hid the bus. We clambered up the gangway as Beppe purred arrogantly on to the ferry seconds before the jowls closed, behind the wheel of half a million euro worth of brand-new, mirror-shiny, two-door Maserati. Luigi winced when I could not suppress the female instinct and commented provocatively that we, too, had a Maserati, albeit not so shiny and new, sitting doing nothing back at Montalcino. It is antagonizingly hard to draw fight out of Luigi; he is passive. The calm sea crossing was uneventful. Once we docked at Elba, and unloaded, we trailed behind the team who lugged bags and balls and banners and bottles to the hotel, a modest seaside establishment. Rooms were adequate, no cause for complaint, with rice-paper-thin walls. 'Listen,' I hissed to Luigi through gritted teeth, 'I can hear our players breathing!'

Bomber Vito, our star goalscorer, is one of two players who have been with the team for years, and he is captain, forming our attack with Yuri the Wardrobe. As we rise through league ranks Beppe buys players befitting our category, which is how Yuri came to us. Something of a bruiser, Yuri breaks through a defence not confident in their ability to halt his tank-like progress. Not only devastatingly handsome, Michele is a graceful bird on the field; more like a swooping kestrel than a gazelle. Then there is our nut case. The Mister, trainer, despairs of him because nothing can wipe the grin from Crazy Cristian's face, even when he is trampled, flattened, kicked in the shins and carted off on a stretcher, which is every week, because he plays as if he wants to be the first hero to fall in a war game. And we have a running screamer called Alessandro, all curly headed and busy. Curly locks runs for ninety minutes, even to the dressing room and back at half time, executes full length body push-ups and tortuous triple leg twists whenever he finds five empty seconds, and screams at everyone else because he reads the play, even when he is not where the ball is. With hair like Nicole Kidman and the face of an angel, Sauro is our tenacious terrier in the centre. His team mates order him to the showers first after every game because it takes thirty minutes to dry his flowing ringlets; he carts a supersonic hairdryer in his kit bag. Defence is orchestrated by terribly sensible Graziano, kept rock solid by illusive Mirko, who never hurries but reaches the ball in the nick of time, and strengthened by artful spiky-haired Nicolo. We have a trick card, a joker, brought on when our trainer, Valerio, thinks it is time to deal a jolly. This is Pippo. It is not his extraordinary ball skills – even I, watching football from a naively feminine standpoint, recognize these as something out of the ordinary – that foil the defence, it is because Pippo looks as if he is not physically able to do anything. He has not the build of a wardrobe, like Yuri, he is not frighteningly fit, like busy Alessandro, or unpredictably crazy, like Cristian. Just when an opposition defence is a tad complacent, watching him tie his boot laces and mess about around the fringes of the bouncing ball is when Pippo leaves a devastated defence trailing in his wake. From a standing start Pippo rockets up the field for sixty metres and, weaving like a frenzied thoroughbred, brings a lofted ball to a dead stop on his toe and, before it stops spinning, he flicks it airborne, dancing straight to Vito, or ploughing into the net. Meanwhile, Pippo motors off the field of play and out of sight, trying to decelerate.

With this band of heart-warming acrobats we encamped at Elba; awarded the honour of occupying the room next door to Crazy Cristian. Soon he was joined by our mature, soberly minded goalkeeper, Vincenzo, which did not make for a convivial mix. My reasonable plea to Luigi that we should dine on succulent Mediterranean seafood in a romantic waterside trattoria met only with astonishment that I would even contemplate missing the joy of dinner with the boys. We dined on a strictly carbohydrate energy boosting menu of boiled white rice dressed with nothing at all, green salad similarly clothed, and bland steamed chicken. Luigi rose on Sunday morning swearing he heard nothing all night; no crashing bottles, interesting language, mournful cellular calls to sweethearts, nor even caterwauling music. Fortunate for him. We passed a tedious morning with a drugged taxi-driver who traipsed us around the lowlights of the island; but soon enough it was time for the match. That game, not worth recounting, passed in an eminently forgettable slow-motion saunter up and down the field. Elba scored, but the game was without synergy. The Mister, seeing our team wanting, drew out our top gun and the joker dealt one of his maverick hands to equalize the score. *That* was a sweet moment.

By the time Sauro dried, pressed and pleated his locks and Luca, our medico, received the doctor's permission for grinning Crazy Cristian, battered from head to toe, to be released from hospital and we decamped from our cute seaside hotel, night was falling. The ferry heaved and hove across the sea because the weather changed, and, with no victory to celebrate, grumpy players fell asleep, and so did grumpier Luigi. We reached the mainland to be greeted by a blackening night, pelting rain and bleak winds. Maurizio charged off to fetch the bus, muttering that he would telephone Vito if he could not get the engine started, but bad-tempered players told him, in ripe and unkind words, to forget that idea. Uncomfortably damp and tired, we left port facing a three-hour drive home through the rain in a dilapidated bus with dodgy wheel nuts and an oil leak. Beppe was long gone; I watched him glide effortlessly away from the dock.

Peering blindly through the streaming windscreen into a cindery sky, Maurizio did not pause in his black–white argument with Illiano about why we failed to win the game. It was a circular debate, going nowhere, until: 'Porca miseria!' he shouted, braking and pulling the bus towards a non-existent shoulder along a narrow road. Sleepy bodies around me and snoring players wakened at the back wondered what had happened, but I watched with a sinking heart as one windscreen wiper collapsed and shattering pieces vanished down the side of the bus. One wiper was grinding away, but it was the wrong one. Maurizio thrust his head and shoulders out of the window into pelting rain, one hand on the wheel, while Illiano peered through the windscreen and Zampa conveyed his garbled messages to Maurizio to steer left or right. Maurizio is a competent driver, but even he was petrified. We crawled along in this hair-raising predicament, passing darkened service stations until, two hours later, the lights of Grosseto rose over a hill. Some players live at Grosseto; they telephoned for taxis, but I could not convince perversely stubborn Luigi that we, too, should desert this sinking bus. At midnight, when the fortress of Montalcino was before my eyes, dead envious that Beppe had been tucked up in his cosy palazzo for hours, I swore an oath, within earshot of my passive husband, that never again will I put one foot on the island of Elba, or on that hysterical pink bus.

Tonight the journey home from Elba is but a distant memory. We are winding down from the spring festival. It is the end of a holiday weekend and only a handful of visitors have delayed departure for home. A musical ensemble on this final night; Angelino's band is playing and he serenades a tipsy couple dancing in the keep. Customers are finishing their meals. A weary smile creeps across Olga's strained face. Hands on hips, with a knitted brow she surveys the midden to which our marquee has been reduced, then, to my astonishment, pulls her cap over her hair and stokes the fire. Onelia is waltzing with Giancarlo, but the dancing breaks when Franco calls him to the barbecue. Lucia and Marisa drag two empty tables inside the tent and join them end to end, and, together with Onelia, set places for twenty-five of us to eat dinner. Luigi and I verge on bodily collapse, but I gird myself, conscious that exhaustion must be defeated. All of us, bone shatteringly weary, both physically and mentally, huddle in the tent enclosed by the fortress walls, yawning, sighing, massaging our aching feet and lolling one against the other. Beppe is with us, but this is not the night for speeches; we seek only the mutual closeness our remarkable effort affords. Giancarlo is not flipping pork steaks on the grill. He dashed home and fetched half a daino, fallow deer, from his freezer. This succulent buck from the woods, brushed with rosmarino, is grilled by our two carbonized barbecue kings, and accompanied by spinach doused with a generous fistful of peperoncino, and slippery cannellini beans, dressed exquisitely by Onelia. Empty Brunello bottles gather on the table. Luigi sits with the men, as is the way in Montalcino, and I am with the women, all of them our friends.

As the final minutes of the Festa di Primavera expire, my jaded mind turns at last to Beppe. His eyes are like blackcurrants, missing nothing, and he pays meticulous attention to impeccable dress, which is tonight in marked contrast to my grubbiness. Black, perfectly creased trousers, white shirt, grey jacket and a contrasting tie sit well on a slight man, not tall, and, to his dismay a span of more than sixty years has passed him by. It does not seem to me that he could be a noble, one of the mysterious elite of Montalcino, but just the same, I am the more insistent to find out why his Brunello carries the name Ciacci Piccolomini d'Aragona. Glancing around this table, rubbing Marisa's toes, which wiggle on my lap while Lucia kneads my shoulder blades, I believe we may be earning a trusted place in the hearts of our friends. When the night is done, Beppe, standing in the shadow of the fortress gate bids us goodnight with an affectionate kiss, surprising me by assuring Luigi he will telephone next week to fix a time for dinner with his family. My mind thrashes about, tugging at conflicting emotions that grapple with the oddness of the life we are constructing. We take our leave; perhaps one day the rewards *will* outweigh the sacrifice.

CHAPTER FIVE

A Wee Bell and her Chatelaine of Keys

Down in the valley a quilt of soft green tips is on the move. The wind huffs between clouds drifting in a wide sky and whistles across a multitude of spires which collapse into each other until it sweeps low, gathers them up once more, and they rise and lean into the emptiness of their own vacillating waver. Watching over the walls which girdle Montalcino a breathtaking choreography unfolds at my toes, a hypnotic dance of drowsy impulses constructing and decomposing the landscape each new day.

Easter is almost upon us. In short weeks the summer solstice will signal a renewed calendrical mood. Tuscan hills *are* more beautiful than dreams have feigned; contour-ploughed fields rise and fall, are lost and picked up once more in the folds of the hills; a never finished work of art. Smiling poppies bare scarlet cheeks, waving from banks left raw by gaping furrows where a farmer's tractor bumps and rattles. Next to a hill flushed with tufted luxuriance and bouncing scarlet heads infant sunflowers burst through; but they are still dreaming – it will be weeks before slender stalks search for the light, or weak heads bend with limp grace, turning petals to the sun. Sunflowers demand the fullness of a scorching summer. Cypress look darker than ever in the pale horizon, far below, where a tell-tale line of chestnuts chases a serpentine brook.

The temptation to linger above the eastern wall is not easily overcome but my goal this morning is to circle east to west. I am on my way to see if Enzo is in his vineyard. Having listened to his revelation of what was happening beneath my feet in a dark subterranean world, when I thought the vines were passive, I find myself smiling when I scrutinize his vineyard day after day, watching for the very first bump to bubble on a branch growing close to the track, which will tell me that wriggling rootlets found moisture and minerals sufficient for their task and are transferring life up through the trunk to the budding branches and the waiting sun.

Entranced by the science fiction rite Enzo elaborated, I am sensitive about whatever else it is that I do not know about wine

made from the grapes growing on this hill. With dispro-
portionate attention I have studied the vines nearest my morning
path and am certain that for two days something extraordinary
has been underway. I intend to find out what. In any case, my
morning is empty because Ingegnere Padelletti is not well
enough to see me. So, I am on another trail. A few days after our
recuperation from the madness of Festa di Primavera, true to his
word, Beppe rang to arrange an evening together. I beseeched
Luigi to accept straight away lest the last weeks of spring speed
away too quickly. The Montalcinesi accelerate into the great
outdoors for a brief sundrenched summer and I do not want to
find myself sat under a tree in a shady garden. I want to see *inside*
Beppe's palazzo. I am fairly tingling with excitement at the
prospect of this evening at palazzo Ciacci Piccolomini
d'Aragona. This empty morning, I am bent on grapes.

Turning from the east a dirt road circles below the wall
bringing me at last to a steep climb and breathlessness at the
bricked-up gate in the rear of the church of the Madonna. I am
back on my customary gravel track. A momentary glance
towards an olive grove is all I intended, but my eyes reel back for
a piercing stare. Something is new here, too. Spindly branches of
coarse, cutting leaves are studded with miniature four-petalled
flowers. Peering into the hollow at the base of a tiny white flower
I spy a ball of green. I have been an annual witness to olives at
birth. It is the birth in the vineyard I have never witnessed.

'This is a crucial moment. If it does not go well, then all could
be over for my crop this year. Sometimes it takes just a handful
of days, but a week might stretch into two. There is nothing I can
do but wait, and pray. Walk over the rise with me, to where the
sun has not reached. Vines to the west are two or three days
behind and we'll see more.' For Enzo, winemaking is an

exacting science. This critical moment is cloaked in subversive behaviour, as were his wriggling rootlets. We backtrack to the edge of a row of vines and cross a succession of stony ruts, walking for fifty metres. Knowing precisely at which plant to stop, Enzo motions me to come close, brushes leaves aside and lifts a thin stalk which quivers under the weight of a blurry mass. 'This vine is ready to flower but you need powerful binoculars, your naked eye cannot see hundreds of miniature flowers which are opening as tiny unfolding petals slip away.' It is less disconcerting now that I understand flowering is not visible. 'So, these are the grapes?' I suggest impetuously. 'No, not yet! This is the miracle. It is called fruit set – poor fruit set can mean no grapes, or not enough grapes. If you can, picture in your mind just one flower. As the petals slip away and the flower opens, grains of pollen, which were hovering at the tip of the stamen, drift down. A vine is a hermaphrodite! It fertilizes itself – and a grape is the fruit of its own fertilization, the pollinated ovary from its own flower!' It is difficult to share Enzo's admiration for this herma-something-dite. Fortunately he does not test my naturalist ignorance, but enthuses: 'With amazing speed each flower will fertilize itself and instead of a cluster of flowers, if fertilization is fruitful, there will be a cluster of grapes!' The humorous pun is not lost on me. We both laugh. 'How is it going this year, Enzo?' His smile fades and a worried frown creeps over his brow. He drops his head to one side, and raises his thumb and forefinger into a pointed gun, angled so that his fingers point upwards with a writhe and twist. This is winegrower language. 'Too soon to tell. Flowering began a day or two ago . . . I expect a certain amount of failure . . . unfertilized flowers are already falling to the ground . . . but the minuscule pinhead clusters are beginning to grow. But look at those tendrils!' His pained voice emphasizes his terrible fear. Curly tendrils race away from the plant, wrap around each other and push upwards. 'Do you recall I told you the soil here is uncommonly deep?' Hesitantly I nod, cautious in case he springs a scientific question to which I will not know the answer, but his voice lowers in despondent desperation. 'I have a vigorous vine on my hands. It is not weak enough and I will have to make it suffer, otherwise the wine from these grapes will not be elegant. It will be ragged around the shoulders and would not age to become a noble wine, which Brunello di Montalcino is.'

A noble wine? Everywhere I poke my nose an unexpected but ambiguous clue is thrown into the pot of mystery. Enzo is anxious that I understand his worry. 'These vines are only a few years old, but they are greedy, impetuous sprawlers. If the vine is putting too much energy into growing leaves the danger is that it will not have enough energy left to nourish and grow beautiful grapes.' Enzo moves from plant to plant, examining branches, frowning at the abundance of shooting tendrils and green leaves. He will walk the rows for hours, inspecting each plant. We exchange farewells and he invites me to visit any time, unaware that hardly a morning goes by that I am not on the track above this vineyard. I pick my way carefully out of the row and climb up the hill, over the rise, and on to the track. A noble wine, or a wine *made* noble, or both?

The village of Castelnuovo del Abate is a clutter of stone houses piled on top of one another between narrow lanes and shoulder wide pathways leading to piazzette, little piazzas, on a hill overlooking the Abbey of Sant' Antimo. It takes its name, New Castle of the Abbot, from an abbot of Sant' Antimo who once lived in the village, although I do not know of any castle there, and is a peaceful, sleepy idyll, perfect for those who seek immersion in a Tuscan village unchanged for hundreds of years. With only an alimentari, grocer cum newsagent, and a post office, one bar run as a co-operative, and little else, Castelnuovo del Abate cannot be described as a thriving metropolis, even in an ancient Tuscan village sense. It is silent and weary, a sad reminder of days gone long ago; but I *do* like coming here. When we are on the way to some other village hanging on the slopes of Mount Amiata, a solitary mountain which hovers over the valley like a purple giant, we sometimes dine at a trattoria close by and passeggiata through the village to see if anything has changed. Castelnuovo del Abate changes not.

This evening, later than anticipated, we are on our way for dinner at Castelnuovo, not to the trattoria, but with Beppe. We planned our departure in good time but one of those unexpected Montalcinesi hiccups got in the way. Luigi led the way down the stairs and I, with unsuppressed excitement, bearing a mandatory gift, clipped down in my stiletto heels. He closed the door behind me and turned to walk . . . to where? He looked at me: 'Whenever did we last use the car?' What he meant was he did not remember where it was parked. Cars and parking are a nightmare for mayors of medieval villages sitting on mountains and one the Mayor of Montalcino is caught in the throes of resolving. Most residents have a cellar four or five steps lower than the roadway, but garages most of us do not have. Numerous parking zones are designated for residents and, depending on circumstances, such as time of re-entry, time of year, weather and good fortune, our Maserati is parked wherever we are fortunate to find an empty space. We have not taken the car out of the walls for nearly a month; a pleasurable thought, because one of the advantages of living in this community, where we want for nothing inside the walls, means we rarely need the car at all.

Luigi checked the car park down the hill, but our car was not there . . . so up the road to the Madonna he strode and I tottered – but it was not there. Possibilities then lay in opposing directions. The hospital car park is a last resort on a windy night, or, less likely, Sant' Agostino, where the weekly market sets up. If we had left it anywhere near there, blocking market caravans, we would have heard about it by now. Fifteen minutes passed. Luigi took the plunge and called Andrea, the village polizia, on his mobile phone. 'Andrea, ciao, buona sera, it's Luigi.' I impatiently drummed my fingers while they went through the courtesies. 'Si, Isabella is fine, and you?' Wise implementation of village etiquette before he got to the reason for the call. 'Certo, I'll pass on your regards . . . and let me know the result of those tests, won't you? Er, ascolta, listen, Andrea, have you seen my car lately?' He had. 'Where exactly did you see it?' Andrea's memory served him, and us, well. Down the hill to the hospital Luigi marched and jumped into the Maserati, which had been gathering dirt for a month. I elected to remain at Bar Prato, but soon we were racing round the walls and beginning this journey to Castelnuovo del Abate.

Leaving the village infrequently means a journey in the Maserati is something of a concourse; during the long months of winter Luigi is compelled to drive down to the valley purely to roll away flat spots in the tyres. Sometimes, on a double mission, we passeggiata in San Quirico or Pienza, both villages we can see across the valley. But we do not invade enemy territory. Over the years a lingering subliminal bitterness between Tuscan villages has implanted the seed in our minds that if it is not essential, then we do not visit the enemy. We have not been to Montepulciano for years. That village and its inhabitants are no fonder of us than we are of them. Centuries of war and siege have alienated men and minds, albeit the last battle was hundreds of years ago, physically speaking. Turning their backs on Montalcino in Sienese territory, the people of Montepulciano face Renaissance Florence and they will tell you that the only thing that comes from Siena is bad weather that will ruin their crops and their wine. We have been contaminated by this ancient animosity that drifts among the hills and our allegiance to Montalcino is manifest by territorial fidelity. Imitating our friends, we go to Florence if we *have* to, but to Siena because we *want* to. Castelnuovo del Abate is friendly territory . . . the village and the Abbey of Sant' Antimo in the Valley of Starcia belong to us, and we belong to them.

Car owners at Castelnuovo enjoy parking freedom reminiscent of the way it was ten years ago when we came to live in Montalcino. Drivers stop anywhere they wish, bumpers and bonnets facing every direction, poking over drains, sticking out at corners and blocking exits. Guiding the cumbersome Maserati along a narrow road, Luigi parks in front of the oil mill. We squeeze out and shortcut through a narrow lane into the village. It would never have been feasible to permit motorized traffic in Castelnuovo. Alleys and arched passageways linking dwellings one to another are no more than a metre or two wide. Most homes are rough stone, the gaps in-filled with terracotta chips. Terracotta eaves crowd overhead, narrowing the gap to the sky to an arm's length. Half-opened slanted wooden shutters offer the only evidence of habitation. We make our way to the solitary bar and ask where Signor Bianchini lives. A dubious expression is accompanied by a dry 'Here.' At length, following a curt explanation that we are guests for dinner, the barman comes to the door and, with a tolerant voice, indulges us: 'There.' Thirty metres along the pathway chiselled blocks of stone protrude from a deep embrasure out of all proportion to the alley that leads to it. Because we are shut in close by dwellings and overhanging eaves, vision is restricted to the next stone house and modest doorway as we draw level. Pretending, conveniently, to be from somewhere else, we thank the barman and before we have taken ten paces are walking beside a massive structure, grey and grave, bearing impassively down upon our heads. Shocked by the volume of stone I quickly count the tiers of iron grated windows high in the walls of a stern Renaissance palazzo. I cannot imagine why I have never seen it before. Our eyes widen, but lips are tightly closed. Imposing wooden doors stand ajar, framed by a bevelled architrave that curves round the doors into an arch. An iron key, noticeably long, is wedged into a roomy hole. I imagine locking and unlocking to be troublesome.

At length, Luigi spies a brass buzzer, ridiculously wee; it seems hardly likely that pressing this inconspicuous point could summon anything . . . but before his finger is off the wee bell we are warned off by a righteous barking dog. This German Shepherd knew we were on the other side of the portal; he lay wary, nose on his paws, not alerting us to his duty until we dared seek permission to enter. Beppe, handsomely accoutred, emerges from somewhere, pats the dog, and the door swings wide. This is all too exciting – I find myself in a state of euphoric optimism, certain I am going to uncover fabulous things. But not yet, alas! 'Buona sera, Luigi, buona sera, Signora.' We proceed through the preliminaries, but then Beppe says: 'Luigi, I hope you don't mind if we have dinner later, I am filling in a few football club schedules, can you give me a hand?' Not a request easily refused by Luigi, nor does he wish to, but it leaves me in an awkward predicament. Thinking on my feet, but not *of* my feet, I offer a solution: 'Why don't I take a walk?' Luigi steps in and I step out. This was not in my fantastic plan, but a sign at the end of the road where we parked the Maserati reminded me that when I walked to the abbey a couple of months ago I had no time to explore the cava, quarry, where the monks cut onyx. When the sun creeps into the Valley of Starcia, onyx is the precious stone picked up by light rays that cast the abbey in pinkish and golden hues. I set off, already painfully conscious that my footwear is glaringly inappropriate, to find the road to the cava.

Mount Amiata is an extinct volcano; a cool retreat from the heat of summer where pine and beech grow thickly across the summit, and in winter, a blanket of snow lies deep. The cleanly drawn mountain rises majestically, out of scale to its sur-roundings, dwarfing lower glades hiding mineral springs in chestnut woods. The sign told me to walk four hundred metres along this stony road running steeply from the village. After two minutes a jumble of terracotta roof tiles are out of sight, the road curves downward into bushy scrub, and in another minute an eerie quiet, not frightening, but as if I am not alone, descends. No barriers hinder my entry to the cavernous pit. I stiletto awkwardly between the slabs into the quarry, teetering on top of the first slag heap. A gaunt precipice rises forty or more metres and tie-wires unroll like measuring tapes, trailing away to an opposing cliff, but the face of the stone is striped and streaked, layered in striated bands tracing a circular wave around the cliffs. Chiselled cracks and fissures through this mountain of onyx have been gouged out and honed by centuries of wind and rain. I could walk inside these crevices, now a refuge for birds, without stooping. The weed-choked floor of the pit is scattered with giant blocks, tossed up and fallen down, held rigid by their own tremendous weight. Quarried from the wall forty or fifty years ago, they look like sad, forsaken playthings. Watching for slithering vipers, for this is an ideal den, I venture deeper into the pit, nervously clipping my way down to a gully. I cross a plank bridge to examine a rusty conveyor anchored in weathered stone which must have shuttled buckets, or quarrying monks, back and forth, suspended from corroded cables looping up the wall. Thus carried upwards, my eyes rest on a pair of languid hawks hanging in the air, adrift above these disturbing images. I turn impulsively to leave, now in a melancholy mood, and my dangerously tapered heels trip over fragments that clash together, making a pretty tinkling sound in the pristine silence, contrasting with this massiveness, an overwhelming down bearing weight all around me. Scooping up the pieces I let them tinkle in my open hand; glassy white and blushing sand tinged with ochre, the gorgeously reflected colours of the rising sun on the abbey. Sliding three or four slivers into my pocket I listen to them tinkling. Removing my dusty stilettos, in stockinged feet I climb swiftly out of the pit. I am glad to have come here.

Perhaps the curious rhyme I hear repeated in Montalcino has something to do with quarrying monks? 'What Siena could not do in a decade, the monks of Sant' Antimo did in half a morning.' I am growing cold and had better start back because dusk falls rapidly under the purple mountain. I steal one last glance into the cavern from the rim of the pit. Elongated shadows prowl across blocks of stone. This sad cava transmits not fear but broken grandeur, evocative in its abandonment. A thousand years ago white hooded monks, I know not how, quarried this onyx to adorn a magnificent abbey to the glory of God.

The door to the palazzo is gaping; raising his head and pricking his ears, the dog does not bark at my buzz. He sees it is me, and waits for Beppe. His tail wags when I step over the threshold and his stretched limbs, into a vestibule lit by an iron chandelier hanging from a great height over a vase of red berry branches on a refectory table. A wide stone staircase rises to my right, but Beppe leads the way down a corridor just as wide where rounded corbels underpin stone architraves spaced along the wall. At the end of the corridor, piercing an iron grated window, the last dim light of day falls dully on stone flags. Beppe opens a door to the left and we step into a lively gathering.

Dinner is soon to be served on a long narrow table. I exchange an affectionate kiss with Beppe's wife, Anna, who says she was half demented by my lateness; she is giving the final critical stir to wild asparagus risotto. Luigi relaxes on a wooden bench *inside* a fireplace, along with Paolo and Lucia, son and daughter of the household. Both in their thirties, Paolo and Lucia live here too, working the family business. I merge into what is going on but the crossfire of pre-dinner chatter makes it difficult to know what that is. I am content to absorb the atmosphere in this brick-vaulted room which may once have been a stable. Anna calls for us to be seated, because the risotto is ready . . . and chit-chat dies. We launch into the joy of eating and drinking as if it were rare. Table talk, being less deliberated than conversation, is difficult because of the speed with which short spurts, conclusions and disputes feed across the table. By the time I consider a response in Italian we are three sentences into the future. Beppe politely asks if I walked to the abbey, it being a few hundred metres from the village. Recalling the pretty musical notes of tinkling onyx, I reply eagerly: '*No, no, sono andata alla Cava di Onice! E bellissima.*' He is astonished. 'Signora! The cava is extremely pericoloso, dangerous, I hope you did not go in? The pit is full of vipers!' Too late he warns me of terrible danger and of evil-eyed serpents who surely shared my adventure, but I am saved from condemning myself when he amplifies: 'At last I have secured a signature from the Minister in Rome . . . if anything collapses, I'll be ready.' Seeing me nonplussed, he transfers his gaze to Luigi, but his eyes, too, are puzzled. 'I have always wanted to reopen the quarry for Castelnuovo; I purchased it a long time ago. The onyx in those cliffs could be quarried for another century but we would have to start from scratch. What with safely practices and bureaucratic red tape the Minister for Mines tells me it would cost a sack of money. But, with the help of the monks I put him in a corner, crept up on him through the back door and he had no option but to relent. Because the monks from the abbey quarried onyx a thousand years ago, if at any time in the future onyx slabs or ornamental carvings need to be replaced at the abbey, the onyx will be extracted from the monks' quarry, which is mine.' If nothing else fabulous happens tonight I am utterly satisfied. Incriminatingly I withdraw the musical slivers of onyx from my pocket which are passed around the table, tinkling on the rims of our crystal glasses.

Beppe works his way around problems that cannot be resolved front on. I wish I had his knack. I cannot think how to blurt tactless questions about a nobility to which he may not belong. Anyway, I wonder why are we down here, on road level, when at least two rows of curling-iron-fronted windows jut from this massive palazzo? Something does not add up. Who lives above?

Anna carries a tray piled with meat to the table, deferential to our preference. A choice between steak, rabbit, lamb, chicken, sausages and pork. In the end she passes the tray to Paolo who stokes the fire and spreads some of everything on the grill. Anna brushes the sizzling meat with sprigs of thyme and rosmarino dipped in olive oil, sending herbaceous aromas swirling around the room. Enraptured to be in this palazzo, even if only the ground floor, I am eager to learn why, when and for what reason it was built here, in sleepy Castelnuovo del Abate. Beppe, preparing for the secondo piatto, glances to a dresser, rises, and returns cradling two bottles of Brunello di Montalcino. Squinting along the table, I read the label: Ciacci Piccolomini d'Aragona. We progress to cheese and fruit. This is a simple family meal, after which, without a doubt, Anna will attend to the washing up, Paolo and Lucia and their partners will rise and revert to plans of their own, and I have no illusion about our familial host entertaining us into the wee hours of the night. Politeness decrees we offer our departure as soon as Anna unwraps my mandatory gift. Each of these anticipated customs verifies itself, leaving Beppe, Luigi and myself at the table breathing in the bouquet and sipping splendid wine. The precision of Tuscan lore is then validated by Beppe himself: 'Before you go home . . .' He knows our time is at hand and I am resigned to our departure, but he surprises me with '. . . I'll take you upstairs and show you where La Contessa lived.' Catching my breath sharply, even noisily, terrified Luigi may feign polite resistance to such a personal intrusion, I close my eyes, exhale, and pray to hear him murmur acceptance. He does.

At the first stairhead, before we turn upon ourselves to sally the next flight, I look back down from where we rose. Tramping feet have worn grooves in wide stone stairs, and, peering from the landing, each hollow groove dissolves architecturally into the groove on the stair below as if water running down a funnel has eaten away the middle of each stone. Rising with us up the stairwell loops a thickly ribbed cord; there is no balustrade. Along a corridor, replicating the one below, we pass more stone architraves on which Latin inscriptions scrawl across emblematic shields. Beppe turns left and we follow him beneath a stone lintel, where we stop. Turning involuntarily, reacting to the existential flutter of something or someone lighter than a feather brushing my shoulder, I am unnerved to find no one, nor is there an open window that could have admitted a wilful shifting of air.

We listen attentively to Beppe for ten minutes. He perceives my fascination with La Signora Contessa and when he pauses I am able at last to pose a tentative question. He shakes his head: 'If you want me to tell you *that* story, make yourself comfortable . . . we will go back to the beginning.'

Beppe's parents, and their parents before them, laboured for the friars of the Abbey of Monte Oliveto Maggiore, a secluded monastery across the valley from Montalcino, but easily seen from the walls. They were not mezzadri, but employees, his father doing whatever was needed at the abbey, and his mother, a lacemaker, repairing lace collars and surplices for friars. There were eighty or ninety friars who, his father endlessly bemoaned, because of the daily work in the vegetable garden, ate as much as ten pairs of cows! Raised within earshot of the teachings of the church, Beppe was a student of the friars and was accepted to study the higher teachings of the church at a monastery at the Cinque Terre, but instead he enrolled in agricultural school in Siena, cycling ninety kilometres to school and home each day. At school he controlled contraband, rapidly earning a reputation for fast thinking by tracing geometric drawings and selling them to his friends so that everyone passed the exams. During summer holidays he helped bring in the harvest, scything and tying up bundles of hay alongside the contadini who worked the land for the friars. Life at the abbey

114

was hard, there was a lot of misery, but, living humbly in three rooms below a brick furnace that belonged to the friars, his family had sufficient to eat. Besides, Beppe grew the best carciofi, artichokes, in the district, and sold them to everyone. Beppe has maintained his friendship with the friars except that now, when the abbot invites him to their annual festival, Beppe takes the Brunello, repeating every year: 'You are fortunate you did not make me into a friar, because I'd have wanted to be the abbot, and what would you be now?'

Although he barely studied he always passed the *last* exam ... but he understood how to solve problems indirectly, thinking laterally. His schooling finished and as his eighteenth birthday approached he was accepted as sotto fattore, a kind of under foreman, on a two thousand hectare farm. As well as the annual harvests to bring in, Beppe frequented the animal fairs in Montalcino every week where more than six hundred beasts were traded for work and breeding. In 1956 there were almost no tractors in this part of Tuscany; teams of oxen, or contadini, pulled the ploughs. Quick of mind, Beppe had the capacity to look at a beast and know its weight and condition in seconds. He was soon being sought by contadini whenever they noticed a cow having birthing complications; he was called out at all hours and the contadini would make him pasta at midnight, or four in the morning, until the calf was born and the mother safe. The sotto fattori on the widespread farms met at animal fairs, and by chance Beppe learned that the head foreman was retiring on a pension from the farm of Conte Piccolomini at Castelnuovo del Abate. But, he was warned: 'It is not the Count who runs that farm, it is his wife, La Contessa Ciacci Piccolomini d'Aragona.' She married the Conte whose genealogy goes back centuries to a noble family from Aragon, in Spain.

'So you see, Isabella, I do not come from a noble family,' Beppe smiles indulgently, 'but at twenty-four years of age I put in my application to Conte Piccolomini and came to see what this noble Contessa had to say. My friends told me to be careful: she makes all the farm decisions, they said, not the Conte. The first thing she lamented was: "Signor Bianchini, but you are so young!" So I retorted: "Signora Contessa, then you can train me in your ways." Ten days later the Conte advised him a contract was ready. "Signor Bianchini," patronized the Contessa, "I'll have the old foreman show you the boundaries and the ledgers." But Beppe refused. "No, Signora Contessa, just give me the books, the boundaries I will find, and when you have half a morning we will go over the ledgers together because you and I and the contadini . . . everybody must understand."'

And so Beppe began work at the farm at Castelnuovo del Abate, bringing with him his wife Anna, and their first baby, Paolo. In those years there was no wine production on a commercial basis, only for farm consumption. He was responsible for the harvests, buying and selling animals for work and breeding, and overseeing the year's work for hundreds of contadini who lived in twenty humble stone houses on the farm, with whom he developed an excellent rapport. He kept the ledgers up to date and the farm accounts were filled in daily because La Signora Contessa was exceedingly fussy, wanting every single transaction recorded. They lived in Castelnuovo; the village boasted a population of around a thousand but most were woodcutters who gathered at dawn in the piazza which was packed with baying donkeys. Paolo's first words, at little more than one year old, were: hee-haw!

Then came the red hot years. A sign of political fervour, red banners flew in the piazza. 'Tomorrow,' the contadini declared, 'we do not harvest.' Union bosses sprang up among contadini farmers, uniting the poor and inciting strikes called by union leaders. Other farms were at a standstill and it was only days until the grain was to be harvested, the largest and most valuable crop of the farming year. 'Don't worry,' Beppe said to the Contessa, 'I will work out how to fix things.' To the union boss he said: 'Pietro, are we going to harvest this year?' Came the expected response: 'Depends on conditions.' Beppe countered: 'Tell me what it is you want.' 'Soon,' the union boss assured him, 'a 3 per cent rise will be awarded to contadini and it is going to become law – until then, we will not harvest.' 'Right,' said Beppe, 'you can have 3 per cent whether it is passed by law or not. You make sure the farm is profitable . . . I will give you the rise.' To La Contessa he reasoned: 'If they were lazy I would not give it to them, but they work hard and keep the farm profitable. But you must insure the grain, Signora Contessa, because if we get hit by a temporale, a lightning storm, then you would lose the lot.' She said to him: 'Giuseppe, do what you think is best.' The union boss and contadini were taken aback – they were used to the old ways of the Contessa – so they tried another tactic. 'We demand the right to fly a red flag from the centre of the haystack.' Beppe countered: 'Put one in every haystack if you like, magari, I'll buy one myself, but I will say this, we will have two flags; alongside your red one will be the tri-colour red, white and green of Italy.' The harvest began, union leaders arrived, but Pietro stayed loyal. 'Whatever we ask for he gives us,' he told unionists, 'so we are bringing in the harvest.'

Beppe always found a way to keep La Contessa and the contadini happy, and the farm was profitable. He worked hard and managed to accumulate a little money. One day he told the Contessa that he had money saved and thought to invest in a parcel of land next to hers. It was a few hectares, but at that time it cost a pittance, and a professor from Florence was selling. She approved, so Beppe bought it and worked every Sunday, officially his day off, to put it in order, planting four hectares of vines, learning about winemaking, buying second-hand vats and building a modest cantina in which to ferment and age his wine. He took over the lease of Hotel Giglio in Montalcino and Anna went to work; he established Pizzeria San Giorgio in Montalcino and young Paolo went to work. Lucia, his daughter, was not yet ten. Beppe was thirty-five years old, steering the farm for La Contessa and gathering the means for independence because social changes loomed. One harvest followed another, but the mezzadria was disintegrating and the Conte and Contessa were entering old age. Beppe needed to prepare for the future and look after his family.

The Count died in 1975, whereupon everything passed to the ageing Contessa. She was now alone. At night, after dinner, Beppe would go to her room and they would chat and look over the books. One night she said to him: 'Giuseppe, I hear you are making wine, you've got your own cantina set up. Those couple of hectares of vines on my farm, do you want to lease them from me?' He accepted and the Contessa's couple of hectares of vines were leased to him. Around 1975 Brunello di Montalcino was taking timid steps towards its ultimate stardom, and Beppe, now with six hectares on which to plant vines, felt that his future would be in wine.

At last it is becoming clear. 'Beppe,' I smile smugly, 'so you *leased* the land, is that why you are able to put Ciacci Piccolomini d'Aragona on your wine labels?' Beppe shakes his head and chortles: 'Porca miseria, no! It is getting late, do you have time to hear the rest of the story?' Knowing it is impolite to be holding

Beppe back from his bed I glance at Luigi, but he is just as fascinated. 'Yes, Beppe, of course we do!' I encourage him with my grovelling voice.

Giuseppe had more than ability. He had will, and passion for the land. He knew when a plant was suffering or when an animal had difficulty with a hoof, or when an olive tree was not fruiting. He knew every hole that could trip a wandering cow and when a stone dislodged and rolled down the hill, he saw it. Knowing every corner of the Contessa's farm like the back of his hand he steered the enterprise wisely, ending each day in her presence. Ten years after her husband La Signora Contessa died. Beppe was ready to meet the future. His own small vineyard was producing good wine and business investments in Montalcino were successful. But first he was obliged to comply with the wishes of La Contessa. Only he understood the financial standing of the farm and La Contessa's funeral would have to be arranged. He telephoned her fourteen cousins, all her direct relatives, some of whom lived not so far away, but others down towards Rome, rarely journeying to Montalcino. He told them of her death; within a day, everybody arrived.

'I listened to them talking,' Beppe sighed, giving a disparaging wave of his hand. 'They did not come here to cross themselves. "What are we going to do with the farm?" That's what they talked about. "After the funeral we'll get together to sort her things out." This is what I heard. "We had better lock the whole place up and bolt the windows." I let them talk on and once I had the funeral arrangements sorted out I said: "Excuse me . . . you will find the books and ledgers of the farm are up to date, everything is accounted for because you know how fastidious La Signora Contessa was, she demanded everything be recorded, even down to the last quintal of wood, every hoe and every rake the contadini used. But, I will say this: you will not close up anything, nor will you do anything, because La Contessa has secured her will in a bank safe at Grosseto. When the funeral is over and the Contessa is laid to rest I will arrange a meeting at the bank and when the will is read, then I will know who the new padrone is, and to whom I should hand her keys. Until that moment I am the foreman. This farm is my responsibility.'

'When they left I called the Marshal of the Carabinierie at Montalcino and we secured all the windows and locked all the doors, and at the end, I handed her chatelaine of keys to him with instructions that they were to remain in his possession until her will was read. You see, during all the years I worked for the Contessa she lived on the piano nobile, the first floor. Farm supplies and machinery were kept in the magazine downstairs, where we had dinner, on the ground floor. I lived with my family in quarters on the top floor, above her, but a set of stairs runs up the outside so I never needed to enter the palazzo to go to my home. A couple of years before her death La Contessa said to me: "Giuseppe, this is the key to a security box in the bank at Grosseto where I have deposited my will. Put this key in the safe in your apartment along with the ledgers for the farm. When I die, I implore you, I command you, do not give the keys of the farm to anybody. I know what my family is like. You must give the keys to no one until my will is read."'

Riveted by Beppe's tale I watch his blackcurrant eyes pierce into the past as if it was only this morning that he listened to those instructions from La Signora Contessa. 'Two weeks later I summoned everybody to the bank. Some said they could not come, they were too busy. Others said they would try to be there ... but at twelve o'clock fourteen of them stood outside the bank at Grosseto. The manager made a room available, lined with chairs, and they all sat down and I introduced the Contessa's lawyer whom I asked to be present. At exactly one o'clock I handed the bank manager the little iron key and he opened the box, handing a yellow envelope, sealed with red wax, to the lawyer who first held up the unbroken seal for everyone to see. He broke the seal with his own fingers and unfolded pages of handwriting. "La Contessa wrote this will ten years ago, within weeks of the death of the Count," her lawyer informed them all. I was surprised by the date . . . she consigned the key to me only a couple of years before, but they could not see my surprised face because I loitered at the back of the room. The lawyer commenced to read: "I leave everything . . ." and I thought to myself that she had chosen to leave everything to one of them, rather than something to all of them – then I heard: ". . . universal, everything that is moveable and non-moveable, everything which I possess and own, all my real and personal belongings, all my worth and my property holdings . . ." It was all in lawyer language, and I thought, well, that's not so bad, if I keep my job at the farm I will have one boss, not fourteen. I felt relieved. These thoughts were flying through my head as I followed it all, and then I heard: ". . . to Giuseppe Bianchini, who is today my faithful foreman, for his sole use and benefit absolutely." You could have heard a pin drop. I was stone cold frozen. The lawyer went on reading, but nobody was listening.'

'Beppe! She left you the lot?' My voice is not insensitive, just astonished, and Beppe's face is charged with memories. 'Si, Signora, forgive me if I am a little emotional.' He can say nothing more because his eyes are filled with tears and his throat is tight.

'What happened next?' This is a thrilling serial . . . I cannot believe it to be true. 'Well, I was stunned.' His voice is quavering, but it is not false humility. 'I could not react, did not even blink, and they were stunned into silence! They turned and stared, twenty-eight penetrating eyes waiting for me to open my mouth, so I thought laterally, like I always do. There is a restaurant downstairs, I said, if you would like to accept you are all invited to lunch . . . and I will pay! They accepted, but as soon as we were seated in the restaurant, one after the other they sprinted to the wall phone to ring families. I did not telephone anybody. I paid for their lunch, bid them goodbye, and drove back to Montalcino to find my wife.'

'You inherited Ciacci Piccolomini d'Aragona, the whole kit and caboodle?' He looks oddly at me, not understanding the Australianism, but catches the drift. 'Not without a fight,' he says, raising his eyebrows, 'not from the cousins, but the Government.' I am not ready for the Government. 'But, did you find Anna in Montalcino, what did she say?' He laughs as he remembers: 'She was working at Hotel Giglio and I went in with a long face. How did it go? she asked me without enthusiasm. Come on, hurry up, I pulled her arm gruffly, we've got to get home and pack our bags, the new owner is putting us out of the apartment. She started towards her jacket, it was not unexpected, but then I became emotional.' His voice shakes again as he relives that moment. 'In a rush the enormity of what had happened poured down on me, at that moment I realized *I* was the new owner, the palazzo belonged to *me* . . . and, amid tears of joyous disbelief, I told Anna the truth. I had not really said anything except the truth because in her testament La Signora Contessa had written a private message to me. "Giuseppe," she wrote, "it is my desire that you and your family

122

move out of the top floor. I want you to come down to the piano nobile, live in my apartment and sleep in the room I have slept in. It is you who are the nobles."'

Her presence washed over me the second I stepped into this room. I was shadow-boxing her spirit, a spectre secretly guarding Giuseppe, her faithful foreman. My sense of shock abates but not my presentiment that her shadow travels like quicksilver and this room is haunted by her spirit.

'I'll show you the rest of her apartment,' Beppe offers, 'and after that we'll go downstairs. Before you go I'll tell you the ending, which won't delay you long, over a glass of Brunello.'

Five or six rooms: high and painted coffered ceilings, florid and moulded architraves, stencilled friezes in concave cornices, rosettes encased in squares, rectangular windows set deep and high, stone fireplaces, indented wall niches with chiselled surrounds, low wooden doors weighed heavy by stone lintels and crests. This is the membratura, the membrane, of a fine Italian Renaissance palazzo. But none of it encapsulates what is really here. As if this night has not yet brought joy enough, her wilful spirit tickles my shoulder again; gently she turns herself into the wind and pushes me into her life.

Almost twenty years ago the earthly body of La Contessa Ciacci Piccolomini d'Aragona was carried from these rooms. Here is her piano, glossy black ebony, ivory keys gleaming, music propped, and a dozen long stemmed roses stand on top. This is her chair, floral cretonne upholstery, and her reading lamp with a linen shade glows down on the marquetry bureau at which she sits to write her last wishes. On the table a sepia photograph in a silver frame: at eighteen she is so pretty, curls falling about her face, a laughing signorina chosen to wed a noble Count. Rising in shelves, the dresser along the wall is filled with her porcelain, her silver, and here, on the credenza, two etched crystal glasses and half a bottle of crème de menthe, undisturbed, waiting beside. At eleven o'clock she retires to this bed; an unadorned iron frame, but yellow appliqué roses ramble across the turned down lace, rolled feather pillows are puffed. She opens the wardrobe door. Tonight she chooses her morning clothes, handing the choice to her maid to be pressed. Swinging from the door, on a satin-covered hanger, a white plissé nightgown floats in a current of air pushed around when she, and I, sailed into this room; tiny covered buttons march down a braid of lace tatting. Concealing shapeliness, her nightgown hangs demurely, an unbroken line from neck to ankles. Beside her bed, the wedding day; she with her dashing Count in a warm embrace. His kiss rests softly on her lips.

In all these years Beppe has not moved a single thing. These are *her* rooms, and he will not permit so much as a doily to be lifted. Should the cleaner not return a trinket to her bedside table, Beppe sees. 'She liked it there,' he will crossly reprove, 'and that is where it must stay.' He once became angry when Anna thought to rearrange a chair that did not sit right. 'Put it back,' he instructed, 'it may not look right to you, but that is where La Signora Contessa wanted it.' He moved his family down, according in part with her wishes, but cannot bring himself to turn her out of the piano nobile. Instead, the ground floor has been renovated into a comfortable family home.

Hushed and pensive, I move to a corner and brush looped up carmine curtains to the side. From the grilled window I stare down upon the valley while Beppe wanders round, turning off lights and closing doors. Down in the sleeping valley, moon shadow and star light filter over the travertine and onyx adorning the Abbey of Sant' Antimo. La Signora Contessa stood here often, watching white-hooded monks in the olive grove, or filing one behind the other into the abbey, sandals padding the stones, to chant praise to God. Hand in my pocket, the pretty music of tinkling onyx muffles, but the abbey, and La Contessa, are clear and close. All my soul is capable of, I have absorbed. Beppe closes the door on the wilful spirit of La Signora Contessa.

To halt any possibility of the contesting of her will at law, the Contessa stipulated that Beppe must give each of her fourteen cousins the sum of ten millione – in old lire – approximately five thousand euro each, and he was obliged to make these payments within a period of seven years, with no interest payable. The Contessa knew there was no cash asset in her bequest, but she felt Giuseppe was up to it. He sold his own small vineyard next door, leased out the hotel, sold three apartments he had struggled to purchase in Montalcino, and, within one year, all fourteen cousins had been paid their share. But the Contessa had bequeathed outside her family; succession tax on his inheritance was enormous. The collateral was real, but Beppe would not borrow from a bank, nor go into debt. Believing that his future would be in wine he promised himself, and La Signora Contessa, never to sell the farm or her palazzo. Sacrificing everything he had accumulated over two decades, allowing himself and his family no luxuries, slowly he worked to pay the taxes. He recalls clearly, fondly, that on many an evening he had sat with the Contessa on the piano nobile looking over the books and chatting about things banal. He would encourage her thoughts, reasoning that Brunello was gaining a market, making great strides, perhaps she ought to relinquish some of her grain fields and plant her land with vines? Her response was always the same. 'No, Giuseppe, I do not think so; the one who comes after me is the one who will plant the vines.' He thought nothing of it, the murmurings of a vecchietta, an old signora, alone and weary of life on the land.

Beppe is at the end of his tale. Our mellow mood befits the opening of a second bottle, loosening our emotions; we consume rather more bel vino than we ought. 'I have told her to wait for me,' Beppe grins, 'because I will be buried in the same place . . . but I said, Signora Contessa, it may be a while, I have a lot of work to do down here – can you wait a hundred years?' He never once addressed her other than formally: La Signora Contessa, and she, respectfully, called him only Giuseppe, never Beppe.

Every month a Mass is said in the chapel where La Contessa is sepulchred beside her Count and on the Day of the Dead Beppe's family hold a service in the family chapel among the hills. The value of the farm has escalated beyond all logic, and continues to rise. Beppe has thirty-eight hectares planted with vines. From seventeen hectares his Brunello is talked about reverently by connoisseurs who probably have little conception of, or breeze lightly over, the threads of a remarkable story and a remarkable man. An aristocrat Giuseppe is not, but I do not believe there could be a more noble wine produced on the hills of Montalcino than that labelled Ciacci Piccolomini d'Aragona.

'Beppe, one last thing . . .' Nagging at my mind are the shields and emblems with the inscriptions above the architraves. It is one o'clock in the morning and we all are yawning, but this umpteenth glass of ruby bel vino at my elbow, and our mutual rhapsody as we savour the sips, loosens my tongue, encouraging me to field the last question. 'What is the significance of the shields and emblems above the architraves?' 'Porca miseria,

Signora, don't you know? This palazzo was built for the abbot of Sant' Antimo. Those are his emblems . . . and this is his castle – the Castelnuovo del Abate.'

CHAPTER SIX

Untouchable Medicinal Compounds

Luigi grappling with a mop is not indicative of a hostile mood; we share chores, even if we live in a society where males are infrequently to be found beating a rug hanging from a window or crashing a broom head against a sill. Sometimes, in order to prop up my shaky reputation, he covertly executes domestic chores unseen by my elderly neighbours, concealed behind our curtains. He knows his way around our cleaning cupboard but I am downright astonished in the stark light of day watching him with lofty sangfroid swish, toss, fold, stretch and turn cleverly in tight corners a rag at the end of, but unattached to, a stiff broom. This morning the marble floor of the church of San Pietro is at the mercy of Luigi's hostile strokes at our working-bee in Pianello. Maurelia called us together for this united quartiere duty and at eight o'clock this morning our gang began shoving and pulling the heavy wooden pews. Ofelia and I balanced an unruffled Madonna on a rickety pedestal and carted Her hither and thither. Strong Cinquino and Francesco lugged the altar table up two steps and lowered smoking black lanterns from the sky while Cecilia and Gloria emptied numerous vessels as tall as me of gaudy plastic lilies. Vases of faded daisies vanished and half burned candles were tossed into boxes by Samuele. Young Dottore Francesco tried out the priest's throne, cunningly cushioned in velvet, but his heavy rear end dropped and he folded himself right through the seat! Beneath the cushion was only a hole. Davide hauled him out while elders admonished his irreverence.

Quartiere Pianello, following an historic sanction by a holy but absent power under whose care it has remained since it rose on this spot in the 1100s, has accepted ownership of the church of San Pietro, a noble and solemn pile of medieval stones right next door to our sede. A Vatican hand scrawled across a contract, between friends, transferred to Pianello, all of us collectively, the responsibility and liability to maintain this Christian house of worship in a manner befitting a consecrated church. Luigi swishes and folds, Cinquino and Michele take an end each and shove cumbersome pews aside as the intimidating mop advances; pushing the pews back into place is easier because the floor has a wicked slope from the altar. A morning's work from willing hands has removed layers of dirt and dust and although our vigour does not conceal the want of renovation in our church, at least it is tidy and clean. Now for Saint Peter himself. Men gather at the base; Davide, Dottore Luciano, Cinquino and Francesco heave and ho with Luigi. I am with Maria-Teresa, Ofelia and Cecilia, holding aloft his head. Maurelia looks on presidentially while Ercole and Lola, by dint of advanced age, resign themselves to offering useful technical strategies, such as, oughn't we turn him over? We are unanimously resolved to grasp this gigantic Saint Peter by the ankles and neck and manoeuvre him into the church and up to the altar. When we held our last working-bee to clean the Sacristy, which had, thirty years ago, been the modest home of the priest, but which had not, in my conservative estimation, been cleaned for sixty years, we dug Saint Peter from a hallucinatory mound of rubbish. The very notion that it is conceivable to lose a monstrous double-life-sized saint in the Sacristy elucidates the way things were in there. Damp marble does not simplify the journey of our saint, for which Luigi accepts beaming credit, nor the uphill gradient, for which he takes no blame, but, amid teeth-gritted grunts, squashed fingers and crushed toes we encourage one another to the task and Saint Peter tosses and turns on his way up the sloping aisle to the altar. When he is finally upright, facing the wall, chirpy Lola cannot resist: 'I told you to turn him over before you got him here!' By the biggest toe I have ever grabbed we swivel him to face an absent congregation.

'Allora!' sings unexerted Maurelia. 'Everything was such a mess last week. Thank goodness that's done – everyone will be pleased to see San Pietro ready for Mass. Luciana and Onelia are upstairs with a jug of iced tea, let's have a cool drink.' Iced lemon tea is a refreshing reviver. Rewarding ourselves we tuck into a merenda, snack, of crocetti, which Luciana and Onelia traditionally make before Easter. This afternoon we will be back at our sede to meet an architect and hear his report on the church of San Pietro. When the contract was signed with the Holy See we took responsibility for repairs to the terracotta roof for which we have been raising funds for restoration for a couple of years. The archives of Montalcino went up in smoke in 1460, putting flame to any drawings by priests that might disclose precisely how this medieval church was raised on bedrock. Onelia steps over stretching legs and slumped bodies to stumble around us with a second platter of crocetti. Lifting one from the pile, I throw back my head and let it drop into my open mouth, icing sugar floating over my face and down my chest. Tangy lemon and orange mingle with sweet Montalcino honey; crocetti are scrumptious balls of dynamite rich with eggs, and, when the exact amount of flour is added, which is, as Onelia inexactly measures, however much you need, in goes a glass of vin santo! As they disappear from the platter she calls: 'Luciana, the crocetti are almost gone, there will not be sufficient for this afternoon, we had better mix another batch.' Wiping icing sugar from our lips and brushing it from everywhere else on to the floor, where it vanishes into nothing, we return our glasses to the kitchen. The work is done. Maurelia reminds us to be here at four o'clock, we exchange farewells, take to the roads of Pianello and stagger wearily back to our homes.

Quartiere life opens the way for Luigi and I to share social and cultural traditions of Montalcino. Would, I speculate, my Protestant family or metallic skyscraper colleagues from the world I once inhabited find pleasure in sharing my Saturday morning sitting at a wooden table munching crocetti and gulping homemade iced tea, weary after dragging a massive Saint Peter up the aisle of a Catholic church? Perhaps they would; those that yearn to find a way to break out of a circle, and who, for varied reasons, cannot. Not all Tuscan villages maintain a social structure that binds generations together, like our quarters do. This afternoon the gathering will range from children to the elderly and all have a role to play in the evolving life of Pianello, and Montalcino. The wandering roots of the oak tree on this hill run deep and nourishment for growth is rich. Even unpleasant accusations and arguments among our young, their pleas for fairness and demands that rules of archery tournaments be updated, unresolved questions still percolating below the surface, are clear evidence of their passion and attachment to *this* village and *this* quartiere, and the desire for victory for Pianello. Dottore Luciano has wisely called a meeting at the practice range, summoning our junior and senior archery squads. The outcome of this council will be critical for Pianello as the summer tournament draws near, but Dottore Luciano is adamant; the best way to restore harmony on the firing range is with a democratic airing of opinion. Nobody dares mention his threatened resignation and if, after a war council, our archers take a united stand either way, the young have, initially begrudgingly, but with a little persuasion from Maurelia, sensibly agreed to abide by whatever decision our archers reach.

Our afternoon meeting is convening and Maurelia is chatting with the architect who is accompanied by an engineer; together they will give their report. Maurelia looks up from her conversation, and using one of her favourite words, calls us to attention. She introduces the architect and the engineer, both grave faced, who nod sagely while she trips lightly over the reason for their presence. The architect opens his report. 'As you know, the roof is in a dreadful condition. Rain is seeping through old terracotta tiles, and, although it may be possible to save some, in reality, you have to face the probability that all the tiles will need to be replaced.' This is not news to us, we have been hearing about it for years; the precise target of our fundraising. 'Your largest expense, though, is not the terracotta, nor the repairs to the timber skeleton.' This is news. A murmur ripples round the room and Michele interjects. 'We already have a quote. The roof will cost at least fifty thousand euro . . . what do you mean?' The architect agrees the cost of replacing the tiles is sizeable, but he has investigated the next step. 'The probability is that to hire, erect and maintain scaffolding for the months' duration of the work will cost more than replacement tiles.' After all the aggravation we have suffered, because buying San Pietro has been a protracted, painful process, our shoulders sag; we sit glumly, unable to raise a protest. But worse is to follow. Maurelia halts his elaboration to prepare us, adding, 'That is not all.' The engineer opens a discourse that we do not want to even visualize, and as he talks our drooping heads fall even further and we sink deeper into our seats.

'Experienced as I am in these sorts of renovations,' he assures, 'I have never seen anything like it. It isn't just the rising damp, which is evident on the walls behind the altar and which is weakening the structure near the door. I have tested with scientific instruments to make sure I am right. There is water of some description, perhaps a shallow creek or even a seepage canal running beneath your church. I have ascertained that it feeds into an ancient well, which nobody knew existed, and I have traced the rim of the well. It is right outside the door.'

'Ragazzi,' sighs Maurelia, a hopeful endearment directed to glum young and hand-wringing old, but even she cannot disguise the utter despair in her voice. 'That is not all.' She sits down and the engineer rises.

'A seepage canal is not unheard of. You must remember you are dealing with a medieval construction, and, because of the geological composition of Montalcino, the resultant repercussions are magnified.' What on earth is he talking about? We glance moodily at each other, stealing looks that confirm our disquiet – is he patronizing idiots? We *know* how old our own church is. One look is all you need to bear witness to a thousand years. He ignores shifting heads and downcast eyes, rushing on. 'This is what has caused the floor to slope downhill, and the reason your beautiful marble altar leans to one side. If it is not restored very soon, your altar faces collapse.' Every one of us stares at the floor, crushed into submission. I do not remember attending a Pianello meeting at which not one voice utters a single word of protest or dissent. Meetings are renowned screaming matches where everybody has something to confirm or deny to which nobody else listens. Michele half rises, then sits, thinking better of it. There is nothing to say.

'Because of this unexpected finding I have been forced to comply with the law and have submitted a full report to the Comune. I am afraid things are now out of my control and definitely out of your hands. The gravest finding is that the church of San Pietro has been built on the bedrock of Montalcino; beneath the church there has been laid not one foundation stone that I can find, nor is there a structural trench or footings below any wall. Nothing is holding it up!'

For months we have been troubled with nothing less picayune than the impossibility of our task to raise the money to repair the roof. Fifty thousand euro is a fanciful dream, an unlikely goal, but we voted, in faith, to buy San Pietro when it was offered by the Vatican because, as well as the church, we bought the Sacristy. We have been able to extend our sede, thinking to provide better facilities with which to raise money to repair the roof. Until the opportunity to buy San Pietro came along we did not think we would ever be anything other than long-distance tenants of the Vatican. Now we are faced with replacing the roof, resolving the rising damp from an underground water course or seepage into a mysterious well, and, to crown the disaster, our beautiful marble altar is about to crumble to the floor and no footings or foundations exist! 'Until the Comune delivers a finding,' the engineer concludes, 'you are forbidden to use or even to hold Mass in your church.' What a lemon we have landed ourselves with!

Maurelia escorts the architect and engineer to the door, sensing, accurately, that none of us wishes to see either of them ever again. Even she cannot think of a thing to say but others take an earlier cue, commiserating with barely audible curses. Maurelia, eternally the diplomat wanting only our happiness, perks up and reminds us briskly that the committee assigned to design our new quartiere banner and scarves has accomplished its task and that soon we will be celebrating Pianello Patron Saint's Day, for which our new banner will be ready. 'And our saint,' she proprietorially adds, none other than Peter, 'was this morning courageously hauled from the Sacristy into the church and dragged up the downhill aisle by a party of volunteers who risked life and limb on behalf of all!' She breaks the spell of gloom. Bursts of spontaneous laughter, bragging shoulders and broken fingernails are boasted and Cinquino and Davide recount the melodramatic details of our mammoth haul. 'He weighs a ton,' quips Samuele wittily. 'Serves him right if the floor collapses under his feet and he spills into a river. He'll be carried down the hill with the crumbling church! Then we can inform the Vatican it is all the fault of Saint Peter . . . we won't have to pay!'

An exaggerated image of a tumbling four-metre Saint Peter rollicking down the hill splashing about in a creek is picturesque enough to have a chorus of yelling youngsters volunteering to drive to Rome to put this thrilling scenario to Saint Peter's earthly descendant, or ascendant, whichever. Resigned to the hideous news, there is nothing we can do but laugh. Maurelia, inevitably, has one more announcement before we devote our wounded senses to a sugary heap of wickedly cholesterol-laden crocetti that Onelia is bearing in on a loaded salver. By the time our meeting comes to an end Samuele and Michele have parleyed with Samanta and Gloria and the young vote on a date on which they will begin serious physical training for our footrace around the walls, which takes place after Easter.

Easter week brings the warmth for which we have longed. Waking to cloudless blue skies, convinced that the sun is firmly in control, overcoats that have been kept handy for the evening and occasional keen morning are at last relinquished. An unspoken semaphore passes through the village and, one by one, musquash and mink hang from shutters, tightly clamped, and each signora allows a current of air to ripple through the fur, turning her coat inside out as the afternoon sun lowers. It strikes me a mite incongruous, walking between a row of huddled medieval stone houses and, looking up, watching outrageously expensive furs flailing about. No longer a sign of poverty, the huddled medieval stone houses in Montalcino are indicative of wealth, riches enough to possess more than one fur coat to zip into a moth-proof bag until December.

The Easter Friday procession is preceded by a traditional dinner of tuna, white cannellini beans and purple onions. To partake of this tasty but unremarkable feast, traditionally, Ercole and Lola, our sprightly landlords, invite us to their home. By nine o'clock, when the procession begins, Lola declares, we will unite with the village and take part in Cristo Morto. A decisively moving procession in the Christian calendar, shrouded in symbolism, at least in Montalcino, Cristo Morto is carried through the village with obeisance. Coming from a Christian family and brought up in a church where a bare empty cross is the only symbol of a risen Christ, Cristo Morto procession immerses me in the sacrifice of the Redeemer and passion of the faithful.

It does not take long to eat tuna, beans and onions. By the time the procession is winding up Via Mazzini we are huddled in a darkened doorway outside Ercole's home. Many decades ago Ercole nailed two flat planks together to form a cross, wired it and attached five light bulbs running lengthwise, and four across. The wooden planks are painted in Pianello colours, of course. Unlit, it leans against the window grille beside which we huddle, and Ercole has his finger on the button to switch on the lights when the procession draws close. Lola urges him to switch on early, but Ercole refuses: 'No. Everybody's lights go on one after the other as He comes up the road so that He is walking from darkness into light . . . it is symbolic.' With a measured tread the village band at the bottom of the road advances, playing a mournful dirge. A few doors down lights flash on and flood the window of the butcher's shop where the butcher has slaughtered a lamb which stretches forlornly across a wooden frame. This symbol of the Lamb of God sends a shiver up my spine, but other heads nod firm approval. The mournful dirge is nigh; a grim reaper shrouded in black from hood to toe comes into view fluttering a lowered black banner. Behind him a Roman soldier in breastplate and helmet, red cape flowing, menaces onlookers with his sword. 'Ercole!' Lola is agitated. 'Turn on the lights!' But when he does, we are exposed in a blaze of electric stars. Lola is mortified. 'We cannot stand here in the light! Christians have got to be in the shadows!' Up the road we flee, diving into some else's darkened doorway. The tableau reaches our hidey-hole and once the Roman soldier passes by, realism and symbolism merge. It is Armando, a scrawny man I associate only with tombola and festival fun. He is wrapped in a scrappy white toga, and from a pouch at his waist, secured by straps reaching over his shoulders, a wooden cross forces him to stagger under the load to his calvary. The Crucifixion passes. Next comes Cristo Morto; a transparent veil floats around a prostrate Deposition. Six pallbearers bear Him along while white-hooded Fra Giancarlo, sandals poking from under a black cape hiding his white cassock, and Don Guido, habitually clad in grave black, with his trademark berretto, evoke by their faces the agony of Christ's sacrifice and death.

I am filled to the brim with passion mixed with grief, but we cannot yet move, because the Addolorata, the sorrowing Mother, is passing. A halo of twinkling lights beams on to Her face; I can see teardrops on Her wan cheeks. I wonder if Mario is really here? Yes, he is one of Her bearers and his face is charged with emotion. Mario is a handsome young man not yet thirty. Tears ran from his eyes when he learned he had been chosen to bear the Madonna because this Mother comes from the church of the Madonna and is brought out of Her sanctuary every twenty-fifth year for the Easter procession, symbol of all sorrowing mothers. 'A once in a life time privilege,' Mario told friends. 'I will be more than fifty years old before I see Her in our procession again.' Broad-shouldered Mario staggers not a jot under Her weight and I marvel that it is conceivable, in this day and age, to find young so attached to the traditions of Montalcino, even religious ones, that they are moved to tears by their own participation.

A pole in the sky to which microphones are fixed transmits the prayers intoned by Don Guido and a multitude of lamenting women mouth the never forgotten responses, stretched in wretched disorder behind their Madonna. I have never been part of a religious ceremony filling me with pity, evoking such suffering, the way this does. Pale starlight brings out no colour in the faces of the women I know so well; they are stricken by betrayal and sorrow. As they fade into the darkened roadway ahead, tiny glimmering wicks flare along the road, showing the way step by step, flickering in the gloom. At length the grieving women pass and we Christians spring from our hiding places in the shadows and tag on to the rear of the procession wending our way through the village to midnight Mass.

This, most assuredly, is not a village procession that could be tangled by the mind with a pageant. By the time the cortège of the faithful reach the Cathedral I am wrung out, caught up in teary emotion. The funereal dirge comes to a halt with the opening of a sorrowful peal from the bell of San Salvatore, ushering everyone into the church. Luigi and I, disentangling our arms from Ercole and Lola, turn for home. She whispers: 'Next year I am going to demand the right to switch on the lights.' Next year? Venerdì Santo is a hard night for a Protestant.

*

139

The footrace around the walls of Montalcino will meander a gruelling four kilometres. It opens with a bone-jarring climb up a rocky gully, is punctuated with a knee-wobbling descent through treed thickets and finishes with a tortuous climb from the lowest reaches of the village where stone arched springs drop into a ravine. The inspiration for the race came from Ercole who meticulously mapped the course to take runners past ancient towers, some standing and others crumbling into ruins, outside the defensive line of the walls and sometimes inside, depending on accessibility, passing through the territory of all four quartieri. But the start and finish line is in Piazzetta San Pietro, outside our church in Pianello. The Giro Podistico delle Mura, or Footrace round the Wall, is part of our celebrations for Saint Peter's Day, Pianello's Patron Saint. This year I am determined to enter the race. Instead of strolling up and leaning over the walls, this Easter Sunday, to the chime of joyful bells proclaiming a risen Christ, I am in training, jogging at a gentle pace, breathing evenly, checking my pulse. As the race date nears I will step up a gear but today I jog unhurriedly along a route not dissimilar to that which will be demanded of me in the Giro Podistico. A few hundred metres along a grassy path leads me out of the lanes of Pianello. Slowing down for my first breather I look over a broken wall to see if a brown rabbit is nibbling grass and a rooster squawking at hens nesting among a conglomeration of junk piled around a ramshackle chicken shed. Perched on the rims of iron buckets, ungainly fowl leap over a wood pile and, wings flapping, crash land on a rusty refrigerator, scrabbling from the fridge to bales of unravelling straw. Farm implements, strangled into permanence by weeds, wedge against trees. A scrawny-necked wrinkle-faced signora is perched on a wooden chair among the clutter. From an iron pail she scatters kitchen peelings towards clucking fowl. She is deaf, I have concluded, and does not hear me. A farm outside the walls is where she began life ninety years ago. Now an ageing widow in black weeds with pride in her contadina roots, she is unable to adjust to life as a cittadina. Relieved to see the rabbit nibbling, for I am sure he is destined for her pot, I jog on, passing under a magnolia, bursting white blooms scenting the air around, past rows of mignonette lettuce and feathery carrot tops. I run panting through a gap in the wall. Under a canopy of horse chestnut and wild oak purple crested birds, perhaps finches, puff out white chests and chirrup. The air in the glen is bracing; boughs from tall trees close over the track. Wild boar, I have been warned, climb from the ravine in winter and rummage about in the undergrowth. Out of the dank glen I jog until I reach the edge of a vineyard and draw to a halt; an ideal place to catch my breath, and see what is happening to the grapes.

Once flowering finishes and the fruit is set the grower hopes newborn grapes will get off to a good start. Spring rain has been infrequent, but light showers, which growers prefer, soak slowly into the ground and the grapes begin to grow. Scanning the rows, I gauge, with limited knowledge, that many vines are impetuous! Foliage is tangled and tendrils roam randomly. Stepping closer, curiously I notice trunks rising high up the stakes. This is not sangiovese grosso for Brunello di Montalcino – but the next vineyard is. Less foliage, and leaping tendrils are curtailed. Free of overhanging leaves, green clusters of growing grapes bask in the sun; they are only as big as a pip. Backing up to the track my feet dislodge a clod of earth. The soil is drying out already and we are not yet into summer. Picking up the clod I think back to what Enzo told me about soil. He broke a clod in half with his hands, which did not seem particularly significant

141

but it was not the breaking apart he was showing me, it was the holding together. Like everything else I am learning, it is the things one cannot see that are essential to growing sangiovese grosso for Brunello. 'If the soil is too sandy,' Enzo said, 'a clump of soil will not divide, it will disintegrate. Too much clay means I have to tear the clump apart because of the moisture it retains, which means the roots of the vine will be waterlogged.' I have heard the word structure pronounced by gurus who evaluate wine in a glass, but Enzo said structure, a vital element, begins in the soil. The clod he broke divided in clean seams, as if he were pulling an orange apart. In this vineyard clusters are receiving warmth and nutrition, the vine is sagacious and the grapes are growing; the soil has structure.

I have tarried too long and my sweating body feels cool. Back on the track in the glen the air is disagreeably dank and I feel a sharpening edge to the cold. Before turning for home at the end of the track I clamber up a bank, grabbing at tufts of grass and scrub which help me climb to a knoll. Below me the Orcia Valley is turning brown; dun earth in fallow fields merges with hills of ripening hay. Not yet, but soon, tractors will be skimming the hilltops; the farmer is counting the weeks till the first cut of hay. He hopes the rain will stay in the sky and the sun will grow hotter. The winemaker prays for a pact with the strengthening sun; he needs a few weeks of warmth as well as soft showers to fall on his vines.

Past a familiar line of garlic I cruise, never without a smile. Puffy lilac balls at the end of long stems deceived me for years. Luigi, pulling up weeds sprouting at the base of the well in our courtyard, tugged on a stem and out flew a garlic bulb. Dozens of purple flowers form this garlic hedge; thankfully this is not a Pianello garden. The path behind the cathedral of San Salvatore in the neighbourhood of Ruga takes me under a walnut tree, past a terracotta urn of cascading white roses and from here I patter down the steps in front of the church where at midnight on Venerdì Santo I left the procession. It is growing dark and the air is clammy on my cold skin but I am ecstatic to have accomplished my circular route and head towards home, the final leg of my first training run. Bursting through the door I call to Luigi that I am taking a shower, but with a start he pulls me up. He has unexpected news.

An inky hand addressed envelope; why has this been delivered to our door on Easter Sunday? Luigi says nothing, letting me savour the pleasure of discovering its contents. Buff coloured card, gold embossed swirls, and along a dotted line it reads: *Mr Luigi & Mrs Isabella Dusi*. A formal invitation to dinner. The date, time and place is followed by: r.s.v.p. – only days away!

Not accustomed to formality in Montalcino we are puzzled. Our circle of friends does not extend beyond the walls of Montalcino, except to families of contadini growers, like Primo Pacenti, whom we visit as often as we can, and friends like Beppe at Castelnuovo del Abate. When we came to live in Montalcino, we realized that to build a permanent life here we needed to be prepared to alienate ourselves from outsiders so as not to be automatically inserted by village people into the parade of passing foreigners. This causes us, awkwardly at times, not to socialize with perfectly pleasant English-speaking people who live part of the year, or even all of the year, in nearby villages in Tuscany. Not wishing to offend folk who are content with their lives – otherwise they would not be here, or come here – we are wary of falling lazily into an ex-pat circle. At the risk of appearing pompous or at worst unfriendly we find a genuine excuse not to attend a dinner party here or a garden lunch there. Our hesitance arises from the danger of spending our weekends with English-speaking people who unconsciously drift dangerously close to discussing, not always in glowing terms, what they find to be oddities about the country in which we have all chosen to dwell. In ten years we have not dined or socialized with a single Italophile except to invite visitors to dinner at a trattoria but that relates to our work, not necessarily our pleasure. It shocks visitors when I admit to be unacquainted with Americans or British who live at Pienza, or Australians at Buonconvento. I am under no illusion: they are loving their life, just as we do . . . they have chosen to do it differently, that is all. Undoubtedly many others hide themselves away, less visible than us.

None of this, I am relieved to note, offers justifiable reason why this invitation from foreigners need be resisted. It is from an American family, Brunello growers who are the owners of a ninth-century medieval castle a few kilometres from Montalcino. An invitation to dinner with Mr John and Mrs Pamela Mariani, at Castello Banfi, is an invitation we will accept – with puzzled perturbation.

The story of John Mariani Senior and his brother Harry, whose descendants are the family owners of Castello Banfi, is vaguely familiar to the Montalcinesi. The gracious headquarters of Banfi Vintners in New York is the pivot around which oscillate the wine affairs of Banfi reaching far-flung continents. Theirs is a generational Italo-American success story that has rippled across the world. But what sort of offspring generate when two small boys are whisked away from a struggling life in Connecticut, brought back to the European country from which their hopeful parents emigrated, to a strange life under the piercing pince-nez scrutiny of a stern and ageing aunt, whose entire world moves around a red-hatted Cardinal who was destined to lead the whole of Catholic Christianity? Aunt Teodolinda Banfi, head of the household for the Cardinal Archbishop of Milan, led a pious life, perhaps austere, judging from scant references to a formidable, diminutive Signora cloaked always in black, never once seen without her head tightly bound in an unflattering black scarf. Did she not appear, to two wild American boys, a matriarchal nun of the strictest order? None of this must have escaped the ambit of John and Harry who found their way back, in their twenties, to an America at last equipped to offer the great American dream which had been dashed by the early death of their father.

Americans who grow Brunello will not, I do not think, intersect one iota with my quest to resolve the social curiosities of Montalcino. The Mariani family cannot be elusive aristocrats entwined in the upper level of a nobility here; nevertheless, this invitation to dinner presents the chance not to talk, but listen. Snuggling under warm blankets, curious about what sort of people John and Pamela Mariani from America are, I sink towards sleep, musing that on the morrow my best Giorgio Armani must go to the cleaners.

The walls of our apartment in a palazzo that rose from the ashes of the 1460 fire are, in keeping with an unbroken row of medieval stone houses stretching along our road, a metre thick. When our home is warm in winter thick walls maintain the heat, and in summer a number of hot days in a row are required before it becomes uncomfortable. Last night in bed, puzzled that a steaming shower did not relieve my chill after jogging home as darkness fell, it did not occur to me that more than physics was to blame. This morning we dress, ignorant of the calamity that has befallen Montalcino. The telephone rings, and, listening to Luigi's voice, transmitting anxiety up and down the line with our friend Primo, I race to the kitchen and throw open the shutters to look over the gardens and hills beyond. Hands automatically rise to my face in dismay, the way one reacts to awful news which cannot be revoked. An overnight meteorological disaster: the temperature dropped below zero and the slopes are blanketed with a layer of deadly white frost.

Clusters of diminutive grapes hanging from vines are blaringly exposed. Sangiovese grosso is a generous plant well adapted to the microclimate of Montalcino; it finds an equilibrium here unlike anywhere else in the world, but I am certain it cannot override a crisis of this magnitude. Brittle, transparent water crystals stiffen, forming icy tears of death as they melt. A late frost is rare in Montalcino but there could not be a moment more disastrous than now for an ice attack on the vines. Looking down, I see that hoar frost has laid low plants at the base of our well; wilted and motionless leaves are fastened to the ground by icy granulations. Luigi replaces the receiver. 'It is too early to tell,' he says, frowning. 'It may not be widespread – reports are coming in that not everyone has been hit. Let's visit Primo this afternoon. By then he will have assessed damage in his vineyard. But it *is* disastrous.'

The piazza is where we find out more. Forsaking breakfast we head out the door and in two minutes are sipping caffè at Fiaschetteria, listening to disheartening comments. In some vineyards the life has been frozen out of vines, branches that yesterday reached for the sun have this morning collapsed to the ground. Grape clusters covered in icy crystals gleam hypocritically because tiny balls of fruit are frost burned, splitting and shrivelling out of existence. There is no salvage operation, no alternative plan; flowering and fruit set is over, the vine will not recover momentum and it cannot fertilize itself a second time. This chilling account comes from growers whose vines lie at an altitude of between one hundred and two hundred and twenty metres. Reports seem less severe at higher altitudes where dawn frost did not reach. My garden plants are covered in hoar frost, a freezing watery vapour caused partly because they grow in damp morning shadows. The vines of my friend Enzo are undamaged; his vineyard lies at an altitude higher than four hundred metres, but lower down the valley, where Primo is, reports are mixed. It will take a few days for a full analysis because damage must be individually assessed depending on the exposure of each vineyard.

Listening to one report after another accentuates the colossal repercussions for growers, large and small, but, like a row of falling dominoes, the aftermath of this calamity will ripple through our community. Montalcino is a village with an economy in agriculture, wine is at the apex, followed by extra virgin olive oil, grain and honey. Damage to olive trees is yet unknown. Carlo, the Travaglio archer, walks into the bar. Ten people crowd round his shoulders, eager for news and we hush our conversations because Carlo works at Castello Banfi, the largest vineyard, where we are invited to dinner. 'Out of our eight hundred hectares sown to vines,' he tells us, 'three hundred are compromised. The situation is critical. Some of our vineyards lie at the crucial altitude where the frost was at its freezing worst. Already our winemaker prophesies that this year's harvest, if damage is as suggested in initial reports, will be reduced by half.' The cost, in monetary terms, is incalculable, and Carlo's final words accentuate the astonishing reason. 'In twelve hours the temperature dived from twenty degrees Celsius to three degrees below zero.'

With just a handful of hectares Primo and his family may be light years away from losses on the massive scale of Castello Banfi's, but, conversely, damage here is magnified by its very diminution. All the family work in the vineyard: Graziella, Primo's daughter, and her husband Piero, their three children, two of whom, Simonetta and Marco, are married with children of their own. Their youngest son is Francesco, a junior Pianello archer, who reminded us weeks ago of his bottling endeavours when we were planning our work at the Benvenuto Brunello lunch. The eleven members of this family dwell in apartments in a rambling farmhouse surrounded by vineyards, olive groves and grain fields. The farm is their life. Often, when we are here, the children rowdily chase around the kitchen but now it is the hour of siesta and they are asleep. Francesco is studying, Piero is in the vineyard walking the rows, surveying damage, while Simonetta is in the cantina with a German couple who are hopeful of buying Brunello; Marco is on the tractor. We sit in front of an open fire with Graziella and Primo toasting Tuscan bread and dribbling it with olive oil from the trees outside the window. Primo's clipped black moustache is turning grey, so is his hair, but his eyes swivel about sharply; he is not many years shy of eighty. 'Most of our vines may be all right,' he tells us, 'but if the quality of the grapes is affected I will not be able to make Brunello this year. We must guard against damaging our product.' The exceptional quality of Brunello is an established international benchmark; growers are obliged to meet connoisseurs' starry expectations of a wine of excellence from these hills. Primo warns: 'We can anticipate rumbling when the Consorzio assesses this harvest at Benvenuto Brunello next year because not all vineyards have suffered damage to a critical degree. How do you qualify the vintage of a dozen microclimates where in some the grapes were protected by altitude or the shoulder of a hill, but in others partially or totally exposed? Some growers may suffer irreparable damage, others are barely touched. For those like me it all depends on the hand we are dealt between now and harvest.'

The heady aroma of wood smoke and toasting bread wafts around the farm kitchen; straying in the open window the smell of cow dung from the animal stall accentuates the honest simplicity of farming Tuscans who need not the trappings of the wider world. We sit at the hearth, cradling a glass of rosso, taking it in turns toasting bread with a wobbly fork. Graziella rubs each crunchy slice with garlic and sprinkles it with salt. Holding my bruschetta out, Primo expertly swishes the neck of a bottle with a hemp tow and drizzles it with golden green oil. A serviette is our only etiquette; wanting not to lose a drop we lick fingers and wipe dribbles of oil from our chins with our thumbs. Tuscans are more Tuscan whenever food is involved, if that be possible. The love of the land and all it produces is bound up in the simplest of pleasures: a piece of bread dipped in oil.

A winding road among an ocean of vines leads to Castello Banfi. Faint lights from farms in the valleys and arcs of brightness hang in the sky above villages crouched on hill tops and a twinkling landscape stretches to the faraway slopes of Mount Amiata. The floodlit tower of the castle has been visible for half of the twelve kilometres between us and our destination, but coming to a halt in the car park I am perplexed to see only three darkened and deserted vehicles. Pulling the invitation from my bag I read it out loud to Luigi to be certain we have the right night – and the

149

right castle – fearing the worst. But we are not mistaken. Pushing the car doors gently, letting them close with a thud, we pass between an avenue of terracotta tubs overflowing with polished ivy alternating with inky cypress, step as quietly as we are able down an echoing iron staircase to a path edged with flowers, which leads to the doors of the restaurant. Still we detect no sign of guests milling, or voices, even muffled, from inside; the interior is wanly lit. We are unsure of what to do, desiring not to find ourselves ensnared in an embarrassing faux pas, but the head waiter, immaculately attired in black tie, materializes on the doorstep and bows. 'Buonasera Signori, benvenuti al Ristorante Castello Banfi.' There is nothing for it but to charge into the maw. I slink behind Luigi, and he, courteous to the extreme, announces we are expected this evening for dinner with Mr and Mrs Mariani. The steward drops his solicitous head to one side in acknowledgement of this truth and says: 'Certainly, Signor Dusi, your table is ready Mr Mariani will be five or ten minutes late, he begs your patience, he is talking to the States . . . May I offer you and La Signora a glass of Spumante while you wait?' Breathing deeply I feel myself gulping to unwind the knot in my stomach, but passing through the restaurant to the bubbly Spumante I am ever more perplexed because no other diners are apparent. Riveting my eyes on his black back, my peripheral vision catches sight of one table dressed with a multitude of sparkling glasses and a bevy of gilded candles standing ready to be flamed into life at a private dinner.

In supremely elegant surroundings we wait. I have heard it expressed that the Ristorante at Castello Banfi operates under the auspicious care of a mightily regarded chef but I am mentally unprepared, although thankful to all the Gods and Bino that he was able to have my Armani ready; and that Luigi dressed for dinner. Thus, when Pamela breezes into the salon clothed in nothing more than utterly simple grey slacks and a knitted top, I am taken aback. A second glance confirms her slacks to be tailored to perfection around her slim frame and the knit hangs on her shoulders as if it were knitted on her very self; she is a flawless understatement.

'*Helloo*, Isabella,' she coos, 'how *fabulous* to see you again . . . This must be Luigi, how do you do? I am Pamela Mariani.' We shake hands and exchange smiles. I am bewildered. Not solely because of the graciousness of her greeting, but by her warmth; as well as struggling to tune my ear to her unfamiliar accent at close range. She addresses Luigi: 'We had such *fun* last year at afternoon tea, didn't we, Isabella? John and I return to the States in two days, tonight is our only free night, thank you so much for coming to dinner.' She recalls when our paths crossed at afternoon tea twelve months ago? I was one face among fifty women that day. We have never met or even seen John Mariani, except in photographs. He arrives and apologizes for his tardiness, welcomes us to the castle, pronouncing *castle* with a funny *a* that makes me smile. Barely can we conceal our bewilderment when he is followed into the room by daughters Cristina and Diana, and their partners. Diana works in New York, she tells us, but Cristina is frequently here at the castle. I am embarrassed to admit never having seen her before. Thus we deduce, not knowing why, that it is we who are awaited at the glistening table laid for eight. Thinking on my feet as they glide me into the dining room I feel Luigi nudge my elbow, but no clear reason for our honoured presence hits me. The atmosphere is restrained luxury with eight waiters waiting to wait on eight. Settling to our pleasant fate I am more than anything delighted that we will not be compelled to partake of polite conversation with unknown persons volunteering forgettable chit-chat. Instead, perhaps we will be privy to lively table debates offering snapshots of this family. Maybe, after all, I will glean a snippet about the winemakers of Montalcino.

As the first antipasto is born aloft on a row of silver salvers, set down upon the table in race-start unison, my eye is drawn to the range of eating implements. There is no menu. This dinner is personalized by the chef who, I learn, is none other than Signor Guido Havercock who has deigned that we commence with crustacean morsels stacked precariously and dripping with a clear syrup. Wine magically appears in the glass closest to my hand. Our familial night is under way and I am keen to immerse myself in the bosom of the family Mariani.

'Well then, heck, I said to him, this is what we're gonna do. You get me ten thousand cases this year and I'll order twenty thousand next year. What d'ya say?' John is recounting to Luigi how he snaffled the market with Lambrusco to replace soft drink and orange juice on the dining tables of America. I am half listening to Cristina give her mother a rundown on the clonal tasting of Brunello she is scheduled to conduct in California next week, but I cannot resist eavesdropping on John's tale. In 1967 John came to Italy to source a wine to compete with Beaujolais, which was making an impression with a burgeoning wine-curious generation of Americans. A senator here in Italy was desperate to increase exports to America. 'You have a deal,' said the senator, shaking his hand on the promise of twenty thousand cases of wine. 'Y'know what happened?' John sounds as if he has just remembered this story after thirty years. 'Well, America went crazy for Lambrusco! In the second year I didn't order twenty thousand cases, did I? Hell, no, I ordered one hundred thousand cases! Now the senator went crazy! Right off the planet . . . and he says to me, John, if you get to two hundred thousand cases next year, I'm gonna give you a car! I thought real quick. Senator, I said, what sorta car would that be? He said some name, I can't recall, maybe it was Fiat or something classier like Alfa Romeo. Senator, I said straight up, if I get to a million cases are you gonna give me a Ferrari? John, he said, if you get to a million you can name the colour!' He has probably told this fun story many times but it offers insight into the man and the challenges he meets. He added: 'Lambrusco was the right wine for Americans in the sixties. I had the drive to find it for them and I had a target to meet!'

'Daddy!' moans indignant Cristina. 'Please! Not the Ferrari story!' Quickly covering any confusion motherly Pamela clears the air. 'Oh, Cristina, I remember when . . .' but Cristina claims possession, deciding to be the one to tell. 'That red Ferrari—' she begins, but Luigi interrupts: 'You got the Ferrari?' His astonished words are directed at John. 'You betcha!' He laughs. Cristina and Diana were eight and ten years old when John took delivery of the red Ferrari. He was travelling to source wines from French négociants and slowly making headway, learning how to make deals with Italians. Pamela sat beside him in the front but the two young girls, Cristina recalls with disgust, were crushed into nothing more than a shelf below the back window and carted in sweltering heat, hot skin sticking to sweaty leather, unable to stretch their legs, seeing next to nothing from minuscule windows but continually nauseous with the smell of burning fumes as John powered that Ferrari, for three weeks, from vineyard to vineyard. We laugh at Cristina's dramatic face and Pamela throws in the punch line: 'When we got back to America the girls were changing school so on the first day, when

Cristina came home, I asked her was everything okay, you know, just being a mother. But she burst into tears. Mommy, she said, school was fine, but I'm never going back . . . the school bus smells just like that horrible Ferrari! I hate it!'

We eagerly consume dainty farfalle, a portmanteau of prawns and scampi, sprinkled with a layer which crunches, but in front of me an invisible waiter has heartlessly replaced the farfalle with a rectangle of turbot oozing aromatic cheese and something or other. The wine glass, although I keep drinking, is mystifyingly never empty. My freshness of vision is dimming, but John pours out numbers, dates, facts and statistics from a computer like brain; has he forgotten nothing that has brought him to this moment in sixty or more years?

'How did you know America was going to go crazy for Lambrusco?' I ask, seeking depth to the story. 'Well, you know my father founded Banfi Vintners? He was kind of led into knowin' about wine by my great Aunt Linda, because when my father lived with her in the palace of the Cardinal in Milan she was responsible for choosing the wines. Even though he was young, she taught him somethin' about wine. When he got back to the States he started up in imports, but was almost ruined twice, the first time was when America voted dry.'

Nobody imported alcohol in the weird years of Prohibition about which I know only that Elliot Ness and the Untouchables saved the morals of the state from spiralling decay in weekly television shoot outs in parking lots with notorious black-hatted cigar-smoking gangsters who illegally trucked crates of hard liquor over state borders. The image of John's father importing only medicinal compounds and health elixirs for thirteen years of Prohibition smacks of improbability. Nothing can shake my belief in the Untouchables; Elliot had his nose, or perhaps it was his ear, to the ground all over the wicked country.

Prohibition came and went, and so did the war, so John Senior got his wine importing business established and in 1963 John Junior joined him just as Americans were shrugging off pious vapours about the evils of alcohol, the economy was improving and the swinging sixties were coming. Sensing change was in the air, John knew Americans were experimenting with Mateus Rose and Beaujolais and decided to find a rival Italian wine. Just a few years later Lambrusco hit America.

It is entertaining, catching bits of his life as he wanders through the years, but it is also charming to hear him talk of his journey, his father, his upbringing. John Senior started the company but John Junior has the vision and the drive. By the late sixties, intuitive manoeuvres began to pay enormous returns, the business was expanding, and while John was working the vineyards around the world, sourcing wines, making deals and setting targets, his brother Harry, who shares company ownership with him today, was back in the States, taking care of the administrative side of running a growing family business.

'In 1972 I went to see my father in hospital. The doctors wouldn't tell him, but I knew he was dying. I said to him, Dad, that doctor won't tell you, but I will. You haven't got long, and nothing can be done. I gotta priest outside the door, what about I let him in? He agreed. After that, as a son does, I said, I love you Dad, and he said he was real proud of both Harry and me, but then he said, I never asked because the company belongs to you and your brother, and I didn't want to interfere, but is everything okay? Are you and your brother managing? I didn't feel like talking about work, but he insisted, so I told him: in half a morning we are doing more business than you did in a whole year! He was real proud . . . we cried a little, and two days later he died.'

The fish has vanished! Maybe I have eaten it. But already two medallions of pink veal repose in a pond of their own sweet juice and the wine has turned ruby, and the glass is bigger.

Pamela chats amiably. She is utterly relaxed listening to John and her daughters, which consolidates my impression of Pamela, but neither does she forget to listen to Luigi's responses. She must have sat through a thousand evenings all around the world, brilliant dinners with divine food and witty table guests, yet her eyes light up as she absorbs and comments on what Luigi offers.

We fall silent around the table as we set to work on the succulently sweet pink baby veal. Diana grabs the initiative: 'Daddy,' she postures, 'if you really loved us you'd let us fly Business back to the States tomorrow.' Everyone tightens up, feeling a thread of tension as we wait for John to unmask his munificence. Only Pamela has a smile on her lips. 'Heck no, darlin', that wouldn' be right. You know what? You don't just *get* Business, you gotta *earn* it. Economy is just fine, you'll sleep most of the way, anyhow.' Diana mumbles about air miles, but tolerates the paternal verdict. Pamela changes the subject.

'We had such fun in town today. I took baby John to Montalcino for gelato. He is so cute. We stood in front of an icebox with twenty gelati to choose from, pointing at this one and that one, and we sat on the step outside the store lickin' till they were done. Then I took him down to the baker. He just loves those cookies with chocolate in the centre, but I only had a one euro coin left in my pocket, so I held it out to that lovely lady with the knotty scarf and said: How many of those cookies will you give us for one euro? She probably thought I was a crazy American tourist, but she put some in a paper bag for baby John.'

Baby John Junior is a year old. The next generation of John in the Mariani family. Pamela is a doting grandmother.

I am stunned by the ostentatious circumference of the glass which is half filled with wine and sitting in front of my eyes. Whose arm was that? And who put those two baby quail on the table? We have all got them! Stuffed with a mixture of ricotta, parsley and crushed walnuts, tiny bodies break apart with the prod of a fork. This glinting ruby wine is Castello Banfi's Brunello di Montalcino *Riserva Poggio all'Oro*! The bouquet wafting around the belly of this crystal is sublime; so is the quail.

John is launching into a story, this time recounting to Diana's partner. They are soon to be married. Probably he has not heard this one, but in seconds we are all listening and laughing. 'We had this resort at Jumpy Bay, you know, Bermuda.' Warmed by wine and flexible of tongue, Luigi and I exchange a grin and nod vigorously and Luigi comments: 'Of course! Bermuda, where we all go on a spare weekend.' John is disconcerted by the oddness of Luigi's seldom-used southern hemisphere humour, but presses on undaunted: 'Yea? Do ya? ... We still go there ... Anyway, it was real nice, tropical and all that, but we had this problem. Every night around eleven o'clock the British Airways flight took off loaded with fuel and it made this tremendous noise when it passed over Jumpy Bay, shudderin' the whole place and shakin' the socks off everyone – and it was never on time, darn it, just when you got to sleep here she comes, shudder and shake, the place would vibrate around our ears. So one day I thought, I gotta do somethin' about that aircraft. Well, at the airport I see this group of business men and I recognize the badges they are wearing. They were British Airways officials and with them was a pinstriped Lord someone or other and an Earl of somethin'. I asked one of the staff for an introduction, told them who I was, and explained the problem, right there in the airport. They were real polite, listened and apologized and said they would look into it. But nothing happened, night after night we'd get our socks rocked off with this darned plane taking off and circling right over the top of us. Once I booked passage on the British Airways flight to London and sure enough that baby took off and circled over Jumpy Bay. I spoke to the steward: can you take me to the cockpit, I'd like to talk to the captain. Sure, Mr Mariani, he said. So I told the captain that the folks down there at Jumpy Bay were gettin' their socks rocked off because of his bone shatterin' take-off. Why couldn't he swing out to sea? But he said he had instructions to take off to the left because he was loaded with fuel, blah blah blah. So I said, give me a look at the flight manual. I knew my way round this manual and nowhere does it say that the plane has to take off over Jumpy Bay, so I showed him. Oh, you are absolutely correct, Mr Mariani, he said.

'Well, we were back in Jumpy Bay a few months later but sure enough, at eleven o'clock, over came that baby and we got our socks rocked off every single night for two weeks! I gotta tell ya, I had to admit defeat, no one and nothin' was gonna stop that rattler! Months later I was lying in bed at Jumpy Bay, waiting for the eleven o'clock bone shatterer, no point in tryin' to sleep till it left, but there was silence, nothin'! Next night, nothin'! Pamela, I said, we haven't had our socks rocked off for two nights, something's happened! That's right John dear, she says, sweet as apple pie, I had my hair done in London last fall and met Lord someone or other's wife, so I told her about Jumpy Bay. She said that if her husband didn't move the path of that plane she wouldn't ever talk to him again! For two years I'd been tryin', I'd talked to all the Lords and Earls and British Airways officials all over the world, even the pilot! Hey, I thought I was someone, but I got nowhere! Two women having their hair done fixed it all in two minutes . . . I tell ya, she taught me a lesson!'

I am determined to leave not a thimbleful of this superb Brunello, swirling and sniffing in paradisiacal contentment as the bouquet wafts into my nostrils, although getting the wine into my mouth is testing my ability to drop my dizzy head sufficiently far back over my shoulders – the wine is way down in this Titan's chalice! One quail I will leave; I am reaching capacity, but looking down I am astonished to see that it has flown away. Perhaps there was only one, after all?

'So, we were so excited about this castle Daddy bought,' Diana is telling me, as the waiter replaces her napkin for the fourth time, 'but when we got here Daddy was real upset when he saw the signs. We ain't a villa, he said, we're a castle, and on the first morning he made me bicycle up and down all these hills with fat rolls of electrical tape in the basket. I had to stick black tape over every yellow and black sign because all the signs said Villa, instead of Castello Banfi!'

'Well,' John excuses himself, 'I couldn't do it, I had to move earth. An' I had to keep my head down . . . we could hear rumbling all the way from Montalcino. I tell ya, some of them were still in the stone age, they'd never seen anythin' like it. They came by in slow motion, in three-wheeler trucks . . . we were spendin' millions a' dollars! I had to walk on egg shells and go real careful.'

A fascinating story is unfolding which *does* draw in Montalcino growers. In the seventies Banfi began buying up sizeable tracts of land, mostly virgin to the vine, on the south-western slopes of the hills of Montalcino. John's nose was to the wind, he knew intuitively that in not many years millions of

Americans were going to grow past Lambrusco; they would be looking for quality, not quantity, and he wanted to be ready. 'I got a battery of earth movin' equipment, not just tractors, these monsters were big enough to move haf a mountain and we started movin' that dirt around, creating a vineyard out of rugged country. I just told them, get that dirt right outa' there . . . shift it and remould the whole darn hill!'

I don't wonder he could hear rumbling all the way from Montalcino. Terror must have circulated among farmers whose ancestors worked this land using farming practices unchanged for centuries. 'Oh, yeah –' John has a good head of steam up – 'it was awesome. They told me they were the ones who'd been making wine for centuries, they had a *history* of winemaking. That was true, but some farms still had olive trees and cobs a' corn growin' in with the vines! And they didn't know how to export. Some farms were owned by aristocrats with titles who had been making wine for a hundred years. They were real edgy, frightened we were coming in, because they had no money, only land, and I was buyin' land and spendin' millions because I had to make a wine millions of Americans would want to drink!'

Ilio Raffaelli has told me what was happening in Montalcino. The economic misery of a small village struggling to maintain efficient running water so the women did not have to draw water from wells. Most houses had only primitive kitchens and bathrooms and needed to be restored, and many farms had been abandoned. Social upheaval was underway; the contadini sought to shake off the oppression of subservience to landowners, the woodcutters lost their livelihood and the cittadini were desperate to hold businesses together in a community in which no cash was circulating. Decades dragged by and, just as a dim light flickered at the end of this dark social and economic tunnel, when they formed the wine Consorzio and turned the corner into the seventies, wild, earthmovin', gun totin' Americani careered over the hills and started pushing back frontiers! In an astute move, knowing their farming neighbours were aghast at stranieri from America hurtling into a tradition-bound community, terrified they would flood the market and ruin everything the growers had been struggling to do for decades, John caught up with an old friend. He sat down with Cavaliere Ezio Rivella, an eminently respected oenologist, and he put before Ezio his visionary dream to make this superb Italian wine a household name in America. By the time they were finished, Signor Rivella, tears in his eyes, said: 'John, I share your vision, I have the will, but there is nobody in Italy who believes me. We have to get Italian wine production on a higher plane. We can work together on this and I promise you we will do it.'

The frontiers were pushed back and the hills of Tuscany changed shape; vines were planted for optimum exposure to sun and circulating air currents. John Mariani and Ezio Rivella, two brilliant minds, were decades into the future. A cellar took shape and the most technically advanced winemaking equipment was shipped to Montalcino, creating a fermentation facility straight out of *Star Wars*, it was so futuristic. Computers controlled ranks of buttons blinking off and on, screens flashed up data exposing exactly what millions of yeast cells were doing inside a galaxy of stainless steel tanks, each as big as a space ship. There was nothing like it, not just in Italy, but in the whole of Europe. It was probably the world's most technologically advanced wine cellar.

'One day, I was sitting at home in New York and the phone rang. It was Signora Maostropaolo, one of our neighbours in

Montalcino. She said, Mr Mariani, I have decided to sell my castle. Would you be interested? I said yes, I would, and added, would it be all right if I send over my lawyer to talk with you? She was happy about that and said she'd get her lawyer up to the castle. My lawyer had been there a few days when he rang to say he had not reached a deal. So I said, is the Signora in the castle right now? She was, so I asked if she would be so kind as to come to the phone. Signora, I really do want to buy your castle, I said, would you be prepared to listen to an offer? She said two words. Yes, John. So I made her an offer, and waited. She said, That will be just fine, John. I had her put my five-hundred-dollar-a-day lawyer back on the line and told him to pack. I had just made a deal millions of lire less than he was talkin' about!'

The Mariani brothers purchased the ninth-century castle increasing their land holding to several thousand hectares. John flew to Rome to do the deal and the Signora politely invited him and Ezio to stay at the castle for a few days to sign the papers. 'You know what?' he says, still sounding amazed. 'The Signora had lived there *for-e-ver*, but that castle had not been restored. There were no corridors, all the rooms ran into one another so when someone showed me to my room we walked right past beds other people were sleeping in! And it was arctic, I tell ya, there was no heatin'; I think I just about died that night! In the mornin' I got up early, dreaming about a hot shower to warm me up, but I couldn't find a shower . . . there were not *any* bathrooms! Someone put a bowl of water on the dresser in my room and I tell you without the word of a lie there was a layer of ice over the top – it would have chilled my teeth to the roots – and folded next to the bowl was one of those stubbly paper-thin dishcloth things! Heck! I did not know you could stay alive like this! I am used to turnin' on the faucet and having a high-pressure hot-water cannon spray me over, with five warm fluffy towels to counteract the chill factor! I *had* to do somethin' about that castle . . . I reckon they were warmer back at Montalcino, even in the stone age! Anyway, I went downstairs, remembering there was a fire down there, and huddled in front of it with his teeth chattering, about a hair's breadth from the flame, was Ezio! I tell ya, it was barbaric. Ezio, I shivered back at him, we gotta get the hell outta here and back to Rome!'

The waiters wait until our laughter subsides before shouldering in silver-hooded salvers. Two improbably vertical circles of fluffy chocolate sponge encase a delicately balanced wheel of crimson cherries drizzled with lime pistachio sauce dripping over a scoop of chocolate gelato. Splinters of pistachio cascade with unbelievable equilibrium over an avenue of plump cherries marching counterclockwise halfway around the rim of the plate. This is uncommonly divine. The wine has definitely changed colour, again, I think. These grapes were grown, vinified and bottled with this heavenly dessert in mind.

John draws us into his dream. We cannot help being caught up with this man's dynamism, but it is more than that – he speaks not with selfish pride, but he shares his excitement. There is a slight ruddiness about his face, his grey hair is thinning but sparkling eyes are permanently in a state of searching for more of everything. I cannot imagine he has made enemies on his journey. He can remember the exact cost of ten cases of wine he ordered thirty years ago and the name of an obscure French Domaine from which it came, and the name of the winemaker. Now in his sixties, a lightning-fast mind captures and holds infinite detail and although he races away on a tangent, recalling some past challenge, at the end he pauses, waits for you to tell him your thoughts . . . and he hears.

It is an enigma, but a just finale to our gargantuan meal, that on eight plates not a crumb of chocolate or scrap of cherry is to be seen when the waiters return. They discreetly remove the evidence of six superb courses and six sublime wines and Pamela suggests we stroll to the courtyard for coffee. The waiters knew; sheltered from the gentle wind, iron tables have been drawn under a scented wisteria pergola where coffee is served, and a selection of grappa.

Like a kid in a candy store Pamela drools over chocolates. Sucking air in through her teeth, hand hovering over a bowl of fabulous creations, she dives for white chocolate, then, cuddling herself with glee, pops a fairytale spun sugar concoction into her mouth. 'Isabella!' she enthuses, 'You must try one of these. No! Have *this* one first, it is divine.' How many dinners with lords and ladies, barons and knights has she sat through? Simply dressed, little make-up, hair pulled from her face and oozing personal warmth; she does not position herself for display like some conspicuous caratage. But her hidden asset is her marvellous ability to transfer her importance to whoever she is with. She makes *me* feel important . . . she appreciates *me* having dinner with her family. You would think, if you were with us, that Pamela and I were bosom friends, that we had shared secrets all our lives. Aristocratic or not, Pamela has class.

We rise to make our departure but do not reach as far as the avenue of cypress because John, throwing out his arms, draws our eyes to admire the tower of the castle, silhouetted from behind by a rising silver moon, casting a faint light over the hills. 'Isn't that a fabulous tower . . . the way it dips and kinda leans over? See where I'm gonna put those big white umbrellas?' He points to a terrace. 'And lots of terracotta, it will be gorgeous, I can just see it. Folks can book one of our fabulous suites under the turret and we'll serve breakfast on that terrace. See what they'll be looking at from that wall? This is the Tuscany of their dreams! Work will start in the fall, but first, what do you think? Let's have that patch of scrub cleared, we could kinda curve one of those half round amphitheatres . . . You know what, why don't we do opera under the stars at the castle in summer? I reckon the locals would like that, don't you?'

A few days ago we toasted Tuscan bread, rubbed it with garlic, sprinkled it with salt, and drizzled it with olive oil sitting at an open hearth with Primo, sharing his compulsive Tuscan generosity and talking over the repercussions of catastrophic white-frost damage to vines. John Mariani has gone past it; damage limitation strategy is in place, white frost ceases to figure in today's thoughts; that was yesterday. He is light years away.

Half a million bottles of splendid Brunello di Montalcino every harvest is an achievement of significance in this community. But the measure of this man, John Mariani, is that from the cittadini and contadini of Montalcino I have heard nothing but praise, nothing but gracious words about what this Italo-Americano has created and how he has gone about it. *That* is his most outstanding achievement.

CHAPTER SEVEN

Fiddly Bits on Sticks

Cylindrical bales, gathered from the first cut of hay as it spewed in the wake of the harvester, topple and roll, scattering until they come to rest at random angles in the gullies at the bottom of slopes. Farmers, surrendering hope, have taken the only option, reaping and baling with unhappy resignation because the hay is desperately needed fodder for cattle in the north and, although a damp, weedy sheen to the bales is visible proof that the hay has not matured, farmers are unwilling to gamble on whimsical weather. Since the temperature plunged on Easter Sunday the weather has baffled Tuscan farmers whose lives, for centuries, have been guided by the saints and seasons; farmers who faithfully sow and reap in loyal accord with the wax and wane of the moon. A Tuscan farmer upholds the wisdom of driving his tractor across the hills in readiness for celebrations for Sant' Antonio, saint of the harvest, because that is the day gathering and reaping begins, never a day early, or late. But this year one Tuscan proverb after another has been turned on its head; even peas and beans religiously planted on Easter Saturday dither in the soil, refusing to leap on to bamboo tepees. Days of insipid sun were followed by gloomy grey skies. At length, the sun gathered warmth, but clouds persisted and half ripened hay stagnated in a crucial phase. And then, perversely, instead of a hot summer sky and wetting dawn showers, the sky opened, dumping pounding walls of water on crops for three days in a row. The cloudburst was a forerunner for immoderation; now the farmer faces a deceitful adversary – sweltering heat, laced with steamy humidity. Humidity is an insidious enemy, perplexing farmers who bemoan an upside-down summer and prophecies of doom have begun to circulate among winegrowers. Many escaped the severity of the Easter freeze, or suffered sporadic fruit burn, but growing grapes have not recovered from the violence of a freezing shock, and crucial summer days are wasting away.

At Pianello, three days of torrential sheeting rain found nowhere to run to except indoors. Working its wretched havoc, rivers of water seeped through terracotta tiles and soaked dirty rings in the ceiling of San Pietro. Cakes of soggy plaster fell into the church and threatening moisture creeps along the walls towards our marble altar. Mopping up the mess, we relocated a startled Madonna to unblinking blessedness at the feet of titan Saint Peter. Today is Pianello's Patron Saint's Day, but, as we were warned, the Comune has forbidden us to use San Pietro for quartiere celebrations. Our working party to clean the church was to no avail, except for delicious crocetti, because our church is a damp, squidgy, mouldy mess and we have no alternative but to defer Saint's Day Mass until community elders pronounce upon the engineer's horrible report, which could take several months.

Mass-less we may be, but we are not bereft of the spirit of God and our saint, for Brother Giancarlo from Sant' Antimo is with us to bestow his blessing. Maurelia, satisfied to find so many quartiere members packed into our sede on a muggy Sunday morning, signals to Francesco to pull the ropes and the bells in the twin tower above San Pietro swing into a celebratory Saint's Day chime. Today we are unveiling our new-age banner under which we will go into battle in the summer archery tournament. We have fought valiantly under our old emblem, but the time has come to expand our horizon and our image, so, leaving geometric diamonds behind and, in keeping with white purity of mind and blue blood in our hearts, at least where archery is concerned, we commissioned the creation of an emblem that harks to our red-blooded fighting spirit and the glory of victory at Pianello. Behind Maurelia, leaning against the wall, splashes of blue and white peep from a stack of new banners sitting immobile, wrapped tightly around long red poles, tied securely with ribbons.

Sunday morning Mass is traditionally followed by a celebratory pranzo in our quartiere, but we have said no Mass, and we have eaten no lunch. Instead, we are unveiling with cocktails, something of a sophisticated switch. After cocktails and an afternoon siesta the Giro Podistico will begin at six o'clock. Tuscans are not inclined to flex sensible rules about the proper moment at which the stomach is ready to receive a wise choice of food, nor how one should go about such endeavours, these rules being paramount to benessere, or well being. Our sensational cocktail initiative is the subject of merriment to some but apparent stressfulness to others who allude to the perfectly sensible benches and wooden tables sitting empty in our downstairs dining room. Elders extol the foolishness of a vertical posture, milling uncomfortably with an odd looking cocktail – hybrid and murky blue – in one hand, and awkwardly picking at fiddly bits on sticks with the other. I find myself smiling at memories from another life floating before my eyes, mingling at cocktail parties in the seventies where a chic hostess would offer the very same sputnik-like spheres of cubed cheese and wee onions speared on toothpicks plunged into oranges. This test of adaptation to finger-eating while balancing a glass makes us comical and boisterous, but Maurelia succeeds in drawing responsible committee members to her side. At the coming tournaments we will adorn ourselves with our smart new emblem as a mark of fidelity, although not everybody wears their scarf looped round their neck; the young are particularly inventive in finding ways and places on which to append a scarf to body parts. A few words about the cost of printing our colours on silk come from Cecilia, committee co-ordinator, and generous applause and cheering comes from everyone, and then, whoosh! she unfolds a blaze of white and blue and red, and our new emblem, held by the corners in the tips of her fingers, unravels and floats into a square so that, after months of speculation, we gape open mouthed at the design. 'Ganzo!

Fabulous!' Michele yells. 'But who is it?' Professor Bruno is summoned to divulge the noteworthiness of a warrior emblazoned across white silk, the design democratically settled on by five voting members commissioned to go forth and find, among the battle symbols emblematic of the courage of Tuscans in a millennium of wars, a fitting embodiment for Quartiere Pianello. They did not, as it transpires, need go far.

'In ages past Montalcino was divided into three neighbour-hoods, not four quarters.' We all nod we-know-that at the Professor. 'But the first Ilcinesi who came to dwell on this hill put down roots and built a settlement right here, on *our* side of the hill. On this accommodating site they were concealed under a canopy of oak trees, beside the church of San Francesco, here in Pianello. A defensive fort, almost a castle before the year one thousand, rose, and a century later was granted its name by the invading Longobards who claimed, as their victorious saint and spiritual protector, San Michele Arcangelo. And so, ingeniously drawing from the very origins of the name of our territory, honouring the traditions of our ancestors, we call upon Saint Michael to protect us as he did our ancient founders. San Michele Arcangelo is our symbol of justice, power and victory!'

Wound up into jubilant high spirits, led by Doctors Francesco and Fabio, the young burst into a Pianello chant. It is a new refrain! I will have to ask Ofelia to translate, but as always it ends with a rousing Pia . . . Pia . . . Pi-a-nello! Everyone is overjoyed with the retrieval of our glorious battle history, proud that the committee has revived our very own paternal protector, right here in Pianello. Fra Giancarlo bestows the blessing on us, our sede and our colours and Maurelia and Cecilia first hand scarves to the girls, letting Gloria and Samanta flap them into the air so we can admire a fluttering Saint Michael, wings outstretched, the scales of justice balanced in one hand, and in the other he brandishes the sword of victory. San Michele submits to being hastily, even irreverently, wrapped, strung, bound, twisted and hung from various parts of the anatomy. We are punctiliously clothed, hungry for battle!

Grabbing the banners stacked along the wall, Fabio and Francesco unfurl two which swoop and swirl above their heads. Michele, Davide and Cecilia each take one and call the younger members into a huddle and in a trice Samuele, Francesco and Filippo balance a banner on a pole over a shoulder. The long poles clash and the banners momentarily tangle when, in full flight, they collide, racing down the steps. They toss the banners into the tray of our three-wheeler Ape in which Cinquino already sits behind the wheel, revving the engine, whereupon Samanta jumps into the tray along with the banners. Crowding around the window we watch until they disappear from view, laughing at them running behind the sputtering Ape as they screech to a halt and, one by one, flutter magnificent banners from iron holders on the walls of stone houses along the cobbled lanes of Pianello. One banner they will triumphantly drape above our insignia on the arch of the cappellone loggia in Piazza del Popolo; but it will only fly today, because today is Pianello Patron Saint's Day.

Leaving the banner hanging to the young, Maurelia checks with senior members who carry the responsibility of ensuring the race route is clearly marked, and she confides with those whose work it is to direct confused runners in and out of gravel tracks that wander through the wall and back inside, to be certain each person has identified an allocated tree or post at which they will be stationed. Excitement heightens as hours to race-start count down. More than a Sunday afternoon run, or a spirited scamper around the walls, this race is a link in a historical game uniting the defiant populations of the antique neighbourhoods of Montalcino; it is a symbol of their very identity. We finish up the fiddly bits on sticks, an outstanding gastronomic success with some, but a ghastly aberration to good sense to others, and Maurelia reminds us that our next meeting, after the race, will be on the practice range with our archers who are in training for the summer tournament. I tuck my blue and white scarf discreetly into my bag because quartiere colours are only worn at official functions and tournaments, never as taunting dress decoration, and turn homewards for siesta. It would not have been wise to expose my lack of knowledge, in front of all my friends, or to query Professor Bruno, but I must find out who these invading Longobards are, or were, and why they came to Pianello.

Jogging smoothly into the piazzetta at five o'clock in whiter-than-white shirt and shorts, an immaculate competitor in the Giro Podistico, I run straight to Giorgio, our ambulance driver, to have my statistics recorded. I did not foresee myself stretching calf muscles and tightening my abdomen encircled by quite this many young boys and athletic looking men. Where are the women? Fiorella and Maria-Rosa are fussily setting tables with chequered blue and white Pianello cloths, and now they are heaving watermelons and jugs of iced tea from our sede down to the piazzetta. Samanta arrives, appropriately dressed for a footrace, but I am assailed by doubt. Where are the Signore, the mature women of Pianello? The register fills with the names of entrants from other quarters, and a few stranieri as well, so I creep up on Walter, noting his pristine Nike strip, who enters in the under fifteen category and wins every single year. I venture a vague remark about the lack of females, but he says, 'Don't worry, Signora, they will be here soon.' And here they are . . . as we flock towards the start line, but, unknown to me, my Pianello lady friends, straw hatted and femininely attired in breezy skirts that float about their ankles, assert that as it is always boiling hot on race day, Pianello ladies do not run, they walk! Charitably wishing not to shatter my self-deluded enthusiasm in running in the Giro Podistico, Fiorella, Maria-Rosa, Luciana and even mischievous eyed Lola decided not to tell me! And I am distraught to discover that my best friend, Ofelia, is not here – she is having a holiday at the seaside. Their sultry forecast is precise because at six o'clock it is thirty-six degrees Celsius with suffocating humidity. But the race is on; there is nothing for it but to run!

Fabio fires the pistol, scaring me half to death, and we are off, a group of scampering athletic young bashing their way through a sluggish line of hesitant others moving self-consciously beneath the boughs of a brilliant magnolia towards the first gruelling hill. Not exactly certain to which track I will be directed, for the young have bolted out of sight, I sensibly tarry towards the back of the pack. The young vanished through a gap in the wall and by now will be tearing uphill towards the first crumbling tower. Certain they must be far ahead, and not wanting to disgrace myself with ignominious conduct, nor yet to remain in sight of the told-you-so eyes of my we-knew-this Pianello traitor friends, I move into a rhythmic jog and tackle the first ascent. Words of encouragement float to my ears as I draw away: 'Dai, Isabella, dai!' Go, Isabella, you can do it. Grimacing, but obstinately haughty, I accelerate until they can see me no more. Puffing mightily, I scrattle across corrugated ridges, my feet sending stones rolling down the track in little landslides, round an unfamiliar corner, and am astonished to be staring straight into the sweet face of my Madonina! I have never reached Her from this track . . . but I smile conspiratorially, taking comfort from secrets shared, and, gathering power from Her enigmatic smile, break into a gallop, catching sight of someone's backside as I lean into the hill and dive stubbornly upward on the familiar track leading to Porta Gattoli. This is the second of four hills which I must conquer. Emerging, crimson faced, gasping and with my body drenched in sweat, in Travaglio, Roberto of the nonsensical tongue, from the football festa, rushes towards me with a cup of water which I toss down my parched throat. 'You are doing fine, Signora!' But why is youngish Roberto handing out water instead of running? My third ascent is through Borghetto, up a path where lumps of jagged stone deter rhythmic progress. Sneaking a glance behind, and seeing no one in front, I slow to an amble, gulping air that is not there, letting my muscle-jarred legs choose their own bit of upward path until the fortress tower is in sight and at once I see Gabriele, a Pianello archer, motoring noisily on his scooter, leading puce faced runners to the drink stand at the fortress gates. Thirty per cent of the race is behind me. I have no idea where anybody I recognize is, having only spasmodically caught a glimpse of hypnotic swaying white bottoms. Emptying a whole bottle of water over my head, not thinking of the hideous consequence of such a wild uncaring gesture, I cannot utter a single word. Cruising on, with a smile plastered to my face as if I have not a care in the world, I approach the middle stretch, taking me across a road and then past familiar vegetable gardens. Peripheral vision takes in black cap and baggy trousers uprooting potatoes and forking them into a wooden crate lined with newspaper, and the rumble of an unseen tractor; perhaps it is Enzo. Ahead is only a shimmering mirage because this exposed track is laid bare to the west and the hazy sun is beating upon me one by one its thirty-six degrees.

Sweat pours down my forehead and stings and blinds my eyes, making my nose run, but I am not deaf, and jog into consciousness when I hear my friend Amelia call to me: 'Ciao, amore!' I glance up, wiping my nose with my hand and smiling just in time to see her blow me a kiss. With a hand half raised I wave at my dear friend, but continue jogging, and sobbing, until, out of her sight and outside the wall once more, I am directed into a chestnut wood. This terrible descent is vertiginous. Trembling legs and creaking knees have minds of their own. Snapping twigs in the undergrowth my feet leap ditches in a spiralling ride, identical to that which The Man from Snowy River must have faced; but he was on a horse. Not daring to turn my head in any direction, lest momentum topples me into a ravine, I sense rather than clearly define bodies lying prostrate amidst the bushes. Ganzo! Some have given up. I will not be the last mad runner home! The crumbling church of Santa Maria delle Grazie gives no sign that the ground beneath her foundations rumbled with the pounding of younger feet than mine, but from here, when legs are beyond feeling, my fourth wicked ascent to Porta Burelli lies in wait. Then, merda, a treacherous cobbled road down the steepest hill in the whole of mountainous Montalcino to the bottom of a gully in Pianello. Will I cheat? I could take a side lane and wend my way between narrow alleys and houses, arriving at the finish line in roughly two minutes. Too many onlookers stand expectantly on corners, watching glassy-eyed pools of sweat stagger past; I have no choice but to be the source of their continuing entertainment.

Inside the walls again, I run towards the hospital . . . and a moment of distracting joy! A diversion enables me to think of something other than my wobbling knees because poking from open double gates is a black Mercedes which I believe belongs to the Ingegnere. If he has been out in the car he must be well again. If I survive this day, I can visit him.

The ancient fount at the bottom of the gully near the ruins of Porta Castellana offers no refreshment because a wire barrier separates me from the mountain spring, and anyway, clear water is not on my mind, I crave only the finish line. With mounting madness and a dash of stupidity I draw level with a female form. 'Non c'è la faccio', I cannot do it, moans eighteen-year-old svelte Samanta who droops like a wet rag. My proud nose goes in the air as I rock by, immediately catching sight of a tantalizing male bottom rounding a bend up ahead. Is that Gabriele from Banca Toscana, an honoured national distance runner in the sixties? He hears my slapping feet and turns to look, whereupon, determined that I shall not catch him, he lengthens his stride, and, galvanized by pride, I lengthen mine, and we battle out the last hundred metres in a death defying sprint as if Olympic gold depends on this alone. The crowd at the finish line senses the struggle, cheering as we contest this pointless war. Flattening them against the wall we cleave the crowd in two as we race over the finish line, Gabriele marginally in front. An arm rips the number from my soaked shirt while I collapse dramatically at everybody's feet, just like Cathy Freeman. Eyes closed, heaving and gasping, I sense anxious Giorgio of the ambulance crouching at my side. Opening my eyes, blinking into the haze, I am crushed to see Walter and a heap of runners crowding over the steps to San Pietro, slurping watermelon . . . How long have they been here?

Samanta and a few more runners stagger over the finish line until, thirty minutes later, threaded arm in arm, cooing like a brace of pigeons, Pianello ladies waltz around the last bend, rosy cheeked under straw hats, hardly having raised a heartbeat. Stepping up to receive my award, a silver goblet engraved with the date of this Giro Podistico, a camera snaps, and my victory, the first female home, goes down as recorded history in Pianello. Walter receives his award, and one trophy is reserved for Venerdì Santo cross-carrying Armando, class of 1927, who has never failed to finish this race since Ercole, bless him, was inspired to invent it.

'He must have been a competent architect because Giovanni the German was recompensed for his work to fortify the fortress by the gift from the Comune of Porta Burelli and Porta Castellana.' It is puzzling to understand how the Comune could just give away two entry gates into the village, but the Ingegnere clarifies, along with his disgrazia, bad fortune. 'Porta Burelli is a medieval arched gate with a guard room and a house built over the top. Porta Castellana was like that once, too. Do you remember, the last time we talked, I told you that after Giovanni fled Germany and came here, the Padelletti multiplied and within a few generations fifty families with the Padelletti name dominated Montalcino?' My nodding head satisfies him. 'Porta Castellana passed down to me, and I still own it today, but it is my destiny that things go badly. One of my ancestors rented Porta Castellana back to the Comune – I have a copy of the contract – and, cannily, the Comune used it as a storeroom . . . for gunpowder! You can imagine the consequences. They *made* it explode. There is nothing standing but a bit of ruined gate. Even back then the course of my destiny was predetermined, my family patrimony was going up in smoke.'

We are not in the biblioteca, nor in the Gothic salon. In the heat of summer the Ingegnere moves into subterranean coolness. Laborious and distressing was the journey from his front door, which he must have sat behind for ten minutes waiting for my finger to press the buzzer, for it swung open immediately and we passed through the vestibule and the gorgeous Gothic salon and he surprised me by continuing through a glass door, stepping on to a balcony, and from there, one by one, with the aid of his cane, he manipulated unwilling legs down a flight of stone stairs. My heart was in my mouth as I silently followed, hardly daring to breathe. At the bottom of the steps he paused, and, pointing with his cane, because he was gasping and could not speak, he motioned me to a rambling garden. There is no structure to the garden; collapsing benches are entangled by plants gone wild, leaping from fretwork arches. Climbing roses clamber from upturned urns, threading crimson between terracotta fragments and hand-forged iron. He wanted to tell me about the ruined garden, but was struggling, so I discreetly left him to battle breathlessness and wandered from the garden to the wall from where I could see Primo's vineyard in green lines on the lower slopes, and framed in a vista beyond is San Quirico, then further, overtopping it, lies Pienza, while far away, on the horizon, the lordly village of Montepulciano hangs in the air. Hearing muffled choking sounds I looked back and to my horror his face was as crimson as the climbing roses. I dared not move; he steadied himself with his cane and, terrifying me, with one shaking hand clenched into a tight fist he banged hard on his own chest three or four times, then a pause, then he banged hard a second time. An eternity passed. He sucked in great gulps of air and I watched his chest rising and falling. Thankfully, he began to breathe regularly; so did I. We stood like this for some minutes until he felt composed, and then I followed him, still trembling with the fright, through a low door and into a room beneath his house, heavy with age. It is undeniably cool, but I am not convinced it is due recompense for the agony of our frightful journey. He lowered himself on to a dreary settee. We are surrounded by the clutter of the Ingegnere's overflowing collection of maps and manuscripts, but in this underground gloom is also assembled a curious collection of memorabilia. Dusty glasses of every size and shape are crammed on shelves and enamel candle holders prop on the edges of tables and the arms of chairs. Two deep settees with flat wooden arms are upholstered in printed linen, but matted horsehair escapes in clumps from bursting cushions. The webbing supporting the cushioned seats has slackened, collapsing to the floor, so that when I sit I flop down, hardly able to peer over the arm. Perhaps this was once a summer party room. Before taking up his story, the Ingegnere reverted to the garden. 'It was laid out in the twelfth century and it is one of my unfulfilled dreams that it be retrieved from that unkempt tangle. But it is too late,' he sighed resentfully, 'I have been robbed of my third age, my elderly years are useless ones.'

And so, once Giovanni the German was accepted as a cittadino of the first order of Montalcino, with the help of ancestors who had taken alternative names to avoid persecution as heretical puri, it seems that things went profitably, because these Padelletti became uncannily wealthy. Other Montalcinesi married into the important Padelletti family and industries like tanneries flourished because the Tuscan Maremma between here and the coast was like Texas. Padelletti traded in animal hides which were sought by a hundred shoemakers; they employed tinters and dyers, and they also had a factory for making candle wax. Some were wealthy possessors of enormous tracts of land, while others succeeded in the professions as lawyers and doctors, probably benefiting from privileged places at the University of Siena. 'Generations passed, but something began to go terribly wrong,' the Ingegnere says, taking up his story, 'because by the time Antonio's name appears at the end of the 1700s, he is one of only two Padelletti families surviving in Montalcino. Antonio was immensely wealthy; he was an industrialist and much of his wealth derived from his emporium for buying, tanning and selling hides, but he also owned Castello Romitorio and tracts of farm land. He was my great-great-grandfather and now the story takes some surprising twists because the Padelletti threw up one genius after another. Antonio had taken a wife, Elisabetta, who was a liberal from Rome, and she had born him two sons.'

I would love half a chance to ask him what happened to the hundreds of other Padelletti. How could they inexplicably vanish from records? But it will distract his thoughts and it will take an hour for him to return to Antonio and the geniuses who follow. Instead, I let him go on and in a roundabout way he sheds insight into what will follow, alerting me to the French Revolution, at which the Montalcinesi rejoiced with wildly exaggerated happiness, even getting married around a tree instead of in a church, and French collusion with Austria. 'And so the Church,' he says, 'with the help of invading Austrians, seeking vengeance sent immensely wealthy Antonio into spiralling bankruptcy. Perhaps,' he concludes, 'this was influential in his suicidal tendencies, or perhaps he just made up his mind to gamble his life away.'

It was winter, and perhaps because he needed money, Antonio laid a bet that he could ride his horse from the church of San Salvatore down the hill to the church of the Madonna. A ride made treacherous because of the cliff-like steepness, but also because a stone quarry had been gouged out of the hill between the two churches, through which he would have to pass. His horse slipped, Antonio broke his neck and falling dead in the icy quarry above the Madonna, he lost the bet. His widow, Elisabetta, was left with two sons and little else; Castello Romitorio was sold off in bankruptcy to the Tamanti family of Montalcino; all she possessed was a couple of farms. Refusing to listen to counsel that she should forthwith send her sons to learn a trade, Elisabetta said: 'No, in my family there have always been Dottore . . . *My* sons will be scholarly men of letters.' She sacrificed herself, scraped a living from two farms called Paradiso and Paradisino, and her sons were educated. 'Both of these boys were exceptional intellectuals,' the Ingegnere states as a matter of fact. 'One was a professor of oriental languages, he was progressive, also a liberal, a rector at the University of Pisa. But it is the tutelary spirit of the other, Pierfrancesco, that we must trace, to arrive at the end of this story. He is probably the least known Padelletti, but he was an amazing genius because at twenty years of age he had attained a laureate in law. He soon came under the observation of the Grand Duke of Tuscany who dispatched him to learn German, among other useful arts, at Vienna at the royal court. Returning three years later, Pierfrancesco became trustee for the Grand Duke of Tuscany. He carried tremendous influence, wielding more power even than the generals in the Duke's army because as a fiduciary it was Pierfrancesco who, a kind of military judicial, commanded all the troops in the territory of the Grand Duke! Pierfrancesco was my great-grandfather. He married a Florentine woman of high birth, her family name is incised in the cathedral of Florence, but that is another story . . . and we will not digress. We must now follow the brilliance of Pierfrancesco through his two sons, one of whom is my grandfather, and the life and death of both of these intellectuals, Guido and Dino, was to have an enormous impact on my father, and me.'

I am struggling to keep up with who begat whom. We have travelled from 1529 when Giovanni the German arrived and then fifty Padelletti families, all wealthy, lived generation after generation in Montalcino. We met Antonio who married strong-willed Elisabetta from Rome, a liberal – but I am not yet aware what that means. Anyway, Antonio was sent into spiralling bankruptcy by the Church and the Austrians, and broke his neck riding his horse down an icy slope for a bet, leaving two sons, both geniuses, one a professor of oriental languages, a liberal progressive (again not something I yet understand), and the other, Pierfrancesco, went off to learn German in the royal court of Austria under the patronage of the Grand Duke of Tuscany, and returned to occupy a position of immense power, controlling the Duke's army. All those generations have passed since Giovanni the German came back, and the Padelletti are still fraternizing, indirectly, but through a powerful Duke, with Germany! I think I have got it. Now he will tell me about Pierfrancesco's two sons, one of whom is the Ingegnere's grandfather. I think it is opportune for me to ask the Ingegnere for dates. I have desisted because I do not want to cause him to go rummaging through a pile of papers for dates which I probably will not remember, but now that he has reached his more immediate family, I am anxious to get this story into chronological order in my mind.

'My grandfather, Guido, was born in 1843 but lived only to see his thirty-fifth birthday. The story of his life is insight into the brilliant mind of this man, and I will tell you more in a moment.

His brother, Dino, was nine years younger, born in 1852, but tragically, he lived only five years more, and left this world at forty years of age.'

It runs through my less brilliant mind that both these brothers were born in an age of immense turmoil in Italy. Garibaldi, Mazzini and Cavour were in the early stage of their struggle to rid Italy of foreign invaders who had divided and ruled her territories for centuries, and from the grasp of a Papal State not willing to relinquish temporal power. The Ingegnere, as if reading my thoughts, goes over the same ground, adding an afterthought. 'Anyhow, the Church always impeded unification of Italy. Even when the Longobards were beginning to unify fifteen hundred years ago, the Church would not allow it to happen. They called in the French kings, but when the French began taking control they did not like that either. Hysterical again, they turned to the Spanish who were the next invaders to rupture Italy for hundreds of years.' Mysterious Longobards pop up once again; I must do something positive about my deficient knowledge.

A knock on the door breaks into his thoughts and his concentration wavers. He calls out for identification from the intruder, but none is offered, so I push up out of the settee and throw open the door. Three strangers of oriental appearance, with some ingenuity, have found his house and ask me about buying Padelletti Brunello. The Ingegnere is not pleased, but harnessing momentum, leaning on his cane, he rises unsteadily and motions for me to come with him. Further into the darkened cavern is a windowless cantina and I am greatly taken aback to find a worker pasting labels on to wine bottles by hand. The strangers taste Padelletti Brunello, with much appreciative bowing, and decide to purchase, but when they hear the price they change their minds, suggesting, politely, that it can be purchased more economically in an enoteca in the village. Bowing profusely, they back away and, somewhat irritated, the Ingegnere comments, for my ears only, with a wry smile on his face, 'They will not find it in the shops . . . Nobody will sell my wine in the village because I am not a communist.' I let this red-hot morsel pass, and instead, I digress to labels. 'The Padelletti,' he says curtly, 'would not accept titles from any pope, but my ancestors called themselves Gentiluomini, Gentlemen, and the label for Padelletti wine has always been written, 'Made by the Gentlemen Padelletti', and I have carried on the tradition. Anyway, I do not believe one should make up nobility; it annoys me that this has happened in Montalcino and one day I will tell you about it. Money and notoriety does not bring nobility – there is only one pure noble in the whole of Montalcino and he is a noble Count. Even after the fall of Siena they could not take his nobility away because it came from the Doge of the Republic of Venice, not the Grand Duke of Tuscany, nor the Pope.'

A comment from nowhere delivered like the blast from a cannon! In his mind the Ingegnere holds so many amazing tales that are supplementary, perhaps sensational trivia, but whether that be so or not, there is immense depth to the history of an astounding family stretching back a thousand years. Much of it exists only in his head, or, if it is written, it is probably scratchy notes underscored in manuscripts that none of his remaining family will have the time or patience to piece together. When he is gone, and, sadly, I suspect that the day is not long away, this marvellous story will go with him to the grave. I selfishly cling to the hope that he will tarry on this earth long enough to finish his family saga; to tell me more about nobles who are not really nobles, and those who were stripped of nobility. And if he does not tell me himself then I will ask him, for I must know about the Count who cannot be stripped!

Half an hour has been wasted not selling wine to three strangers from Japan who are destined to a fruitless search in the shops of Montalcino. Probably they were blissfully unaware they were tasting Brunello with the Ingegnere Padelletti himself, a Gentiluomo. We return to our cave and compose ourselves. 'Let us continue and see if we can reach my father. There are some disastrous issues to pursue, and that will mean that when next you come I can tell you about the life of my father and mother, which people around here will deny.'

'The lives of the outstanding brothers Guido and Dino,' he warns, 'need to be related individually, but they are entwined, with overlapping repercussions, as you will discover at the end. Remember though, both died young; the first to die was Guido. You have noticed that weaving in and out of my family is an insistent German thread, not only by birth through my ancestors, but through education and circumstances of career. From Guido's father, Pierfrancesco, who learned German at court for three years, an implicit link can be inferred. It is not surprising then, that his son, Guido, about whom I now talk, was something of a Germanic industrialist; he thought on an intellectual level, and inherited great wealth.'

I have to interrupt. 'Do you mean, Ingegnere, that all through these generations, all these Padelletti lived in Montalcino?' He nods. 'Yes, even though many came and went, Montalcino was the pivot; this is where my family wealth and heritage has always been anchored, and I am still here.

'Even though Guido was influenced by rapid Germanic industrial development he loved Montalcino which, for the times, was progressive in mentality even if money was scarce. By his eighteenth birthday Guido had been awarded his degree in law – in fact, in many universities all over Italy they still teach from books written by Guido, and he was a colleague of Professor Wilhelm Zumpt, an eminent German archaeologist. The science of antiquities was liberated in Germany, seats of archaeology in German universities flourished well ahead of France or England, and my grandfather, with Professor Zumpt and Heinrich Schliemann, frequently travelled to Greece and Egypt excavating buried temples and opening up pharaohs' tombs among the pyramids. As a matter of fact, you probably remember that Schliemann was obsessed with finding the ancient city of Troy? My grandfather and Schliemann ended up in an almighty scholarly dispute because my grandfather would not concede that Schliemann had found Troy, which he claimed . . . but that is another story . . . although my grandfather has been proven correct – it was not the city of Troy.'

An incidental story, casually elaborated then brushed away, makes my eyes boggle. I want to know about the sack of Egyptian scarabs engraved with ancient symbols that were brought back to Montalcino, and about thrilling campaigns to dig up the lost city of Troy, but, frustratingly, we must refrain from diverting to Egypt and Greece and, saying that he will come back to Guido, the Ingegnere says no more about his grandfather's exploits, except that he married and had a son called Carlo, 'who –' he points his finger accusingly at me, instructing me to remember – 'was my father'.

'Now we must move sideways, turning to Guido's brother, Dino, otherwise you will not understand how the lives and early deaths of these two brothers are entwined in the story of my father. Dino, too, had intellectual brainpower and as a young mathematics professor was lecturing in this abstract science at

Naples and Palermo. He had a sparkling future ahead, he never fell out with anyone and was well liked in Montalcino; a warm affectionate man. Guido had appointed him to be the guardian tutor of his son, Carlo, who, I told you to remember, was my father. At the time Guido died, after a long illness, the mother of both boys, the Florentine of high birth, was living with Dino and his lover, down in Naples, where he was lecturing. In service for Dino in Naples was the son of a contadino from Paradiso, one of the family farms in Montalcino. It was normal, in that unimaginable social structure, for a contadino with too many mouths to feed to surrender one of his children to the padrone, as a servant, where they often stayed until old age. When Dino's nephew, Carlo, my father, reached eighteen years of age, Dino intended to return to Montalcino to grant the boy his inheritance and accordingly he withdrew a substantial sum from the bank in Naples.'

Empty seconds tick away as he reflects on how best to proceed; he resolves to jump forward. 'The bodies of Dino and his mother were never examined because they had been buried in lime . . . the excuse the contadino servant and Dino's lover gave the police chief was that Dino and his mother had died of the plague. My father, young Carlo, took two days to reach Naples and in the house where his uncle Dino lived with his mother and lover there was not a stick of furniture, not a book, not a paper, there was nothing. Every single possession of Dino's had been stolen, along with Carlo's inheritance, by Dino's lover in collusion with the contadino servant who cunningly had poisoned both Dino and his mother!' He could not have presented me with a more horrifying picture, but is this really plausible? A puckish laugh escapes his lips, and then, as if to emphasize the terribleness of the deed committed, he says, 'I will recite for you what is written on Dino's tomb, in Montalcino: "What treasure we have lost when our Dino has only forty years, and, when your body is at rest in our cemetery, alongside that of your illustrious brother, Guido, this is a glory to our village." My father returned to Montalcino with nothing, his inheritance was never traced. His own father, Guido, his grandmother, and guardian uncle, Dino, were all dead. All he possessed were the farms.'

'But what about Guido's wife, Carlo's mother? She is the only person you have not told me about.' He is exceedingly pleased at my perspicacity. 'Excellent! Now we will return to Guido's wife, who was *my* grandmother and a remarkable woman . . . but where to start? This part of the story has a deplorable impact on my family in Montalcino.'

'She was a Berliner, and her name was Hilda Zumpt – you see, Guido fell in love with the daughter of the eminent archaeologist with whom he dug up tombs and temples in Egypt and Greece. He brought his German wife to live in Montalcino and it was Hilda who had, not unnaturally, an intense love of Gothic . . . this home *is* Hilda Zumpt and her stamp is forever on it. But this was a time of great social upheaval in Europe. Professor Zumpt and his daughter were close friends of Engels and his companion Marx, an association that did not bring great fortune. I have seen photographs of my grandmother standing alongside Engels and Marx, taken shortly before the development of socialism which turned into communism.'

Grave social implications of a grandmother with such conspicuous companions are not lost on me. Twisting himself round he points to a dresser and asks me to fetch a black and white photograph so that I can see Hilda Zumpt. Four refined sisters, Fernandina, Clara Marie, Augusta and Mathilda, shortened to Hilda, in a set pose for the camera. Hilda is gowned in folds of shining taffeta, with a goffered frill of lace on an upright stiffened collar, ropes of pearls loop round her neck and gems sparkle from ears and fingers. One sister leans on a parasol, another raises an open book; hair styles are elegant chignons at the nape of the neck; polished, educated and sophisticated young German ladies.

'Now I will tell you the cause of intense distress, aside from an association with Engels and Marx, and the thing that aroused the Church's hatred of my family which escalated and evolved into a wicked vendetta. Hilda Zumpt was a direct descendant of Cavaliere Benantoni, who was counsellor to Martin Luther, the German religious reformer who preached justification by faith alone and nailed a Bill to the door of Wittenberg Cathedral in the early 1500s! Hilda, you see, was a follower of Luther – a live-wire German Protestant!'

I am hard pressed to believe these tales relate to one intricate story of a single family. Truth is assuredly stranger than fiction, but I have no doubt it would be inconceivable for anyone to make all this up. The Ingegnere has brought me to his German grandmother, friend of Engels and Marx, descendant of a mysterious counsellor to Martin Luther. The implications are explicit and dangerous.

'Hilda, finding herself locked into a Catholic society, needed somewhere to pray, and at that time there was plenty of money, so she initiated work for a Protestant chapel to be built. The Catholic Church tried every possible means, including inciting the population and imploring the Vatican, to stop her, but they could not. Hilda's chapel lies adjacent to my front door. One day I will show it to you, but we will need to have a workman with us because I do not have any strength in these old bones and the wooden doors have not been opened for years. I cannot slide the bolts without help.'

These, I recall, are the weather-beaten wooden doors that I mistakenly hammered on the first time I came to visit the Ingegnere, believing I was at his front door. With this unexpected disclosure my mind is occupied with repercussions of the entanglement of church and state, catholicism, communism and socialism, patriotic marches inciting intellectuals and students to risk their lives, to expel invaders and unify an Italy torn asunder by foreigners for centuries. And the heavy-handed consequences wrought upon a Christian woman who wanted somewhere to pray. But the Ingegnere is not ready to let go of an oppressive attitude: 'The Catholic Church has never forgiven my family for bringing a heretic to Montalcino. The Padelletti have always been free spirits, they were liberal in thought and mind. My grandparents, Guido and Hilda, wanted to take this village into their hearts. They gave so much of their wealth to Montalcino but they were hated by prejudiced priests, considered shameful heretics left over from the days of the puri, and the Church would not tolerate competition against their shop!'

We fall silent, exhausted from the different exertions of our minds. The enormity of these revelations weighs heavily in the air. His eyes dwell accusingly on me. 'Signora, do you not believe me?' I assure him I do, but, being the offspring of a Protestant family, it pours confusion into my already disconcerted mind. 'Upstairs,' he goes on, 'I have the original cartoons for the frescoes inside Wittenberg Cathedral, the door to which the rebellious priest Luther nailed his Bill. The cathedral was destroyed in the last war. These drawings came to my family because the artist, Gustave Spagnanberg, was godfather to a

Padelletti niece.' In his excitement his diction is muffled, but I nod, pretending to recognize the artist's name. 'My grandmother Hilda had a great mark against her and one of her saddest moments was right here in Montalcino. Being a descendant of Benantoni, through her family she came into possession of one of the bibles interpreted and translated by Martin Luther himself; she unselfishly wished it to be preserved in a museum. She handed it to the Comune of Montalcino, but naively did not request a written receipt – and they made this incalculably precious bible vanish! It was never seen again and the Comune denies it ever existed. This is not something she, nor I, can forgive.'

'Now you can see,' he says, 'the extent of the hostility my father Carlo faced, when he returned from Naples without his inheritance, about which I will tell you when next you come.'

The Ingegnere is weary and has politely signalled my discreet departure. His mind is wound into overdrive and I am conscious of arousing embittered memories, not to mention his racing heartbeat. But his words do not seem to me (to recall the way Beppe described La Signora Contessa) to be the words of a vecchietto, an old one. Frail of body he may be, and I am not at all convinced that I may hear the end of this tale, but the Ingegnere is not frail of mind. Each link in the chain of history fills his face with emotion, shows in his watery eyes and is stressed with a wry smile or impotent gesture with his hands. I am fairly worn out myself, absorbing the emotion of the story, and that of the Ingegnere is piling on top of my own. I take my leave, grateful that he remains seated, offering me departure through the garden gate instead of up the staircase through the house. Not wishing to leave him in this dark cave alone, I protest, but he is intending to return to the cantina and assures me the worker will provide assistance, should it be required.

My smile widens as I turn out into the daylight, through the garden gate and walk past the doors of the Protestant chapel shut tight. Wooden barriers that could not be broken down by the most willing heart. That *will* be an interesting visit; when I telephone for our next appointment I will volunteer to bring Luigi to slide back these rusty bolts and prise open the doors. My shoulders drop and my smile creases into a frown. Am I fooling myself, harbouring spurious illusions? After all I have listened to today, is there any possibility that a Protestant like me could ever find long-term acceptance in Montalcino?

At last the clouds creep away, carrying stifling humidity to some other hill and scorching heat brings the kind of sun-drenched summer we have come to expect. In Travaglio roses and falling petals daub stone paths and walls in hot pink and canary yellow while blood-red climbers scale garden walls and droop lazily down the other side, finding nothing more on which to exert themselves. At the church of the Madonna miniature white roses ramble through a garden and sprawl on the well, cloaking the iron cover like a white mantle. A sweet perfume sweeps through the air, a musky scent hard to find in florist's roses.

Luigi is unable to come with me today. He has departed to Siena in the Maserati, which is why I am walking to Pianello archery range, a couple of kilometres outside the walls. I am pleased we have a bright summer afternoon in which to gather and encourage our archers before the coming tournament. Soon I will be outside the walls, but, anticipating a thirty-minute walk in the heat, I have chosen to divert from my usual exposed track, preferring to walk downhill through the village in the shade, while I may. I made slow progress in the first ten minutes, pausing to see what two weeks of sun has wrought in the gardens; apricots yield to ripeness and peaches show a first flush. I watch a man jump down from a bank to a strawberry patch, a high-handled lattice basket swinging over his arm. Lifting the leaves he plucks the reddest berries, letting them plop softly into the basket. In three minutes the basket is full and he begins tearing shallow blades of grass from between the plants. I hope these strawberries end up at Laura's shop; I can practically taste them and the aroma of furry stems and ripe fruit makes my mouth water. I pass a bed of rucola and four kinds of lettuce marching in tight rows, enviably healthy. Where are the insects? Why do snails or other pests not nibble these tender leaves? Jasmine camouflages a wall, blazing white above a terrace in the neighbourhood of Borghetto; on this jagged path my feet squash overripe apricots pecked from the tree above. Birds are so wasteful – one peck per apricot is all they take. At Porta Cerbaia, the gate through which I leave the walls, spindly wildflowers skirt the rim of a broken stone parapet behind which Montalcino's archers once crouched, and, below the gate, banks of wild dill have gone to seed.

In the open now, the sun beats upon me as I keep to the shoulder of the shadowless road, stopping only when I reach a magnificent vineyard. Cultivated as harmoniously as an ornamental Japanese garden, each avenue is a mirror image of its neighbour, clipped into discipline, instincts subdued by years of training. Approvingly, I nod my head; not a blade of grass grows in the rows, but between the trunks spires of sword grass and thirsty thistles fight for survival. I bend closer, peering at the clusters hanging free; the grapes are growing bigger than chickpeas. No Easter white-frost damage here, although I am not certain that I know precisely what to look for; perhaps there is none because this vineyard is at high altitude. Turning from the road, shafts of sunlight pierce the shade from overhanging oaks as I begin to climb through a wood to reach the practice range, but as I rise higher a forest of tall pine trees blocks the light and the drone of wasps is dulled by my feet crunching dry needles. Ten minutes sauntering beneath sighing pines brings me to a clearing where cars are parked, and from here I step through the undergrowth and on to a grassy path, invisible unless you know where to put your first foot.

Winding down the last few metres I respond to a hail of ciaos from everyone watching our archers. Ofelia points to her daughter, Chiara, who is preparing to shoot. Girls and women are eligible to enter tournaments, it is not exclusively a male realm, but selection to shoot is dependent on many criteria. The bows are not equipped with technically advanced sights; this is a mental and physical skill, taking measure of wind currents and the lofting flight of an arrow. The bows are lightweight, compared to those used fifty years ago, but if a tournament is prolonged, which happens if scores are tied, it may be that an archer is compelled to shoot for an hour, sometimes longer. Raising arms to a rigid hold, continually fixing arrows and dragging back the string, pulling the arrow to tautness for that length of time is beyond the strength of many Pianello girls. Today we are gathered on the practice range and everyone shares the fun of practising with our archers; Chiara and Maria-Teresa are shooting a few arrows into the target. A round robin between the archers will soon be under way, which will assist Dottore Luciano, our trainer, in gauging the preparedness, the level of mental and physical skill at which an archer is shooting, so that he can confidently nominate our archers for the tournament. We have all been dutifully informed, after the brouhaha our youngsters raised a few months ago, that Dottore

Luciano held his council of war with the archers and, talking through the cause and effect of a damaging quarrel with the Captain of the Tournament, this close to the event, it was unanimously agreed that complaints should be put to one side until after the summer and autumn tournaments. Then, the Dottore wisely counselled, during the winter pause he will call an open meeting and in a democratic way, if there is cause, our quartiere will lodge a request for an official inquest into the scoring regulations at tournaments. He warned, however, that if one quarter lodges a request for change, it is unlikely to meet with success. The young are obliged to seek a consensus with members of other quarters.

Ofelia's husband, Massimo, is our veteran archer with more than two decades of experience on the archery campo; he is dedicated to archery and will continue shooting for Pianello until our younger archers, like Samuele, Francesco and Filippo, rise through the ranks and prove their skills on the practice range. We are hopeful that Filippo will shoot for Pianello in his first tournament this year, but the final decision for selection rests with Dottore Luciano alone. As well as veteran Massimo, Alessandro is a steady-handed and accurate marksman, and Davide, too, has been shooting for many years for his beloved Pianello. Besides these three we have Gabriele, Gaetano and sometimes Dottore Fabio. All of them will participate in the round robin, together with our junior archers.

Chiara sends all her arrows whizzing down the range and then, unstrapping the leather sheath at her thigh, she hands bow and sheath to Cecilia, who, in clearly a conciliatory action, dismissing divergence between their views, laughs alongside Dottore Luciano, shooting for the sheer fun of it. Excitement at the thought of the approaching tournament is building and senior members have come to the range to encourage our archers, not shoot arrows, although many of them, in their youth, were archers for Pianello. When the round robin competition is under way we break into groups of four or five and gather behind the twenty-five metre line, hushing into a respectful silence during each shoot, applauding and cheering when we count five arrows thudding one after the other into the target. Maurelia flits from one group to another ensuring the young, because it is their responsibility, are organizing the cleaning and mending of our medieval costumes, and are deciding among themselves who is to parade through the village in the historical pageant on the day of the tournament. We need a dame of Pianello, and her knight, several ladies in waiting, pageboys, or girls, and each will dress in a costume in Pianello colours. As well we need soldiers who wear a leather breastplate and brandish a sword to protect our dame and knight, and the symbolic thrush hunters wear pointed hats with plumes, pantaloons to the knee and long socks with gaiters, slinging hunting nets over their shoulders. A couple of halberd-bearing pages will lay offerings of a pheasant or a hare at the feet of the Lady of the Fortress who will sit on her throne in Piazza del Popolo. But Maurelia need not concern herself; this is a tradition in Montalcino and the young have grown up dressing for the pageant, year by year advancing from one medieval costume, one Pianello identity, to another. Most navigate the early years of their life parading as a page for the dame and they continue dressing and parading in the cortège until they are old enough to wear the costume of the dame or knight. Gloria and Cecilia, officially in charge of costuming, confirm they have brought our costumes out of storage and all are hanging in our sede; buttons have been tightened, red pointed shoes polished, hems adjusted, pantaloons darned and the halberds and helmets, nets and bows are lined up against the wall. Lastly, on tournament day they will drag from the cantina the wooden chest that holds the jewels: a pretty tiara for our dame and ropes of pearls and lockets and chains for her ladies.

No Pianello gathering is without a civilized banquet, not even a picnic on the practice range on a sweltering summer afternoon. As the round robin competition reaches its final stages, Ofelia and I, together with Gloria and others who are not shooting, follow one another back up the grassy path to a clearing where Luciana and Onelia are preparing bowls of insalata di riso, rice dressed with oodles of pungent shredded basil, freshly diced tomato and olive oil, and acciuge sotto pesto. The first time I tasted these astringent anchovies steeped in pesto sauce they took my breath away. Standing at a table under the trees Fiorella is adding the final condiments, olive oil, vinegar and a few leaves of basil to chopped onion, celery, cucumber and tomato – whatever is ripe from the garden goes into her panzanella. She mixes the dressed vegetables and herbs with day-old Tuscan bread that has been soaked in water and then wrung out. Apricots and peaches bathe in bowls of water, ready for dessert. Before we sit down to our picnic a demijohn of red wine is upturned into flasks and we pour the wine and boisterously applaud our archers as they spring one after the other up the grassy path. Dottore Luciano divulges the scores of the round robin, accompanying each tally with loquacious comments, but knowing we are eager to begin our feast the archers urge him to babble no more and, with much brio, he gives us the winning names. Massimo and Alessandro attained the highest scores, but Dottore Luciano praises the accuracy of young Filippo's arrows. Filippo is embarrassed when we whistle and cheer. Perhaps this will be the year Dottore Luciano will nominate Filippo for his first trial on the campo. We raise our glasses and toast our archers, not knowing any more than they do who among them will carry the responsibility to shoot for Pianello in the coming tournament. Spirits are high, but will this be the year that Pianello will take the victory at a tournament?

Plenty of hands, including mine and Ofelia's, help clear away the picnic and in no time ceramic bowls and plates, glasses, cutlery and blue-and-white tablecloths are packed into the cars. Massimo is with the archers, gathering bows and arrows and securing the target, but Ofelia spoke with him earlier; we are resolute that our plan need wait no longer. Having talked about it for months, the timing is finally ideal because Massimo's fire brigade duty is taking him away from Montalcino for a week, and Chiara will be in Sicily on a school excursion. Ofelia and I are taking a train and spending two days in Rome.

Despite protests and offers of a seat in a car I insist on walking up the hill and home. Pianello friends, young and old, shake their heads in dismay; I have sought to explain, but I do not think they understand that walking through the hills of Tuscany is exactly what thousands of visitors dream of doing. I am fortunate to be able to do it whenever I wish. Since the Giro Podistico, of which I am happier not to be inflicted with reminders, Isabella has been labelled the fastest woman in Montalcino. Raucous laughter rises when Ofelia reminds me yet again of her astonishment to be reading *La Nazione* newspaper, when on holiday at the seaside, and there, in black and white, she gasped at a most uncomplimentary photograph of the first female home. I should have known pouring water on my head and a flashing camera would bring an ill end . . . I wave Ofelia away in the last car; she toots and disappears in clouds of dust.

Reaching the sealed road I turn towards the village; in front of me is an uphill climb for two kilometres, hence I neither rush nor tarry. My mind dithers where it will, imagining an adventure to Rome with Ofelia, and praying for a longed-for victory for Pianello on our return – a victory I have never witnessed. My eyes graze on a pocket of hill slope, a radiant palette of dullish dun, gold and grey parched fields. Some patches lie fallow and in others dark earth shows through where dry rings of stubble, left behind by the harvest, shrivel into blackness. Luscious vines run gallantly in serried ranks down a slope away from my left. With my head turned to the vines, I am brutally roused from my reverie because I fall awkwardly over the legs of a recumbent figure on the edge of the bank. 'Bruno! Are you all right?' It is Amelia's husband, the woodcutter. 'Buonasera, Signora.' He is breathing in short shallow gasps. This is worrying. His handsaw is lying on the bank, but I can see no cut branches. 'Bruno, are you on your way out or back?' He points up the hill to the village – he is on his way back, but has not cut any wood. Bruno goes to the woods each morning; why he is out this late on a hot day? His face is pale . . . I suspect he is dehydrated. Fortunately, everybody knowing each other on the hill of Montalcino means someone quickly sums up the situation and it only takes seconds before a car pulls over and a man pleasant to look upon jumps out and walks towards where I am bending over Bruno. He comes to the village; we have exchanged buongiorno in Fiaschetteria and Caffè alle Logge, if infrequently. 'Buonasera, Signora. Bruno, do you need a ride?' He agrees with my prognosis and we help weak Bruno into the car. The good looking man insists we go first to his home, which he says is only a hundred metres on, to let Bruno drink some water. Then, if necessary, we will call a doctor, or, after a rest, we can take Bruno home in the car. In a few seconds he turns the car on to gravel between rows of immaculately manicured vines.

Bruno implores me not to telephone Amelia, but succumbs to lying down and sipping a glass of diluted juice. Between myself and the young man with a very fine profile we settle Bruno on a day bed in a darkened room. He is soon breathing without strain. 'Signora,' I hear a whisper from a well tanned face close to mine, 'I was on my way to collect my son from football training, he will be wondering where I am. Would you mind if I leave you here with Bruno while I fetch him? By the time I return Bruno should be rested and we can take him home. You live in the village too, Signora, don't you?' This gives me the opening to introduce myself, a pleasantry Tuscans rarely initiate, and in response I learn his name is Andrea. He leaves me with Bruno and for the first time, as Bruno's eyes droop and he drops into an easy doze, my eyes grow accustomed to the gloom, and I stare around the room.

A pair of sharp grey eyes behind wire-framed glasses peer down at me. An inquisitive stare, and penetrating, from a balding man with a fuzzy white beard. The room is extraordinarily high, ten metres square and hanging around the walls are heavily framed portraits of sombre unsmiling men and stern bosomy women. An ornamental fireplace centred on one wall faces on to a refectory table – apart from Bruno's day bed and a carved armoire that could lead to a secret room of its own, holding books and bottles behind glass panelled doors, this is the only furniture. A tapestry hanging from a rod breaks the sequence of portraits along one wall, and two curlicue holders for candles project a metre into the room. From pelmets over the windows linen drapes to the floor and looped swags across the top are fringed with cotton bobbles, which bob in front of diamond-shaped leaded panes. The room is something of an understatement with nuances of restrained austerity. Leaving Bruno to a snuffle, I stare at the portraits, going swiftly to the largest from which the stout figure of a man with curly black hair, reddened cheeks, an abnormally long nose and glinting eyes half turns his shoulders towards me. But it is not his striking looks which astonish, it is his armorial bearings; one hand rests on a steel helmet, the other on his sword. He is a warrior, a soldier in battledress. The handwritten date is not easy to read because the portrait has been blackened by candle smoke, but I think it reads 1503, and, if I am right, he is Cavaliere Crescenzo Costanti. Crossing back to the sharp-eyed balding man with the white beard, his name is legible. He is Avvocato Tito Costanti, but the date is smudged – perhaps 1850, but I cannot be sure. Three hundred and fifty years separate these two men, but they are related. Whose handsome house is this? Looking round the room I focus on a prancing bull carved into the stone fireplace with the crest of Montalcino in one corner. My legs carry me off before my mind affirms that a winged screen is not a fireguard as I had assumed, the middle panel is painted as if it were a tree trunk and spreading tentacles over the hinged panels are outstretched branches of a family tree. Cavaliere Crescenzo and Avvocato Tito must be among these branches somewhere, but, goodness, there are hundreds of names and dates and wriggly tendrils going hither and thither to offspring shoots and dead ends. Crouching on the floor, I hastily scour one branch after another, hoping the end of a limb may tell me what I want to know. Here he is, second from the bottom, Andrea, the beguiling young man who brought us here . . . that would be right, born in 1960. Something is written underneath his date of birth. I drop to my knees and lean down, resting on an elbow with my head angled, hair brushing the floor, and this is the excruciatingly embarrassing upside-down pose in which I am ensnared when the door swings open and Andrea and his son walk in. But I have read the words and am blown away because this handsome young man is *Count* Andrea Costanti!

Blushing scarlet from head to toe, exhibiting not the sheerest modicum of feminine poise, I leap from the floor, but, barely battering a curling eyelash, he walks straight to Bruno, pretending he has not seen my childish prank; a true aristocrat? Bruno is awake and anxious to go home; he walks slowly but unaided to the car. On the way to the house, preoccupied with Bruno, I had not noticed the lilac wisteria sheltering the courtyard, or a trimmed box hedge that, in a maze of intricate angles and curves, switches back and forth around magnificent trees. In a few minutes we reach Montalcino and Andrea parks the car opposite the garden at Bar Prato because Bruno insists we not make a fuss – he does not want to arrive home accompanied by good Samaritans, otherwise Amelia will dissolve into tears. This seems reasonable, but I warn that in an hour I will call at their home. 'Bene, Signora,' he says brightly, 'I'll have a drop of my liqueur waiting for you.' We watch him shuffle towards home with his saw under his arm, but neither of us is convinced he can fool Amelia because he has no chopped wood. I am trying to formulate words to excuse my earlier lack of decorum, at the same time thinking maybe I should take the easy way out and say nothing . . . but Andrea, gentlemanly, as one would expect of an engaging Count, says: 'Signora, if you are not going to see Bruno and Amelia for an hour, why don't we go to the piazza for an aperitivo?'

'Your vines looks so well, Andrea, did you not suffer damage in the Easter freeze?' A clever way of steering conversation a long way clear of warriors in shining armour. 'No, my vineyard is high, the frost did not reach three hundred and eighty metres. But you know, even nature's wrath can bring positive results. In some vineyards the grapes may be behind, but nature is better at it than we are. They may harvest fewer grapes and they may harvest later, but the law of nature is that only the best will survive; those damaged clusters struggling to survive may well end up optimum quality grapes and give a wine of great elegance. It depends what happens between now and harvest. Five-star vintages do not always come in a perfect growing year.'

He is wholly relaxed. Our easy exchange is broken from time to time as we salute passing friends because we are highly visible, sitting beneath the bell tower outside Caffè alle Logge. Sebastiano is aimlessly wandering with an empty drinks tray in his hand. In half an hour the piazza will be animated as passeggiata time brings everybody out for a walk on a warm evening. Andrea is young for a winegrower in Montalcino, and alludes to a guiding philosophy lurking behind the bottle. 'Have you grown up with the vineyard?' I ask, thinking to stay well clear of family trees and bottom branches, but I have fallen into a snare. 'Oh, no, Signora, I have my degree in geology. I was a young man of twenty-two not intending to be doing this, but even though I had never even tasted a glass of red wine, it was my destiny to play a small role in the secret of Brunello di Montalcino.'

His destiny, and the intriguing scent of the philosophy of a young geologist growing one of the great wines of the world, capture my imagination. Even being caught grovelling upside down on the uneven stone paving of a Count's lodging is not awful enough to cause me to halt!

'Did you see the portrait of Avvocato Tito Costanti?' My throat is blushing crimson, but I detect no censure in his voice. 'I would be happy if Tito had left me a few bottles of wine instead of pieces of paper hanging on my wall, because bottles would be worth a lot of money and I would be famous . . . but just the same I am proud to tell you that Tito was one of the first of four families to enter a wine identifiable by the name Brunello in an exposition. Two were the Tamanti and Anghirelli, both Montalcino families that have all but disappeared; thirdly, there was the Santi family, and in the same document, my family, Costanti. All four entered a wine called Brunello in an exposition in Siena, and that wine, from 1865, is, I believe, the earliest written positively documented historic time the word Brunello can be identified.'

Ingegnere Padelletti emphatically told me there is one true noble in Montalcino and Conte Andrea Costanti has fallen into my lap, thanks to Bruno; am I finally getting to the noble root of Brunello di Montalcino? He has said not a word about creation, but identification of the wine Brunello is a link that may help me solve the jigsaw, and now I have a date of identification.

'However, there was a significant difference between the four families because only one of them, from the inception, was occupied at a professional level with making wine. Tito was a lawyer, and his farm was grander than it is today, producing crops as well as olive oil. Tito's wine was for family consumption. It was rarely bottled and if it was sold, then probably in demijohns that customers brought to be filled. Tito chose to enter competitions, and I am immensely proud of his foresight, but merit has to go to the Santi family – of the four, only they were making wine with superior techniques, bottling wine and labelling it as well.' I probe, tentatively, but Andrea will not allow swinging debates about the paternity of Brunello di Montalcino to clutter his mind. 'That argument,' he says, 'has been circulating underground for a hundred years and serves no purpose. The document with Tito's name on it, and the word Brunello, is enough for me. But,' he says with a smile, 'it would have been handy if Tito had saved me a few bottles of the 1865! Then again, Tito was not to know about my adoption.'

Adoption? In Montalcino, knowledge is a river deep and dangerous, I know not to where it may run, but I cannot hold back. 'You are an adopted Count?' The words fly out . . . but Andrea is unperturbed at my rashness.

The Costanti genealogy can be traced to the 1300s. Honoured for bravery and loyalty, by 1500 they were Nobili Senesi; brave men of war who went into battle on the side of Siena against the eternally despised Florentines. Giulio, Carlo and Crescenzo, the one in battledress in the portrait, were three warrior brothers looking for another war because Siena was in ruins. An opportunity for battle befitting their bravery arose at a time when the Republic of Venice was at war with the Turks, so the three brothers left their families in Siena and went to war on the side of Venice. The Doge rewarded their bravery by bestowing on them the title of Count, adding the vital words that it be a hereditary noble title to be perpetuated through the male line. Conte Giulio and Conte Carlo begat large families but a couple of hundred years ago both branches died out through lack of male heirs. Cavaliere Conte Crescenzo was fortunate to give life to a branch of the family that flourished. The Grand Duke of Tuscany and the Pope conferred noble titles but as power fluctuated with victory or defeat in centuries of war, noble titles were frequently revoked. The Costanti never lost their nobility because it was bestowed by the Doge of Venice, not in war-ravaged Tuscany. On his death Conte Tito Costanti passed his noble title and the farm to his male issue, Emilio, who became the next Count, but Emilio had no children and it seemed all would be lost. Conte Emilio was uncle to Andrea's father, but he is not a Count. In 1982 the ageing Conte Emilio was growing sangiovese grosso for Brunello which his father, Conte Tito, had initiated, but he was also ill. To Andrea's father he reasoned: 'I have no male heir, our family nobility will be lost because the title will die with me; if you will agree to let me adopt Andrea, your oldest son, I will legally hand to him my hereditary noble title as Count Costanti, and the farm.'

'And so, at twenty-two, I found myself with this patrimony, a hereditary responsibility and sense of duty to my ancestors. Many smallholdings like mine were exporting a little wine but few were gearing up for the international stage . . . and Signora, reflect on the year! The Americans were moving into Castello Banfi. Some people were terrified! But Costanti have been making wine for hundreds of years, we do not make wine to *create* a market, or to satisfy a fashion on the other side of the world. Conte Emilio died within weeks of passing me the title so he had no time to teach me how to make Costanti wine. How I would love to have harvested just one vintage by his side, but it was not my destiny to learn from him. I was young, but I had to understand the philosophy and spirit in which to make our wine. If it rained, when I did not want rain, I used to get angry. But making wine is tied to events that I do not control and every day in the vineyard is a lesson in accepting what nature gives me. A million years ago the hill where my vines grow so magnificently was an island and down below was the sea. Rocks deep in the bowels of the earth were thrown to the surface but could not withstand the atmospheric conditions; limestone is the evolutionary result. My vineyard sits in miserable poverty, there are no nutrients for the vine, so the bunches fight for existence. But how can I claim credit for this geological phenomenon? Now that I understand the secret I try to make a balanced wine, like an orchestra, elegant, a fusion of colour and flavour and aroma. Every bottle that leaves my vineyard has Conte Costanti on the label, and it must be a Costanti wine, with the personality of my vineyard and my family written upon it. I have to be careful of using my noble title, and if I did not have it, I would not use it – unlike some who invent it – but for foreign markets Conte Costanti signifies the long tradition of a noble winemaking family. I cannot convey the emotion I feel when I see even one bottle of Conte Costanti Brunello in a New York or Munich restaurant!'

Two things puzzle me. Both the Ingegnere and Andrea obliquely refer to false claimants to nobility; and another thing, Tamanti is the name the Ingegnere mentioned, talking about Antonio and his bankruptcy, and Anghirelli is a surname I have heard, but Santi on its own makes no sense to me. The grower using Santi has double-barrelled it with Biondi. Curiosity entices me to plough on with my investigations, there can be nothing for me but finding the answers, if I can, but nagging apprehension warns me that I may not like what I discover. For the moment I am led, by virtue of Andrea's earnestness to have me understand, back to a description that caught my ear several minutes ago. 'Andrea, tell me then, what is the secret of Brunello di Montalcino?'

'This is what I believe. The most important factor in making Brunello is not the clone of sangiovese grosso, it is not barrels or barrique, nor that the wine ages four or even five years. It is not the winemaker or the harvest. Perhaps, someplace in the world they make a superior wine, but nobody in the world can make *my* wine. They may plant sangiovese grosso and follow our technique, but they do not have our secret. Brunello is unique because the earth is what makes it Brunello . . . Montalcino is the secret!'

Passeggiata has come and gone and we have not stirred or joined the swell of citizens on the evening ritual before dinner. 'Signora,' he finishes, 'many people do not know this story and unless they ask I do not explain. Apart from jokes that football friends play on my son Emilio, who will one day carry on the family nobility as Count Emilio Costanti, a noble title is of questionable value in today's world. If someone is looking for a geologist, they are not looking for a geologist count, are they? Perhaps it serves to help sell a bottle or two of wine, but, aside from duty to my ancestors, that is the only purpose to which I will put my nobility.' About to shake hands, he pauses: 'Signora, ci possiamo dare del tu?' He seeks my permission to take the liberty of addressing me by my first name. Relinquishing the respectful but distant Signora and claiming to be friendly Isabella is an achievement I work relentlessly towards. I smile politely and, tongue-in-cheek, reply: 'Only if you will relinquish my responsibility of addressing you as Count Andrea Costanti.'

Hearing pots and pans clattering as I reach Amelia's shuttered windows, I can be sure she and Bruno have not yet sat down to dinner. She opens the door quickly, saying Bruno told her I was coming, and I am mute when she suggests he is in the cantina, stacking the wood, getting washed before dinner. A delicious aroma rushes from the stove and she lifts the lid on a pot of ragù sauce, a meaty dressing for her pasta. I inspect and approve Amelia's cooking regularly, to her happiness. We spend time together at least once a week; sometimes she rings my bell and comes upstairs to my kitchen for a chat, but more often I knock on her door in the afternoon when Bruno is chopping and stacking wood in the cantina. Amelia is a tiny woman, approaching her nineties, with a seraphic face and kindly eyes; I count her among my dearest friends. She has a daughter living in the north of Italy but I sense a clash of personalities; Amelia is stubborn, rigidly obstinate about her simple way of living in her tiny home. She reacts with a tongue of fire if her daughter suggests a sojourn in the north, finding no need to go further than the Friday market or the baker; but she walks alone to the cemetery early every morning to visit and lay flowers on the grave of her first daughter. Sometimes we watch television together, or water her azalea, and sometimes she lets me help her roll the pasta or stir a sauce, and we often sit and she talks about her past and I talk about mine. Bruno gathers wild fruit in the woods and yesterday brought her a sack of apricots. She has baked an apricot crostata and I am offered a slice along with a goccia of Bruno's homemade liqueur. Bruno bangs the door of the cantina downstairs and I begin my departure, a bag of apricots under my arm. Remembering, I turn back, and remind Amelia that soon I am going away for a couple of days – she must not expect me again until the end of the following week. Whereupon she has me reeling, warning me of the terrible dangers awaiting two women in a wicked city like Rome, baffling me with her fatalism, until she answers my last question. Amelia has never been to Rome in her life!

CHAPTER EIGHT

Don Michele and the Disco Rumba

Summer visitors approach Montalcino overjoyed to be winding upwards between rolling hills that swoop downwards into deep gulches, in an inexplicable conflict of brittle fragility and yielding curves. Couples scan ploughed slopes for glimpses of romantic farmhouses, half fallen down, overshadowed by chestnut and oak, with cypress standing guard at the end of a gravel road. Seldom, on a hot summer afternoon, do they find evidence of life, except perhaps a barking dog. Rising up towards the village, eyes are hypnotized by ribbed tyres from a farmer's tractor, choked with dried mud cakes, relentlessly creeping across the hillside. A listless trail of pale blond chaff blowing hither and thither, carried away by the breeze, drifts out of the valley. At last, eyes feast upon resplendent grape clusters hanging from vines that clothe the hills of their dreams. Heads twist from side to side, but eyes cannot focus on, let alone count, a thousand blurry rows flashing by. Narrowing eyes at a bend where an outstretched hand can almost finger the vines, they stare at bunches through car windows, amazed that Tuscans erect no barrier between the passing world and these precious grapes. Into the car they packed smart straw sunhats together with the latest guide with which to track down the secret places of Tuscany. But in Montalcino the paradisiacal picture is shattering because when dreamy-eyed, hot and thirsty visitors approach the summit of the hill, wend their way around the wall to the fortress and look for somewhere to park, our Mayor declares that the dream comes crashing round their ears. Visitors with vehicles present difficulties, but in comparison to the political war our Mayor is facing, they are, in truth, a lesser component of a monumental dilemma facing mayors of medieval villages. Living in a picturesque walled village offers security, tranquillity and social infrastructure, among many privileges, but it does not offer enough spaces for prosperous citizens to park cars. Not only those who dwell within the walls, but a couple of thousand who live on the vineyards and farms who come to the village to socialize, or to visit the butcher, and there are those who require a bank, or even to post letters.

Our Mayor, waving a red flag to a bull, aware that it is not feasible for things to continue the way things are, in keeping with his belief that the only way for Montalcino to move is in a forward direction, proposes a new car park inside the walls. Unfortunately, the appropriated stretch of land is one of few remaining wild growth hillsides sporadically planted with olive trees. Walking this early morning along a dirt path in the wildness above the olive grove I drop gloomily on a bench and listen to chittering birds, and in a few minutes I will chat to Nani, the basket weaver, who, in his ninety-fourth year, can be found nearly every morning sitting on a stump from where he weaves wicker baskets for the olive pickers. This morning he is not yet here because, sensibly, he first calls at the bar for caffè. Wild blackberry rambles over three stone walled terraces built by the Montalcinesi centuries ago to protect the village from invaders. Distressed by the Mayor's proposal, citizens who care have formed a committee pledging to fight mayoral madness; they do not want a car park inside the walls, nor do they want to see this olive grove destroyed. And they are defiantly, passionately opposed to the bulldozing of centuries-old dry stone terraced walls.

This is troubling to my mind and, needing to examine my conscience before signing a proffered petition, I sit on the bench and look out over a valley that offers everything to be wished for in the way of a Tuscan dream. Olive trees are so close that I can touch the fruit; the skin is flecked and pellets brick hard. Along with twittering birds, olives are a distraction to my wrestling mind, as is the prickly green ball that I plucked from a chestnut tree along the way and dropped into my pocket. Sharp barbs prickle and irritate my thigh, although when I brushed the fronds the spines rolled soft and pliant over my hand.

Politics in Montalcino can be difficult to comprehend; the village has been governed by socialists and communists for as long as anyone can remember, and although there are opposition parties of the centre right, they hold no power. Just the same, struggling with myself, to support the fighting committee perhaps I need not visibly enter either camp; but to take a stand in a hot political debate could be imprudent. My mind loops around the pros and cons, unmasking my inability to accept what my conscience tells me; but the village is small; in half a day all my friends will know.

The snapping of twigs and tearing sounds from bushes clutching at the terraces interrupt the birdsong, releasing me from maudlin self-examination. 'Buongiorno Nani!' I greet him with a happy voice so as not to startle him when he looks up and sees me standing just above on the path. 'Oh, Signora, buongiorno, but it is not a good morning, is it?' Can Nani be referring to the threatened olive grove? Probably he does not know about the proposed destruction of the trees and these brambly terraces. 'The humidity is too high, Signora, it is no good for anyone and makes my work harder.' Watching a ninety-four-year-old at work distracts my mind from car parks. Nani holds a clasp knife in one hand, and with the other, suitably gloved, he tears at blackberry, stripping a tendril from an entangled mass. When he has three or so metres raised above the thicket, he cuts through the tendril and, folding the knife and slipping it into his pocket, loosely coils the thorny whip and tosses it to the ground. The tendrils are moist and he is cutting and coiling to dry them out before he turns them into lashing for weaving into baskets. Nani is of another epoch. He labours in his

Sunday best, always to be found with a tie knotted round his neck, and a smart brimmed hat never leaves his head until he is sitting on his stump – unless he passes me on this path, whereupon he lifts the brim of his hat and sweeps it through the air in a gentlemanly gesture. If the olive grove and brambles are destroyed Nani will not be able to come here and weave his baskets; he will have nowhere to sit out the remaining years of his long life. Perhaps the Mayor's proposal will not, after all, proceed.

Leaving Nani to his work my thoughts turn brightly to Ofelia and our impending visit to Rome. Since we sealed our plan at the practice range vacillating weather has sent summer somewhere else. The sun is beyond a haze of cloud, glaring down upon us while we swelter in moisture laden air. By mid morning, suspended vapour saps our energy, wilting the most spirited who venture to the piazza, forcing us home and behind medieval walls in melancholy afternoon siesta, always longer than intended. The long-range weather forecast is uncertain; farmers pray for a drop of rain and growers pray for sun, the rest of us pray for a decision by the gods in one or other direction, so long as summer returns and we are relieved of close and heavy air. The President of the Consorzio is driven to counselling in daily bulletins the dangers in the remaining weeks before harvest. 'The season has not changed its features,' he announces. 'We hoped for stability, but we suffer week after week with wild swings in the weather, and fears are growing. The Easter freeze was destructive in lower zones, many vineyards suffered a violent shock; days of useless torrential rain poured from the hill and was followed by a burst of scorching heat . . . but the sun has not endured and the days have descended to rare flashes of blue heated by a sick sun. Monotonous days marked with insidious danger now follow one upon another; I have seen nothing like it in fifty years. Vines are suffering prolonged stress.'

This morning a shimmering haze hangs in the valley. Breezes and soft air currents are needed to aerate the vineyards but for a week not a leaf has been lifted or shuffled from its canopy along the rows; every day increases the likelihood of disease. 'If you have not already done so,' advises the President of the Consorzio, 'delay no longer: get rid of foliage, thin down clusters, cut off what is not needed. Maturation is late, the struggling clusters must be circulated by air or your grapes will putrefy.'

'Buongiorno, Enzo.' I suspected he would be here this morning; defoliation is underway. 'Do what we may –' he waves a hand at workers – 'if we do not see the sun, the grapes will not ripen. Leaves are of no more use, they shelter grapes and shield air currents. Conditions could not be more suited to powdery mildew attack. Look at the grapes – the skins are weak and with moths breeding in this humidity it only needs a few insects to pierce the skins and the juice will ooze. We will face disaster.' His words remind me of a sommelier I listened to at Benvenuto Brunello. I was intrigued to see him hold a chalice of red wine to the light, explaining that he was looking for the sun in the glass, telling us that it is not only the changing colour of the grape skin, although ripening toughens the skin, increasing its impervious-ness to insect attack, but purple skins give Brunello its marvellous ruby hue in the glass. No sun means pale, weak skins, and it means the grapes will not be sweet and juicy. Sunny countries produce sunny wines; the microclimate at Montalcino, blessed by air currents at altitude, allows connoisseurs to judge Brunello a sunny wine. Perhaps not the coming harvest. 'I am doing what I can,' Enzo shrugs, 'I have chopped away weak clusters, reduced my crop by a third, and all shadowing foliage will be gone by lunch time. Mildew and moths are a danger that I must leave in the hands of the Almighty . . . and pray for sun.'

Luigi drove us in the Maserati to Chiusi, a fifty-minute ride. The summer Apertura tournament will be held days after we all return – Massimo from his fireman's duty, Chiara, who is in Sicily, and Ofelia and I who are on our way to Rome. In a little over an hour on the fast intercity train we will reach the eternal city. Lightly burdened for our overnight adventure, we clamber aboard and, settling ourselves in an empty compartment, girlish chatter occupies half an hour, but steadies to a dribble of banal exchanges once travellers from Orvieto climb on board and occupy the empty seats. Whereupon continuous babble suffices for everybody, because Italians are unable to maintain silence in group travel, and soon, once preliminaries are out of the way, and everyone is politely acquainted through points of departure or destination, they revert to perennial discussions about planting, tendering, harvesting, cooking and, eventually, eating all the food they grow in garden plots, diverting on occasion to when, where and how all these essential harbingers of benessere, well-being, can be accomplished. Our journey and culinary lesson at an end, we all bid each other farewell, quit the train at Termini Stazione, and a few minutes in a taxi races us past one picture postcard after another, heightening our sense of awe, exalted at the sight of Rome's washed and weathered monuments flashing past the windows.

Our boutique hotel is a few steps from Piazza di Spagna. It was never our intention to spend every minute of our days in Rome together; Ofelia and I approach Rome from different directions, so to speak, each giving ourselves over to pleasures to quench our yearnings. Ofelia has lived within the walls of medieval Montalcino her whole life; she married Massimo, an Ilcinese, and they, together with daughter Chiara, are surrounded by each other's parents, grandparents, uncles, aunts, nephews, nieces, cousins and in-laws. Chiara has telephoned Ofelia from Sicily twice a day for nearly a week, jubilant with her excursion to witness the spewing lava and fiery night spectacular over Mount Etna. Once we check into our hotel Ofelia telephones Chiara suggesting that, for the next couple of days, she should ring Massimo instead. We simultaneously switch off mobile phones, laughing mischievously; we are adrift and unreachable! We unpack, and over caffè plan our itinerary. Ofelia relishes a visit to this bustling city where she is anonymous in shoals of frenetic Romans. She is on her way to spend happy hours battling chaotic crowds in a triangle between shops and stores from the Corso to Piazza del Popolo, and from Via Veneto to the Quirinale. Whereas I want naught to do with frenzied feet and honking Fiats, savouring hours alone. I stroll the banks of the Tiber, find bookshops in Trastevere, cross the river to Via Giulia to stare at once-proud pediments glowering from blackened palaces. Then, repairing forthwith to a bar I sip campari, watching Roman arrogance at being Roman, reading, or half reading, and, finally I thread my way through tortuous alleys in hotchpotch warrens towards Campo de' Fiori.

At the end of our first afternoon we meet at the stone brim of the fountain at the foot of the Spanish Steps, satiated and brimming with tales of things old and new. Strolling down to Caffè Greco we sip outrageously expensive thimblefuls of caffè. Ofelia pulls out her purchases: a box of glittery bangles and a pretty skirt for Chiara. I unwrap my unimpressive battered second-hand book, which she disdainfully leafs. But I am not offended – Italians tend to be justifiably vain and are not good at someone else's cast-offs. 'Ah, si,' she at length concedes, 'but we did all that at school.' Ofelia is a good deal younger than me, but we are close friends and pass weekly hours over caffè, debating the complex merits and demerits of our lives in Montalcino in comparison to living in the world's great cities, like Sydney or Rome. Her ability to put forth eloquent substance to sway me to her argument frequently confounds me. But today we are lent to luxury, enchanted by Rome. 'Andiamo!' she urges, pulling me up. 'Let's go! Everyone will be in Via Condotti.'

The ticklish art of passeggiata . . . elegantly dressed and walking nowhere in particular with the purposeful air of a destination, at a pace that allows you to brush past other well-dressed persons as if you have not moved, but they have . . . a slow nod of the head or benign smile in mutually ingratiating acknowledgement of courtesy and breeding. Arm in arm we passeggiata, caught up in the animation, giggling at modish hair styles, admiring too large necklaces draped on plush cushions, we pull each other from one side to the other, zigzagging to ogle and swoon at gorgeous gowns and shoes and bags and diamonds in spectacularly dressed plate-glass windows ablaze with rays of golden beams. Ofelia pulls at my elbow to keep me in line because my legs want to bolt, seeking to arrive somewhere, anywhere! I am amazed at her capacity to passeggiata to nowhere for two whole hours.

Dinner is characteristically Roman, one of Ofelia's favourite haunts, carrying her mind back to her own school excursion to the papal city when the custodian of monasterial lodgings directed her class to an Osteria frequented by nuns. We order chicory shoots with anchovies and salmon carpaccio, move on to clams and fettuccini and risotto with radicchio and walnuts. We have eaten so much that we are barely able to consume our secondo of saltimbocca, and we *are* unable, at the end, to squeeze in even lemon gelato. Apart from the soporific vibrancy of Rome, and our choice of this amusing Osteria where waiters with high brows and aquiline noses race between tables playfully calling over our heads in a flat drawling dialect, we are lured, by our sense of utter freedom, into letting go of all the strings from which life dangles when commitments are somewhere else. The neglected gelato we succumb to, licking as we dodge the crowd in Piazza di Spagna until the bells of midnight beckon us wearily back to our hotel. We leave the Roman masses to their confusion knowing that the piazza will not quieten until the wee small hours.

Breakfast we take on the run, caffè and brioche, Roman style, then we part once again for a couple of hours before a promised lunch. Ofelia heads for a market and I head for a museum. Two hours at Villa Giulia is a top-up . . . to read the adoring faces of an Etruscan husband and wife, united in death, on a banqueting couch, to marvel at bronze shields and broken tablets, studying one letter more of the Etruscan alphabet, and once again to be dazzled by the sheer ostentation of granulations and prancing lions on the clasp of a golden brooch. Our time has gone; we meet at the corner of Via Giulia and Via Flaminia and a tram and a bus carry us back to our hotel where, happy but hungry, we retrieve our belongings, and Ofelia's stunningly wrapped and beribboned shopping. Trajan's column and the triumphant arch of Helena's son and Nero's Golden Palace flash past the taxi window, taking us to an exotic lunch, the grand finale to our brief hours of liberation. The love of the Italian table and every procedure to do with it cannot be underestimated, and Ofelia is a true disciple; yet she is also young, curious and adventurous. We repose in the exotic ambience of silver ram-head chairs facing each other over saffron tablecloths. Triumphant elephants trumpet over our heads and a maharaja watches from his throne – all in banquet scenes along the walls. This glittering Indian restaurant is our arrivederci to Roma. 'Ganzo! I love the names,' Ofie laughs, and the dishes come out with an odd twist of accent: 'Murg peshawari, chicken and herbs.' Both of us breathe in exotic aromas and the spicy scent of vindaloo lamb and tandoori shrimp. Blissfully we sail away on a magic carpet, extravagantly ordering white wine from the Veneto. Even to drink white wine is an adventure to those who hail from Montalcino! We are giddy, our unfocused vision entranced with a shimmering maharanee in a gilded frame on the wall. Her veil is sheer organza and almond eyes peer into the face of a bird she caresses. Topaz and jade adorn long fingers and delicate filigree tinkles when suspended tracery sways . . . or is it we who sway? Ofelia raises her glass and we clash them together. 'To the exotic princess!' We are exhausted by our gustatory pleasure, made pensive by excessive wine, but just the same, unable to resist Kulfi, pistachio and almond ice cream. We return, ever so gently, wafting on our magic carpet with pistachio and almond, back to Italy. Ofelia agrees to forgo the obligatory end to any Italian meal, so we do not order caffè, because we have been to the east. Encumbered with bulging shopping bags we rock and sway arm in arm to the railway station, sauntering and stepping rhythmically in time like Indian elephants. Crumpled tickets eventually feed into a cantankerous validating machine and we scramble aboard the train, thankful for an empty carriage. We slump into seats and pass hardly a word, allowing aromas and flavours and our faraway maharanee to linger in our minds. Drowsy, we give ourselves up to napping, barely aware of the tranquillizing wheels of the intercity clicking and clacketing, rattling us north past the plains of Lazio, thundering in and out of tunnels, and, only after we roll across the Tiber more than once, do we stir and open our eyes, recognizing forested hills topped with crumbling castles.

We are deposited at Chiusi. 'Ciao! Ciao caro!' I wave to Luigi on the platform as the train shudders to a halt. He looks sombre, but we ignore it. 'Luigi!' shouts Ofelia. 'We are going to Venice for two nights next time!' But Luigi is unsmiling. 'Isabella, listen,' his tone of voice fills me with panic; he is preparing me for something. 'You will have to hurry, get in the car. Bruno died last night; Amelia is asking for you. You have less than an hour to reach the church of the Madonna in time for his funeral.'

Bruno is the first of our elderly village friends to die. I knew the day would come when I would face such a death and have pondered the depth of my emotional armour. Death was not often part of a migrant family's life; there were no elderly in the neighbourhood. I was twenty-seven years old, mother of a baby daughter, when forced to attend my first funeral, which was my husband's, and her father. Terrified, I had no idea what to do, nor did I know what might happen, and when my eyes rested on a polished coffin on a table at the front of the church I recoiled into self-protective unreality. Betraying no emotion in a surreal world, my mind secretly did not correspond to the motions of my body. Turmoil and fear were so intense that I closed out the pain, pretended not to be hurt, ignored it, and got on with working to raise and educate my daughter, Rebecca. In anger I twisted a shiny gold band from my finger and determined that I would never wear another – and I do not. There was no grieving because I do not believe I understood what was happening to me. For a span of twenty years I stood away from the pain, though it did not go far from the surface of things, but when I found Luigi,

Isabella Dusi

or he found me and brought me to Italy, and we began to make our life in Montalcino, a sense of serenity – the security of finding myself somewhere where I was nobody in particular – led me to understand that, here, it could not hurt me. I could go through the emotion of grief and leave it behind. Ofelia and I shared happy hours of liberation in Rome, but my liberation from anguish and waste after so many years in a wilderness, until Luigi brought me here, is unimaginable.

As the car wheels hurtle towards Montalcino I feel an emptiness that awakens my memory to fear. Ofelia drags a dark jacket from her bag so that I will not need to go home and change from my consciously unsuitable one. Approaching the church of the Madonna a crowd is gathered, many of our friends are here. Luigi slows and the car stops. I get out just as the bell is tolling mournfully for dear Bruno. I glance over as Amelia is being helped towards the church doors. She looks so fragile, wizened, stricken by the suddenness of Bruno's death. In my mind I was standing back, looking at her from beyond myself, but my legs must have carried me forward because as she lifts her face towards her friends our eyes meet and in an instant her face uncreases into a thousand hurting smiles. Her soft eyes entreat: 'Amore, you are here!' she whispers, and runs half childishly into my arms, her body so fragile I fear she will break. Tears flow unchecked as we unburden the ache, the intensity of need, each to the other. With her second daughter on one side and me the other, Amelia's head does not leave my shoulder, nor her hand unclasp from mine, during monotonous intoning until finally the priest rings a tiny bell that sends Bruno on his way, blessed and entrusted to the care of the Madonna. Amelia expects that I will go with her to the cemetery where Bruno's casket will be cemented into the wall, one spot away from her first daughter,

222

Silena, who died of a ruptured appendix at the end of the war. I did not see my own husband's coffin lowered into the ground, any more than I kissed him one last goodbye. A well-meaning doctor thought to shield me from . . . what? Something too terrible to behold? For the rest of my life I have only empty frames of what my handsome young husband looked like, when in death we did part. When Giovanni the bricklayer prepares to seal Bruno's tomb Amelia tosses a handful of dirt into the recess, which scatters across the casket, and then, oddly shifting focus, she withdraws a tissue from her pocket and busily swirls the dust from the marble angel that decorates the grave of Silena. There is one empty hole left in the wall.

'He came home,' Amelia tells me, seated around her kitchen table later, 'and, Isabella, it was strange, because he brought no branches from the woods.' Perhaps I should have told her about stumbling upon Bruno at the side of the road, but no purpose can now be served. I let her talk on. 'He said to me, Amelia, I am going down to the cantina to hang up my tools. I will not be going to the woods any more. I said to him, Bruno! You have been going to the woods all your life, how will I cook your dinner if you don't bring me any wood? But he just shook his head and said, no, there will be no more woods for me. I wanted him to go to the doctor, but he just smiled. If you wish, he said, but it will be of no use. And he was right.'

Amelia ran away from home in Pianello, a girl of fifteen, to be with Bruno; the cause of an unhealable rift with her father who never spoke to her for the rest of his life. She had nothing, except Bruno, and a capanna, a mud and timber shanty, which they built with their bare hands in the woods when Bruno began his life as a woodcutter. Neither of them had ever been to school.

They still had nothing when their first daughter, Silena, was born. Amelia has told me the story so many times, forgetful of memory, that one day, in 1944, when Bruno was needed to work at a mercury mine, during war years, German soldiers stormed into her primitive hut in the woods, pointing their guns at her and the child, threatening to kill them. They turned the place upside-down looking for Bruno; it was a dark time when young men were ordered to enlist in Hitler's occupying army. After the war she came into Montalcino and worked at Albergo Giglio, bleaching the sheets, a weekly rite when the hotel whites were piled into a terracotta tub under a cloth over which ashes were thickly strewn. She poured pails of boiling water through the ashes, and it filtered through the sheets until it streamed unblemished from a spigot at the bottom of the tub, bleaching the whites on its journey. Her second daughter was born, named Silena after the first, and eventually, when woodcutting for a living was no longer viable, they came to live in this two-roomed house in the village. She holds out one hand, spreading her fingers flat on the table and with the other hand she plays with a worn gold band on her finger. She smiles through tears at the thin, dull band and does not even see tiny black holes all in a row where twinkles of glass once sparkled. Bruno gave it to his fifteen-year-old bride.

Bruno must have known his thin and wiry body had had enough. He reached the end of his life cycle and he knew death was at hand, so he stopped, and waited. Is it the certainty of the cycle, the rhythm, the knowledge that things will continue just as they were, which prepares one for death? Bruno reached the point where even his own approaching death ceased to be a shocking change, but a part of the rhythm of his life.

*

Gossip about the morning headline rockets through the village. 'Agitated Waters in the Land of Brunello,' the paper screams. A provocative communication issues from the Consorzio, not about the weather – there has been no rain here for weeks. Purists are frantically trying to scotch a rumour aired on the internet yesterday accusing the Consorzio of relaxing disciplines for the production of Brunello. Indignant denials stream from the office of the Consorzio; but an emotional tempest is intensifying from irate purists who believe that Brunello is a traditional wine, and must remain so. First to bash at the wooden doors of Palazzo Comunale, headquarters of the Consorzio, is the Colombini family, whose wounded words were reported in the morning paper: 'My family,' declares Stefano Cinelli Colombini, 'won our first medal for Brunello in 1842, one of a handful of growers, not hundreds.' I read the report twice, to be certain my eyes are not fooling me, checking the quoted date because this is big news to me! Eighteen forty-two is twenty-three years before Tito Costanti, and three other families, entered an exposition in Siena and the word Brunello is said to have been historically recorded for the first time. Could the date be wrong? Jogging my memory, I feel sure someone has commented, sotto voce, in a whisper, that Colombini were among those who held the view that contadini should not be allowed to grow Brunello. But then, reflecting on the Ingegnere's words, the peasant society of those times is unimaginable today, and anyway, Tito Costanti also held that view because it was, as Andrea put it, unthinkable to him that contadini would have the money, or the expertise. The Colombini are one of those elusive Montalcino families I have never met; but the morning paper assures that they are a founding wine family with ancestral roots – but it does not say where. A loaded weapon dances in front of my eyes . . . The final salvo is perpetrated in the paper as an unimaginable blow to the prestige of the Consorzio, akin to a loss in the fashion world of Armani or Versace, and on a par with selling out Ferrari! The article has awakened percolating trouble, because, with excruciatingly precise timing, the founding wine family Colombini threatens to resign from the Consorzio! The plot thickens as I read on that Biondi Santi, that double-barrel-named family that Andrea referred to only as Santi, have neither come out against the rumour, nor in support of purists. Whispers around the piazza, partnered with tapping of noses, winking eyes and swift hand signals, not beyond my interpreting ability, are that with Colombini resigning from the Consorzio, Biondi Santi will, after nearly forty years, apply to take up membership. Is this a gross exaggeration, or a power struggle between two elite families? Do I smell a forty-year-old aristocratic rumble?

The day began gloriously well. Tables cloaked in blue and white were laden with a refreshing feast well ahead of the arrival of drummers and trumpeters banging and blowing their way through the cobbled roads of Pianello. Our saintly protector, San Michele, angelic wings outstretched, flutters from windows and flies from iron holders in the walls of our homes. With white and blue wound round our necks, or other parts, we gathered in our piazzetta, listening to the clip clop of horses that signalled the closeness of the sacred emblem of Montalcino: six round hills topped by an oak tree. The banditore, town crier, secured the ancient scroll under his arm and, once the reverberation of blasting silver trumpets and stirring drum rolls died, we waited in hushed quiet, emotions soaring, to hear once more the words of proclamation hundreds of years old calling us to battle for Montalcino. The banditore took a majestic stance upon the wall;

crimson pantaloons, fitted doublet and lacy cuffs of pristine white cutting a fine medieval figure, and, with a toss of his head, which sent the plumes upon his pointed hat into a jostled dance, he unfurled the scroll. Quartiere Pianello, one of four, is summoned to obey the command of the Lady of the Fortress, to find our most skilled and bravest archers and bring them to the campo on the morrow where their skill and bravery will be tested on the archery range. The reading of the proclamation by the banditore and his regal company never fails to raise goose bumps on my neck . . . the splendour of medieval costumes, the snap of the drumsticks and haunting call of the silver trumpets echoing across our roofs is spine tingling. Weaving so much of the ancient past to the now, behind shields and breastplates, beneath the helmets and plumed hats, are the defiant faces of the Ilcinesi who claimed the right to dwell on this hill a thousand years ago. The faces of today are historically identifiable, identical to those of yesterday; ancestral names have not changed, nor has their defiance. The banditore, feasted and refreshed, marched his trumpeters and drummers through the winding roads of Pianello towards Travaglio where fly rival red and yellow banners. Nourishing ourselves for battle, physically and morally, we eagerly finished off the salver of crostini and bowls of peaches and wedges of watermelon, indulged in a bottle or two of Pianello wine and then, as Luciana and Fiorella whisked away plates and glasses, the young, overburdened, swayed and shuddered all the way down the hill ferrying trestle tables to Via Moglio, the blue heart of our quartiere.

Apertura della Cacce is the summer archery tournament in celebration of the nearness of bountiful autumn hunts, hence the name, Opening of the Hunt. Centuries ago archers went to the woods and hunted wild boar, hare and pheasant, but

Montalcino, strategically desirable to the superpowers of the middle ages, Siena and Florence, found itself constantly under siege. Village archers, risking death in the woods at the hands of a Florentine axe or a Sienese sword, were desperate to bring inside the walls a boar or brace of pheasants. If it were not for their bravery and hunting skills the stubborn defiance of the besieged could not have endured; starving citizens would have fallen into the hands of the enemy and their liberty and their right to dwell in self-determination on their hill would be lost. So the archery tournaments between the four quarters of Montalcino are not staged as a strenuously contested competition between sporting teams. Deeply rooted in the blood and defiance of the past, archery carries with it the symbol of survival and sacrifice, bravery in the face of death to protect families and defend Montalcino from behind its girdle of ancient stones. The Ilcinesi have, through many centuries, passionately expressed their refusal to accept external suppression, their willingness to endure starvation, pain and bloodshed, until triumph brings hope and the liberty to be who they are, under the sacred emblem that binds and unifies them to this hill.

At midnight the tables the young ferried down to Via Moglio this morning are carted, by clumsy stumbling legs, with hissing and smothering of giggles, back up the slope and stacked unceremoniously into the Sacristy of San Pietro, clattering noisily one on top of the other in disarray. We are exhausted, but emotion and adrenalin run high and our hearts are brimming with hope for a Pianello victory on the morrow. Our elders went home hours ago, having eaten a delicious four course eve-of-tournament dinner, and having listened to rousing speeches by President Maurelia and trainer Dottore Luciano, all vigorously applauded. Our archers were heartily cheered, slapped on the back and kissed a thousand times. Egged on by Ofelia, who pleaded, 'Dai, Isabella, come in the middle with us', I implored Luigi to go home without me. Ofelia pulled me on to a bench along with Cecilia and Gloria. Not willing to cry off from this unifying closeness, yearning for inclusion in the deeply rooted passion in the hearts of our loyal young, I lingered till the end. Midnight is the deadline at which music must cease, otherwise Andrea, the polizia, cruises down in the patrol car and demands we restore the peace in respect for elder quartieranti whose shuttered windows are hardly more than an arm's length from our tables set along a medieval road. Some secretly invited themselves to the celebrations, and Michele, possibly under the influence of Francesco and Riccardo of the fabulous voice – or possibly an alternative influence should be blamed – stood on a chair on the cobbled road and, gyrating to 'We Are the Champions', a deafening blast to ensure they could hear us in Travaglio and Borghetto, if not the next province, he lost his balance when the girls distracted him with sensuous gyrations of their own. He toppled off the chair and vanished. We rushed over to see that he was not hurt, but he was not there! Looking at each other in dismay, our puzzlement turned to waves of belly bursting laughter when a black door creaked open and a white-haired Pianello nonna, eighty if a day, smiling conspiratorially, explained she had been standing behind a crack in the door watching, when Michele tumbled straight through the door into her cantina! We hauled him out, but shaken Michele would not return to that chair, so we finished the night around a table, banging glasses and bottles and fists in a rhythmic chant, raising the roofs of the houses and disturbing every living thing from here to the valleys far below. Riccardo with his melodic volume always leads our chants: '*Noi vogliamo questa vittoria!*' Over and over again: bang, crash, bang, thump: *'We want this victory!'* When midnight came and we had demanded victory a hundred times, Fabio switched off the music and signalled we were obliged to stop. We had not a bang or a thump left, and anyway, there remained not even a drop of water with which to quench our raspy throats, and, knowing our archers should be in bed, we sent them on their way home. Parting from Cecilia, Ofelia and Gloria at the sede door, I am mindful that it is time for me to stagger home because I know their night has not finished. Grabbing each other, with Riccardo and Fabio leading, they turn their voices and their weary legs towards the piazza, gearing themselves to face quartiere opposition squads hurling derision under the cappellone in a traditional midnight war of words.

Dottore Luciano must nominate three archers. Three names go into a hat and, balloted by the magistrate, the banditore, from a high window above the piazza, and at the revelling of a silver trumpet, announces which two of the three will shoot the arrows for Pianello. Each quarter hopes and prays that archers one and two will be drawn, but it does not always work out that way. Occasionally archer one misses the draw, and a quartiere must shoot with their second and third best archers. Dottore Luciano nominated our veteran Massimo, steady marksman Alessandro and sixteen-year-old Filippo. A wild card . . . Filippo is young and, although an archer may shoot skilfully on the practice range, no one knows how Filippo's mind and body will cope with the electrifying atmosphere on the campo. Hundreds of members from each of the four quartieri transform themselves into a bombastic mass of hysterical screeching, crying, cheering, passionate supporters for their archers. With all this distraction it is easy for an archer to lose concentration, but, more dangerous than the noise, more compelling than the whistles and jeers and bloodcurdling yells, is the tension that sits upon the shoulders of an archer. A rush of adrenalin and constricting muscles can destroy an inexperienced archer before he has fired a single arrow. He, with his firing partner, takes on himself the accumulated centuries of sacrifice, bloodshed and defiance, and the anguish of the whole quartiere for a liberating victory. One victory, in Dottore Luciano's words, is all it takes to wipe away the anguish and the pain of all the times we did not win. Tension hangs in the air, transmitted from the heart and soul of everyone from every quartiere, praying that their two archers are the bravest, the most skilful in Montalcino.

On tournament morning the historical pageant of more than a hundred citizens in splendid medieval costumes parades through the village. Each quartiere cortège is easily identified by the colours worn by their dame and her knight and court attendants. This year Chiara, Ofelia's daughter, is page for our dame, petite Gloria, and our knight is handsome Davide. Exquisitely costumed drummers and trumpeters and regally gowned magistrates with ermine collars, who implement the rules, as well as pages in pantaloons who hold up the scores, and rows of hunters with nets and soldiers with spears and serfs with axes, take part in the pageant. Along the way, each quartiere offers a gift, brought in homage to the sumptuously gowned Lady of the Fortress and her lord, who repose on velvet thrones in Piazza del Popolo. Once homage is given, with typical Italian sensibility to strongly held tradition, everyone retreats to their quartiere for last-minute tournament strategy sessions, and a hearty (no less than five-course) lunch. The afternoon pageant weaves through the village once more, but this time the captain of each archery squad escorts his two balloted archers to the firing range, following slowly behind the Lady of the Fortress and her lord, as well as the cortège of the four quartieri, and all take up position in front of gaily striped peaked tents on the campo. By the time the parade files through the gate at the campo, the archery range below the fortress, carrying aloft the sacred emblem of Montalcino, members of all four quartieri are already seated in the stand or have gathered down at the fence, united under quartiere colours.

Filippo missed the ballot. His friends Samuele and Francesco comforted him – they have been firing partners on our practice range for years. It is a joyous moment when a young archer, nurtured through the quartiere from childhood, dedicates himself to archery and works his way through the ranks, and finally steps for the first time on to the campo that can bring him, and Pianello, greatness. But, at the same time, we cannot be disappointed with the draw. Massimo and Alessandro, handsome in their white and blue medieval costumes, stand composed; bows are slack and in pouches at their sides five fletched arrows lean against the leather. The magistrate consults his pages to ensure four targets in the shape of a wild boar, along a sliding rope, swivel freely and unhindered. He checks that pages have scorecards in their hands, and that the captain of each archery squad is satisfied with the accuracy of the distance markings, the wild boar targets, and the arrows which he and the archers examine.

Rules are not complicated: distances are marked from the target, the first at twenty-five metres and the final round is shot from a maximum of forty-five metres. The reward, at the closer range, is one point per arrow, increasing to two points at thirty metres, again to three points for thirty-five metres, until, in the fourth and final round, at the greatest distance, each arrow is valued at four points. Every archer, and there are two on each squad, must shoot five arrows in each of four rounds, but five arrows must fly from his bow within the space of forty seconds. The penalty for time failure is rejection of his late arrow, and he is denied the points. Theoretically, with four rounds of five arrows, each archer will shoot twenty arrows, unless scores are tied, and if this happens the quartieri whose scores are tied are forced into a shoot-out until victory, or defeat. I sit in this stand with my heart in my mouth, with every year an increased awareness of the emotional significance of this day, and gaining a clearer understanding of the sacrifice demanded of our archers. But I have never experienced the joy of a Pianello victory, only the anguish and bruises of crushing defeat – often at the cost of one wayward arrow.

The magistrate signals; a fanfare of rallying silver trumpets rises across the campo and then, as it dies, a faraway sound, low and long, seems to emanate from the woods. We hush and listen to the haunting moan of a hunting horn . . . long and low it resounds across the campo. The tournament can now begin. Ofelia and I huddle against each other in the stand, our hearts beating furiously as the first archer from each quartiere strides to the twenty-five-metre marker and steadies himself for the shoot. Alessandro is shooting first. This means – Ofelia clutches her stomach with anxiety – that if the rounds get tough the stress and heightening tension will rest on the broad shoulders of our veteran archer, her husband, Massimo. As four archers draw the first arrow from the pouch strapped to their thighs, thousands of screaming quartieranti rise from their seats and with deafening shrieks and pleas, the tournament is off to its usual screeching claims and counterclaims, exchanges of insults, heckles and jeers, chanting and waving of quartiere scarves as friends suddenly become enemies. The air is scorched with taunting slurs.

The first round is over and no archer has missed the wild boar target. Alessandro, head shaved bald, and Massimo shot with a serenity that belies the madness rising from this crowd. Shoulders relaxed, they passed a word or two between themselves and nodded to their captain Francesco as they swapped places at the marker; it is as if they do not even know we are here, even as we go half crazy counting the arrows one by one, thudding into the boar, and cast our eyes to enemy targets to see what has happened to Travaglio, Ruga and Borghetto's arrows. Retreating five metres for round two, the tension begins to mount. Thud, thud, thud . . . the arrows sink one after another into the boar, until an anguished shriek goes up . . . our heads twist . . . it is Travaglio! The first arrow has missed the target at the thirty-metre mark. Our eyes swivel back to Alessandro, one more arrow and . . . oh, no! Where did it go? We have dropped an arrow! But so have Borghetto, and where is the other one? Ganzo! Ruga missed as well. An attack of nerves rippled through the other three archers when the first arrow from Travaglio went astray. But what is happening down there? Time is up, the boar swivels as a late arrow sails over the target and ricochets into the fortress wall. That is the second thirty-metre miss for Travaglio! Relief! Our stomachs unknot and Ofelia's whole body droops into my lap. The second archer from each squad moves forward, steps less confident, but veteran Massimo shoots his five arrows flawlessly, packing them closely into the heart of the boar. Francesco is absolutely correct, they really do seem to be splitting shafts. But, merda, the other archers have clear rounds too. At the end of the second round Travaglio has fallen behind. Captains harass their archers, urging concentration, using their own hands to simulate the flight of an arrow, desperate to rectify what went wrong in the previous round. But there are two more rounds to go; victory, or defeat, is a long way off.

At the start of round three the tension rests with Ruga, Borghetto and Pianello but, determined to keep pressure on Travaglio, the jeering crowd goes berserk hexing and lewdly distracting their downcast archers. Round three progresses; the first archer for each quartiere thuds five arrows into the boar, everything is steady, and now the second archer is back at the line. Ofelia and I do not know where to turn, where to put our arms; our eyes are shut tight, unwilling to accept a bad vision . . . but they spring wide open as soon as a thunderous roar goes up. Someone has missed . . . no! Our eyes sweep the young gathered down at the fence for a signal . . . it is not Massimo! It is Borghetto! We know because their supporters have turned their backs to the campo, scowling in despair. Borghetto archers are prone to exhibit petulance; instead of getting on with the round, firing his fifth arrow, the Borghetto archer remonstrates with his captain. 'Shoot, shoot!' the livid captain orders, and the archer flicks out the last arrow and more by luck than judgement turns and aims roughly down the range, shooting the arrow into the swivelling target, where it hangs by a thread from the tail of the boar. Travaglio and Borghetto are several points behind; Ruga and Pianello have scored the same number of points.

The pressure is indescribable; thousands of moaning, crying, anguished quartieranti bury faces in hands, cover heads with scarves and sickened by tension turn away from the campo, unable to bear the dragging seconds before the last round begins. Ofelia is pale and faint. 'You do not know what Massi is going through,' she moans, 'his stomach churns, his arms are heavy and the tension on the bow has doubled. He has to close everything out of his mind, to think only of the arrows, but archers who have missed an arrow are niggling at each other, unable to hold back bitter disappointment. It is not as calm down there as it looks.' Our fine marksman Alessandro raises his bow and in perfect unison the Ruga archer and he send scorchingly accurate arrows down the range. We clutch ourselves and count the thuds, one, two, three, four . . . where is the fifth! No! Alessandro, what have you done? A jubilant roar goes up from Ruga quartieranti. Seeing Alessandro's arrow fly wide triggers their passion, but it is short-lived – their fifth arrow sails away, their archer unnerved when distracted by the fletch of Alessandro's arrow wavering in flight! Borghetto and Travaglio are out of it – too many missed arrows and we do not bother to count. But Pianello and Ruga scores are once again equal and Massimo has five arrows to shoot. Down at the fence, Pianello young are in agony, raw fear and emotion is writ upon their faces. Ofelia and I fall silent, but our hearts thump like bass drums. On the campo our dame and knight and all the pages have scurried inside the blue and white tent. Chiara's head peeps out of the flap; she watches her father, nibbling her fingernails.

Only Massimo is unmoved. Here we go. One after the other he rhythmically draws an arrow from the leather pouch, fastens it to the bow, pulls back the string and away it flies; like a singing bird it whirs down the range and sinks into the boar . . . one, two, three, four . . . five! But, damn! So has Ruga! Behind me a Ruga family are in tears, a nervous mother comforts her crying daughter, while an anxious father sits a small boy on his lap who buries his head in his chest. When I turn back, Ofelia has vanished. She could bear it no longer; she jumped from her seat and struggled through tiers of quartieranti, racing to the fence.

Now she is hugged and enfolded by Pianello young; they seek comfort in each other. We are in a shoot-out, but from here the level of difficulty rises. All arrows will from now on be fired from forty-five metres. Instead of five arrows in forty seconds, the archers must shoot six. Less time to fix an arrow, less time to pull the string taut and less time to sight and let the arrows fly. The archers have already fired twenty arrows down the range; arms are beginning to ache and concentration wanders. Doubt creeps in; can he make it through the next round?

Ruga and Pianello archers take up position. Alessandro's shoulders wriggle into relaxation, words of trust and confidence come from captain Francesco. The round is finished; no arrows missed. We suffer through Massimo's round, no one misses. One after the other, we witness three more astonishing perfect rounds. The crowd, exhausted by emotion and tension, is hushed; nobody dare move or utter a curse that may distract or force a result. During the last round Alessandro used up precious seconds bending and unbending his legs; holding position for so long, the muscles tighten and knees go weak; this is a test of endurance. All four archers, to keep arms from cramping, sweep them in circles between rounds; every arm that rises to shoot an arrow is now a dead weight. Perhaps we have the slimmest glimmer of advantage because Massimo is an exceptionally strong man and his shoulders incredibly broad; but mental endurance is paramount.

The next shoot-off round begins. We cringe in fear as one archer from each squad flounders, dropping an arrow, but the crowd cannot scream now, we recoil into our seats, sighing, gulping air in and huffing it out again in long pained breaths. We can do no more than exchange looks. Massimo and Alessandro go into a huddle with their captain; draped arms join them and foreheads touch. Fifty arrows have left their bows. Massimo and Alessandro put down their bows and swing arms anticlockwise to loosen up muscles, keep the blood circulating. Time is passing, the magistrate is worried because it is getting dark; he is hurriedly searching the rule book to see what he should do if the tie cannot be broken before darkness makes shooting impossible. The crowd, finding something less explosive to scream about, yell to him that there is no such rule. They remember twenty years ago when, with archers shooting in pitch dark, after each round they had to wait on the magistrate to tell them what had happened! We are too weak with anxiety to jeer or hiss opposing archers, but when Ruga drop an arrow in the next round we send ourselves ballistic . . . too soon.

'Stay calm,' thunders Riccardo, because, unbelievably, Massimo's last arrow misses. The collective despair is heart rending. Massimo does not blink an eyelid; shows no emotion, no disappointment, no anger. Walking back he drapes an arm around Alessandro, who, poised for the next round, accepts the challenge to fire six arrows, which will take him to fifty-six arrows for the shoot. The archers rub their eyes, screw them shut, then open them wide. Shoulders are low, not from dejection, but physical and mental exhaustion. A sensation sends Ruga supporters into hysteria; tension explodes and frustrated shrieks of damnation and curses carry across the campo. Their first archer has missed not one but two arrows at the beginning of the round; he struggles bravely on amid the tumult, and his remaining four arrows miraculously sink into the boar. Heeding Riccardo's warning we hold back our jubilation, our eyes switching to Alessandro. He misfires the last one! With fire in his eyes he turns to Massimo but his anger extinguishes in a flash and the two men, arms around each other, make a triangle with captain Francesco. We have a one-arrow advantage, with six more arrows left to shoot. Ofelia has vanished from the fence. Chiara dives inside the tent, while our dame and knight race in and then back out; pages lie face down on the ground, not bearing to watch yet, unable to close it out, they roll over and squat. Tears are welling in my eyes; the stress and anxiety is far greater than I could ever have imagined.

Massimo has six feathered arrows in his sheath – all six arrows must sink into the boar to take victory. His chest rises, he breathes deeply in and out, his broad shoulders ripple as he sheds the tension, closing his ears and his mind to the shrieks of fear from Ruga, suddenly finding their voices, aware they may lose. But their archer is brilliant, he has brought them many victories, and still could triumph. Their real hope, their every prayer, is for Massimo to miss one arrow; the rabble gears up for a crescendo of jeers and insults, but Massimo no more hears their wild abuse than our imploring prayers.

Alessandro and Francesco take several paces back, leaving Massimo with a bow and six arrows, to face the boar alone. My throat is taut; holding my breath, these seconds are eternal and the light is fading, long shadows cast along the campo. Six arrows in forty seconds. Go Massimo, you can do it. The frenzy of piercing whistles and taunts from Ruga is thunderous. The hopes and dreams and prayers and pride of our whole quartiere rest on Massimo's broad shoulders as he raises leaden arms, fixes the first arrow to the bow and sends it whirring down the range. Thud, thud, thud . . . three times our eyes race from Massimo's hands to the target to await the flying arrow, to hear the thud as it plunges into the boar. We are overwhelmed by the unbearable burden of the peril of not winning. I cannot take my eyes from Massimo, dare not swivel my glance to Ruga's target . . . only

Massimo's last three arrows matter. Thud, the fourth sinks in . . . why is it taking so long? Massimo, you have only forty seconds! Load, load! Thud, the fifth arrow sinks into the boar. One arrow to shoot. Thousands of quailing and praying beings are on their feet, screaming in horror at what might or might not happen. I see nothing but a blur because my eyes are filling with tears and my mouth clamps tightly. Massimo raises his head, dropping it in measured inclination to one side. He draws the last arrow from the pouch and sets it to the bow, the bow rises and sweeps in a perfectly balanced upward arc as his arms draw taut the string and broad shoulders hold; the last arrow leaves his skilful hands and shoots from the bow with a whir; the feathered missile hums, the fletch does not quaver . . . its path along the range is an eternity, we are hypnotized, Massimo is motionless, his bow hangs in mid air and arms are ramrod straight until that last arrow, carrying with it all our prayers, our pride and our joy, with the fletch flying faultlessly, plunges, with a dull thud, into the very heart of the boar.

Like a flock of startled pigeons, Pianello erupts, shocked into disbelief that the victory is ours. People are screaming no! when they mean to be screaming yes! Massimo is on his knees, arms reaching above his head, the bow swinging wildly; Alessandro flies towards him, clasping his hands to his head, they shake each other by the shoulders and fall towards the turf and the added weight of Francesco's flailing body topples the three of them, who roll over and over, releasing pent up emotion, bursting with joy absolute. Every elegant costume from our tent is racing inelegantly across the campo, spears are discarded on the turf, swords jangle, velvet skirts are hitched up, helmets crash to the grass. But first on the range is Chiara. She throws off her pointed hat, opens her arms and runs as fast as her legs will carry her, screaming: 'Babbo! Babbo! We have won!' Massimo hears, he sits up and twists on to his knees, and opening his broad arms her slender body slams into his chest and in a flurry of arms and legs he wheels her effortlessly into the sky, whirling her round and round above his head in a wild exotic dance of victory.

I clamber half blindly from the stand and begin my own race towards the campo, desperate to join the throng heading towards our waiting archers, but someone grabs at my shoulder. Tears streaming down our faces, Ofelia and I lock into an emotional embrace and run together, to Massimo. He is waiting for her. In seconds a tangled mass of young and old are united in joy on the campo with our heroes Alessandro and Massimo and Francesco, who disappear beneath an ever growing swarm, hugging and kissing, pushing and shoving each other in a show of stunned pride. After so long, so many barren years, this is an outpouring of utter joy. Dottore Luciano is numb; a drawn out victory that took six shoot-outs and fifty-six arrows over two tortuous hours. The young find their voices; Riccardo's melodic chords rise into a chant, and with a flourish, the swords of victory from our San Michele banners swirl and swoop wildly above our heads. The victory song is ours to sing.

> We of the great Pianello
> We come from Via Moglio
> We are the pride of the oak tree
> You owe us respect!

Linking arms and chanting, we shed the tension, and, draped in our battle colours, banners emblazoned with our warrior angel San Michele, and with Tomaso banging on the drum, it is time to begin the triumphant march back to our quartiere; we must ring the victory bells from the twin towers above the church of San Pietro. Our tears fall freely, uninhibited, young and old. Nothing in my life has prepared me for, nor did I ever imagine, the depth of emotion, the innermost joy and pride of victory for something outside of myself. This is a collective triumph, not just for our archers, but it is *ours*, the victory belongs to Pianello and will live for ever in the honour of our quartiere. Our archers have carried the burden, but we have shared a ritual that unifies our hearts and minds; this victory is a part of each of us. We have the bravest archers, the village is safe, the girdle of stone walls secure, we will have enough to eat through the bitter winter because our bravissimi archers have proved their skill. Weaving a fugue with our chant as we sing 'The blue is in our blood and the white is in our hearts', triumphant, we make our joyful way from the campo, round the fortress, winding noisily through the narrow roads till we reach the piazza where our victory song echoes ever more loudly until, eager to be home, our jubilant throng moves off again, only to be stopped by Danilo at the pizzeria who has bottles of Spumante ready . . . not to drink . . . he shakes them up, spraying us with bottle after bottle. Laughing and licking our wet arms we are clapped and cheered by smiling old heads poking from shutters as we pass under their windows, finally arriving at our sede where, to my astonishment, Luciana, Maria Rosa, Onelia and Fiorella are frantic in the kitchen rustling up pasta for a couple of hundred. Our first victory dinner begins right now! The bells in the twin towers above the church of San Pietro ring out the news: Pianello has taken the victory.

Dragging out trestle tables and benches, a hundred hands have cloths and plates and glasses in place in minutes. This is the most marvellous impromptu meal I have ever sat down to. Out come steaming cauldrons of tagliatelle with tomato and basil sauce that never tasted so sublime! Luciana clucks and clangs lids and orders us to eat, but as soon as our bowls are empty, spoons and forks start crashing on the table and a demanding chant to be fed is thrown towards the kitchen. Our cooks rush back with more iron cauldrons, ladling penne with zucchini and onion into our empty bowls. With hoots of joy and counting our victories, that quickly disappears as well. The kitchen is ready! Out they come, now with shallow pans of sizzling orecchini, little ears, and more tomato and basil sauce, but we do not care! We devour our third plate of pasta with total joy, as if it is a rare exotic treat! Cecilia tells me that one year, when Ruga celebrated their nineteenth victory, they held a dinner with nineteen different plates of pasta. Oh, Dio, this is our nineteenth victory!

Fabio and Riccardo pull wires and plugs from San Pietro; as soon as we exhaust a year's supply of pasta in the pantry we are going to party! Then, a sudden hush. Coming down the hill are the Presidents of Travaglio and Borghetto, and their archers. They have come to honour the victors. Shaking Maurelia's hand, then those of our archers, they are offered a glass of wine, but this is not their night. They quickly retreat, having paid their respects. But where is Ruga? Next to arrive with a swish of white is Fra Giancarlo; he greets us all, shares our joy and blesses us and our victory, and we plonk him down on a bench with a glass of bel vino, which he happily accepts. The climactic moment of tension is here; Maria, President of Ruga, is approaching down the hill. Ruga leads the count in victories in the modern era of archery, they have celebrated many magnificent wins, but are they good losers? Behind her, crestfallen but resigned to their cruel defeat after a mammoth battle, walk the two losing archers. I am touched to see the warmth of the embrace between four archers who bear the responsibility for their respective quartiere. They all accept a glass of wine and we respectfully halt our singing and chanting until Maria and Maurelia affectionately kiss and shake presidential hands. The archers salute us with a wave and turn to go, whereupon, before they are out of earshot we are into it . . . a rousing crescendo of voices explodes with our victory song! From I know not where, our three youngest archers, Francesco, Samuele and Filippo, light firecrackers that explode with thunderous booms. Ruga archers disappear round the corner, and we count our victories one more time.

The elders rise to go home. At this signal our bowls are hastily cleared away and tables pushed aside to clear a space in the piazzetta. We are partying to a disco rumba and melodious Riccardo is our disc jockey. Tonight I do not hesitate – I could not miss this – and anyway, not all the elders go and soon a ring of benches enfolds us and Riccardo switches on the music. Cecilia and Ofelia pull me into the twirling mass of legs along with Gloria and Caterina and young Samanta and all the rest, and we writhe to 'Another One Bites the Dust'. Davide, Cinquino and Gabriele spray us with water, and then soak us with precious bel vino! Delirious with joy, we are not exactly dancing, but cavorting like idiots one minute and jumping up on tables and forming lines for the Macarena the next! Elders, hands up to their faces, huff unbelieving gasps but their eyes watch on enviously. 'Pick Me Up and Turn Me Over' is followed by 'We Are the Champions'. Then Fabio and Riccardo and Caterina lead a blasting rendition of our victory song, loud enough for Travaglio, Borghetto and especially Ruga to hear, and we count off our victories all over again. I dare not meet the eyes of our elders, my hips swirl and I sink into the same intoxicated joy as everyone else, all respectability has deserted me.

'YMCA!' I have not heard that one for years, and one of our members whose name I do not know, because he works in Pisa and only comes home for the tournaments, is an expert with the actions. We are YMCA-ing for ten minutes until someone spies Michele gyrating . . . he swore he would never do it, but he is back on a chair! Riccardo announces into the microphone: 'Signori! Il magnifico Don Michele of the Disco Rumba!' Maurelia gasps, 'No! Ragazzi basta!' Anxious elders look swiftly round. Has Fra Giancarlo gone? Whether he has or not, Michele is hoisted from his wobbly chair on to the wall in front of the little Madonna standing in the open doors of San Pietro, two metres above the rest of us, where, incited by our shrieks, and possibly an overindulgence of that other bel influence under which we all seem to have fallen, begins to unbutton his shirt! The sensuous Latin rhythm has us all gyrating, so off comes his shirt, which he throws to adoring females lapping at his feet. His mother, Carla, horrified at this uncharacteristic outburst from her circumspect son, attempts to retrieve his shirt, but Gloria will not give it back. Michele flicks his belt from the last loop of his jeans, and pulling up his singlet, exposes his bare chest. Belt and singlet are dispatched into the wrangle of writhing girls. In Pianello such flamboyant exhibitionism has never been witnessed. Cinquino and Gabriele whistle and cheer. 'Don Michele!' Davide and a chorus of girls implore him. 'Go on, go on!' And he does. Jeans are dropping from his bottom! We girls raise our arms in feverish tremor in homage . . . he turns his back and we feign horror as his Armani underpants come into view! His mother is going spare! 'Oh, Dio, Michele, basta!' Massimo jumps on the wall and throws off his shirt! Dear Don Michele, whom we all adore, is blessed with a sexily gyrating but not remarkable body . . . but our Massimo is Mr Universe! Tanned, bulging biceps, rippling chest, immensely broad across the shoulders, now we feign gasping vapours as Massimo draws an arrow, the last one which flew from his arms on the campo, from his thigh and thrusts it triumphantly into the air, whereupon the chanting and swooning rages all over again. We push our other victorious archer on to the wall and lowering an arm Massimo clasps hands with young Filippo, and, lifting him like a featherweight, props him like a puppet, beside himself, Alessandro and Don Michele, on the wall. Filippo is the future.

For six nights in a row we are gyrating in that piazzetta! Don Michele performs his now notorious striptease every single night. Such is our Don's fame that other quartiere members hear about it and cannot resist creeping down to Pianello to see if it is true. We see them peering round corners and, because they are friends, we drag them into our party. By Wednesday night we entice Dottore Luciano to gyrate at our disco rumba. Michele's mother throws in the towel; our Don is indefatigable, and his father, dear Giro Podistico Armando, relieves our pasta-crazed cooks and makes delicious pizza. Celebrations go on and on until the following week when, around one disco-rumba midnight, the patrol car creeps threateningly down the hill and Andrea, having leniently ignored our outrageous eardrum-bursting rave for a fortnight, begs that we quieten. We cheer him good naturedly, insisting he drink a glass of wine before we send him on his way. He did not know we had taken bets, gambling on how many nights we could rock the neighbourhood senseless and drive the whole village crazy before he turned up. All it takes is one victory to wipe away the anguish and the pain of the years we did not win. This is *our* victory.

CHAPTER NINE

The Chicken Shit Library

Leaning over the stone sill, curiosity the better of me, the haranguing cry of a spruiker grows inarticulate. A man bellows into a microphone, descending our road in a barely moving vehicle on the roof of which is mounted a loudspeaker reminiscent of the horn from a 1940s gramophone. The pleading hawker splutters promotion of a gas hot water boiler, but the amplification, bouncing into stone walls, muffles and disintegrates his invitation to purchase. For a few weeks each year we harken to a plethora of commands and pleas from these harbingers of merchandise that will ease our pain, make us richer, or cosy up our lives and homes. A knife and tool sharpener comes all the way from Arezzo once a week for a month; first he cruises the quartiere hailing us: 'Oggi Olivio e qui . . . in Montalcino.' Today Olivio is here. 'Bring me your knives and scissors,' he commands, 'only two minutes and costa poco', it costs so little. Olivio never broadcasts where he can be found; anyone who has worn-down knives and blunt scissors knows he is in the piazza. Wheeling antiquated apparatus down a ramp from the rear of his truck, he sharpens on a whetstone, polishes on a whining grindstone, and sends acrid smells and particles of powdery flint skittering into the air. Restaurant owners deliver a sack of serious culinary tools, gardeners turn up with all manner of sickles and scythes and blades for reaping and cutting and lopping, and a coterie of gossiping signore wait their turn with an assortment of slicers and choppers and peelers.

I wonder, in this age of television, if a loudspeaker on the roof of a crawling car entreating us to buy will endure beyond a few years more, even in Montalcino. Itinerant spruikers are a lingering trace of past insularity when vendors in carts drawn by oxen plied the roads every morning with steel pails of milk; from Mount Amiata they brought sacks of glossy chestnuts and carried them on their backs through the village. A year or two after our arrival in Montalcino, two elderly men who swung wicker baskets of walnuts or cherries or seeds over their arms, singing in melodious voices as they passed our windows, ceased their daily street-call only when death overtook them. They had no need of money – a couple of eggs or an artichoke was seldom spurned in exchange. Colourful images of life that vanished long ago from urbanized Tuscan villages survive all that much longer within the insulating walls of Montalcino. It is not many years past that Luigi opened the door to badged and uniformed Graziano who, before giving us our new telephone directory, cautiously phrased searching questions. Questions, and answers, he candidly recorded, flicking the switch on a mini tape machine fastened to his chest with anti-theft straps wound round his neck. 'Are you Osvaldo Luigi Dusi?' 'Si, sono io.' 'Do you swear that you have a telephone in your apartment?' 'Si, lo giuro.' 'Please tell me your telephone number.' Luigi reeled off the number. 'Do you acknowledge receiving from me at ten o'clock on this morning –' here he checked the day, month and year – 'a telephone directory for Siena and Montalcino?' Luigi acknowledged this truth, but the unbelieving uniform did not hand over the new directory until Luigi relinquished the tatty out-of-date one! Accustomed to a heap of directories uncaringly dumped in an elevator, or thrown thirty metres on to a driveway from a featureless van, nobody giving a toss whether you had a telephone or not, much less what you did with last year's directory, I found the cross-examination charming. How long did it take Graziano to deliver a thousand directories? What happened to the sworn testimony from a couple of thousand citizens? Smiling to myself, I dreaded the graveness of the penalty if you lied and Graziano triumphantly slapped damning evidence on the judge's bench!

The last festival that traditionally bids farewell to the summer is held at the church of Misericordia beside the hospital, which is joined to the abandoned church of San Francesco. Always bewildered at the ease with which Italians unite the sacred with the profane, we stroll arm in arm to the church for the festival, and yet again I am astonished to find nails driven into the centuries-old façade. This House of God is adorned not only with devotional prayer cards, but also peppered legs of prosciutto, strings of pork sausages, squat salami, bottles of Brunello... hanging in pairs dangerously dangling from lengths of rope, and donated gimmicks such as lavender pouches and zoccoli, wooden clogs for the beach, eau de Cologne and lacy jackets for toilet rolls. Luigi, pure of blood, is unperturbed, but I am speechless when a roulette wheel, devilish temptation to sin and iniquity in the Protestant world, is rolled into position outside open church doors. Armando wiggles the shaky under-structure to identify wobbles, chocks the base with slivers of cork, and all is ready for the annual gamble to raise money for our hospital. Luigi buys a book of tickets, crossing fingers for a bottle of Brunello, but everyone around us is praying to take home a leg of prosciutto. Early spins allocate toilet roll jackets and lavender pouches, working towards coveted upper nails, where prosciutto, salami and Brunello thud and clink against the stone. It requires an hour or more for a reasonable crowd to build. When four hundred eyes are riveted on the wheel, a collective groan goes up whenever one prosciutto less swings from the wall. Hence, when Luigi's ticket numbers correspond to the spinning wheel twice in a row, and he dashes up the steps to claim a prosciutto *and* a fat salami, a wail loud enough to scare the devil rises from despairing holders of tickets for dwindling rewards. Struggling home under the burden, not of our prize, but the predicament of not being the possessors of a stainless-steel razor-sharp saw for slicing prosciutto transparently thin, we debate the senselessness of hacking at a leg of prosciutto with a blunt bread knife opposed to the sagaciousness of donating our

250

prize to a worthwhile cause. The cause Luigi has steadfastly in mind is our heart-warming football team.

Caprices of the weather are driving us half crazy; mopping brows and fanning faces day after sweltering day, wilting and drooping in drugged stupor under clouds which do not unload their burden, each evening we pray for rain and release from sultry sameness when at last we spy darker clouds prowling round a taut sky. But it is illusory; rolls of thunder grumble angrily, whipping into a dark frenzy each evening, only to rumble into oblivion. A veil of haze smudges the hills and valleys every morning, but the rain will not fall. In this demented state, clothes sticking to our backs and beads of sweat upon our brows, a boil-over was perhaps inevitable when injustice on the football field found our team in dire straits. The last home game, a fortnight ago, seemed lacklustre. Our eleven players ran on to the field and the whistle blew, but a biased referee dreamed he saw a handball in the penalty area and angel faced Sauro was unconvincing in his plea of innocence. His red-carded departure from the field did not augur well, stirring up the referee to deal out punishment for every niggling foul . . . and red-carding Yuri for the dainty thump he administered to a cadaverous defender. None of *us* heard any bones snap. Beppe, our club president, white hot with rage to be fielding nine against eleven, threatened to sack the whole team. 'I'll throw the lot of them on the bench for a month,' he menaced, 'they are out of control!' From whence a stone sailed I am not certain, but this wicked indiscretion erupted into calls for the Carabiniere, who emerged, seeking to isolate the hurler. Did Crazy Cristian see the satanic act from his position on the field? Why did he not leave inquisition to those *outside* the fence? Out flashed yet another yellow card. Derision and profanities scorched the air, and an abominable utterance flew straight to Beppe's ears from, I am assured, the thrower of stones: 'An evil curse upon you and all your house ... may God send hailstones on to your rotting grapes and destroy your harvest!' The referee was escorted to his vehicle and out of the walls by the Carabiniere. We suffered the absence of the two red-carded players at the following away game, and Beppe, trainer, team manager and medico, who all reacted with animated aggravation, have been banned from accompanying our players on to the field for the next two matches. Inexplicably, the team dressing-room door was kicked to shreds.

Summer, in name only, insidiously refuses to cycle into autumn and today a buffeting wind sends tawny clouds scudding across the sky, billowing through a persistent curtain of haze. Luigi delivers prosciutto and salami to sustain our players and I walk to the football field arm in arm with Ercole who is prodding his walking stick into fluttering leaves. His head nods sagely, and prophetically he mutters: 'This wind is a promise of no good.' In the stand along with us sit all the banned officials who are normally on the bench down at the field to manage our players. Only incomprehensible Roberto is not banned because he was retrieving a ball out of play when the fracas erupted a fortnight ago. Today's match promises to be interesting; a micro-skirted female linesperson is taking the field.

I cannot be sure when I began dreaming about football; reliving the agony of that white ball bouncing off the upright, skimming outside the net or being miraculously glued to the arms of an acrobatic keeper. An attractive feature of my fall from feminine grace into fanaticism is that, for reasons of personal security, I sensibly refrain from competing with opposition female supporters whose boorish slurs and hurled derision cut the air venomously enough to cause our burly men to falter. Yuri and Sauro are released from detention, back on the field, and we breathe easy, watching fluid moves that foil a weak opposition. Despite lapses in discipline our team is near the top of the table. Ever busy, frighteningly fit Alessandro orchestrates the midfield and the ball consistently carries forward to Bomber Vito. Mirko stealthily and Graziano blatantly block opposition counterattack. Crazy Cristian's eyes flash as he thrusts and swerves like a mad matador who knows his goal is really to kill the bull. We are two goals up and the game is into the second half. For weeks we have blundered from one sweltering day to the next, wilting under close and heavy air. Why, in the space of a minute in the last ten of a football game does a petulant sirocco treacherously reach our field from the straits of Africa, blowing a veil of grit in weird puffs that mount into gales and turn the sky bronze? We turn backs to shield our eyes from dust swirling around the grandstand but the wind from Africa is breathing hotly down our necks. 'Ah,' Ercole sighs, 'this is good, the sirocco will bring rain.' Next to me a bearded man temptingly delivers a curious invitation: 'Ah, the wind from Africa! Tordi will pass in the morning, are you coming to the woods at dawn?' Tordi are migratory thrushes that fly on the wind from Africa and pause on their northward journey in the woods of Montalcino. Hunting tordi is illegal, but the memory of expeditions with the arrival of the sirocco are legendary in the village – as is the flavour of roasted tordi.

But why did the sirocco blow into a punishing gale against our team? The opposition, backs to the gale, are herded down the field by a filthy wind gust that tosses before them a dense soup of sand, straight into the eyes of Mirko and Graziano. The opposition did not even kick the ball . . . it flew unassisted into the net! The female linesperson, jumping crazily because grit is bouncing up against her bare legs and because her mascara-caked eyelashes are shut tight against the dust, sees nothing; she is not even watching as the opposition foul Michele and push their way forward a second time. The ball is in the net again . . . we do not know how . . . but a blind referee has whistled two goals in one minute! With hands over my ears, in this blustering gale, I am unable to block out violent fulminations from maniacal female supporters lunging for the throat of the leaping line-lady-person! A few seats below me Gianfranco from Fiaschetteria, with a contemptuous snort, ignites the flame of passion: 'All women should be banned from football matches, on and off the field!' The tempest will not abate, an irritable wind ruffles and claws, tossing dust and sand and grit so that by the end we are caked smudgy bronze. An unjust two-all draw. Leaving the field, only red-eyed Crazy Cristian is laughing; not because of the weather, but jubilant that even after cutting and thrusting and picking himself up from the blood-stained field, at the final whistle he is upstanding! A shrill ring, someone's mobile telephone rings as we descend from the stand; word passes faster than the thrashing wind. Last week's stone-throwing low-life has been mysteriously involved in a physical encounter at a rival game. A mellifluous murmur ripples across the grandstand and shoulders shrug; he was on the receiving end of a thorough bashing.

Ercole is wrong. The sirocco brings no good. For two days this petulant African wind rattles the shutters and shakes the windows. It buffets a veil of dirty yellow sand and billows it into our homes. Gritty sand hurries into corners, on to beds, into linen and my fingers trace thick loops across every polished surface. A broom is useless. One push sends a cloud of bronze dust airborne so that at the end of my exertion there is nothing to sweep into the shovel. But, in a matter of hours, the warm sirocco at last sweeps clean the valleys and the haze vanishes. The air is dried by the hot desert wind, and, at length, the sun shines bright. But when the sirocco is spent the heavens too are released from pent-up atmospheric pressure and the next day a Tramontana blows cool after the irritable hot wind, hurrying rain clouds to Montalcino. Knowing rain is on the way, the Consorzio warns growers, but forecasters did not predict the sky to crack open and recalcitrant clouds to drop everything at once. Intervals of furious downpours cut furrows in the hills, clods of mud cling to tyres and tractors hastening to deep plough before winter bog down in muddy earth. Rain pours from the hills, running into rivulets and streams as it races down the valley, piling up summer debris in its wake.

The grape harvest is only weeks away but the Consorzio can do no more than offer words of comfort: 'For the last few years we have been living in a favourable growing period. Montalcino's unique microclimate saves our vineyards from excessively bad harvests, but we must resign ourselves to the facts. If we suffer a bad harvest once every twenty years we can be disappointed, but we should not complain. It is traditionally your preference to harvest as late as possible, especially at higher altitude, but this year the decision of when to begin harvesting is problematical. The forecast is for rain and intermittent sun but already there is an overnight chill in the air.'

'A flush of muted yellow brown, the first sign of metabolic change, is creeping over foliage.' Luigi and I will drive down the valley to talk with Primo later today, but Enzo is with me at Bar

Mariuccia, sharing elbow room with a caffè, so I am gleaning news from him about the vineyards higher up the slopes. His word pictures are filled with imagery because Enzo visualizes the journey of each plant. Purple clusters at harvest time are the remuneration from the vine which has striven for perfection, and struggled to survive the ravages of violence. 'You see, Isabella, I told you the vine reached the point where it closed down growth and instead, pushed all its life force into the grapes; that was a critical moment, but the sun did not beat down for eight or nine hours a day so acids in grapes have not decreased, and because grapes are not mature, sugar content has not risen. My vines are fighting instability from the elements, suffering shock after shock. The Easter freeze, prolonged stress caused by humidity, no showers for months and then a weak sun followed by a scorching one, a sirocco that dried the plants, and now a Tramontana has brought drenching rain. Assault by nature has forced the vine to turn head over heels and inside out; because the future of this live organism is the seed hidden in the grape. Duelling with death month after month the vine is fighting to save its own seed; an instinctive battle for survival. Grapes look purple, but ripening has slowed, which adds to the vine's acrobatic tension because without a boost of sugar, skins are weak, and that means susceptibility to grey rot – the next deadly predator the vine must strive to overcome. The vine, with no chance to retreat and recuperate, has faced a host of hostile enemies since Easter.' I am fairly worn out listening to and absorbing the whys and wherefores. At his altitude, where air circulation is freer, Enzo may chance delaying harvest, gambling on a few days of sun before autumn turns cold. But, if the sun does not shine he could be harvesting rotten grapes. 'Then again, if I harvest too soon,' he frowns, 'when grapes are not mature, the juice will not be sweet; that means less perfume and bouquet. And if the skins are not as purple as midnight, then my Brunello will not refract that ruby hue . . . In truth, how could I call it Brunello di Montalcino?'

Primo's vineyard presents an idiosyncratic picture. A terrace of vines along the lower slope of the hill, facing the rising sun, are, in any year, likely to gather less sugar than those from western slopes. Primo's Brunello is an elegant, structured wine, destined to age – but he faces a dilemma. Rain pouring from the hill has left the vineyard sodden, but with no grass to soak up water from the saturated soil and puddles in the furrows he dare not begin the harvest. He will not risk destruction of structure, the holding together, of the soil. 'When we worked for a padrone, before Brunello made itself famous in all the world, we were obliged to begin harvest on the same day each year – the fourteenth of September. Nowadays we often harvest in October, but my vineyard is waterlogged. Unless the rain stops pouring from the hill and we get a few days of drying wind, or even better, a warm sun, I cannot allow pickers or crates down the rows. A muddy trap awaits boots and crates and tractors laden with grapes. I *must* delay the harvest.'

There is tension in the damp air. Itinerant workers who annually arrive from all over Italy to harvest grapes for Brunello, all of which are picked by hand, trudge from one vineyard to another, seeking a start date. Growers are reluctant, or, like Primo, unable to begin, preferring to delay and see which way nature swings, hoping the rain will be driven away by wind. The only certainty is that between now and Sagra the harvest must be in.

La Sagra del Tordo is the celebration heralding the second archery tournament of the year, held in memory of thousands of migratory thrushes that, in the Middle Ages, signalled the arrival of sweet fresh meat to famished villagers. The first sirocco brings migration, and for a few short weeks the tordi, according to many elderly Montalcino ex-thrush hunters, fly on the wind from Africa, passing through our woods by the end of November. Those that stray or trail behind the flocks were not hunted because latecomers fed on ripening olives and their tiny bodies turned acidic – not at all desirable for the spit roast. This year, so I have heard on the cooks' grapevine, Sagra organizers have ordered more than a thousand tordi for the spit roast in the fortress on the day of the Sagra. Thrush hunting in the woods of Montalcino has been outlawed for decades, in which case, how, and from where, I wonder, are these reputedly delicious birds going to materialize? My friend Ivo Caprioli, President of the Etruscan Association in Montalcino, in a rock-faced cantina under his house has stowed away for posterity not ten or twenty, but a hoard of wicker thrush cages. Sidetracked when searching for a book about Etruscans among a veritable trove of battered volumes, he digressed into recounting the story of his grandfather. If anyone can tell me the truth about thrush on the spit roast at Sagra, I am sure it will be Ivo Caprioli.

Ivo's grandfather, Giovanni Megalli, was a wholesale merchant and, so that he had somewhere to store his merchandise, he rented the fortress of Montalcino from the Comune. Before the Second World War the fortress was in a semi-abandoned state. Crumbling stone houses leaned against the walls but had deteriorated into nothing more than dilapidated animal pens. Barracks that once housed soldiers stood in the middle of the keep and stacks of wooden crates and palings and fodder lay all around. There was a deep well, and a dungeon below the main tower provided cold storage deep underground.

Every day fruit and vegetables and chickens and turkeys and ducks and drakes and rabbits and goats would be brought to Megalli in the fortress. He had the only cold storage for cheese and milk which was sold in iron pails around the village at daylight. Megalli would truss watermelons with rope and lower them down the well, where they chilled in blackness. One thing Montalcino did not have was fresh fish so Megalli would go to the coast and buy baskets of fish and on Friday morning set up a table under the dark loggia in the piazza – everyone would come for miles around to buy fresh Friday fish. In the wee hours one Friday morning Ivo was born, and so excited was Megalli with this new grandson that by eight o'clock Megalli had cushioned one of his fish baskets with a layer of straw and into it he laid baby Ivo, barely three hours old, blissfully asleep in a basket surrounded by octopus and cuttlefish and bloody tuna. Ivo believes his grandfather has contributed to weird happenings in his life.

Megalli, married to a woman in the village, fathered a brood of children. He was a larrikin, fancying the bella vita and he was a gambler (usually lucky) who kicked up his heels, got into scrapes and messed around infamously – in Italian terms, a baldaione. He had another woman in the countryside, brazen for the times, who mothered more than a few of his children. But, for all his wicked ways, Megalli was adamant that his grandson would not take the same road as he; Ivo was his favourite.

Like all the kids in the village, Ivo was drawn to the fortress and, because he was the favourite grandson, Megalli gave him the keys to the wooden doors whenever he wanted. The thirteenth-century fortress became Ivo's private playground. He would whistle up boys from the village and with the iron keys jangling from his hand he would proprietorially open the gates and take them in to *his* fortress to play. One of his cherished hopes was to find the secret of the fortress, because in medieval times it was common to dig a tunnel so that the lord of the castle could escape if danger threatened, but he never could find it. The very best game of all was a real one. Because it was *his* fortress, he ordered his friends into regiments. For hours on end two little armies would storm the gates, race up crumbling stairways sending squawking turkeys flying, creep on to the abandoned battlements and wooden arrows would rain down on the enemy who took cover in the barracks. Leaping from paneless windows into animal pens when the enemy discovered their ruse, battalions would culminate the day's war in a tenacious sword fight to the death. When the battle grew long and they grew weary, Ivo would haul up a watermelon from the well and, splitting it open with a wooden sword, they regained strength and began the battle again. They fired upon thousands of Spanish soldiers every day, retreated when catapulting boulders ripped a hole in the wall, then they would rush in reinforcements and block up the gaping gap. They would shinny forty metres down rope ladders in the towers, fire arrows through embrasures on to Cosimo di Medici and the Florentines prancing outside the walls on their fine white horses, and dive between the stamping hooves of goats and bleating sheep, fantasizing all the while of the heroic siege of Montalcino and the ultimate fall of the Republic of Siena because, so far as Ivo is concerned, the life was extinguished from his beloved Montalcino when capitulation came. The four-year siege by the Florentines and Spanish he learned about at school, and with the fortress at his disposal he relived every minute of history, fighting that great battle day after day. Ivo would never be in the Florentine army – he was Ilcinesi, to the bitter end of every bloody battle, claiming today that Montalcino never accepted Cosimo di Medici, and in 1559, all of Montalcino, when it was finished: 'Went into mourning for the loss of our liberty . . . and we have been in mourning ever since.'

Nurtured by a first-hand love of the history of his village, Ivo was hungry to learn more. 'There was a slippermaker,' he said, his eyes fairly shining, 'not a shoemaker, because he only mended and did not make shoes. His name was Bernardino, and he did his repairs up near the monastery of Sant' Agostino. Bernardino was surrounded by filth because he kept chickens in his cantina, where his workshop was, and these chickens would wander over everything, dropping chicken shit and clucking and laying eggs and messing wherever they wanted. A couple of us kids would call in on our way to school to stir him up. Have those rotten chickens laid any eggs today? we would call, and he would yell, go away you delinquenti, go to school. But on the way home, if I was on my own, I would try and be really nice to him. I would be polite and soften him up because around the walls below nesting hens and filthy perches were heaps of old books and I got curious about what was in the books. One day I said to him, Oh, Bernardino, look at your old books, they aren't much use, not like useful chickens that lay eggs, and anyway, your chickens poop all over them, they are covered in crusty shit and feathers and no good to anyone, would you lend me one? Bernadino nodded and said, Piglia, piglia . . . take one, take one. I went back, told him the book was really bello, and he told me to come and get one whenever I liked. I had to scrub off layers of dried excrement and wash the bindings and wipe down the pages, then I covered them in brown paper. Bernardino had a henhouse library . . . and my love of ancient books and history began in chicken shit!'

Ivo's grandfather was not a gun-toting thrush hunter. In Tuscany, up until the Second World War, principally nobles and aristocrats hunted animals and birds in privately owned woods, but after the war, prompted by a fearful shortage of food, and the social changes brought by exposure to a wider world, everyone began to hunt and eat birds until eventually the Italian government called a halt and bird hunting was decreed illegal. Shot tordi were not a commercial proposition, even before the war, because removing shotgun pellets was not practical and rendered the tordi inedible. Megalli was a legalized merchant and hired boschettieri to snare the birds.

Without cleaning, but after squeezing in a couple of juniper berries, tordi were speared on a stick and slow roasted over embers. Ivo's fondest memory of eating tordi is when his grandfather would say: 'What am I going to do with all these leftover birds?' And Ivo would yell: 'Nonno, let's make a saint's nest!' First Megalli's wife would make a ragù sauce with boiled and roasted chickens and ducks, including all the innards, nothing was wasted, and Nonno would slice up pork sausages and cook a pot of rice. He would get out the biggest roasting pan with high sides and everyone watched as he layered rice on the bottom, then slices of pork sausage, then ragù sauce, commencing again with rice until the pan was brimming and last of all a thick layer of rice covered the top. Taking succulent tordi from the spit, and the odd red robin and purple finch, he would delicately bury each tiny body up to its neck in rice, round and round in a circle, leaving heads and beaks poking out. When Ivo could see only rings of saintly heads peeping from the pie, into the oven it would go ... but a saint's nest was a special treat if Nonno had little flyers left over, those that had not arrived in time for export.

Ivo was one of twenty-three of notorious Megalli's grandsons, who, in autumn when the tordi passed, were all drawn into the export business. Megalli operated within the law, as it stood at the time, and his business created a chain of work for thrush hunters when the need to feed a hungry family overrode deliberations of conscience about nature, and fairness of methods. Megalli exclusively commanded a vast network in the woods of Montalcino, capturing little flyers not only to satisfy the palates of Tuscans, but all of Italy, and daily exports sent them to Marseilles to feed French gourmands as well. Every September, before the tordi flew in, the boschettiere, a thrush hunter, began preparing the boschetto, a little wood, in a patch of forest undergrowth without trees. Bushes like juniper and scrubby close-growing vegetation were ideal. In the middle of the boschetto he built a refuge hut in which to conceal himself and one small boy, because wily Megalli sent one grandson on every hunt to keep the boschettiere honest. Radiating from the hut in the pattern of an artistically landscaped Italian garden of the 1700s, the boschettiere cleared spotlessly clean flat paths that ran for tens of metres, and, bordering each radiating path, the bushes on both sides were carefully manicured into a hedge, artfully rounded, like topiary. In Italian Renaissance gardens the paths were pebbles or gravel, the hedge evergreen with boxwood topiary no higher than your knees, but in the boschetto the paths were earth, and the hedges, crudely but eruditely clipped, were a little higher than your thigh. With no trees in the boschetto, when little flyers swooped to these waiting hedges, they found nowhere to alight except where the boschettiere wanted.

'My grandfather woke me at two o'clock in the morning and told me to get dressed because the sirocco was blowing and tordi would pass at dawn. Our day began when it was black as night.

He sent me out to the woods with a boschettiere called Savino, and we set off together, carrying our second breakfast and walking through the dark to the boschetto. Savino had a lot to carry because in cages, like the ones in my cantina, he carried traitor thrush, and he had a leather bag – a big pouch, filled with sticky porridge mixed from the sap of plants. When we reached the hut we always lit a lovely fire to brighten up the night, and we ate a good breakfast. Then Savino would set the trap for the little flyers.'

Going one by one down all the paths, Savino would balance sticks of chestnut, stretching them from one hedge to the other across the paths. Each stick was an ideal perch for a bird, clean and smooth and notched in one direction. As he went along the rows, Savino, his leather pouch stuffed with hundreds of floppy fronds of juniper coated in slime, would painstakingly insert a sticky frond into each notch in the chestnut stick so that the fronds all leaned at a similar inclination. Then he would fetch the traitor birds in their cages; they were strategically placed among this deadly garden.

'By the time all the work was done a pale dawn was lifting the veil of darkness. We put out the fire, and then we crawled into the hut. In absolute stillness we waited and listened. In the quiet I often heard beetles scratching, or the pattering of mice or squirrels, but I held my breath when my ears tuned in to the distant rustle of thousands of fluttering wings growing closer; the little flyers wheeled across the sky and Savino, with a kind of whistle between his lips, gently coaxed the traitor birds to sing. Without warning, thousands of tordi would wheel and fall into a swooping dive, whooshing over the top of my head with a thunderous noise as their flapping wings stormed towards the singing traitor birds. But when thousands of tiny flyers dropped into the boschetto and prepared to close their wings, they found nowhere to alight, except on the chestnut sticks across the paths. Instinctively, they smelled danger, mostly too late. Some would wheel and fly away, but hundreds wrapped their tiny feet around the sticks. Rising, opening their wings to hurry away, their feathers flapped into the sticky fronds and they toppled to the path with their wings spread wide, pinned, outstretched like Gesù on a cross. We listened to the soft thuds as hundreds of tordi fell and at that moment Savino would race out of the hut on his hands and knees and crawl through all the paths where panicking tordi tried to flap free. But they could not. Savino broke their delicate necks and pulled away the sticky frond, putting it back in the pouch for the next hunt. While Savino gathered the tordi I would light the fire, mix yellow flour and dice dried figs to feed our traitor birds . . . and roast sausages over the flames for our third breakfast. The hunt took about two hours, so we were hungry, and after a glass of red wine we walked home, carrying four, five or sometimes six hundred tordi in hessian sacks.'

I daresay Ivo had a fourth breakfast when he walked back into the fortress. The other grandsons arrived one after the other, but the work was not yet finished; Megalli needed his grandsons for a few hours more.

'We kids had to help with dispatch. Our hands were small so we were the best packers. Picking up a tordo, delicately, because we did not want to break any bones, and they were fragile, we laid them side by side, tucking in little bent heads so each nestled into the tummy of its neighbour. Perfectly lined up in cushioned chestnut baskets we dispatched maybe three or four thousand tordi, all labelled 'Megalli – The Woods of Montalcino', with the afternoon courier, bound for Florence, and a large consignment went to a port, destined for Marseilles, in France.'

By 1960 it all came to an end with government protection laws. Ivo had finished school and began work in a fast-changing Italy. An uncle, who fathered only daughters who could not inherit, bequeathed family artefacts and memorabilia to Ivo, whose personal collection grew, and so did his interest in antiquity. He became a school teacher, but that did not go well because Ivo cancelled lessons and set the kids into squads – armies – and the classroom erupted in a daily battle. So he changed career, and went to work as an administrator at the hospital, next to the church of San Francesco. This church fascinated Ivo because he had never forgotten that, when he was a boy of ten, news arrived at school that the floor of the sacristy of San Francesco had caved in and as soon as the bell rang and school was out, morbidly captivated, he raced over to stare at ghoulish mummified corpses. He remembers well the hands of a defunct crossed on his chest, bones sticking out of cloth wrappings and his head bent at an awkward angle because when the floor collapsed it broke everything apart. Years later, with time on his hands as the administrator of the hospital, Ivo began to study wills and testaments and found records of deaths, and a plan of privileged burials in the ossuary under San Francesco. Not able to devastate the whole floor, which has never been excavated, Ivo and a friend decided that, on their next free day, they would excavate the sacristy – where the floor had fallen in when they were kids.

'But Isabella,' Ivo went on, 'before I tell you what happened, you must understand that I am a believer in reincarnation of the soul. This is the third time I have been on this earth. I was alive during the Republic of Rome – although I have an aversion to the Romans and would have preferred to have been here earlier because it was aggressive Romans who destroyed the Etruscans.

But I know that I came back a second time: in the medieval period I was a minstrel. I am now in my third spiritual and earthly body. I am telling you this so you will understand why I believe it is true, because the night before we decided to pull up the slabs, in a dream, I visualized myself buried in a peculiar way. Well, we heaved up the stone flags and we did not have to look far before we found two mummified corpses on a timber pallet. We pushed away the debris and unwrapped the first body. He was dressed in a Franciscan robe; fragments of cloth were intact and bits of leather and rope from his cincture were still there, so we knew he was a Frate, a friar. But, in the *same* box was a woman who wore a beautiful lace dress and a celestial blue corset! I will never forget this; it was the moment which confirmed my belief in my own reincarnation. I swear to you I had dreamed the night before of being found with a woman and buried alive! Anyway, we put the two mummified corpses in a glass-fronted wooden case. They are still in the sacristy of San Francesco. We established they had been buried in the 1600s because before we put the slabs back I gathered the chewed bits of paper; most were eaten away or had rotted, but there were fragments scattered around the wooden pallet, so I took them home to study.'

If this story had come from someone whose outlook or mind seemed a tad alternative, I could have shrugged it off into the rather unlikely basket. But Ivo Caprioli is not such a man; he has spent his whole life studying facts, and although he is now more than eighty years old, there is absolutely nothing alternative about his mind. When Ivo was painting this morbid anatomical spectre for me, telling me of his triple reincarnation, we were deep underground in his cantina, searching for the chicken-shit library book about Etruscans, and the cantina went black! My heart was pounding, I was never so glad to see his wife at the top of the stairs, but before I left him to his waiting dinner he insisted on taking me into his study. Opening a large book he showed me a half chewed, yellowed sheet of parchment which lay protected within the pages. 'This is one of the fragments that I rescued from the wooden pallet and brought home to study.' The writing was in a shaky hand, black and thick indelible ink, and I could not read the script, but he said, 'No, look down there, at the bottom, where it is torn away on one corner. Read the letters.' Perhaps it is an unnerving coincidence, because only the first four letters of the name of the deceased were visible. Stunned, I left it to Ivo to read the letters out: 'C A P R . . . and the rest is obliterated. But I am sure,' Ivo *Capr*ioli concludes with a smile, 'that I dreamed about, and then dug up, one of my own ancestors!'

It is not hard to find Ivo; he is in the piazza most mornings although he rarely stops for caffè. His snowy white hair is easy to spot between the bookshop and the cappellone. Bringing with me the well-clawed but scraped-clean book he lent me about Etruscans, by the time I drink my caffè macchiato, he is passing. 'Buongiorno, Ivo.' We go through the courtesies and I thank him for lending me the book, which is by an eminent Etruscologist – Etruscology is one of my favourite research projects right now, the other being the Longobards. Ivo belongs to Quartiere Borghetto and, as all quartieri are beginning preparations for the Sagra, it is not difficult to find an opening to bring up the subject of tordi, rumoured to be ordered for the spit roast in the fortress. 'Si, Isabella, si, I went to Florence a few days ago and ordered a thousand tordi from a merchant. I told him they were for the Sagra del Tordo in Montalcino, and he was stunned. "What!" he said to me. "My father and grandfather ordered tordi from old Megalli at Montalcino for fifty years. He had enough to feed the whole of Florence . . . now you are here to buy them from me! Don't you know old Megalli?" He laughed when I told him who I was, but he says the tordi he sells now are not fresh and sweet like those that came from the woods of Montalcino.' Preferring not to know, I did not ask if today's thrushes were hunted or bred for the table. Ivo tucks the chicken-shit library book under his arm and reminds me of the final meeting of our Etruscan Association before winter, but then requests that I keep my diary free for a meeting next year, after winter. 'Is there something special happening?' I am alerted by this advance warning. 'Yes, there is,' he says. 'I went to school with Franco Biondi Santi, we are the same age. After winter our association is invited to visit Il Greppo, his villa. We will have our meeting there and see Franco's collection of Etruscan artefacts.' I am going to meet Signor Biondi double-barrel Santi in person!

As autumn softly mutates green to gold in our hills and valleys our sluggishness dissolves. So much waits to be done before winter closes out visitors and we retreat, withdrawing our lives in cosy shelter from the eyes of the world. Winter heralds a lowering of the flag, a receding of the frontiers and, girdled by our protective walls, our reliance will turn inward and life seclude us inside. Feeling upon our backs the last breath of retiring summer, and, before we find ourselves locked too soon in a freezing winter, everyone is galvanized to an autumn of industry. A sad, unpromising harvest is underway. Those who chanced high stakes on nature repaying patience have lost the gamble. The sun, barely warm, peered weakly between grey clouds with hardly a smile. The vines, wearied from violence, can offer no more; they have reached the end of the battle and must retreat for winter. Hearts grow heavy as selected clusters are severed for the harvest while those bearing signs of mould or carrying shrivelled grapes are left on the vine. Resignation remains the only choice; this *is* the one year in twenty. Nature has dealt a deadly hand, but even so, some vineyards believe they will produce discreet Brunello, others may produce none. The Consorzio will not be able to rate this harvest based on altitude or zone. But wine made with these grapes will not be ready to drink for more than four years. Many growers, resigned to a modest vintage in Montalcino, are already turning minds back to the grapes harvested four years ago. That wine developed its nuances in huge oak casks, slowly maturing in a temperature-controlled cantina year after year until the winemaker, testing and tasting, decided the time was right to bottle the wine. But racking wine, removing it from its stable home after so many years means another traumatic shock; bottling needs to be gentle, and filled and corked bottles must be put to bed for several months to allow the wine to fine, to slowly recuperate in a new environment. Even in the bottle, the wine is evolving, developing into fullness. In a few weeks the sleeping wine from the harvest four years ago will be retrieved from silent chambers, brought back to the light, labelled, and a superb Brunello will be released to the world.

Close to home, before autumn turns to winter, the last village plums, purple and coated in bloom, are busily turned to jam; fat squidgy figs are hanging in the cantina, drying from now till Christmas, and jars of pickled capers, salted and bottled weeks ago, are ready to eat while caper bushes shrivel and shrunken roots withdraw into crevices in the walls. Garlic heads have fallen over and downy puffs from mauve pink blooms have floated away; cleverly plaited clove heads sway from rafters. New aromas float from shuttered windows as bean soup simmers and wood stoves send white puffs curling above the roof. Wild chestnuts, in abundant abandon, let glossy nuts slip from split casings on to roadways; chestnuts are plentiful, a poor man's food. Groaning three-wheeler trucks return from the woods with trays overloaded with logs and outside our windows the chopping and stacking filters the scent of dank forests through the shutters as bark and chips and splinters fly; the smell of autumn leaving.

Filled with compunction for work left undone when sticky summer nailed me to my bed each afternoon, I eagerly awaken in clean autumn air and scribble well-intentioned lists of things not done due to summer ennui. Stuffing photographs into drawers and meant-to-be-tried recipes between pages of books, I close up tight. Next summer, perhaps. This autumn morning is for walking; riddles about nobles and unanswered questions about noble wine race around my reactivated mind. Responsibilities in Pianello are already upon me; friends whose courtesy must be repaid await polite invitations before my preferred season of the year rushes in with the Day of the Dead. I have not the will to make up lost time on undone summer chores and, even before I have time to rise to autumn promises, the mayor is pontifically rushing us into next year before this one is over. Until Massimo became mayor, we rarely heard mayoral rumblings. His conservative predecessor was not inclined to dream up clamorous change, but the earth trembles, and so do we, when Massimo speaks. Meandering around the cobbled roads of Pianello, half in a daze and without directing my feet, I follow no set path, just pleasantly revisiting memories, smiling over my secret places which I last visited before summer heat made the hills too steep and the going and coming back too tiring.

Sooner or later this morning, though, I am resolved to pass the trembling earth where a huge yellow caterpillar is clawing at stones among the wilderness that the mayor is determined will become a car park. As if to mellow the hearts and minds of belligerent petitioners the mayor has dangled a sweetener – reparation of a long-held grudge. The undoable is about to be tackled, he announced. The post office, which was short-sightedly built into the arched loggia in the piazza fifty years ago, locking out a spectacular panorama of the Orcia Valley and Mountains of Umbria will, declares the mayor, be moved. This compromise rouses disgruntled memories, but with nods approving a wrong about to be righted, anxiously we await more news because we know not to where the post office will be moved. On this morning walk, moved by the scent of mayoral concession, I am determined to confront the clawing yellow Caterpillar.

From the low eastern wall the village curves around the hill like the dress circle of a Roman theatre. Tiers of ragged stone houses jut and sink and thrust from the hillside, all sheltered by terracotta roofs that dip and poke every which way over terraces and balconies only large enough to stand on. I have my back to the church of San Francesco where the corpse of Ivo's priestly ancestor decays alongside that of his naughty corseted consort. They have taken with them the obscure secret of an undone tryst betwixt priest and maiden, but, sadly, they do not look amorously happy. I have been to visit the first of my morning secrets because the sacristy conceals more than ghouls. Languishing in that cold room, gouged by furniture scraped along the walls and disfigured by delinquent hands that scratched initials, understanding not, nor caring, that in 1511

Vincenzo Tamagni, piccolo maestro of the Sienese School, figured these walls, is an enchanting Wedding of the Madonna. Scraps of fresco clinging to decaying dampness disintegrate for lack of money, carried away by time, and too many years of not caring. Mary, one hand resting lightly on her swollen belly modestly offers a hand to Joseph whose fingers hold a golden ring. Onlookers have all but vanished, but four divine women with long necks curving into oval faces flushed the softest rose, with sheer veils falling from their heads, are inestimably excellent. Drawing nervously about them robes of rich brocade and silk, watching Mary accept her vows, their almond eyes are alarmed at God's burden on their friend but set reddened lips dare me to raise a murmur in objection to this holy matrimony. As a boy Tamagni worked with Sodoma, a modern painter of the late fifteenth century, and like his master he presented his story as a living scene. His career was short. After he painted at San Francesco he assisted Raphael at the Vatican, reaching great fame, but, after the sack of Rome by the Spaniards, and the premature death of Raphael, there was nothing but to flee. He came to Montalcino many times and four masterful works survive; this one hangs by a thread.

The walk down the uneven stone slabs in Via Castellana is, I think, the steepest in Montalcino. The timber door I am passing separates me from a living room where a gigantic millstone for crushing olives is embedded in the wall. Donkeys plodded in the dirt swivelling a two-ton wheel of vertical stone and through the centuries a house grew around about. To remove the monolithic wheels of stone – for the other stone is half buried in the kitchen paving – would mean demolishing the house, so a pair of four-hundred-year-old millstones live on alongside the compact disc and refrigerator.

At the bottom of the hill, standing under the broken arch in the ruins of Porta Castellana takes my mind back to amorous Giovanni Padelletti. The whole summer has passed and I have not been able to visit the Ingegnere and every month that passes without hearing the end of his story is, I am afraid, a month closer to the possibility of never hearing it at all. Facing two paths which in minutes would bring the joy of seeing the smile of my sweet Madonina, I take neither. Zigzagging through Pianello I puff uphill into Ruga which will, with a few turns, bring me face to face with the caterpillar.

'Buongiorno!' I try not to startle a moustached man sitting on the step outside his house. It is early on market day, and folks are beginning to stir, but that is not the reason for my shock. An iron pail sits at his elbow, and a knife balances across his knee. His fingers move with a fillip, smartly snapping and releasing as he plucks the feathers from a pigeon tucked between his knees, tossing grey plumes into the pail. This is not a common sight in Montalcino; piazza pigeon is inedible, but, having been treated to a delicious meal at the home of a friend, I have the recipe for woodpigeon Ilcinesi style, sautéed in oil and parsley with an onion tucked in its chest, closed into a pot of water with ginger and pepper corns. He is as startled as I, knocking the knife clattering to the ground. 'Sei in anticipo sta mattina, Signora, buongiorno.' You are early this morning, Signora. Is that not a culpable tone? We exchange knowing smiles and I walk on, suspecting this fat pigeon, soon to be pranzo, may have fallen into a ghastly trap.

Up the steps leading to the cathedral of San Salvatore I climb, not pausing to glance over the wall into the vegetable garden but with eyes straight ahead, bracing myself, I walk down the pebbled track beside the church and soon face the hunting woods whence, I suspect, that woodpigeon flew this morning. An eerie quiet meets my gaze; no birds are singing. A menacing yellow beak hangs in the sky above the olive trees. Walking with trepidation behind lurid orange netting that fences me from the battleground, the topmost olive trees are untouched, but lower down the grasping claw has been ripping at brambles and decades of tangled undergrowth, exposing bare stone walls, one of several terraces stepping up the hill. Grimacing, not wishing to hold the image of the digger in my mind, I cross the road and descend below the outer defensive wall along my walking track. Brushing my hand up against the wall of stone as I walk along, I stop at jutting boulders of granite that the angry Sienese tried to knock down when they sought to destroy Montalcino. The boulders are accidentally juxtaposed, shaping a hollow in the middle as if to form the seat of a grand stone throne. Sitting on my secret boulder throne, feet dangling above the ground, I look over autumn vineyards where an entangled mass of tendrils turning orange falls haphazardly. Enzo is here, lifting and tying tendrils along the wires, imprisoning them until spring. But I have more secret places to visit this morning; I will speak with him another day.

My eyes rise over the vineyard to the woods where, in this limpid air, autumn creeps; leaves are washing russet and purple over the distant hills and Castello Romitorio seems nearer than ever. Voices chatting about produce as they walk along the path above the wall filter down to my throne; they are going to or coming from Friday market. I shall probably find Luciana there, along with Onelia, buying crates of tomatoes and sacks of onions because in Pianello we have not finished cooking for Sagra. Luciana programmed afternoon sessions for Pianello cooks, and those with less lofty titles, like me. We all obediently do whatever she directs us to. I never expected to get near a stove, but close friendship and hoots of laughter as the ladies banter and chat is part of the bonding life in Pianello. Borrowing a neck-to-knee floral wrap-around apron from Bruna, my neighbour, because I have only modern ones which tie uselessly around the waist, I turned up a few days ago ready for anything. Luciana grabbed me by the arm. 'Oh, ninni,' she laughed, turning me back out the door, 'you will not be in the kitchen today.' My heart sank, thinking that even peeling garlic had fallen beneath my suspect capability. But in our dinner room at two trestle tables lines of ladies were standing where they worked. I think it was Fiorella – I was so overcome with long awaited joy not to be peeling garlic that I hardly recall – suggested to Luciana that I find a place at the second table. 'Si, si,' Luciana bellowed at me, 'Isabella, you can learn to roll.' The ghostly apparitions at the first table were coated with flour, piling it on the table in puffing pyramids. Those wearing spectacles smeared floury lenses with wet fingers and worked while peering through foggy goggles. At each end of their table sat a bowl of mashed potato and bottles of water. 'You cannot go home for dinner,' declared Luciana, 'until I have forty-five kilos of gnocchi in the freezer!' Empty flour bags piled up on the floor as they combined ingredients and began swiftly to fold and knead, turn and thump. Hands bashed and elbows smashed as the mixture was smoothed into a shiny paste and then, expertly lifting the dough and releasing it with a final thump, fingers poked and wrists prodded as they watched for the dough to react.

I squeezed in beside Ofelia and Gloria. It was noticeable that only the most experienced women claimed a position at table one. With a thud, Maria Rosa dumped potato-laced dough in front of us and I imitated Ofelia as she dug out a handful and, lightly flouring the table, began to work. Deftly and so lightly her flat hand rolled over the dough until a long strand began to form. She showed me how to lighten my stroke, drawing my hand with a feathery swish away from the roll to lessen pressure, but this feathery touch is not easily mastered. Ofelia stored up six or seven forty-centimetre rolls of identical thickness, but my two or three were bulging in the middle and faded away at the ends. I should not have felt so badly if I had only to endure pitying laughs from friends at my table – and had Luciana stayed in the kitchen – but she was back. 'Oh, ninni,' she sternly remonstrated, 'gnocchi must be rolled as thick as your middle finger, how will you be able to shape those skinny bits of string?' Everyone laughed, so I encouraged the fun, letting Luciana hold up my miserable strands. Ofelia took command and did her best to put my skinny strings right, and then, more slowly, initiated me into the rite of rolling gnocchi. We put the strands on floured trays and covered the trays with tea towels. Forming with fork and thumb would come later.

'Buonasera a tutti!' Maurelia pranced in and spilled out the Sagra news, reporting that at our archery range Dottore Luciano is satisfied to have four archers shooting skilfully. The Sagra tournament is drawing nigh, but at Pianello we have barely risen above our Apertura victory. 'Però, I have other news,' Maurelia teased. 'My son Carlo is to be married!' Startled, we stopped gnocchi-ing and looked up. 'Who to?' A chorus rose, because, although we all know Carlo, we have not seen him often this year; he has been working in Milan. 'Allora,' Maurelia settled into an explanation, 'she is a pharmacist, so it is very fitting for our family, her name is Costanza, and –' she took a breath and raised her eyebrows – 'she is from Montepulciano!' What! We all wailed at once . . . Carlo is *not* marrying someone from the enemy village across the hill? It took a full minute before

Maurelia could regain her audience because the women, each turning to another, were tutting and clucking over the awful scenario Carlo will face having to eat barbarian food and dwell among Florentines! Faces winced and frowned and some drew back. 'No, it cannot be true,' they pleaded. 'Ascolta! Listen, wait, wait a minute,' begged Maurelia, 'I have not finished . . . It is not so terrible, Costanza's family live at Montepulciano, and Carlo and she will have a house in the country, but the good news is that Costanza was baptized right here in Montalcino!' Relief was heartfelt and genuine. Carlo had not, after all, taken leave of all his senses and betrayed us. Maurelia promised that Carlo would be home for Sagra and will bring his bride-to-be to Pianello.

Rolling gnocchi was infinitely superior to peeling garlic cloves, but after forty-five kilos under grim discipline from Luciana, who commanded we return in a few days' time, I shall not care if I never eat it again.

Friday market is a social encounter; people flock to the village from all over the valley for the weekly gossip and muddling meander around the travelling road show. Straight away I meet my neighbour Bruna, who passes a message from Amelia asking me to call at her house because she has baked a fig crostata. I exchange greetings with a circle of black suits wearing black hats and leaning on walking sticks, among them Nani, the basket weaver, and a tallish thin man whom I suspect to be a thrush hunter because I hear a plaintiff birdsong rising from the darkened shutters of his cantina, which makes me suspicious. From the fruit and vegetable caravans the vendors call and plead like eloquent orators making public discourse. Overflowing with kaleidoscopic temptation, glossy purple aubergines rub shoulders with Roman cauliflower heads, all green bumps and craters. Bright tangerines ripened under the hot Sicilian sun reflect into shiny purple plums. Summer's peaches and apricots and melons have vanished for a year, but the autumn produce creates lively chatter and a coaxing vendor splits the thin skin of an orange-yellow citrus, dribbling juice and flooding the sweet aroma into the air, offering tangerine segments to clucking tongues. Not everyone is here to buy, some come because they know another will be here, so messages are passed and reports taken – and mothers with prams are halted as the elderly stoop to squeeze the cheeks of a new generation born on the hill. Vendors of pillows and pots vie for trade, less one against the other than seeking to attract by their sing-song voices, tinged with urgency, conversational groups who defiantly resist their incidental challenge.

It seems peculiar that this road show sets up outside the doors of the only modern supermarket in Montalcino, but I have never heard a murmur of complaint from shopkeepers. With a six-hundred-year head start, Friday market has psychological precedence because Tuscans will not exchange, even in the smallest villages, the social opportunities of a weekly market – including the chance of an encounter with three white-hooded monks from Sant' Antimo who, I can see, are halted every three paces to talk with beaming parishioners. Why would the monks of Sant' Antimo come to market, unless it offered the opportunity to catch the eye and ear of parishioners who were not in church last Sunday? Amused, I watch two swishing white gowns shuffle off towards the fortress – where I am going, to run my fingers through my next secret – while the third fairly romps, his sandals making flapping sounds as he claps down the hill towards the piazza.

I sail past the main gates to the fortress and around the towers towards the low doorway cut through the wall. Before the last tower, not hidden but visible only with sharp eyes, is a chiselled cruciform. Sinking my fingers into the worn smooth grooves I trace the intersecting hollows. In 1552 a Spanish Don cut this cross in the rock as a warning of God's wrath with rebellious Ilcinesi who would not heed his words. But his vow was unfulfilled – he never came back to destroy their will, but lost his head at the gates. I remain persistently inquisitive, having heard a snippet from Ivo, about a secret tunnel, strong in the collective memory of the Ilcinesi, supposedly leading from the fortress. Legends grow into folklore, telling so much about the will and defiance of the people because myths and legends are never black and white facts boring us with their blandness. In 1553, when Montalcino fought off a siege and after a ferocious battle the victorious Ilcinesi turned the Spanish and Germans out, they marched a surviving German prisoner through a secret tunnel to Castello Romitorio, with a guarantee of safe passage. He was given a message to take to Germany suggesting to these invaders that they cease wasting young lives by sending soldiers here . . . because the Ilcinesi had massacred the lot with ease. The soldier, overcome to be the last German alive and unable to bear the humiliation of returning home with such a cowardly dossier, took his own life under a tree at Castello Romitorio, which to this day is known as Cesso di Tedeschi – the Pit of the German. I am convinced the legend of the tunnel is not fictitious because when the road to Montalcino from the west was under construction in the 1940s, rumour of a cave-in flashed round the village and Ivo Caprioli was first to arrive. A passage, vaulted with bricks and paved on the sides with rocks, vanished beyond the fitful light of his torch, but on the walls were iron cressets and rings to hold oil lamps. The passage travelled deep underground towards the woods; but a sealed road was sorely needed and the mayor of the time gave the order to speedily fill in the hole, pile rocks and stones over the evidence and lay asphalt before Montalcino ended up with no road. If it is the secret tunnel, it is buried for ever – unless, one day, the continual rumbling of trucks and tractors forces a cave-in. Ivo is ready.

Turning down the hill into Via Boldini I think to rejuvenate with caffè at Bar Mariuccia, but as I walk away old Gina appears, bobbing under the top half of a split wooden door in her plainest dress and house slippers, hair uncombed and a scarf folded around her neck. Gina has a habit of bobbing in and out of her stable-like door hailing anyone who passes. 'Signora!' she beckons me, holding out a light bulb. 'I am in darkness . . . I am too frightened to stand on the table. Would you be kind enough to replace my bulb?' Gina is reluctant to allow sunlight to enter her cell-like home; shutters across windows set deep in the walls seem always to be closed; her apartment is as dark as a catacomb. Nervously I bob under the stable door and, slowly growing accustomed to the gloom, pull a chair from under the table, on which to stand, while she removes a vase of plastic flowers, and I rise on to her rickety table and twist the bulb into the socket. The light glares – all of fifteen watts, barely improving the chthonic darkness, but Gina is beaming. Now for my caffè.

Having not walked to my secret places all through summer, it is like finding them all over again. After coffee I will go further down the road and greet the Duce, then I will walk to Travaglio and visit Queen Helena's legend . . . and I might as well look over the Orcia Valley and see again that vision captured by the paintbrush of Gabrielle de Annunzio . . . and, instead of coming back to the piazza, I will end my gloriously selfish morning in silence, with my eternally smiling sweet Madonina, descending through the chestnut wood and climbing up the hill back to Pianello. My thoughts thus organized, sipping caffè and munching one of Angelo's twists filled with apricot purée, my eyes boggle when I see a hooded white cassock whirling from a door. The monk fairly cartwheels down the road, frolicking in unmonkish sneakers! Quickly emptying my cup, I call to Angelo that I will be back in a moment to pay, and peer in a door, greeting shoemaker Luciano, whose face is set with a bewildered expression. He looks up from behind the bench and calls me in. 'Buongiorno, Isabella, your belt is ready, but what do you say I should do with this?' He holds two parts of one sandal in his hands, the sole separated entirely from the upper and frayed straps holding on to nothing dangle from both halves. Now I can see why I heard a strange flapping when the monk bolted down the hill from the market. 'There is nowhere for me to put a stitch!' he moans, tossing the halves on the bench and sinking his hands into the pockets of his blue work apron, signifying unwillingness to be tainted by it all. The sandal debris is immediately camouflaged by the litter on the bench. Luciano knows I have a fetish about monks and sandals and, because I did not catch sight of the monk's face when he accelerated down the road, Luciano gestures for me to inspect the indentation, which is as big as a walnut – or a toe! It was Fra Andrea! Luciano shakes his head when I ask how much I owe him for the loop he has mended on my belt. 'Lascia stare,' he insists with a wave of his hand. 'Let it be, the work is done, we'll catch up,' is Luciano's response, not wanting payment for a useful fiddly job. Before chasing down the road after Fra Andrea, because that is my direction, I pop back into Bar Mariuccia and pay Angelo for my apricot pastry and caffè, and a caffè for Luciano as well. It is a tiny way to compensate his work, which is more like a voluntary service for friends.

A black Duce watches me walk by. I do not need to stop for it is a mutual stony glare. Around 1924, when Benito Mussolini was beginning his rise to megalomaniac power, a wane in the popularity of fascism, dangerous to Mussolini's delusions of grandeur, was rising. To strengthen resolve, followers of the Fascist Party stencilled the head of the Duce on walls wherever they could. So far as I know, this one, on the wall near our printing shop, is the only surviving black Mussolini head in the village. I know not why it lingers, a sombre reflection of death and tragedy, because others were painted away years ago, but I am glad it is still here, part of Montalcino's history. A sharp left and I am in a lane too narrow for a three-wheeler Ape. It carries me deep into Travaglio territory and past their sede in Via Donnoli.

How many Tuscan treasures are demolished by time, or evaporate from memory? One day I will walk down Via Donnoli and find this one covered and protected, and yet the contradictory truth is that once a transparent Perspex shield conserves, and thus identifies, the stone, it will be robbed of its naive purity; the very nature of its appeal is its unsophisticated expressionism, not meant for the external world. Near Vicolo Gattolini, Lane of Little Cats, medieval dwellings are punctuated by generations of minds made up and then undone. Stone blocks and wedged rocks alternate with terracotta bricks and splinters of carbonized wood because these homes, at least the lower structure, survived the destructive fire of 1460 and were reconstructed. Here an arched window was cut out and then bricked in, a double door to a cantina narrowed to one, there a slab of stone from a fireplace recycled to prop up a mantel – and so it goes, a trove of yes, no, or maybe, the changing needs of countless generations. Here in Montalcino, a naive hand from the fourteenth century, with childlike faith and scant else, has chiselled into the wall of a house the legend of Helena and her pilgrimage to the Holy Land. A Latin cross rises above the curved dome of an Eastern church, and on each side of the cross two cherubim with hooked wings, as simplistic as we drew them in kindergarten, hold candles, I think, or maybe not. Tiny feet paddle in nothing, as if treading air to hold themselves aloft. Beside the fluttering angels, at the hem of each winged child's gown, a Greek letter is incised. The whole scene is partly disfigured by a careless swirl of plaster by who knows whom, or when, or why. Curiosities and legends. Some of the myths and curiosities of Montalcino I have yet to find, like Fonte di Latte, a magic spring, and its cure has been taken by Ilcinesi who live here today; they left at the spring three personal items, perhaps a comb and a handkerchief and a cup of milk. The waters trickle between sharp hanging rocks, I am told, and although I see this mythical fountain in my mind, it must be half buried in stinging nettles because I have not been able to find it.

If I were a visitor to Montalcino I would be intrigued to search for the Fonte di Latte, delighted to sit on the boulder throne and trace in my mind an imaginary secret tunnel to Castello Romitorio, there on the hill. Curiosities and arcane secrets rarely appear in guides, not even those for Italians, but it would be exciting to scrabble around in the dirt where silver coins struck in the name of Emperor Tiberius were found, and to read death warnings carved into a gate of pestilence and flood. Who brought pestilence? Which sweltering August did flood waters rise *this* high? Perhaps the skeletal priest and his corseted consort are not for everybody, but Vincenzo Tamagni's tender Madonna, would, I am certain, enrapture every visitor. Caffè in the piazza, and a glass of fine Brunello, yes, and a delicious dinner, these are the pleasures of every holiday. But in popular legends, magical rites and scratches in walls there is tenacity, patience and faith. While all the world was traumatically whirling in faraway places, humble people who never walked outside these walls left curious traces of their lives.

Somewhere in Travaglio is a carved marker stone, naming and dating an old roadway. It reads Strada Nini 1610. It would be easy enough to ask a friend about this ancient road sign, and the magic spring, but I do not because when my eyes search for and finally focus upon a stone, or a drawing or object of veneration, it becomes preciously *mine*; thus the hunt is a pleasure in itself. Strada Nini is not apparent this morning as I thread through Travaglio and descend to the track leading outside the walls to my sweet Madonina. Turning through Porta Gattoli, I smell rain-freshened grass – it must have rained heavily in the night – and I smile, as always, when little birds, startled, dart away cheeping dire warnings to mates. A morning of secret places and private musing has lightened my conscience of summer neglect; my mind is mixed with legends and magic and plucking pigeons . . . the simple things in life, mingling with a frolicking monk from Sant' Antimo, the mysterious Longobards, and the unwell Ingegnere. And I must not let another week pass without learning from Enzo what is happening to his harvested grapes. Straight after Sagra is the Day of the Dead, the first year for me to join the annual pilgrimage, with Amelia, and visit Bruno. (Mental note: order a pot of chrysanthemums.) Luciana will dragoon us all in two days' time for more cooking for Sagra . . . and Ofelia's message is still on my mobile: an accusation that we have not met for caffè for more than a week!

So much to do and be done – my cluttered mind is out of breath – and I have not yet considered a plan to find out why Colombini threatened to resign from the Consorzio. After winter, when I go to the villa to see Signor Biondi Santi's collection of artefacts, perhaps I will uncover the story of his family. Churning over in my mind are the unanswered questions and riddles about Brunello and the ancient families lurking behind the bottle. If I can think of a way to meet the Colombini, because a Biondi Santi visit is on the horizon, perhaps the pieces will slip into place and the puzzle of who created Brunello, and the elusive nobles of Montalcino, will at last be solvable. The more my thoughts overlap about my busy involvement in so many things in the coming days and weeks before winter, the slower my pace becomes. Absently bending, I pick up a needle-sharp quill dropped last night by a passing prickly porcupine. Shiny ivory at one end, it deepens to pearlescent ebony at the tip. I raise my head, brought back from cocooning thoughts by a muffled hum. I gaze around for its source – it seems to be coming closer, growing louder, rising into a drone, throwing me into confusion, making me hasten my step and turn every few seconds to look behind. A sharp crack, and the droning cuts out. What can it be? I am almost at the Madonina when the droning rises again, alarmingly close, and whacking noises, and with a great whoosh, flying leaves flutter on to the track round my feet. Jumping sideways, gasping, groping my way through a mangle of stinging nettles and ivy, I dive behind the wayside shrine until everything is quiet. Cautiously I struggle back to the path, lift myself on to a rock . . . it is almost on the wall! No! My sweet Madonna of benign simplicity will never again smile into eternal silence! She smiles wanly at a snarling bulldozer viciously uprooting trees and hurling boulders towards the wall, tearing at the fabric of the hill, not three metres from Her head, and mine. Our eyes fill with tears. A flashback devours the years, I am twenty years old, hand in hand, standing here on this path with a youthful husband, smiling into Her serene eyes, calmed by Her benevolent face, not understanding the role She would play in the putting together of my life.

The day is blighted and clouds roll back. The olive grove is under destruction; what do I care about legends and secrets, the stones and the myths? It is safer, and deceptively easy, to claim it not to be my business. But this is my home; am I a carapace hiding in my shell? This sweet Madonina is part of the culture and Her blessings count. Only this morning someone has been here, seeking Her benevolence – a chestnut branch, weighed down by furry casings, droops from a bottle. She casts a forgiving smile, but today I see deep sorrow in Her eyes; pale crystalline tear drops beseech mine. I turn to the track to walk home through the chestnut wood. In the shadowy wood it is cold and dank and the path is muddy; shrivelled leaves float down and brush my face, dropping to the track where my feet dodge puddles and step over tell-tale droppings from wild boar. This is not a hunting wood, there are no rifle shots likely to ring through the trees, but I must not walk here in winter; locals warn me of the danger when foraging wild boar are on the move. Staring at nothing, I decide. As soon as I reach home I will telephone Professor Bruno. I am ready for battle and will join the fighting committee. Perhaps I will chain myself to an olive tree, or camp, immobile, in front of that vulgar clawing Caterpillar. First though, I will make an appointment and speak with Mayor Massimo.

from the wall out to towards the causeway

CHAPTER TEN

Evicted Pigs and Purple Figs on the Rim of an Iron Crown

The tinny Fiat rattles along, bumping over potholes and swerving to roll over the edges of corrugated ridges in the road, which is narrowing with every hundred metres. By the time we turn on to a track to penetrate the scrub, the track is a succession of stony ruts, scarcely a trail. Ilio ends our journey with a spurt, propelling the car towards a mound of bark it rollicks over the hump and the engine dies; he noses the bonnet down the other side, propping the car against a wood pile in a clearing where stacked logs pile up to the sky, waiting to be chopped and trucked into Montalcino. He jumps out: 'From here we begin our walk.' We pull our jackets on and retrieve rucksacks from the back seat of the car. A shroud of mist wreathes us in white swirls.

Yesterday, when I asked Ilio if he could guide me to the ruins of San Michele, he insisted that we go the very next morning. 'Winter is nearly here, the ground will ice over and the track becomes a quagmire when winter frost melts . . . and the days are short . . . who knows, the first fall of snow might come in a week or two. Tomorrow we can walk to San Michele, but we must take the circular track because wild boar are foraging. It is too late and too dangerous to walk the hunting trails.' Accepting his counsel and agreeing to our immediate departure I had not envisaged a cold grey start, and sought not to blanch when he said: 'I'll wait for you at the fortress at seven o'clock. We will walk for five or six hours . . . and return using a slightly longer trail, but it means less hard kilometres uphill.' Ilio is as excited as a boy scout at the prospect of a day in the woods. Borrowing a rucksack from Chiara, Ofelia's daughter, I stuffed it with what I think might be essentials for a day in the wild but as I have not passed a day resembling anything like the wild since my brother took me chasing goanna, and cajoled me into carrying a tiger snake looped round a stick back to our mother, after a walkabout in the Australian bush, I am not overly confident. Walking around the hills and valleys close to Montalcino is a pleasure, but to describe me as even *outdoorsy* is an exaggeration.

Ilio sets off and is soon into his stride, stretching to grapple wild apple, pointing out holm oak and juniper before my eyes and legs have adjusted to the terrain; a tad reticent, I am in his hands. Ilio was Mayor of Montalcino for decades, but he grew up in a family of woodcutters and charcoal burners. Sharp of mind, closer to seventy than sixty, he is a short man, neat and tidy, but at the same time he has the look of a rough, mountain character. He wears overlong serge trousers that flap around his ankles; a weary jacket conceals a waistcoat, in modest contrast to my borrowed padded parka, and sat on his head is a worn peaked berretto while his feet are encased in round-toed mountain boots. His alert black eyes have the penetration of an experienced trailblazer bushman as he scans the vegetation. The bosco is a natural habitat for Ilio and his encouraging smile, between one or two chipped teeth, consoles my cittadina nerves and my apprehension is soon displaced as we spiral down the first hill, into the quiet. We pass elderberry, and he tells me the leaves are food for roe deer, and that probably we shall hear them this morning, and perhaps see one. A few steps further on he breaks our journey once more, holding a branch between his fingers, explaining that when he was sick as a child his mother made a syrup rich in vitamin C from the red fruit of this dogrose. I did not catch on at first that he meant *this* dogrose. Already I am frustrated that I will not remember half of his outpouring of bushcraft intelligence. The track is heavily overgrown with weeds and sword grass, but we travel at an easy pace, without hurrying. The coppice to either side is in a natural uncultivated state, but not dense around because scrubby undergrowth and trees have been thinned by woodcutters.

A stroke of luck – or I wonder if Ilio brought me along this track so that we would stumble upon these strange grey heaps and the blackened traces of a charcoal burner's hut? His excitement fairly explodes as he dances about in his boots, cradling clumps of mud and picking up black sticks and running around powdery piles of carbon dust. Charcoal burners, or carbonai, moved their families into the woods with the first autumn shower and remained there for a couple of months, until the first fall of snow. That is about the extent of my charcoal-burning knowledge, but one question is all that Ilio needs. My loquacious guide assails me with descriptions vivid enough to build the picture. 'Woodcutters and carbonai had to build a capanna,' he says, giving me a stare as if I ought to have known at least that much. 'We built a new hut every autumn, first cutting wood for the frame, upright logs, and then we filled in the walls with clods of earth stacked one on top of the other, but sloping so it was broader at the base. There were no windows. Inside was one room where my family slept, and we had a fireplace which we shaped using slabs of stone. Two beds sat on the dirt floor, one for my parents and one for me and my brothers and sisters, raised off the ground and criss-crossed with branches, on top of which, stuffed with dry leaves, we laid a palliasse. In the night, whenever we moved, it crackled fiercely, but if it was not *us* moving, then a rustle meant I had to wake my brothers and sisters to catch a dormouse. We laid dried grass on the roof of the hut, trapping rainwater, and my mother cooked with tin pots and pans and we had enamel plates, and a small barrel for wine hung on the door. We came into the capanna at night when it was cold and wet. I can still smell the wood smoke, but the fire inside barely took the freezing chill from the air – sometimes our capanna was warm enough to call tepid.'

Carbonai were reclusive loners, never welcoming intrusion much less anyone poking into their mysterious life. I recoiled in fear when while walking I once happened across a roaming carbonaio, although I am told that only one or two now live on the fringes of the woods, and society. A carbonaio spun spooky tales into the night and made up songs about how poor he was and the misery of his life. Mothers in Montalcino forbade their children to speak to the children of the burners; sinister connotations wove a web of intrigue around their nomadic, semi-savage life, and the mystical rites that might be encountered by disobedient children who wandered into the woods. It was filthy work, and the carbonai, and their children, were made the more repulsive by a coating of smudgy black charcoal.

This deserted camp might help me establish where wood-cutters, like old Bruno, and carbonai slot into the social classes of Montalcino. I do not think they are the same as contadini, oppressed under a life of subservient debt, but nor do they fit into any of the four classes of cittadini. 'How *do* you make charcoal, Ilio?' He looks stunned that I do not know. 'First we chopped down trees, mainly Erica arborea, which is a kind of tree heather. The branches were as thick as a man's arm, sometimes a bit more or less, and cut into lengths of about a metre. When we had a heap of wood piled up we constructed the carbonaia, the burner. There had to be a hole down the centre for the fire, and we arranged the wood to form a rounded hill, maybe three metres high, and when all the wooden lengths were in place we dug clumps of earth as thick as the shovel allowed. The wooden mound had to be covered with a blanket of earth so that it was sealed, except for the hole down the centre. Climbing to the top on a curved ladder a carbonaio lit a fire by dropping embers down the hole and from that moment we could not take our eyes from the burn. The watchman opened and closed air vents because the temperature had to be constant; we did not want it to be fanned into flame. The mound smouldered, taking maybe four or five days and nights. We had three or four stacks smouldering and smoking at once and the carbonaio, with nothing but his wits, kept the temperature constant, filtering the air or blocking a breeze until the burn began to sag as the wood carbonized. When the burn was over he gently forked away the blanket of earth and the carbonized wood, black, brittle and hot, was left to cool and then bagged into hemp sacks.'

'What did the women cook, out here in the woods?' Perhaps this might bring me a clue to social class. 'Every night mother mixed a pot of polenta –' Ilio smacks his lips and grins – 'that was our staple, and after a hard day's work it warmed us up when the night was freezing. Fruit we had, because there are plenty of berries and wild pears and chestnuts, but we did not have the luxury of meat. And there was always charcoal burner's soup, which we made with wild mushrooms. We did not eat as well as a contadino, who never went hungry, but we did not depend on anyone – we found our own food in the woods.'

'So, Ilio, carbonai were not like contadini?' I am closing in. 'Diamine, no! A carbonai had his independence, he was not beholden to a padrone. We lived poorly and there was plenty of misery, but it was a way of life. We had a certain dignity because carbonai did not fall into never-ending debt like a contadino. We might owe the shoemaker for repairs to our boots, or the carpenter for mending the yoke for the oxen which pulled the cart, but we earned our own money, selling charcoal to every forge and furnace in the region.' 'But what did you do when the charcoal burning season was over – did you come back and be cittadini?' 'What! We could never do that! Village children were terrified of us!' Ilio is amused, explaining that for months they washed in a basin of rainwater, which never got rid of carbon powder because it wrinkled into ridges all over their faces and bodies and piled up in their ears and knotted their hair. 'We looked like black monsters! We worked hard and the family ate well enough, but we had to supplement our income. Some carbonai took part-time work in summer, perhaps reaping the hay with the contadini, or if there was road making going on we shovelled stones.' Just as my findings rise towards a conclusion, they are dashed . . . he is distracted, changing the subject. 'Look at these berries, we call them coccola. Juniper berries ripen in July and August so dozens of us came back to the woods and picked berries for export from our bosco.' Oh, we *are* still on the same subject, just tangentially. 'Coccola were picked to make jeen for the English market – for jeen and tonico.' It is my turn to be bemused at the image of the English swilling gin and tonic with no idea they drank the berries from the woods of Montalcino. So, the woodsmen were not contadini, and not cittadini. A class of their own, kind of half and half, with a measure of independence, but segregated because of their mysterious life in rough isolation from society. I am not sure if these woodsmen slot into upper-lower class or lower-middle class!

A ten-minute halt at the carbon burner's camp puts a chill on my back but Ilio seems not to feel the keenness of the air. He wears no gloves and has only a cotton shirt under his waistcoat and jacket, whereas I zip my arctic parka over a woollen jumper and pull my hat down to my ears. We set off down the track. Walking warms me and Ilio's chatter about bushes and birds and berries diverts my mind from the bracing air. He points out the trail of a deer by its droppings, exposing, with studied examination, odour and diet with the prod of a stick. He crouches over a habitat for weasels and a lair for a porcupine whose shed quills give his home away. Ilio, more than a bushman, is a naturalist; this bosco is his second home. He knows all the birds, pointing out blackcaps, which I have seen feeding in gardens in Montalcino, singing a melodious song. We are not walking in ideal mushroom territory, but a humid summer and autumn rain means mushrooms in all shapes and colours are rising everywhere. Luigi and I are already growing bored with black-capped porcini; the scented aroma of tagliatelle with porcini sauce floats from the kitchen windows of my neighbours after every dawn raid.

Ilio signals with his arm for me to stop, as he does. I search around, believing he may have seen a deer, but can see nothing. 'Lo vedi?' he whispers, do you see it? I shake my head. He points to spindly scrub low to the ground. A tiny bird, a few centimetres long, feeds on insects in the foliage. It looks more mouse than bird. 'They are hard to find because they are so tiny, we are fortunate to see one . . . It is a Scricciolo, but the local name is Re di Macchia, King of the Woods.' He seems far too wee for a king, but I knew this little bird existed. I have heard a legend about Re di Macchia to do with the abbey of Sant' Antimo, but before I can question Ilio, he, and the wee bird, have darted away; the bird is gone in a blurry flash.

We turn from one narrow track into another, large enough to walk abreast, then switchback on ourselves to barely more than a path that flattens as we push into it, leaving a beaten trail along the grass. We have travelled up and round hills and crossed valleys, so that I am hopelessly disoriented with no inkling in which direction Montalcino lies. Ilio falls silent; birdsong and his boots crunching stones keep us company. We leave the stony path and work our way through trees and dense vegetation; Ilio suggests we keep walking and eat breakfast when we reach San Michele, which is not far.

When I asked Ilio to bring me to the ruins of San Michele I did not make apparent my interest in the Longobards. Even propped up with pillows, dozing, and with books sliding from my chest and crashing to the floor in the hot, soporific summer, I have learned something about this tribe whose justice and valour we claim in Pianello. I have also learned that for a long time Longobards were ignored by historians – not many books are extant – and even Italians refused to accept these wanderers from over the Alps.

'This is the tower, but it is in ruins.' Ilio points. 'San Michele, a chapel, was added later; the tower seems to have been an early outpost.' Immersed in a canopy of trees invading each other with limbs and feeler branches entwining, creeping vetch and brambles sprawl over blunt walls. Peering through a hole in the wall, the tower is larger than I imagined, perhaps thirty metres in length and twenty wide. A rounded arch exposing earth and broken stone is imprisoned by noxious nettles that bind it in spiky chains. It is a chaotic mess, and appears impenetrable, but Ilio is at once hacking at brambles clinging fast to his legs and bashes at nettles swinging around his head, hooking the shackles on a stick. He batters and I follow, until we are through the arch. Ruskin came here, I read in the summer; poking about in the rubble, he was fascinated by nature and its tenacious grip on romantic ruins. It *is* pure romance, a place of mystery and its very decay is a kind of loveliness, but I wonder if it were quite so ruined, back then. The tower has atrophied. Its energy has gone, along with the stone parapet behind which the guards warned of the approach of an enemy. Dislodged by weather and eaten by time, loose stonework from the upper half of the walls juts and hangs at defiant angles, an inexorable descent into rubble. A haven for flocks of woodpigeon, they rise and circle warily, distrustful of our intrusion into their private tower home; beady eyes follow our prying path. A menacing crevice widens above the arch, cleft by weather and tree roots thrusting the stones apart; it trickles water, sprouting glossy ivy and a crowd of ruderal flowers – perhaps asphodels, blown on the wind. Snapping underfoot tells us we are stepping on shards of shattered terracotta and stones, all fallen into a convulsive heap when walls yielded to pernicious time and the roof caved in. The chapel, added to one end, is the reason why this ruin is referred to as the church of San Michele: he was the favourite saint of the Longobards, and the reason we have claimed him for our banner in Pianello.

Swishing leaves from a ledge and flicking stones over the broken wall, upon which he rests his rucksack, Ilio breakfasts, and I breathe easy. I have guessed well for breakfast in the wild. We have the same menu, except that my prosciutto is tucked into neat round panini, whereas his flaps out in folded tiers from doorstopper wedges of Tuscan bread. The woodpigeons settle and throaty coos indicate they would like to be invited to our picnic. Over the summer I read an extract cut from an Italian magazine. Less weighty than pompously pontifical tomes, which confused me with dates and unpronounceable names, it gave me a feel for Longobards, rather than bland cold facts. Here in the wild their story is coming to life.

Longobards have been treated poorly by historians, they suffered bad press, were accused of all kinds of wickedness, some of which was justified, but their reign of peace is rarely exalted. Historians taught, and students learned, that Longobards were disgusting barbarians. But, I think we should wonder, were they nothing more than barbaric hordes who quenched their thirst on blood, invading Italy after the fall of the Roman Empire?

It is the year 568. A Longobard, King Alboin, rides through an Alpine pass in melting snow and reins in his horse at the border into north-eastern Italy. Behind this king, in their tens of thousands, swarm his shivering foot-weary subjects, guarded by an army of horsemen with a reputation as merciless warriors. Is this king a blood-thirsty invader, looking upon the rich plains north-east of Venice, greedily rubbing his hands and seeing booty in front of his eyes? Is he lusting for plunder in an impoverished land, feebly dissolving, inhabited by leaderless tribes of survivors of the once great Roman Empire? Scarred from the horrors of endless Gothic wars, powerless for a hundred years in the face of wave after wave of barbarian nomads, were these wretched people facing a new wave of terror? Did the crossing of the Alps by the Longobards bring an apocalypse, the destruction of civilization and the end the world as they knew it, taking them into the dark ages?

Can historians not find a distinction between these and other barbaric wanderers who crossed the Alps with the melting snow for a hundred springs? The Longobards *must* have been more than plundering invaders, because they did not, as others had, carry booty back over the Alps before the winter snow fell. King Alboin penetrated the snowy passes with his people, who pushed carts loaded with tents and sacks of corn, carried farm tools and pots and pans and beakers and barrels, with goats and bleating sheep tethered to carts running along beside a human chain stretching for kilometres. King Alboin brought old people who had to be carried on wooden pallets, and pregnant women who gave birth to their babies on mountain trails. Children stumbled under the weight of bundles balanced on their heads. The

Longobards left nothing behind. They had nothing to return to, north of the Alps, because they brought with them every single thing they possessed. King Alboin led a hundred and fifty thousand subjects into Italy! The Longobards had been on an awesome march, conquering one after the other nomadic tribes in their path, on the move for more than forty years. They were not looking for booty, for golden trophies or marble statues hidden beneath the rubble of Roman villas and palaces. This was the transmigration of a whole people . . . the Longobards were looking for a new home.

Paul the Deacon wrote the history of his people and although his story is couched in legendary terms, romantically biased, it is written in Latin and sheds light on the deliberate crossing of a whole people over the Alps into Italy, in the year 568.

But my mind goes back to those miserable remnants of the Roman Empire, the last flickering hope of the great civilization that had conquered the world. They were by now a forlorn population, exhausted, dwelling in a land devastated by war, an anarchic society where the only liberation from misery was slaughter at the hands of pitiless invaders. Rome's citizens were reduced to scavenging wretches, but through their elders they knew about the glorious days of their ancestors who studied ancient manuscripts, spoke Greek and Latin, and who had travelled east and west and lived sumptuously in golden palaces in a magnificent eternal city of marble. Stories had filtered down through the generations of fearless generals who marched iron-clad legions thousands of kilometres and conquered Greece and Egypt and Spain.

When you think about it, Italians are not large people. To these descendants of a fallen Rome the Longobards were a horror beyond all imagination. They towered more than two metres high, were broad of shoulder and chest and wore their reddish-fair hair shaggy, straggling down either side of the head and streaked with warrior-like red dye. Longobard eyes were not brown, but crystal blue and these gimlet eyes glinted from freckled faces. Dressed in rough tunics of woven flax, this was a tribe too unspeakable to contemplate. After a hundred years of suffering, the Italian people could think of no barbarian they had faced that was fiercer than this tribe who grew long bushy beards that straggled down their chests, streaked red like their hair – from which distinguishing feature they earned their label as Longobards. But the ultimate horror was that Longobards hacked at their enemies with murderous, mutilating axes!

Paul the Deacon apparently moved in the upper stratum of society in the Longobard kingdom because he educated the daughter of one of their kings, who was named, deliciously, Adelperga. He wrote the ponderous story of his people, narrating their epic journey, not from Germany, although they tarried there and in Pannonia, swelling their numbers; but he says that when the Longobards packed up the pots and pans and the goats and grandma, and set out to find a new home, they decamped from a humble settlement at a ford on the lower course of the River Elbe . . . in Scandinavia!

But back to those wretched Italians. Italy lay wide open to exterminating conquerors. Little was saved from violence, cities were razed to the ground, descendants of Roman nobles swept away, massacred like pigs. King Alboin consolidated in the north-east, at Cividale di Friuli, and it became a dukedom that endured for the whole of the Longobard reign. For thirty-five wretched years, cruel Longobards waged insurmountable carnage, destroying and slaughtering anything in their path. Facing lacklustre resistance, spreading west, they took Milan, laid siege to Pavia and then moved south, closing in like a swarm of locusts on Ravenna, Lucca, Arezzo and then down to Siena, which is when this ruined tower was probably built, and also when they settled at the castle in Pianello. But the Longobards saved their cruellest oppression for the clergy, killing and maiming and ransacking monasteries and nunneries.

By 603, once they had conquered almost the whole of Italy, amazingly, the king and queen of the Longobards saw the evil of their ways. The Longobard court converted to Christianity! Illuminated by this divine light, within a few years these wild, blood-thirsty creatures became devout Christians. Burdened with guilt at their reign of terror, their repentance overcame them. They rebuilt monasteries that had been pillaged and burned, they promoted the rebirth of agriculture so that those Italians who were still alive returned to the desolated land and farming life began again; even literacy made a comeback.

Perhaps, then, after thirty-five years of mayhem, the Longobards deserved a new reputation. But from historians they got nothing. They were stamped for ever as the pagan barbaric hordes who killed the last flicker of hope of a once-great people. But historians refuse to acknowledge that for one hundred and seventy years peace returned to Italy, arguing instead that nothing good happened until, when Christian Longobards no longer wanted war and tried to negotiate peace, the Pope called in the conquering liberator, Charlemagne and his iron army, which scared the indolent Longobards half to death. The great Longobard king, Liutprando, died in 744; within a few decades Italy fell under the power of whimsical French invaders.

It is a great loss that Paul the Deacon did not finish his story, choosing instead to close the book and put down his pen in 744, exactly when King Liutprando died; he did not tell us of the last thirty years of the Longobard reign. But there is a clue to a hidden, or ignored, truth. Cividale di Friuli, the only Italian city that has retained a Longobard name, was, for two centuries, a splendid artistic dukedom. Has some historian incidentally spoken of art? In Cividale, not only weapons and the iron crown of a Longobard king, but monuments of noble conception and sacred relics were left behind in a city that has never let go of its Longobard identity. A tiny temple has miraculously survived the danger of twelve hundred years of incense burned by monks in the monastery. Fragile stucco, a profusion of delicate leaves within loops, borders laced with ivy and flowers and stone filigree of tasteful elegance swoops around the altar of a temple. In thirty-five years they penetrated Italy, creating dukedoms from the ashes of the imploding Roman Empire. For nearly two hundred years they reigned peacefully, entwined their society with the remnants of the population, and created and left behind sublime art – though much of it was carted back over the Alps by later barbarian hordes because shallow Charlemagne changed his mind and did not stay in Italy.

'So, we really need an archaeologist to dig around.' I am dreaming of a king with an iron crown and a princess called Adelperga, but Ilio is handing me a tin cup of red wine, philosophically facing the truth. 'We cannot restore the tower, it is too far gone, and the chapel of San Michele is no more than broken walls, but if the paths were cleared and signed people could walk through the woods, I am sure they would like it. There is scant documentary evidence, but the tower existed exactly when the Longobards penetrated Tuscany, and we know for certain that King Liutprando was here.' Ilio's words ring in my ears: the king of the Longobards was here, making a new home for his people. Maybe that is why I am so enthralled by the

Longobards. Like me, they came to find a new home. There is a lump in my throat that I am unable to swallow. Perhaps Longobards do not deserve all of their dreadful reputation. Did they wickedly stamp out the flickering flame of the collapsed Roman Empire? Or, if historians are misleading us, should the Longobards be honoured for *lighting* a tiny flame that flickered and rose from the ashes of a crushed civilization?

We are not able to walk all the way around the tower and chapel; the vegetation has a stranglehold and it is impossible to see where to put our feet because of collapsed walls and precarious blocks of stone. But I am satisfied, desiring no more than to fantasize about the presence of Longobards in this romantic ruin. We set off, backing out through our own trampled pathway towards the track, and when we step out of the scrub Ilio continues in the same direction as before. We are on the circular path that will swing back to Montalcino. The temperature has risen one or two degrees and the white veil of valley mist has whispered away; we walk in clean, sharp air, but without sun. Ilio is quieter now, giving me noteworthy morsels as they rise to mind about wild pears or the bark of a tree that he boiled to make something I am not at all sure about, but he is not showering me with botanical names and medicinal remedies. We stop briefly to examine a dead trunk where a woodpecker has been drilling, then move on in companionable silence, listening to the sounds of the woods.

Ilio knows every track and almost every tree; I would never have the courage to venture into these woods alone. He points to a pile of stones and says one word: 'Prehistoric', nodding sagely when he sees my puzzled face. 'It is a pile of rubble, Ilio, how do you know?' He smiles benignly, but does not respond, lifting his eyes towards a bend in the track and quickening his pace.

Dragging my eyes from prehistoric rubble I run three or four paces to catch him up, but he has only accelerated as far as a large tree. Broad leafy bowers spread over the track and branches droop under the weight of ripe purple figs. 'Let's rest. Do you like figs?' I am closely acquainted with figs by way of my neighbour, Bruna, but never have I eaten ripe figs in the wild. Dark purple jackets are splitting open, bursting millions of black-red seeds, and sweet milky sap oozes. Ilio plucks two, turns them over in his hands, and offers one to me. Sticky syrup dribbles between my fingers and seeds cling to my chin. Some have been tasted by birds but after one peck have splattered to the ground in deflated heaps where a battalion of black ants cart away the seeds. Sitting on a bank with our legs straddling a trickle of water in a ditch, it feels bizarre to be here, plucking purple figs from a tree in the wild. I did not even know how to peel them until Bruna taught me. Gently release the skin at the vertex, tear it cleanly away from the pith in three or four runs, leaving it at the base as if you are peeling a banana, she instructed. Why is Ilio making a strange noise, *tzi-tzi-tzi*, pushing the sound softly out between his teeth? '*Tzi-tzi-tzi*, can you hear it, Isabella? It's the call of a thrush . . . He is around here somewhere but you won't see him, a tordo flies too fast.' Purple figs and a little flyer! My eyes search the trees and watch for his flight – I would adore to see a thrush in the wild, but Ilio is right. The little flyer is calling to Ilio, a to-and-fro naturalist-to-bird conversation. 'He is waiting for wind from the south, probably left behind when his flock winged away. He'll catch the last flight out.'

Ilio drags a lidded tin from his rucksack into which he layers green fronds from the fig tree, and then, plucking one at a time he lines the tin with purple figs, lying them side by side. 'Ilio!

You knew these figs would be ripe, didn't you?' The imperfect bloom of the wild brushes the purple skin of the figs in the tin, like some luscious impressionist still-life. Folding the fronds over the fruit he fastens the lid, and settles the tin horizontally, securing it into his rucksack.

Bruna, my next door neighbour, does not have a fig tree, but her son does, and he brings them from his garden. 'Luigi, Isabella,' she implores each autumn, 'my son is here, we are having pranzo, come and help us eat the figs.' It is an aromatic autumn lunch in front of a log fire. Strings of purple onions and sometimes coppery red corn cobs in bunches of two or three and little cloth bags of herbs and nettles for flavouring sauces hang from the mantel over her fireplace. Bruna has an alcove in her kitchen where she keeps tomato sauce bottled in summer, but at this time of year she has mushrooms in a basket, gathered by her son. Her table is spread with jars of preserves and little bowls of dried peperoncino and fragrant thyme. There is no ceremony at lunch with Bruna – she surprised me the first time, but now I know we can begin when she says, 'If you want bread, cut it yourself . . . and if you seek God, *you* pray!' So much for saying grace! Arms dive across the table towards loaves of unsalted Tuscan bread. Bruna wanders behind our chairs holding a loaf to her chest and cutting into it at odd angles, hacking off wedges and tossing them on to the table which is already laden with antipasto. All colours and shapes of onions, tomatoes barely cooked in the oven and drizzled with oil, salty melanzane and zucchini grilled over the fire, and her own pickled artichoke hearts, which are simply divine. The wine is poured into squat jugs and seems to grow more delicious as we drink. Then we always eat pork sausages that smell and taste of wood smoke and, if she has mushrooms, she lays a shallow pan over the flame, dips them in batter and then fries them into odorous balls. At the end, from the same alcove in the corner she retrieves a wicker basket piled with purple figs and we peel and talk and peel and drink until we care not a fig about anything else. The coffee, gurgling into readiness, sends that wanton aroma into the room as we demolish the whole basket of figs. Fortunately, when we stumble out of Bruna's front door, we have one step down and only two paces along the roadway before turning into our own.

Rinsing our sticky hands in water trickling in the ditch and shaking them dry, we are ready to move on. The track curves down a slope and around a hillock and we enter a valley where chestnuts are dense, but the oak scrub grows thinnish. Grasping at tree trunks because my feet skid on damp leaves in the wake of the morning mist, I try to follow Ilio's exact footsteps and in a few minutes we walk more easily across the valley floor. Ilio watches for deer at the forest edge and scans the sky for falcons that hover on the current and dive to the valley floor, lifting in their talons unsuspecting field mice. We turn from the valley and skirt the next hill, crossing a bridge spanning a creek from where the lapping sound of water plashes, then drops with a splatter into a millpond, where it is carried along in a swirl to a ruined wall. Ilio tells me this abandoned mill once ground corn for monks. 'Ilio! We cannot have walked that far!' I am astonished that we could be anywhere near the abbey of Sant' Antimo. 'Porca miseria!' he uncharacteristically exclaims. 'Well, yes, and no, Isabella, we will not see the abbey, but we are circling Montalcino to the south, where the abbey lies, passing between hills behind the Valley of Starcia.' I have not walked to the abbey since last spring when I watched the monks prune olive trees – that was the first time I heard the singing stones. As soon as winter passes I will walk to the abbey again, once we are into spring. Ilio is not yet agitated by my inquisitiveness so I ask a question that has bothered me since we left the ruins of San Michele. 'Why *did* King Liutprando of the Longobards come all the way to San Michele? It is so isolated and doesn't seem to lead anywhere.' His look is that of a stunned mullet, which is to say, in Australian colloquialism, dazed into a stupor like a thumped fish. Unable to find his voice he purses his lips, then whispers, his poignant tone a touch sardonic: 'To adjudicate in a quarrel between avaricious bishops which led, later, to our betrayal to Siena by the abbot of Sant' Antimo.'

The provocative rhyme! Woven into the history of Montalcino is the last great Longobard king with the iron crown! 'Tell me, Ilio!' I plead, promptly sitting myself down on a log.

'Way back at the beginning of the 700s the bishops of Arezzo and Siena were locked in a brawl, each of them claiming ownership of parish churches on Montalcino territory, including Sant' Antimo. Spiritual disputes were really about temporal wealth, and in the end, when King Liutprando came to San Michele to adjudicate in the fight, the whole of Montalcino's territory was donated to the abbot of the Abbey of Sant' Antimo. The monks became rich and powerful because the abbot had Montalcino under his veil; poor vassals worked the land and the money went into his coffers. The abbot had spiritual and temporal jurisdiction over our territory, which has always been strategically vital, not just the village of Montalcino. Both Siena and Florence wanted Montalcino but it was a three-way conflict because Montalcino did not want to link its fate to either Florence or Siena, so we rebelled. Siena could not expand to the north because the Florentines were defending the borders, so they began to expand south. They assaulted Montalcino, putting us under siege. But we defiant Ilcinesi defended our walls, like we always do, for a decade; during which partisan monks from Sant' Antimo, privy to all the war councils that went on inside our walls, fought alongside us in the name of liberty. But there were three conflicting parties. The abbot did not want to cede his money-making feudal interests to Siena; Montalcino had been at war with Siena for a decade, and Siena's goal was to expand south at any cost, including, insinuations were clear, taking the territory of the abbey itself. On the morning of the thirteenth day of June in the year of Our Lord One Thousand Two Hundred and Twelve –' with a flourish of theatricality, Ilio dramatizes – 'a treacherous accord was signed by the abbot. After ten years of fighting alongside us, he sold us out, ceding one quarter of his territory, including *our* village, to Siena, our enemy! Eight hundred years have passed, but we Ilcinesi have long memories of those who betray our liberty.'

I never want this walk in the wild to end. Will I ever be able to discover all the precious fragments about these defiant people who dwell on a hill in a small walled medieval village in Tuscany? Another riddle is solved . . . dastardly betrayal by monks. What the Sienese could not do in a decade, the monks of Sant' Antimo did in half a morning. 'Have you walked to Sant' Antimo?' For once it is Ilio asking something of me. His mind is also on monks and the abbey. I tell him about my marvellous walk last spring, and my just-made decision to do it again, after the winter. 'It would not be worth going at all if we had not saved it from the Diocesan Curia who systematically went to sleep when anything concerning that stupendous abbey was involved.'

Over a number of years I have touched upon anti-clericalism

in Montalcino. Not only over domestic hiccups, like the blocking out of a glorious panorama by a bishop who insisted the post office be built under the cappellone, but also the oppressive measures employed by priests during the mezzadria when contadini were debt ridden. The Ingegnere, too, has alluded to the unwillingness of the Ilcinesi to be dominated by church rule. Montalcino, now and throughout her political life, is overwhelmingly left and has stayed that way through the decades, including when Christian Democrats held the seat of power in Rome. Now that the riddle of betrayal by monks and the abbot is solved, it is apparent that ecclesiastical tension between village and church reaches back to the beginning of Montalcino's history. What *else* is Ilio going to tell me? I suspect he realizes he is provoking the newshound in me by dangling an anti-clerical bait.

'In 1963 a tourist drove in his car to find the Abbey of Sant' Antimo. The road was unmade, full of holes, and the car skidded dangerously as stones splayed about. It seemed inconceivable to him that this could be the only road to an important religious monument. Seeing the abbey from the road, he felt compensated and became emotional at the beauty of the Valley of Starcia and the travertine abbey. But his emotion turned to fury when he entered the abbey and he angrily scrawled into the visitor's book words tinged with irony: 'Signori Governanti, you do a great job spending our money . . . here I see what you have the capacity to do.' The place was in a state of criminal abandon. It was sacrilege, humiliated in its most revered parts, hardly more than a farmyard, a place where chickens wandered wherever they wished, and bleating sheep and goats snuffled the grounds. The walls of the abbey leaned menacingly and the antique cloister was crumbling into a pile of rubble because grain was piled against graceful arches, pushing them outwards, and one end was used for a duck pen. Inside the abbey flocks of pigeons flapped their wings, chasing one another around the entablature. All manner of birds nested around thousand-year-old pillars where Daniel is menaced by lions and ovoid-headed oxen peer down with slanted eyes. They coated every frieze and roundel with filth and grime. What is more, it was also a storage depot for muddy tractors, bales of hay and sacks of animal feed . . . but, even worse, cattle wandered tranquilly in and out, dropping cow-pats and swishing tails at filthy flies breeding in the squalor where dung and feathers and chicken excrement piled up on the paving, desecrating the stones.' I am aghast. 'Ilio, you are making me ill! That is repulsive!' His face does not change; a half smile, but still written upon it is his own disbelief. He shakes his head, hushing me with a finger to his lips.

'One day a truck unloaded a pile of wooden stakes, dumping them at the doors of the abbey. The custodian, an incomparable fellow, demanded to know what these deliveries were for, and learned, to his horror, that the stakes were for a new pig pen. Don't worry yourself, said the driver, intanto, at any rate, it is too late, the place is already fit only for swine. Those responsible for this negligence had decided to rear pigs, quietly constructing a sty in which they could root and snort at the abbey, ignoring pleas from the inhabitants of Castelnuovo del Abate. Soon, the folk on the hill grumbled, Gesù above the altar will be smelling the stench and listening to squealing pigs roaming around, grovelling at His feet below the cross. The custodian wrote to the Mayor of Montalcino, begging intervention, and the mayor raced like the wind to the abbey demanding that not a single stone or stake be moved. Then he contacted the Superintendent of Belle Arte, those officially concerned with heritage monuments, who informed him they knew about the old abbey in this valley because at that very moment they were working to block an application for a multi-storey concrete hotel to be built on the hill – facing the abbey!' Now the hairs are standing on the back of my neck, and I cannot be hushed. 'But Ilio,' I accuse him, 'in 1963 were you not the Mayor of Montalcino?'

'Yes, it was I! Thank God we were saved from that vulgar hotel . . . but the abbey, a pearl dating back to the 800s, was in a state beyond all comprehension, squalid, fit only for swineherds. And the slothful Curia, who owned the abbey, casting around for excuses, clutching at anything, hid behind the secrecy under which they operated, blandly claiming that it did not really depend on them! He, who is above them, should have opened their eyes to the despoliation of an incomparable Christian monument!'

Ilio, then Mayor of Montalcino, began a campaign of fury and for six months gathered comments in a visitors book before the bishop even knew the book was there. Armed with ironic comments the mayor disclosed all to the House of Deputies in Rome. 'I waited for a miracle,' Ilio sighed, 'because at that time, in Italy, without a miracle, nothing went forward.' The Curia, under immense pressure, was forced to hand the Abbey of Sant' Antimo to the state, for which they received not one single lira. Lax monks had been turned out of the abbey and it had been abandoned for hundreds of years, it was disintegrating, but at least it was saved from squalor and swine. In 1979 three young men left Normandy, in France, believing this place of antiquity would be their spiritual home, but another twelve years passed before these brothers, wandering on Tuscan soil under Mount Amiata, rested their sandalled feet under the table in a barely habitable monastery.'

The Canons Regular of the Abbey of Sant' Antimo have exorcized man's negligence. In my mind's eye I am on my pew in the abbey and see the rising sun pierce the arched window and radiate the apse, falling lightly on the hoods and capes around the shoulders of the chanting brothers, a glad melody rejoices and the sacred stones in the Abbey of Sant' Antimo begin to sing.

Rounding the shoulder of a hill, the village coming into view along the ridge in the distance is Montalcino. We dip into a gully where olive trees clothe the hill in neat rows, but the hill and grove shut us off from our home. 'In ten minutes we will be at the gates of the fortress,' promises Ilio. Overwhelmed by our walk in the wild, for it is two o'clock in the afternoon, my mind is cluttered with birds and berries and kings and their crowns, with betrayal by monks, evicted pigs and purple figs. For the first time since our walk began my eyes blink with tiredness; struggling up the last hill my legs drag. As we turn down the slope towards the gates of the fortress, something is going on. Two carabinieri on black motorcycles are speeding away, following a police car, and the fire brigade truck, engine rumbling, is parked over the road. But there's no fire. Yelling into cellular phones, all at once the firemen jump into the truck and with the engine screaming, roar past us back up the hill. 'Seems like they are going to the woods,' Ilio asserts. 'Ilio!' I am again aghast. 'We have forgotten your car . . . we left it at the wood pile, we *drove* to the woods this morning!' He laughs as he opens his rucksack. 'No it isn't. As a matter of fact it is sitting in my garage. My friends picked it up ten minutes after we began our walk.' Relief flows over me – for one agonizing moment I thought we might have to walk back to the woods. With relief comes a yawn wide enough to bring tears to my eyes, and when my mouth gulps in wallops of air and my jaw bangs shut I am obliquely considering how to thank Ilio. Words seem banal after he has shared so much with me. But he would not like me to shower him with praise. 'Allora,' he defeats me, 'these are for you and Luigi – can you leave the tin at Fiaschetteria for me? Anyway, we'll see each other there in the morning.' I take the tin, weakened by his generosity, and we part. Ilio walks to the nearest bar to find out what all the fuss is about.

Yawning distorts my face and I drag my aching legs down the hill, clutching the tin lined with leaves hiding rows of beautiful purple figs. Some we will eat this evening with prosciutto, but I think I will use some in a recipe with duck. My friend Maria Pia's recipe. She sometimes cooks duck at Taverna del Grappolo Blu, which she manages with her husband, Luciano. Disentangling my shoulders and arms from the rucksack as I climb the stairs, trying not to tilt the tin, I see in front of my eyes a glass of red wine, and recipes, and a longish siesta. Luigi opens the door at the top of the stairs and looks out. 'Ciao, ciao!' I say, stifling a yawn. 'Ciao,' he replies. 'Did you meet anyone else in the woods?' Yawning widely, I shake my head, at which he says: 'Strange, the place is crawling with carabinieri and tracker dogs, hunters have gone to help as well. They have been in the woods since early this morning.' 'Why?' is all I can say, my yawns suddenly gone. 'Because before dawn Piero, from Osteria Porta al Cassero, took his eighty-year-old father-in-law porcini hunting – he goes every year – but somehow they got separated and the old man is lost. Piero tried to find him, but could not, so he raised the alarm and thirty hunters who know the woods got a search going. The carabinieri and fire brigade are searching too, combing the woods on foot, and a helicopter is on the way, but if shrouds of white mist envelop the hills the helicopter will be useless.'

Ilio and I walked for seven hours hearing nothing and seeing no one. The image of an elderly man struggling through dense undergrowth sends a shiver up my spine. Those wild woods stretch for thousands of hectares, and wild boar are roaming, foraging for food. 'Piero is frantic,' Luigi goes on, 'cannot believe that in two or three minutes he could lose him, but his yells were useless, so are barking dogs and whistles because his father-in-law is sordo . . . deaf as a post. They have got to find him before the white mist comes down – he may not survive a freezing night in the woods.'

Collapsed on my bed, scanning recipes, dreaming about the iron crown of a Longobard king and evicted pigs, sipping a glass of bel vino and peeling a purple fig, I suspect Ilio has, after all, gone back to the woods to help with the search. But Ilio is rather more than a rough mountain man.

CHAPTER ELEVEN

Flowerpot Men Prop up
the Crumbling Altar

Of all the intriguing festivals and feast days in Italy, none, on the face of it, is quite as bizarre as the Day of the Dead. Buried, so to speak, somewhere in the psyche of the nation is an untroubled and convenient demarcation between death and the dead.

Unwritten etiquette forbids the first to be spoken of face to face, and if whispered, the sign of the cross is swiftly sketched to avert simulacrum lest it bring the worst of all deaths, a violent one, upon the living. A cosy coexistence of opposed feelings brings mental equilibrium. A good part of the morning of the Day of the Dead I passed with Amelia and, as this is the first Dead that I, too, have a departed friend to remember, I found the commemoration bewildering. We walked arm in arm to the cemetery carrying potted chrysanthemums and squat red candles, uniting along the way with friends, all smiling and similarly burdened. Together, a band of chattering pilgrims bound by our wistful journey, we beautified the cemetery, spruced up the gravestones and swept the marble doorways along the roads to sepulchral vaults, watering and weeding, passing a frond of greenery to a neighbour. Amelia bobbed from one grave to another, conversing amiably with the recently bereaved sitting on the edge of marble tombs while the beautiful dead in their black and white photographs watched on. By the time an hour had passed even the humblest tomb looked spectacular, bright with gorgeous blooms and flickering candles. When it was time to leave cheery ciaos and arrivedercis ricocheted across the lofty sepulchres and echoed round the marble slabs. Amelia, giving Bruno a final rub round with a damp cloth, half turned and blew a kiss to her first daughter, calling: 'Ciao, ciao, amore, un baccio, si vediamo domani.' Goodbye darling, here's a kiss, I'll see you in the morning.

Back in Australia, my first husband reposes in a deserted place where only the most recently grief-stricken can be found crouching by a new grave, shedding tears, submerged in the rawness of separation. My rare visits were made under angry sufferance. A crushing sense of affliction enveloped me when I walked between the tombs of the dead and iron picket fences, passing graves on which spindly flowers died months ago and plots were overgrown with weeds and thistles. Finding his grave occupied a few minutes, and my emotional state was one of cross ridiculousness at even being there, because my mind pretended, for I know not what dark reason, that I had forgotten precisely where he lies, and perhaps I should not find him. But I always did. Staring at the cold black marble, reading youthful words of love tinged with the horror of violent death, tears flooded my eyes and within thirty seconds I turned my back and strode belligerently through the gates, determined only to put the affliction under cover.

Italians visit the dead as if they are alive in the tomb. Instead of fear and foreboding, or anger, Amelia and I smiled as we parted from Bruno, spick and span, then she blew a kiss to Silena, enveloped in gorgeous white blooms. Instead of pain, our journey home was filled with loving memories and calm togetherness, and instead of pushing Bruno further into netherland the Day of the Dead binds us ever closer. Perhaps, at Christmas, when for the first time in many years Amelia will not press my door bell, beckon me to follow her across the cobbled road to her kitchen, and, for my Christmas gift, open a square of damask holding Bruno's walnut-stuffed figs, perhaps then, for a while, I will be sad because Bruno, too, walked in the woods to gather wild figs. It is persuasive to imagine him at the leafy tree to which Ilio took me. Bruno would have known the criss-cross tracks to the charcoal burner's camp, and to the Longobard tower.

When the wailing siren sounded it was pitch dark. Piero's father-in-law had been lost in the woods for twelve hours but our firemen stumbled across him at dusk, kilometres away from where Piero lost him, near to Castello Romitorio – but he could not see the castle because of dense vegetation. He was fighting his way through tangled undergrowth, scratched, tired and cold, but his determined efforts had kept his body warm. Fortunately, although he strayed into the hunting wood, he was not confronted by foraging wild boar; if they were watching him he did not hear anything terrifying, because of his deafness. It was almost dark when the firemen, whose calls and whistles he did not hear, tapped him on the shoulder and brought him out of the woods, calling Piero on the radio, who rushed to the castle in a four-wheel-drive vehicle. Piero said the old man had the biggest grin on his face that he had ever seen. 'Don't worry, son,' he said, 'I've still got the porcini, I didn't lose them!' Over his shoulder, knotted to the end of a stick, hung a net sack of porcini mushrooms. Piero fairly cried at his lugubrious wit, but declared his octogenarian mushrooming days were over.

Cold November days close round our hill, the afternoons sink into greyness and petulant winds rise from the mountains bringing a blast of dire winter swirling into our homes when we open the door even a crack. Wood chopping on the roadway at the foot of our stairs has come to an end. Load after load of logs, as fathers and sons wielded axes, were tossed into baskets by mothers in pinafores and daughters in coats, dragged a couple of steps to the door, then manhandled down a stairwell to the cantina and stacked wall to wall in the dark depths; a hoard to warm the hearth, and to cook with, all through winter, near at hand. Walking around the walls in winds which buffet and push, whistling past my ears and occasionally whipping the hat from my head and tugging at my hair, is a stubborn battle of will.

There are no workers in the vineyards; the vines have commenced their decline into slumber. Foliage is sparse and only crinkled orange and golden leaves persist, dancing merrily from stalks where, by a thread from an earlier battle, they hopelessly clutch at the vine. The longest branches were trimmed, cuttings piled into bonfires and the entangled tendrils ignited and puffed back to grey ashes. Thin branches are imprisoned along wires; they will remain tied to the wire through the winter. Soon the last dancing leaves will be stripped away by a determined wind, branches will freeze dry into brittleness and, waiting for spring, the grower will cut them away too; only gnarled trunks will stand, waiting for wriggling rootlets to stir, writhing between tree roots and shale crevices in their dark world under the earth.

In the cantina, predictably, Enzo paints bizarre images, visualizing billions of workers self-destructing in a suicidal frenzy. 'Once the grapes were separated from the stalks a delicate press patted and paddled them, gently rupturing the skin, but without bruising – it must be non-violent because if grapes are squashed and bashed, in the end you will taste it in your glass. The grapes, that is, ruptured skins, with pips, pulp and juice, were fed into fermentation tanks. Come and listen to a ferocious battle . . . enzymes are boiling themselves into a chemical frenzy.' I put my ear to the stainless steel tank and listen to a gurgling, hissing sound, like effervescent Alka-seltzer spitting and dissolving. 'We call it must in the tank, rather than juice, because if it was only juice, I would not end up with Brunello. I need the skins, and the pips and little bits of stalk that may have slipped through, and the fleshy pulp of the grape, as well as juice, with which to make Brunello.' Enzo's penetrating eyes stare brightly into mine when he talks, his hands clapping together with a bang, then breaking apart as he dramatically demonstrates. 'And I need fission –' he claps his hands together – 'by millions of microscopic cells that split and reproduce and release energy into a foaming frenzy of froth and bubbles. What you hear is the must at war with itself.'

What I see, climbing a steel ladder and peering over the rim of the tank, resembles nothing I could ever bring myself to drink. The must is clouded and muddy, cluttered with particles of pulp, bits of skin and stalk, and disengaged pips floating around in the turbid violence. My face, I am sure, looks less encouraging than Enzo's enthusing words. 'Sunshine sweetens grapes and the sugar in the tank is the key to spontaneous metamorphosis, because the amount of sugar affects the degree of alcohol. But the sugar can do nothing alone!' This earnest doctor of oenology is enthusing himself into a mad, agitated scientist, waving his arms vigorously. 'All around us, on the grapes, perhaps carried in the wind, out there on the tractor or on the stalks are yeast cells. Scientists are puzzled because they cannot always find them where they expect . . . but yeasts are in the tank and they need energy to reproduce themselves. They get that energy from sugar.'

His voice softens to whispered intrigue. 'Inside that tank this turbid must is working itself into unmitigated fury. Yeast cells start fermenting the sugar and reproducing themselves, splitting and reproducing again and again . . . astonishingly fast. Just think: if this tank began with half a dozen yeast cells, in a couple of days there will be seventy million deranged cells racing round and round in the turbulence searching for sugar, creating bubbles of gas, carting around the solids and swirling it all into a delirious frenzied mass.'

He sees my doubting eyes, partly I doubt because I do not recall learning precisely what fermentation is, but Enzo is enthralled with his own exploding plot. To me it seems like science fiction. 'Fermentation raises the temperature and under the immense pressure from rising gas, skins and solids are propelled to the top of the tank where they slam into one another.' One hand is out flat, the other bashing into it from below, but I get the picture. 'Slowly the tangled mess is pushed up and out of the must by the force of boiling bubbling rising gas. The ejected solids form a shell, untidily battered together like a badger's habitat, which we call a pomace. The pomace is pushed up and rises higher and higher out of the must and, as you would imagine, begins to harden.' Encouragingly, I nod, on the pretext that I can well imagine the effect. 'Any solids that were too heavy to be propelled to the top of the tank, maybe stalks that have latched on to pips and a bit of skin, drift to the bottom and stay there – that's why the tank is shaped like a cone. That is what is happening right now. Just imagine: the waste solids have dropped to the bottom, but a tangled foaming pomace is hardening at the top, kept up there by turbulent gas and boiling bubbles. But what do you think is going on in between? The yeasts in the must in the middle of the tank are still furiously scavenging for more sugar in desperation to keep reproducing. The boiling turbulence in this tank is awesome! Now I'll tell you the miraculous part.' Enzo can already see the miracle and cannot wait to let me into the final act. 'All this fuss is going to end. The yeasts, delirious with joy while they ferment sugar, do not know that as well as reproducing themselves, they discharge enzymes and, inadvertently, in the process turn the must toxic with alcohol. They can only reproduce as long as there is sugar in the tank – it is chemical warfare – but when all the sugar is converted into alcohol, there is nothing left for yeasts to do, because alcohol poisons yeasts! The deranged yeast cells self-destruct in a suicidal frenzy. This is nature's miracle, the mystery which creates wine.'

Enzo explains that the pomace is not waste because it contains tannins that are important to the structure of the wine, and all those beautiful purple skins trapped in the pomace give the wine its ruby colour, and pips and bits of stalk contribute to the flavour and complexity. He does not let the pomace harden into a solid crackling cap because from time to time he syphons must from the middle of the tank and pumps it over the top, softening the pomace and sending skins and pips and bits of stalk floating right back into the tank. The must turns ruby as hue is extracted from the skins.

'When the yeast cells are dead, and the sugar is converted to alcohol, fermentation is finished.' But Enzo is not. 'Then I will drain away the solids in the cone at the bottom, and when I judge that it is no longer beneficial to extract more colour or tannin or flavour, I drain the wine from the pomace. And then I have to tranquillize the wine; it has been subjected to explosive violence, but it is brimful of the most marvellous bouquets and colour – everything it needs to become a structured, complex wine. Very gently, without shaking the wine around because I don't want it splashing and dispersing bouquet before I get it to the cantina, I feed it into oak casks. Slowly it recovers from the shock of chemical warfare and begins to work its own miracle, beginning a long journey through time in the cool silence of my cantina. The wine sleeps; but I will hear it whispering because the wine in the cask is not static; it is living and growing into greatness. I harvested fewer grapes because I drastically reduced the clusters, but the quality of each cluster was good and unlike some growers whose vines suffered shock after shock during the growing year I believe mine will be a discreet Brunello. But I will not know its individual character until, four years from now, I awaken the wine. You will have to come back in four years if you want to see what this harvest has given me.'

Walking back up the gravel track from Enzo's cantina a demonic wind forces me to bend forward; my coat billows and particles of gravel prickle my legs and, clasping my hat about my ears, I push into the gusts with half-closed eyes. This is my favourite season to walk round the walls of Montalcino. No one else is foolish enough. I have the whole valley, all the rolling hills and the distant purple mountains – the world as far as I can see – to myself. From the wall above the vineyard the vines seem distorted; bashed and buffeted, the stakes tilt at crazy angles, shuddering in the wind. A metabolic change has sent the life force deep underground. Like sleeping wine in the cask, the life in the vine will sleep in darkness all through an approaching winter.

The Sagra tournament is over. No more cooking in Pianello until our thank-you dinner, which we award ourselves, and at which Maurelia usually has us mapping out end-of-year celebrations. The days before the tournament vanished in a flurry of fun and bluster. Luciana bawled and bellowed, as is her want, panicking that forty-five kilos of gnocchi was not enough so she summoned us back to the kitchen and we began rolling all over again. Now we have left-over kilos in our freezer and will be eating gnocchi at our thank-you dinner, and probably at Christmas as well. For my tenth Sagra Luciana relented, but I am not confident that I have not been demoted. 'Ninni,' she hummed unctuously, 'leave the garlic, Ofelia is quicker . . . Go to that bench and peel those sausages.' My relief was short-lived because six-centimetre dried cinghiale sausages are fragments of granite and when I dug a knife in, to prick the filmy skin, wild boar sausages shot from my fingers and bounced on the floor, or skidded under the stove where, on my knees, my fingers felt goodness knows what horrors in the dark. Not once did a sausage fly with dexterity out of my hands and into the pot.

On tournament morning a roar from the piazza and Pianello chanting told us – because we cooks and sausage skinners were cooking and skinning in the kitchen – that young Filippo had been balloted in the draw. Sagra means a day of exhausting work for members with barely time to watch the parade; many are trapped in the fortress cooking and serving at a timber stand for thousands of visitors who feast all day on the food and wine of Montalcino. Those working in the sede kitchen, like me, see our archers and Pianello dame and knight, and the court attendants, when they return to the sede for lunch. We then have a five-course meal to serve to a couple of hundred visitors, and we clean up as quickly as we can and race to the campo, hoping to get in the gate and find a seat before the tournament starts. Filippo looked so small and young, but his friends yelled encouragement and he shot well in his first tournament for Pianello, but we did not win. Ruga are the victors; jubilant celebrations are under way. Their two archers did not miss a single arrow. Our youngsters raced on to the campo after the tournament because they knew Filippo would be distraught, and in a throng of supportive friends he was cheered from the shooting range. After months of dedication and sacrifice on the practice range the day of a tournament is emotionally draining, but Filippo's tears in defeat were soon wiped away as the young wrapped arms around him and assured him we are proud of his skill; he is a great archer, and there will be many more tournaments.

324

'Anyway, Filippo,' they consoled him, 'at least our worst enemy did not win!'

'Allora,' begins Maurelia at our post-Sagra debrief, 'I have some good news and some not so good.' Everybody groans, but this does not halt Maurelia, who ignores our interruptions and gathers us with the help of her favourite words. 'The good news is that the Comune has agreed to exempt Pianello from complying with modern building regulations. The mayor has agreed that, because San Pietro has been standing for a thousand years, it is not likely to slide down the hill this year or next, and although we must undertake repairs, we can have Mass said in our church whenever we wish, and engineers will start work to decide how we can hold up the altar while we try to find some funds.' In a sense this is good news, but as we do not have the money to carry out essential repairs it is academic, as Maurelia knows, and except for a desultory suggestion from Maria Rosa about when we should call the priest for Mass, causes hardly a ripple.

We are in the upstairs meeting room. Vittorio came early and lit a crackling fire; most of us sit on benches with our backs to the hearth letting the warmth seep in while the young rock back and forth on chair legs, twiddling with arrow heads . . . and it doesn't seem to worry Maurelia that Tomaso, drumsticks between his fingers, tum tum tums while she talks. Pianello meetings are known to be volatile, but tonight's meeting is neither challenging tradition nor demanding riveting concentration. And yet, with Maurelia's next words we are woken out of our yawning drowsiness. 'Comunque, it is time to hand over the reins. I have been president for many years, but my mother is ill and I must care for her. Però, we are working our way through the problems to do with San Pietro, and Pianello is moving forward; it seems a good moment for someone younger to take over. From tonight I am handing in my resignation.' At this thunderbolt the gathering livens and we gape in astonishment. Most of us had no inkling, but some of the elders nod their heads because they know the pressure Maurelia is under looking after her ill mother. This means a quartiere election. We are not yet recovered from Maurelia's dramatic declaration when Don Michele of the disco rumba, seizing the moment, jumps to his feet. 'I must tell you tonight. I waited till after Sagra to break the news . . . and it has not been a decision made lightly, but, well, Francesco and Cecilia and most of my friends already know that I am in love!' A cheer goes up from the young: 'Bravo! Bravo! Don Michele.' I thought this might be in the offing because I have spied Michele with a girl who has been cooking in two local restaurants. 'I am compelled to follow my heart, and Alida, my girlfriend, to Canada. We are opening a Tuscan restaurant serving Montalcinesi cuisine in Toronto! And,' he yells over the rising babble, 'in memory of all of you in Pianello, we are calling it Tutti Matti.' Overcome by Michele's emotional news we burst into happy cheers, thumping the table in unison and throwing him culinary advice about what he and Alida should put on the menu in a restaurant called Everyone's Crazy. The elders, who had no suspicion of this international love-match, murmur with consternation that times have changed alarmingly now that Carlo is married to Costanza from Montepulciano, and how peculiar it is that Michele, who was born within sight of our sede and grew from babyhood to manhood under their very eyes, surrounded by friends in Pianello, is journeying halfway round the world to eat the same food as he can eat right here!

'But I make a solemn pledge,' vows Michele, 'I promise that I will return to Montalcino every year for Apertura and Sagra.' Young and old, we crowd around and wish him well, but our elders look somewhat dismayed. It is time for change in Pianello.

The woods are mantled russet and purple, a hiding place for wild boar in cold lairs; only the hunters venture into their habitat and plunge along icy tracks at dawn. The temperature is dropping a degree or two each day. The crack-crack of the hunters' guns echo through the valley and up to the village as clearly as the hollow chimes from an abbey atop the lunar land of the Sienese craters. The ring of mountains that surround us looms closer, villages strung along faraway hilltops or clinging to river valleys are defined with such clarity that we see chimneys smoking, and in the limpid air the commanding ring of their church bells calling them to Mass echoes across to our hill. The sun arcs low and with its last rays a glowing ball streaks the reddening sky with fire and paints the clouds purple before it drops behind a crown of mountains, pulling after it the brilliance of a late November sunset.

One harvest is still to be brought in. Olives are on the verge of maturity, ripening quickly; growers consult almanacs and stare into the sky, waiting, hoping the wind will stay away and these limpid days and flaming sunsets endure. Monolithic grinding wheels and stone canals to carry the murky slush to coiled mats are clean and ready. Nets are unrolled and loosely spread beneath trunks along with olive baskets, and tapered ladders are wedged into branches. The decision to harvest is always a last minute one and when picking begins the hours pass in feverish work to pick and deliver the fruit to the mill in time for the grower to inspect the olives crushed before his. He needs to be sure that his olives will not be tainted if a careless grower has not been watchful because he may have left dirt on his olives, or worse, let them sit in sacks overnight with a risk of mould on a damp dawn.

Our landlady, Lola, taught me how to preserve olives a season ago. Her lessons are not without stern censure – she rattles instructions with the wave of an arm, always alluding to how simple everything is; but this one I memorized because few steps are involved. I am not certain, though, that Lola thinks well of my preserved olives. Over the years Luigi and I have shared scrumptious lunches and dinners of hand-rolled pasta and ragù sauce, roasted livers, wild boar and rosemary polenta, and pasta al forno with Ercole and Lola in their home. In winter we huddle around the girarrosto, rotating roasting spit, in the tiny dining room. Ercole is a retired school teacher, painstakingly deliberate in his ways whereas Lola is a sprightly woman who adores chatter, exhibits an exceedingly dry wit and darts about ordering Ercole to do this or that just when he is settling into a lengthy conversation. When I drum up courage we periodically return the gesture and courteously request they visit us in our apartment, which is why I am not certain of her precise adjudication of my preserved olives, which she sampled last week. When Ercole and Lola come to lunch my culinary artfulness is under scrutiny and I am anxious to make a bella figura, a good impression, because with Lola, as with all Tuscans, and any Italian, food is a philosophy for life.

Concealed behind my kitchen shutter I listen to Lola instructing Ercole which buzzer he should press – notwithstanding we live in an apartment they own, and to which Ercole finds his way unassisted and alone most mornings, buzzing the buzzer and beginning each day passing a few cheery words with Luigi. I do not cook my famous dish, which has become legendary in Montalcino, for Lola and Ercole, although I have been tempted. When Ofelia and Massimo, or Maurelia and Roberto come to dinner, they are thrilled when I cook Indian or Thai green curry – Ofelia is excited to be tasting eastern and Asian flavours, as we did in Rome – but next morning, when I reach the piazza, gossip is in the bar before me. 'Oh, Signora,' they are bursting to tell me, 'we hear Maurelia has eaten foreign food at your home last evening!'

On the other hand, when Lola comes to lunch or dinner I am not inclined to be rolling pasta by hand, fearful that I may fail her scrutiny and my reputation, struggling for survival, may suffer irreparable damage. Poring over recipes that might be acceptable for Lola's taste buds, and within cooee of my culinary ability, I came across pumpkin and chickpea purée, which I thought might be marvellous for an early-winter lunch. Then I stuffed chicken breasts with ricotta, spinach and pine nuts, spending the entire day before and all that morning preparing our feast, including a triumphant dessert of lime and lemon poppy seed cake.

Lunch did not get off to a flying start and my heart wilted under her humour. 'Oh! Cara,' she cooed with a puckish laugh, 'I remember this flavour, when we were poor we made chickpea soup, forty years ago, when there was nothing else in the cupboard!' Murmuring how much I adore the nutty flavour of chickpeas I lapped up two bowls of soup, trying not to turn pink at her vague disapproval. I don't know if word went round the village that I served Lola the dregs from the cupboard that the poorest of the poor always kept to hand, but I suspect not, for Lola admonishes me, never unkindly, but with humorous matriarchal guidance. The chicken was agreeable, so I was momentarily redeemed, but she was genuinely perplexed that I purchased ricotta at this time of year, which she did not think could be had from any *reputable* farmer, because the sheep are pregnant right now, aren't they? And as well, the accompanying salad was not to her liking because I added crispy pancetta to the greens, together with a few walnut halves; these flavours were *interesting*, but *raw* walnuts and *burnt* pancetta were bothersome to bite into for someone as old as she. Pregnant sheep did not enter my thoughts when I planned lunch, but Lola judiciously added to my knowledge – no more ricotta until the lambs are born in spring – and I think, after all, my own mother would probably find raw nuts and crispy pancetta less than agreeable. Hiding in the salad were a few of my preserved black olives, to which Lola did not refer. To the table I waltzed with la torta, confident that this fluffy white creation, borne high on a glass platter and ceremoniously settled between us, would be a sparkling way to end lunch with an impressive flourish. My own hands whisked, for what seemed like hours, the tangy lemon curd and I spent an hour grating undersized limes until the particles were not even the dimension of desiccated coconut. The recipe called for cream, which Tuscans rarely put in or on anything, so instead, throwing caution and waistline to the wind, I extravagantly encased the whole torta in mascarpone, titivated into a fantasy with deft swirls of a knife. 'Your torta is exquisite my dear,' pronounced Lola with a smile, 'but I wish you had not mixed in these annoying gritty black poppy seeds, which get stuck in one's teeth.'

Lunch together, nevertheless, with these two octogenarians, is always fun and Lola's sharp wit keeps me on my toes. They have lived their whole lives inside the walls, and this is where they will end them. After they had left, when washing up I found hiding under Lola's lettuce leaf one small pip, but beside it were three untouched black olives.

A swinging debate has been raging for weeks between the Mayor of Montalcino and those opposed to a car park inside the walls, or, more precisely, the destruction of the olive grove. 'When the rest of the world is banning traffic from cities and towns, when we must care for the environment, when noise and traffic in medieval villages rock the foundations and threaten the safety of our children who go to school inside the walls, why are you obstinately proceeding with this madness?' Letters for and against lead the reader round in circles. My appointment with Mayor Massimo has forced me to turn my mind to the problems Montalcino faces. 'Isabella,' he begged, 'you have to see a wider picture, bigger than the one you see when you walk inside the walls.' Massimo is a young, alert politician. His policies, for he represents the Democratic Party of the Left which broke away from the mainstream Italian Communist Party, he emphatically parallels with those of Tony Blair and former President Clinton. But his doublespeak chain of reasoning left me dumbfounded. 'You are absolutely one hundred per cent right,' he exclaimed, thumping the table with his fist, and then, opening his pleading hands wide, went on, 'but so am I – because it must be viable to live in Montalcino in the modern world, otherwise we force our citizens to move out of the walls, and, Isabella, that rings the death knell! We are a small population with a huge territory, our school buses travel eight hundred kilometres a day and our coffers are never full because agricultural producers are not taxed like factories and big business. I am walking a tightrope. We lead tranquil lives, safe inside our walls, and I will not let

Montalcino die, but there is a cost. The car park must proceed because I will not make life intolerable for our business people and our young. We need hairdressers and doctors, people must be able to see a solicitor and pay car insurance, visit the dentist and be able to purchase more than ceramic plates and bottles of wine, even if Brunello is our greatest ambassador. Have you seen what has happened in some medieval villages? People are forced to travel out of the village to carry out their daily lives, young families leave because the school is too far away, or there are no medical facilities and, vital to a small community, a social breakdown occurs and the very things that bind the village together, like our four quartieri, can no longer survive because members do not live in their quartiere any more, they spread too widely, no longer tied to their roots! In Montalcino we are different: there is too much at stake, we have an identity, values, and we defiantly protect our rebellious history, reliving and teaching it to our children through our quartieri and at every tournament and festival.'

His assertions are confirmed in newspaper reports I have read about San Gimignano, a gorgeous village to our north. Their mayor is worried because another newsagent has closed, and because only one shop in the village sells clothes for citizens and only two alimentari, grocers, are still open for business. Not so many years ago San Gimignano had tailors, shoemakers, woodworkers, butchers, iron workers and the citizens would gather in Piazza Cisterna to discuss politics and football, or read the paper. But the life of San Gimignano is vanishing. Tourists pour through the gates every morning, barely able to see above a throng of bobbing heads to admire the stupendous medieval village around them. Citizens have been forced out, deprived even of buying a newspaper. Massimo pointed out that

Montalcino is not a tourist town. That is not to say that tourists are not welcome, but an economy firmly based in agriculture means we are not reliant on tourism. Montalcino is a thriving village with a life unto itself, whether tourists are here on not, and it is this fluid vibration, this confident sense of being, that perceptive visitors adore when they poke around among our homes and monuments. Nothing is put on, there is no façade, no pretence of *Italy for tourists*. Not even the archery tournaments, which are an expression of the defiance and tenacity of the Ilcinesi, are staged with their comfort in mind. A few visitors wander into the piazza and stay for an hour, not able to comprehend why they are here; others understand, receding into the background, watching, sipping wine and listening to the daily exchanges. They visit the churches, the museums and walk around the gardens; they linger because Montalcino exudes its enigmatic Italian-ness . . . all those paradoxical signals that lure them to Italy are here.

But even as the mayor spoke, thumping jack hammers were drilling into boulders that formed the walls behind which the Montalcinesi sheltered from enemies camped in the valley. Some of the olive trees still stand, shaken, but the hillside is denuded. Anger rises when we walk round the wall and see the mayhem the yellow Caterpillar and thumping hammers are wreaking.

'We welcome visitors,' finished Massimo, 'residents need to park cars, and so do visitors. But we have to keep our eye on the future, even if our hearts are in the past. We dwell in an enviable ambience, no factories pollute our air, our village is immersed in chestnuts and vines on a hilltop in a glorious part of the world, but we have to accept that there is a price to be paid, and if living inside the walls is not viable for young residents, and we force them to leave, then who will pay? We will uphold our traditions, we will never lose our identity, and Montalcino will never fade, but some things must change; that is why we are losing Luciano, our shoemaker.' I am saddened to learn that at the end of the year our very last shoemaker will close his workshop. Once it was profitable to be a cobbler, but now people buy new shoes that cost less than he charges to mend old ones. When Luciano no longer hammers on his last the only reminder of centuries of the tanners and leather workers of Montalcino will vanish. I have passed many happy moments waiting for a hole in a belt, or the heel on a shoe, but payment by way of caffè is no just reward for Luciano. Even so, I cannot accept destruction of an olive grove and ancient walls. I remain firm in support of our fighting committee.

'Dai, ascolta! Ragazzi! Listen up everyone! I have drawn two numbers and here is your clue; the first is bigger than the second, and the total of the two numbers is forty-six. Who has the winning ticket?' Fabio is enjoying himself, drawing prize-winning tickets in a raffle at Pianello using nonsensical mathematical riddles. 'It's mine, it's mine!' The claimant is Cecilia's grandmother, well into her eighties – I cannot believe she has beaten me to working out the winning number. 'No!' thunders Fabio, when she triumphantly holds up her ticket. 'Anyway, you cannot win, because Cecilia donated the prize, so you are excluded.' She wails that this ruling was not explained when she purchased her ticket, but Fabio is not listening, he is yelling over the top of her that the second number is half of the total of the first, plus the number of days in November! Cohorts Lorenzo and Gabriele heighten the confusion, calling out wrong numbers, raising the hopes of baffled ticket holders. The young fall about laughing, watching us frown and shuffle little squares of green and pink paper on the table, trying to fathom ridiculous riddles. 'Yes!' Fabio's voice rises in exultation, 'You win!' It is Luciana, and Fabio directs Davide to give our head cook a flowerpot holding a pink azalea.

The flowerpot raffle is Vittorio's idea. He is always thinking of ways to raise money for San Pietro and is determined to begin fundraising to prop up our collapsing altar, so he organized the flowerpots, and appointed the flowerpot men. Fabio banters good-naturedly, dismisses claims of foul play and feigns throat-clutching horror that he could be accused of skulduggery. Luigi ate with us but was obliged to leave early because he is attending a meeting of the football club, but every table is occupied; many members who came home to Montalcino to help with the mammoth work involved in staging the Sagra have come to the dinner as well. Luciana passed round the table twice, trying to coax us into yet another plate of gnocchi . . . but we are gnocchied out. At the end of the raffle when eight flowerpots have been won, Vittorio dives under a table and brings out a cardboard box and the flowerpot men present flowerpots to all the women who cooked for Sagra. So the winners go home with two – but we all bought tickets in the raffle anyway, so we really paid for our own flowerpots, and Vittorio raised a little money for our altar.

We are enjoying a relaxed night in our sede, thanking ourselves with our thank-you dinner, and afterwards Maurelia will disclose the result of our elections. But first she must report to us on a meeting she attended with the other three quartieri presidents to spare Montalcino from bedlam during the Sagra. The number of visitors who come to the Sagra and drink excessively continues to increase. This year it was beyond our village polizia to control thousands of cars trying to park, because eighteen thousand people made their way here from all over Italy, and even further afield, for a weekend of eating and drinking. The carabinieri marshal was compelled to deal with inebriated visitors from Pistoia who unwisely became involved in a boxing match, with our police! The most titanic carabinieri officer I have ever seen sorted out the tangle with his own hands . . . and Signor Pistoia did not come out of it the better. Public inebriation and delinquent behaviour is foreign to Montalcino. Fighting and such like happen down *there*, they do not happen up *here*, inside *our* walls. 'So,' says Maurelia, 'the presidents are putting a proposal before the mayor and marshal.' We have been facing the prospect of change for a number of years, which is worrying because if we do not have annual income from the Sagra, then we will never be able to raise the money to restore the church of San Pietro. We hit upon the idea of inviting people from all over the world to take up honorary membership of Pianello and donations to our fundraising help. We have honorary members in many countries who want to help us save our altar, and our church, but it will need to grow to an avalanche before we can begin work on San Pietro. With changes looming for Sagra we dare not take out a loan, even a favourable low interest one, lest we find ourselves in a financial bog in the future.

'Però,' Maurelia begins again, 'I need to report back that we in Pianello are in agreement with the proposal.' Nobody says a word, allowing Maurelia to invite us to put forward our thoughts when she finishes explaining. 'There will be no more feasting in the fortress. We cannot accept the dreadful behaviour of a few nuisances who come only to drink to excess and ruin our festival. Instead, visitors can book into one of our quartieri to taste our cuisine and our wine . . . magari, we can have two sittings to bring is a bit more income.' Moaning sounds come from one of the tables, grumbles about a drastically reduced income, but Maurelia is ready. 'You are right, but listen a moment, because instead of concentrating all our efforts on the one weekend of the Sagra we propose that the whole month of October be dedicated to our festival, culminating in the historic parade and archery tournament on the last weekend.' Some of us have been involved with Maurelia in hammering out the proposal, and our verbal support for her words quietens the others, so she goes on. 'Each of the quartieri must agree to develop their own folkloristic and cultural events throughout the month. For instance, Fabio proposes that, because we have so many wine producers in Pianello, for three weekends before Sagra we will offer visitors a genuine Ilcinese dinner in our sede accompanied by the wines of Montalcino . . . including Brunello from our own producers.' Vittorio is standing, anxious to speak, so Maurelia relents. 'Why don't we organize some kind of concert in San Pietro?' he ventures, 'and another thing, we could offer guided visits to San Pietro and our sede. Isabella,' he turns to me, demanding, 'would you and Luigi help? Then we can offer guided visits to foreigners as well.' I nod my head becuase the noise level is rising and no one would hear me above the din. In Pianello, when ideas start flowing it always takes a few minutes before Maurelia can rein in control. Caught up in the excitement, I raise my hand and Maurelia bangs the desk and calls order so that I can speak. 'I think Vittorio's idea is wonderful . . . a musical evening in San Pietro . . . and, well, my mother earned heaps of money every time she organised a cake stall for our church . . . why don't we do that?' Every eye is upon me but not a word is uttered. Maurelia comes to my rescue. 'Isabella! You will have to explain what a cake stall is!' Everyone laughs, trying to pronounce the words and dream up recipes, ingredients which could never end up in a cake stall. I eagerly agree that crocetti will be perfect. Maurelia sums up: 'Comunque, I can report to the other presidents that we are in agreement with the proposal. It means our work will be spread over the month of October, but that will help us recoup a portion of our lost income from the feasting at the Sagra. Most important of all, a month of cultural and gastronomic events means all the quarters can work towards retrieving our Sagra, the medieval parade and archery tournament from the grip of inebriated nuisances. If they turn up there will be no food or drink in the fortress and we believe that after a year of two they'll simply stop coming.' Maurelia allows a few minutes for us to discuss among ourselves the pros and cons of all this, but then she draws us back to the present because we still have to talk about end-of-year celebrations and plan our winter programme.

'I know,' ventures Fiorella, 'let's have a games night. It is always fun when the fire is blazing and we set up the board games.' The young are not enamoured with her idea. 'Fiorella, not again, we have games every year . . . We are tired of Ludo and Monopoly! Can't we do something different?' Maurelia, sensing a minor rebellion, asks what they would like to do. While the young form a huddle and appoint a spokesperson, the rest of us vote in favour of a fish dinner a couple of days before Christmas. 'Va bene,' jokes Riccardo, pulling his head out of the huddle, 'I undertake to order extra toilet paper!' We all break out laughing, clutching our stomachs and yelling comical abuse at him, remembering the last time we had a fish dinner, because something went horribly wrong – we queued up at the toilet for an hour!

The young have worked out their plans and Maurelia sums up. 'Allora, this is our end-of-year programme. A fish dinner two days before Christmas, Massimo is in charge of ordering fresh fish from the fish man when he comes the Friday before, and he will organize his helpers. A pizza dinner the night after Boxing Day, Santo Stefano's day . . . Armando will make three sorts of pizza with help from Cinquino, Gabriele and Davide. And that night the board games will be in the upstairs room for those who want to play. You young ones are responsible for setting up your own bar-disco in the downstairs dining room on New Year's Eve, and you are inviting your own friends from the other quartieri as well. The bar-disco will be open to all quartieranti up till ten o'clock, and after that those of a certain age will go home and leave the disco to the youngsters.'

One by one our plans are finalized. Quartiere life ties us to each other, a pivotal point for social as well as traditional and cultural events, narrowing the gap between family, extended family and neighbourhood. I am unceasingly impressed with the young, not just in Pianello, but in all the quartieri. They have initiative enough to organize their own entertainment in Montalcino and they are cheerfully agreeable to having older quartiere members join them to get their night off to a fun start with music and dancing, young and old together. Their sense of unity and identity, which Mayor Massimo talked of, is accentuated with quartiere life, tying the young to the village.

'We still have to think about Epiphany,' murmurs Maurelia, 'but last year we left it all in the hands of Francesco, Samuele and Samanta who organized a fabulous party with a Befana, witch, for the children. Why don't we do the same this year?' Everyone agrees. The young are growing into their responsibility.

'Va bene,' Maurelia exhales, 'I am about to perform my last duty as President. I have signed nominations here on the table, and all the votes have been counted. Before we announce the results and I join you as a quartierante instead of president, I must give you one more piece of thrilling news.'

Could this be something to do with the Sagra, or San Pietro? When Maurelia keeps news to herself and then prepares us for something we do not know about, we get nervous, but she did say thrilling. 'Allora, Carlo would tell you himself if he were here, but he is working in Milan for a few more months, then he will return to Tuscany and live in the countryside with Costanza, who some of you met at the wedding. Soon we will have a new member in Pianello. Carlo and Costanza are expecting a baby!'

A new baby is wonderful news in Montalcino and we pour bubbly congratulations on the nonna to be. When we quieten, Maurelia announces the result of our election, our new President thanks outgoing officers, and our evening comes to a close. I bid farewell to my Pianello family, Dottore Luciano and Maria Rosa, Fiorella and Claudio, Vittorio and Ofelia and Massimo, and as I turn towards Ercole and Lola I call out arrivederci to our huddled young. They turn and respond ciao, waving arms and smiling, but they are distracted planning their bar-disco. A young man rises from their table and calls to me. 'Excuse me, Signora, before you go, my grandfather has asked me to let you know that he is awaiting your next visit. He has arranged for a workman to unbolt the door of the Protestant chapel.'

Luigi and I live lower down the hill but it is our habit to link arms with Ercole and Lola and walk four abreast up the hill to their doorway. Tonight we walk three abreast. Ercole and Lola do not come to all Pianello functions, especially in winter, but tonight was our thank-you dinner and an election, so even our octogenarians were present. We exchange an affectionate goodnight kiss and, clutching my potted azalea, I walk through the dark towards home. Silvano has delivered a welcome message from his grandfather, which I will heed forthwith, and on top of that, the night delivered a request from our new President. Light blinks through the slats in the shutter; it is almost midnight, and Luigi is home before me. He is full of smiles when I walk in the door, confronting him with the news. 'Guess what? Carlo and Costanza are having a baby!' That said, I move into the main bulletin. 'The results of our election are final; guess who is our new President?' Men do not like participating in guessing games, so I tell him. 'We have a young President, Maria-Teresa . . . but we did not know whether to cheer or cry . . . because guess what?' He still does not want to guess. 'Her boyfriend is a Borghetto archer!' He raises his eyebrows, suitably impressed. I give him the next titbit. 'I don't quite know how,' I feign modesty, 'but I have been elected Secretary of Pianello!' To which he responds, 'Congratulations! We are both up to our ears . . . Tonight I was elected Secretary of the football club!' We both burst out laughing, shaking our heads with amused joy.

In my hand is a gold-embossed envelope that Maria-Teresa handed to me at the end of our elections, saying, 'Isabella, we have both been elected, but I have a problem. Maurelia has given me this invitation, but I am committed to a school teachers' meeting in Arezzo on the date, and, although it is addressed to the President, would you be free to represent Pianello, as Secretary?' Not even knowing what was in the envelope, and sanctimonious about my first responsibility as Secretary, I responded with enthusiasm. 'It begins at four in the afternoon, which is when they will officially open an on-line Museo di Brunello, and Stefano and his mother, Signora Francesca

Colombini, have invited all the quartieri presidents to dinner in the cantina at Fattoria dei Barbi.' My first duty as Pianello Secretary is going to let me meet and talk with the descendants of one of Brunello di Montalcino's founding families.

We have not yet passed the winter solstice but wood fires are burning in the late afternoon, shuttered windows close out the chill and we withdraw into our warm homes, darkened by five o'clock. Our fire is allowed to die and becomes glowing embers in the night, and the house becomes tepid till the hearth is rekindled with dry brush and twigs in time for breakfast. We feed it chopped logs in the morning, so we are cosy for pranzo, but the chill wind in the afternoon turns it greedy and it consumes a basket of logs before dinner. But we know that bitter winter nights and sub-zero mornings are still to be faced; soon the winter solstice will be here and one morning we will wake to the chilling whine of a droning wind from snow-capped mountains. Anticipating our solstitial retreat into the warmth of our homes, the village begins to close eyes, windows are blackened and not a wisp of light escapes into the dark. After the troops of visitors who arrived with spring, and those who sweltered through a Tuscan summer there are now no strangers to be found inside the walls. Winter isolation is not unwelcome; it brings intimacy, shared moments in the bar sipping a steaming pink aperitivo. On this cold Sunday evening the main road into the village is closed to all traffic and four braziers are rolled into the piazza; by six o'clock red embers glow and metal scoops dig into sacks and out come glossy chestnuts which are spread on racks and roasted over the fires. The piazza, dressed with a long table and a white cloth to the ground, is soon animated by gathering friends as the cindery aroma wafts from home to

342

home, tempting us into the freezing night. Rugged up in thick coats, wearing essential gloves, scarves and boots, we huddle around the braziers sipping red wine. Ruga ladies twist pokes from brown paper and fill them with charcoal chestnuts tinged with the bloom of ashes which scorch our fingers as we break away the burned shell. Ruga has brought a sack of autumn chestnuts from Mount Amiata and, still celebrating their Sagra win, offer everyone roasted chestnuts and red wine on this bracing night. Later, when the victor's offering is devoured, their old and young will begin a quartiere celebration; one hundred per cent accuracy is something to sing about . . . we will hear them from our homes, singing and chanting their victory songs, and a few dastardly ones, till midnight. By seven o'clock glowing embers are low and the chestnut roast is drawing to a close. An icy wind forces us to pull up collars and pull down hats and move closer to the braziers. 'Water and ice will not stay in the sky!' a Ruga lady recites the proverb. Snow will not fall tonight, sages assure us, but, be that so or not, she is right, because flaky particles of ice carry on the gusting wind and spit into our faces. Hovering under the cappellone three or four Ruga youngsters, each holding a broom made of wispy switches cut from willow, wait for our departure. They will sweep the steps and from the cracks in the stones whisk away every skerrick of chestnut shell and paper poke, leaving nothing lingering in the piazza except the smoky aroma of roast chestnuts.

Wrapped up against the cold, turning the corner, I am astonished to see the Ingegnere leaning on his cane, sitting on the step outside the Protestant chapel. He is well protected in a coat and his head is covered with a hat, but the morning is windy and the cold penetrating. Silvano's message confirms my conviction that recounting to me the history of his family is pleasing him. When he invited me to walk in the tangled garden, and we went underground to the rock-faced cavern before summer, he was noticeably unwell, choking for breath, and his gait was appalling. It would not have been polite to request that he exert his mind and body over a stifling summer, nor was I inclined to bother myself to more than flop on a chair until autumn, when Pianello kitchen responsibilities weighed me down. And then came the rain, mixed in with unmissible Apertura celebrations that tired me into the wee small hours for nights on end . . . and already the Sagra was upon us. But now at last I can bring my mind back to the family Padelletti and the noble class of Montalcino.

A round bolt as long as my arm from elbow to wrist slides from a socket along an iron plate fastened to the weathered wood; the door loosens and creaks as he pushes it inwards. We are in a vestibule, empty except for a black-headed dragon flaming, not fire, but bare light bulbs. Swirls of dust on grey stone flags rise into the air we break through as we enter cold stillness. The Ingegnere offers no comment, but takes off his hat and with inching steps makes his way in and lowers himself on a pew. There is only emptiness, and loneliness, in this once hallowed place. Accustomed as I am to Italy's exuberantly ornamented churches with angels flying, a hundred candles flickering, robed and mitred popes, saints and prophets frowning from lofty perches and images of Madonna and Child, I am struck by a vague sense of familiarity . . . but shocked by the chasteness. As in the church of my upbringing there are no statues, no icons, no painted images of Mary, or Christ, or God. There is only an empty wooden cross. It is we who bring God into the church, my father would insist, we bring him in our hearts and souls. God has no use for a building empty of his children. How well imprinted in my mind are severe Protestant teachings. A smell of cold stone and damp socks pervades the hall; no devout soul has prayed with God in their heart in this chapel for a very long time. Patchy walls flake white paint, wooden pews are dull but the timber is beautifully grained – once they would have shone. The chapel would seat about forty followers, if it were ever full. A plain wooden rostrum is angled to the wall from which to announce the first song of praise but, sadly, the preacher would be dodging pigeon droppings which stain a stairway to the pulpit. My eye catches sight of a looped pair of plush drapes, timeworn, but shimmering blue. Perhaps it leads to a vestry in which the preacher communed with God before delivering his sermon. Gently lifting aside the fold of blue velvet I face a wrought iron grille separating me from a niche. Nonplussed, I stand still, unsure, but slowly release the curtain from my grasp – I feel the Ingegnere's piercing eyes upon my back – and look away, pretending to not understand. In the niche, settled into a hollow, is an elegant marble lapis lazuli cinerary urn. Perhaps it holds the ashes of Hilda Zumpt, his Protestant grandmother? Whoever it is has a silent, lonely and cold resting place. Taking a breath, fixing a half-questioning smile to my face I turn to the Ingegnere. He has not moved from the pew, both hands resting on the crook of his cane; he offers no words, but, watching me walk towards him, he suddenly gathers his hat. He is ready to bolt the Protestant door.

We closed the door of the chapel, sliding the huge bolt and catching it into the socket to hold it taut until his workman returned to lock it securely, and a slow ten-metre walk brought us back to his front door, which was ajar. We shed our coats and settled ourselves into the warm biblioteca, surrounded by the stories of this family. He breathes more easily, his pallor is improved and he seems in better spirits; the oppressive summer heat must have been damaging for his chest ailment.

'We reached the moment when Carlo, my father, was cheated of his inheritance when his uncle Dino and grandmother were poisoned in Naples, and he came back to Montalcino possessing nothing more than a couple of farms. He had some help from Professor Zumpt, in Berlin, but then two things happened. Do you remember the high-born Florentine who married my great-grandfather?' I nod affirmatively. 'She was my father's grandmother and she had several brothers, all Florentines. One after the other the brothers died without issue, leaving their entire fortunes to Carlo who, in a short time, became immensely wealthy once more.' That is something of a relief. I felt badly for young Carlo being cheated out of his inheritance and I was sure the story must come back to wealth, although I had not expected it to be so rapid. 'The other thing that happened,' he continues, 'is that he married a wealthy woman, not from Montalcino. I shall tell you about her in a moment. There is parallel story that brought more wealth to Carlo, in a roundabout way, from a niece of Queen Victoria of England, a niece by marriage who was engaged to a prince of the Hapsburgs.' Oh, Dio, we are connecting with British royalty! Would it be a wild exaggeration to say that there is no corner on earth to which the Padelletti from the walled village of Montalcino did *not* filtrate? But the Ingegnere has not batted an eyelash. 'This royal English unmarried niece, because her prince charming gave her more than he morally should, and promptly got himself killed before he could marry her, gave birth to an illegitimate child, and the bastard child was taken secretly to the royal court of Austria, and given the title of Count. But he could not stay there, in public view, so he spent his winters at a castle by a lake, and, being the same age as my father, and because of my family's friendships in the royal court, he spent most of his summers in secrecy, here in Montalcino. He grew up with my father, they played in the garden together. Everybody called him Count, but they never knew who he was, nor why he was a Count. I cannot elaborate because it will take too long, but the short of it is that every summer the Count always brought to Montalcino with him a married tutor, who looked after him. The tutor's wife was like a mother to the Count, and became like an adopted aunt to Carlo. When she died, in Berlin, her husband the tutor was already dead, so she left my father all the patrimony, including a castle in Germany. You see, Carlo grew richer, inheriting fortunes wherever he turned.'

Montalcino, I am convinced, is not, after all, an isolated village in Tuscany. I wonder, who else has been told these secrets . . . perhaps only me! As the Ingegnere talks, my mind boggles with secrets spilling from *his* mind.

'My father began to consume his wealth. I have told you he was a saint, but he was also an economic criminal. If he had thought to enter the game of buying up land, he could have bought the whole of Montalcino and all of its territory and still been wealthy. But he was an industrialist, he had seen what was happening in Germany, and he dreamed of industrial revolution, he wanted industry here because he wanted to live in Montalcino like a Berliner. He imported all the machinery and opened a printing press, then he set up a bookbinding business; next it was pipe making, and he built his own oil mill. There was nothing in Montalcino, it was desolate, people needed work and my family had been here for centuries and had witnessed this misery and poverty century after century. Then, probably the craziest of all his enterprises, he began to consume money building a sawmill. Think of the madness of this. The railway was coming through down in the valley, at Torrenieri, but there was no work here, except for woodcutters who could cut railway sleepers, so my father, because he loved Montalcino so much, thought he would help. The railway was twelve kilometres away, but he built the sawmill up here at Montalcino. Chopped trees were carted up the mountain to Montalcino, where they cut railway sleepers, and then he had to cart the sleepers down to the railway. He was crazy! Around 1900 my father had houses in Rome and a couple in Florence – but where did he prefer to live? Where did he build an electrical energy plant? At Montalcino! It is well documented: we had electrical energy in Montalcino, for industry, before Florence! My father employed Engineer Costanti to design an electrical plant that ended up costing triple because it was more like a Gothic palace than a factory – you can still see a few Gothic windows in Pianello. But he did not use conventional combustion engines to create electricity, that was too simple; instead he *built* motors that were fired using gas created after burning carbon. So, as well as making electricity, he helped the woodcutters by requesting more wood, engaged workers in the sawmill, and bought charcoal from the carbonai because he needed to burn carbon!

'My father thought he could create miracles, but he was wrong. His ideas were outrageous, he wanted to do things for Montalcino because he wanted to be loved, and that, I believe, was his great error. The contadini were not ready for industry, they sent grain to a miller who still turned a millstone with a blindfolded donkey, grinding corn and chestnuts with stones! Some let water dam up into millponds, so they could only mill while there was water. They preferred to pray for rain than make use of electricity that was waiting for them in Pianello. And if that was not nutty enough, my father founded the Socialist Party in Montalcino – he saw the oppression of centuries, so he formed a union movement for his own workers! To be a modern-thinking industrialist, as he thought he was, he squandered the family fortune on Montalcino; he also had farms, he had vineyards and he was making Brunello. He did more for the contadini than anyone, and spent a fortune trying to help the cittadini, but they did not want to take advantage of the possibilities of electrical energy. He did it all because he loved Montalcino, but the cruel fact is that they did not thank him for it, not once, and they did not love him. Now I must tell you about his wife, my mother.'

I could never have dreamed that a family story could unravel so shockingly, but am growing accustomed to having my mind thrown from one heady abstraction to another, and hardly turn a hair when he says: 'We shall go to France', as if we are about to purchase a ticket and jump on a train. 'But I shall tell you concisely, otherwise we will be bogged down by French Huguenots and revolution. I am sure you know about Saint Bartholomew's Day when ten thousand Protestant Huguenots were massacred in Paris, and they wanted to kill Henry of Navarre, who was the last heir to the French throne?' What should I do, nod yes, or shake no? One will lead to a captivating story of Huguenots, but the other will lead directly to Carlo's wife. I nod yes, fibbing just a wee bit in the name of expediency because I do not want to overstay my visit; the morning is passing.

'Va bene, King Henry was lowered over Parisian walls with ropes and escaped into the heart of France. Arriving at a granary, he asked for asylum from the padrone, who voluntarily concealed him in there, and thereby saved his life. Henry rewarded this loyal farmer, bestowing on him the hereditary title of Count Grenier. Generations later, a Count of the Granary had a brilliant career as a general under Napoleon. But along came the coup d'état, France became a Republic and Napoleon III declared himself President. But Count Grenier would not swear allegiance, he refused to serve under the Republic and exiled himself to Switzerland. Count Grenier lost his wealth and his French nobility, and was stripped of his title. He had an enterprising son, my grandfather on my mother's side. His name was Philippe Grenier, and in Switzerland he set about making himself a tidy fortune buying and selling fabrics, trading between England and Spain. At sixty years of age Philippe Grenier had not married, so there were no heirs to his fortune. Finding and marrying a sixteen-year-old of good family, by the time he died at seventy-four he had six children, and one of them was Jane Grenier, who was my mother, a descendant of ennobled Count Grenier, a Protestant Huguenot and follower of Calvin. Jane grew up in Geneva, but after she married my father he brought her to live in Montalcino. She, too, prayed in the Protestant chapel and she, too, was branded a heretic.'

The Ingegnere stunned me once more. 'My mother could always find out where I was during the war because of her connections with the secret service in Switzerland, and not only that, she was continually in touch with her good friend Clementine, because they went to school together, and Clementine, who married Sir Winston Churchill, often visited Montalcino; she stayed in this house with my mother during the summer.' I am beyond surprise, shuttled vertiginously from Hitler to the Queen of England to Churchill, adapting to the twists in this switchback story. Hence it was no surprise when he added that his father maintained dual nationality, German and Italian, but that in the war he chose to fight on the side of Italy. They had considered themselves to be an Italian family for generations, proven when the whole of the family patrimony in Germany, including a castle, was confiscated. Here in Italy, however, the authorities froze all the family assets anyway.

'So you see, it was not possible for my family to become Catholic. Padelletti lived and thought for themselves, but we lived in a Catholic society and tried to fit in. It annoyed the Church incredibly, in particular that Protestant chapel, they despised us for it, and put every possible obstacle in our path. My father insisted that I learn Latin and Greek because, as he said, you must get to know the enemy, so he sent me to learn languages from the priests. For my father and I, our Protestantism was more political than religious. Historically, Padelletti have always been free spirits, as you can see from the intricate stories weaving in and threading about my family. My father's story is one of a sad, broken man. He squandered a fortune because he wanted only to help, and he wanted the Montalcinesi to love him, which is why I believe there should be a monument to him in Montalcino. When he returned from the war, their bitterness and hatred was so vicious they wanted to kill him; he was utterly destroyed in mind and spirit, and financially ruined. He fought on the side of Italy, but in Montalcino, by the time he returned they had burned down every one of his businesses and factories. He ran for his life to Switzerland, but, even after all that, when Italy began to shake off the deplorable consequences of civil war, he came back to live, and die, in the place he loved but where he was not loved. In Montalcino.'

'I will tell you one more thing about my mother, and then we must close our discussion for today because my grandson is home for lunch and I must not be late. If you would like to hear a little about my own life, it will not take long, because it is my destiny to be the one to see this great family patrimony dissolve, like salt in water, but you will need to come back one more time.' I nod agreement, filled to the brim.

'My mother, Jane Grenier, died in 1952. There was ecumenical talk on the Church agenda at the time, but the bishop formally prohibited, with threat of excommunication from the Catholic faith, any person from Montalcino taking part in the grieving cortège behind her casket. And the Church, so powerful even then, consumed by hatred for heretics, forbade the Comune of Montalcino from allowing her coffin to be taken in the back of a hearse. My father and I were the pallbearers, we carried Jane Grenier on our shoulders. Within a few years my father was dead.'

CHAPTER TWELVE

On the Lances of the Florentines ... The Citadel Tilts to the Left

We have broken sharply into winter; no more old men with sacks of mushrooms swaying from the ends of sticks return to the village jubilant at the girth of porcini. No more scruffy truffle dogs yap at the heels of hunters returning from nocturnal forays. Truffles are not widespread around our hill, but are hunted in seasons after humidity followed by rain. We have shaved, sprinkled and chopped truffle extravagantly over practically everything edible this season, including gelato and scrambled eggs, which my friend Maria Pia taught me to do. When truffles are plentiful, friends turn up at the bar with bumpy pungent lumps in jacket pockets, small but powerful. All the chestnuts have been roasted, and even the little flyers, lingering tordi, have wheeled away on the wind and flown from our bounteous woods where pear and juniper and purple figs offered autumnal sustenance on their migratory journey. It is an extraordinary beneficence to reap and eat the bounty of the season, to be at the source of these gifts, to live where they are grown and smell the earth where they emerge so loyally from the hills, season after season. Only the olives, gleaming black beads hiding beneath the silver undersides of leaves, must wait a day or two more. When the olives are picked, a year of Tuscan reaping is done, the harvesting over.

For a week we anticipate the onslaught of winter. The horizon is limpid and in crystalline air our breath puffs white vapour as we pause to chat to friends, wrapped, hatted and gloved. On many days a patch of blue brightens the morning, but the sun is shrouded by clouds in the afternoon, and dull coldness forbids prolonging passeggiata through the piazza to more than a quick rendezvous. After tiring months serving cappuccino to thousands of visitors, Luca and Gianfranco close up shop for fifteen days, a quindicina. Luca threatens, next season, to alter the menu at Caffè Fiaschetteria to put a stop to visitors complaining when he wisely serves cappuccino at the temperature appropriate for the stomach. 'Dimi!' tell me, he begs. 'Why do they order cappuccino in the middle of stifling summer boiling like lava flow from Mount Vesuvius?' Cappuccino at Fiaschetteria will, next season, be offered as Cappuccino Vulcanico. But not only Fiaschetteria, Caffè alle Logge, too, is closed for eight days. Sebastiano has gone fishing in Sardinia, leaving us stranded without a pink aperitivo in the evening and no bites and tasty nibbles on trays. Bar Prato is closed on Sunday all year round – but Prato is a bar en route, not one in which we socialize, distant as it is from the piazza. On Monday we are desperate. Bar Mariuccia closes for a weekly day off and Angelo's white apron and hat hang disconsolately from the oven door. Not even the freshly baked smell of his kaleidoscopic pizza wafts into the air. Hence, we dither in knotty huddles in the piazza, not knowing where to turn when we run into friends, unable to saunter inside and shout across the counter for brioche and caffè, and we dicker between ourselves, whining at the unfairness and outright barbaric state of things in Montalcino when not a single espresso rumbles and hisses into a cup from morning to night.

Bearable days carry us kindly, one after another, closer to the first rush of air from Siberia that encourages, thankfully, the return of our wandering bar owners and the familiar hum that signals the delicious aroma of dribbling espresso. On the eighth of December the valley is clean and clear; a wisp of cloud hovers above a moonscape of Sienese craters, but towered skyline of Siena stands clear in front of snow-capped Apennine mountains. Farm dogs bark at foolish pheasants flying low and hunting dogs howl affirmation deep in the woods. Puffing gun smoke and huffing wood smoke float lazily, meeting my ears along with the chimes of the bells at the Madonna where, crunching and crackling through frost laying low the grass, I hear the monotone priest, and the staggered hail from parishioners. A delicious December morning; perhaps two or three degrees Celsius. If Siberia does not hurtle in today, a watery sun will break out and we will reach six degrees by lunch.

For a reason unknown to me, on this specific day, Romans empty out of Rome like milk pouring from a bucket and drive to Montalcino. Festoons of yellow gold chains linked around throats are thick enough to strangle, and with their hair dyed henna red and tyre-sized gold loops dangling from lobes, they sport gorgeous leather handbags and totter on stilettos. A haughty parade, but odd it is, because these exiled Romans greet each other, seeming to have some prearranged December appointment along our roads. The aquiline-nosed men, too, are handsomely set: cashmere coats with topaz buttons, cream silk stringy-fringed scarves and driving gloves with little holes. Two ladies swaggering in fur coats abreast fill the roadway and I cannot overtake. Many Montalcinesi drag furs from storage before the wind from Siberia blows, but furs here are not worn ostentatiously. It is not unpleasant to tolerate a Roman invasion this morning; it lends an air of sophisticated citified approval of our medieval mountain home. In mutual flattery they pose in Fiaschetteria and sip, then select, bottles of Brunello, some knowledgeably, and then cast about for somewhere to lunch. Many have rung Luciano at Taverna del Grappolo Blu, because he and Maria Pia, among our closest friends, hail from the Eternal City and Luciano anticipates friends of friends from Rome booking in for lunch today. He and Maria Pia are about to leave the bar, needing to shuffle tables and uncork bottles before serving lunch at Grappolo. But when the invaders have eaten at our restaurants and drunk our wine, with an imperious wave they take their booty and rattle back to Rome. They are the last visitors for the year, placated conquerors, and Montalcino can dig in, lie quiet, and await the festive season.

Filling me with trepidation about why, as she is preparing to leave Maria says: 'Isabella, where is Luigi?' I respond that he is outside the door, so she calls to him and he joins our cosy enclave of territorial Ilcinesi inside the bar, fogged windows separating us from wandering Romans. 'We have decided to close Grappolo Blu for a break before Christmas. We think we'll drive north before snow blocks the roads – why don't you come with us?' Luigi gulps, but as I don't spring to his aid he has sole responsibility for forming a response, and I am bound by his acceptance. A holiday with Luciano and Maria Pia is a mixed blessing. Not that they are not dear friends – but they are Romans! They rocket about the countryside from dawn till midnight, and after, when Luigi and I are tucked up in bed. We spend happy times together, carefully monitored and co-ordinated by ourselves, because their life, never planned with any certain objective but packed with surprise and often requiring diversionary or salvage operations, wears us to a frazzle. We are delighted that our Montalcino friends choose to invite us to share their holiday . . . and, Luigi is absolutely correct, we would never negate such an offer. Nevertheless, the prospect is daunting. I am not convinced that we will revive in time for Christmas. 'When shall we leave?' sings Maria Pia. Remembering that I have a Pianello commitment to attend the opening of the museum at Fattoria dei Barbi, the farm owned by the Colombini family, we programme our departure for the week before Christmas. 'Right,' attempts Luigi, with hope in his voice, 'where are we going, for how long, and in whose car?' Maria's response turns me rigid: 'Oh, anywhere, non preoccuparti, don't worry, we'll just go, five or six days, it doesn't matter where . . . But we can't take our car, it's too small . . . Can we go in the Maserati?' Luigi, not wanting to disappoint, answers yes, but Luciano perceives his hesitation. 'No! We cannot take the Maserati. We can all fit in the car, but the boot is so small we will never get the wine and luggage in. I'll borrow my father-in-law's station wagon.'

'Va bene,' sighs Luigi, and then breathing deeply, ventures: 'Tell you what, here's an idea. We have told you about our friends in Montagnana; what about if I plan a loose itinerary? We'll set off towards Umbria, then move on to Emilia Romagna for a night or two, where we have eaten at a stupendous restaurant, and then Montagnana – our friend there is a wonderful cook – and we'll see how many nights that takes before deciding where to go next.' Bravo Luigi! Any clue that delicious food is involved wins drooling approval from Luciano and Maria Pia. An intense love of food and wine is second only to adoration of their large family, which extends from here to Rome. They wholeheartedly concur that Luigi should plan our journey. They must be back in time to have Grappolo Blu open for Christmas. My heartbeat slowed into rhythm, at least for the present.

Ofelia will meet me at the Madonna when Massimo telephones to say the olives are on the way to the crushing mill. Today is perfection for olive pickers. The air is blindingly cold, and the sun blindingly bright. We reneged when Massimo offered that Ofelia and I join the pickers. Neither she nor I wish to revisit olive picking. Romantic and Tuscan it sounds, but in freezing air the leaves of the tree are miniature razors; olive leaves do not bend or fold into softness when you run your hand down a prickly branch to loosen the olives; fingers freeze and hands and arms up to the elbows end up covered in cuts and scratches from leaves. The harvest is in full swing and on perfect picking days like this even our bank manager vanishes for the morning and turns up behind his desk with bits of olive tree in his hair in the afternoon. He wears a crown of twigs and leaves but his devotion to golden oil is hailed with praise and approval by his patient customers, most of whom have rallied uncles and cousins to the olive groves. Waiting for Ofelia behind the Madonna I watch the farmer, not bent double, but instead reaching gloveless for the topmost branches, while his scarfed wife gathers olives with a plastic rake. No nets surround the trunks; they cull a harvest for themselves from a handful of aged trees, plopping the olives straight into half-moon wicker baskets strapped to their waists.

Inside the frantoio, the crushing mill of a friend at Castelnuovo del Abate the air is warm and dank. In brittle cold sunshine we watch Massimo tip gunny sacks of olives into a shuddering separator to shake away leaves and bits of twigs, then the black beads funnel through a hole in the wall into the frantoio where they drop on to the circling granite and soon fall under the rotating grinding stone. The monstrous slabs of granite screw and grind against each other grating and vibrating; ground pulp of pips, skin and flesh spews into a stone channel like green-brown porridge, not in the least resembling anything one would choose to pour on lettuce, but this hardly tempting slush is scooped up by Massimo with a shovel and taken to the coiled rope mats stacked like pancakes in cages where, using centrifugal force, pure oil is separated from the sludge. Extra-virgin cold-pressed olive oil trickles green down a funnel, but Massimo spoons some into a china basin where Ofelia and I hover with crusts of Tuscan bread, dipping into the bowl and savouring the piquant oil. We cannot dwell in the frantoio – the caustic air is bitter and breathing in the acrid smell sends us dizzy. Watching the crush, tasting new oil, and jumping back in the car with bottles of cloudy but delicious gold is as near as we deem it judicious to be to the romance of the olive harvest.

'Come on, Ofie, let's have coffee at Caffè alle Logge . . . Chiara can join us.' Chiara is already in the piazza; but we cannot find a space to park the car. Round we drive, in one gate and out the other, down to the hospital, behind the Comune, round by the Madonna, up to the fortress for a second time, but there is not a free car space in Montalcino. It rankles no end when my mind subconsciously concurs that the olive grove car park is sorely needed. Ofelia rings a friend on her mobile: 'Claudia, where are you? Can I park in your garage for an hour or so?' The response is positive. We round the fortress once more, but we both stare open-mouthed at a gleaming stretch limousine with darkened windows, horn blaring and roaring towards us, splaying gravel from screeching tyres. Two black vehicles try to keep pace, not police cars, more like escorts. 'Who is that?' our eyes ask each other. Their speed and recklessness causes Ofelia to pull to the roadside, where Rosetta, a Pianello friend, is pinned against the wall. She waves her arms wildly and yells after the disappearing black monster: 'Aya! How dare you blow your trombone! This is Montalcino . . . and it is *ours*, and the roads belong to *us*, not you!' Rosetta, claiming territorial roots, does not know who is in the stretch limousine, but she and her friends were walking, as Italians do, three abreast, confident that cars who borrow their road will manoeuvre round them, which locals always do. We shrug shoulders, Rosetta and friends move off, three abreast, and we drive on. Ofelia's car is finally stationary in Claudia's garage.

What is going on? So many people are in the piazza, some with heads in newspapers, others staring up at the sky, and Piero from Osteria Porta al Cassero, who lost his father-in-law in the woods, is defending himself against jibes from friends who move from one bar to another, sharing some kind of joke. Chiara sees us and runs over. 'What's happening?' demands Ofelia. 'I don't exactly know why,' she admits, 'but Berlusconi, the Prime Minister, was hounded out of the fortress and has fled Montalcino.' *That* is who was in the stretch limousine! 'But that cannot be in the paper, he only left ten minutes ago,' objects Ofelia. Chiara draws her head back in despair at her mother's obtuse comment, the way a thirteen-year-old is inclined to do. 'Mamma,' her voice is condescending, 'the paper has got nothing to do with Berlusconi. Mayor Massimo has created an uproar.'

In Montalcino we hold our collective breath and quake in our collective boots when Mayor Massimo speaks. What is he proposing now? His last proclamation, moving the post office, met with cautious approval but we waited until he informed, via the press, where the new post office will be before we breathed easy; even if it will be most inconvenient for Pianello and Travaglio pensioners to climb that steep hill. His dream to restore the magnificent panorama to the people met with praise, although he anticipates months or even years of bureaucratic muddling to negotiate the restoration of our view from state ownership. Rushing for a folded newspaper on a chair, we scan the front page for a headline. '*La Torre avrà una nuova scala.*' That is why people are looking skywards! 'The Tower will have a new staircase.' Flipping pages we find a picture of our bell tower, under which we stand. 'How can it?' Ofelia exclaims. 'Massimo was up the tower years ago, a staircase does not exist!'

Mayor Massimo has decided that, after a thousand years, the stupendous panorama of neighbouring villages and hills of Tuscany from the belfry of our tower should be accessible to visitors. He is proposing to invite puffing tourists to climb above the piazza. 'In time it will pay for itself,' he is adamant, 'because visitors will buy a ticket at the tourist office.'

The slender tower, harmoniously fastened to the twelfth-century stone Palazzo Comunale, rises like a sensitive antenna from ancient times; it is a symbol of liberty for the Ilcinesi, of rebellious people who demanded communal freedom which, in 1559, after four years of resistance in bloody war and siege by hated Florentines and invading Spanish, was lost only as a consequence of a treaty between powerful European kings. Ivo's words, when he went into battle in the fortress day after day against Florentines, are not an aberration but the moral convergence of a collective village state of mind that has endured for hundreds of years, just as he said: Montalcino never accepted Cosimo de' Medici, and when it was finished we went into mourning for the loss of our liberty . . . and we have been in mourning ever since. Under this tower the iron keys to six gates in the walls, together with the freedom of our citizenry and Comune, passed for all time into the hands of our enemies.

A hubbub of consternation from disturbed citizens threatens to explode. Some are revelling in the hastened departure of Prime Minister Berlusconi, and, as the initial shock subsides, decide that perhaps it will not be so bad if they, too, can climb the tower. Others are adamant, just like Rosetta and the roads: 'This is Montalcino and that is *our* tower!' Wanting to get to the bottom of these developments, Ofelia coerces Piero to tell her about Berlusconi, while I read that Mayor Massimo has invited the fire brigade to bring the smart new fire engine with the telescopic ladder into the piazza, and will officially announce the architect's plan and cost of the new staircase.

Prime Minister Berlusconi's political persuasion is not that of the left, but centre right, hence his governmental policy does not enjoy great favour with our Democratic Party of the Left. But when he stormed out of the fortress with his minders in tow, raced to his car and slammed the door of the black stretch, fleeing outside the walls and ordering his driver to put as much distance as conceivably possible in the shortest possible time between himself and this mountain village, nobody even knew it was him, nor why he was here. A black shadow tore down the narrow road where Piero's Osteria is, and, not certain which way to turn, obviously blinded by fury reverberating inside the car, the driver braked and propped – whereupon Piero, coming out of the Osteria, threw impulsive words and gestures in the driver's direction because the limousine was blocking the road and cars were banking up. What the hell are you doing? Get out of the way you cretin (or something to that end). The driver, following the wave of Piero's arm, turned on to the road where Rosetta and friends were walking three abreast, only to be met by her arms waving wildly and more verbal abuse, and that is where Ofelia and I careered to the roadside to avoid the speeding cars. Rosetta was third in a line of ministerial abusers, although she and Piero were ignorant of who was behind the black glass.

Cavaliere Silvio Berlusconi, a wealthy man, came to Tuscany scouring the countryside, we understand, for a forgotten about and spare medieval castle and sensibly preferred one that stands in the growing zone for Brunello di Montalcino. Eighteen million euro was, we believe, a point of departure for negotiations. But what lit the flames and sent hostile Silvio hurtling back to Rome? Next morning's paper relegated our staircase project to the back pages, and instead, headlines screamed: 'After his Flight Berlusconi Abandons Them.' What we did not know is that our illustrious castle-hunting Prime Minister, unannounced, saw fit to visit the keep in our fortress, but no sooner had he stepped below the black-and-white Sienese crest above the gate than persons unknown, inside the keep, recognized his swarthy political face, and began hurling derogatory abuse which stupefied even him, accustomed as he is to verbal opposition. Outraged by this rudeness, and the hostility of the caterwauling, Silvio turned his back on wicked communists in our citadel, fumed his way back to his car, screamed orders at his driver, who was mightily confused as to which narrow medieval road would carry them out of Montalcino.

Mayor Massimo defended his citizens. It is difficult, he says, to remedy a brutta figura, an ugly impression, but nobody in Montalcino is guilty. Anybody wandering in the fortress keep at this time of year, when our olive harvest is in progress and the keep is gusted by freezing wind, is not a local but a visitor! Politics, he sums up, is an ugly beast and sometimes one loses patience, fleeing from a hostile climate. Cavaliere Silvio is crushed, and Italy's prestigious knight decides he will not, after all, think to dwell among Tuscans, even on holiday. A multi-million-euro deal collapses. Nobody but Ofelia and I knew about Rosetta, but ministerial minders leak to the press that not only was Silvio accosted so rudely in the fortress, but twice along the roads of our uncivilized borgo. Piero, half proud claimant and half denying discourteous behaviour, is for eternity labelled as the Ilcinese who chased the Prime Minister out of the walls!

Stepping from the car in my cream silk jacket I glance around, see Maria, President of Ruga, and assure Luigi he will not need to collect me for there will be plenty of cars returning to Montalcino following the formal opening of the Museum of Brunello and dinner. I wave Luigi away and walk towards Maria, who is happy to see me because many strangers mingle in their finery at Fattoria dei Barbi. We are joined by the President of Borghetto, black suited and tie loosely knotted, but the Travaglio President, too, is represented by a deputy. This innovative museum, the brainchild of Stefano Colombini, is physically in its birth stage, but virtual reality on the internet. 'We want to conserve our way of life,' says Stefano. 'This museum is a walk in the story of our lives.' My eyes focus on a large black-and-white print on the wall, which intrigues me. Who exactly is Riccardo Paccagnini, labelled a Pioneer of Brunello, and why is he displayed with such prominence in the Barbi Brunello Museum? Interesting name. I am sure that is the family from whom Enzo bought his vineyard below the wall. Important identities are introduced to the audience, none of whom I have personally met, but some are familiar names in the world of wine and literature. I ask Maria to point out Signora Francesca Colombini. La Signora is a dark-haired, straight-backed woman sitting on the end chair with a table of dignitaries. The opening speeches proceed, with an interesting admission from Signor Piero Antinori catching my attention. 'They say you have to pass through suffering before reaching paradise, but Brunello is a wine that has never suffered, and found itself in paradise when it was born. Up in Chianti,' he justifies, 'we are still overcoming an image problem. When Brunello hit the world in the 1960s, Chianti was suffering; it was not as good as it could have been and was born in a raffia flask, identified all over the world as a rough red. We have had to remedy a negative international image and create a symbol of quality. But there has been no suffering here because Brunello di Montalcino was born noble.'

We adjourn for dinner and the dignitaries, including La Signora, make their way up the hall between a couple of hundred guests, shaking hands and pausing to accept congratulations. Seeing her draw near, I nudge Maria. 'Can you introduce me?' La Signora is hurrying to supervise dinner, but smiles recognition at Maria, who quickly interjects: 'Signora Colombini, have you met Signora Dusi?' Nonchalantly I flap a business card in the air. La Signora shakes my hand courteously, but there is confusion in her up-and-down glance, hesitant caution – perhaps she believes I am a foreign journalist come to report on the museum. Hastening the moment, I blurt that I have been researching the Colombini family. La Signora shows interest. 'Are you staying in Montalcino?' she questions with a polite smile. Without declaring that I have been here ten years, I respond yes. 'Well, then, Signora, I will be in Montalcino tomorrow, where will you be? I will call on you at five o'clock and we can talk.' What! Panic rises in me. 'Oh, goodness, Signora, I can come back at any time to suit you, no need for you to go to that trouble.' She holds herself proudly, crooning, 'No trouble at all, I would not dream of it. Is this your business card? I will come at five o'clock.' And she hurries into a crowd of VIPs.

What have I done? Dinner is vaguely delicious, so are the wines, but I am fretful and when Maria delivers me to my door, I pounce on Luigi. 'Do you have any plans for tomorrow?' He hears the urgency in my voice. 'I intended to watch the boys at football training, we've got crucial games coming up and I've got work to do, why?' 'Well, you cannot! Please! We have to clean the apartment . . . Do not ask me how, but La Signora Francesca

Colombini will be calling on us at five o'clock tomorrow evening.'

Luigi and I dwell in modest circumstances in a homely apartment in the village. From the front doorstep two paces take you to the kitchen, and four take you to the living room. From the front door you can see the bedroom, which is next door to a small bathroom and on the other side is our cluttered ironing and storage space. We did not arrive in Italy with a sack of money, and that which we had was spent exploring, because it was never our dream to accumulate riches, only to enrich our lifestyle, begin a different life, and find a new home. I am stratospheric. 'Luigi, can we buy a new sofa tomorrow?' He is dismayed, as only a man can be, at feminine priorities. 'Do you think Bino at the cleaners would do an overnight job on the curtains? The market is on at Buonconvento tomorrow – please, can you drive down and buy a new rug?' The realization that none of this is going to happen resigns me to my fate. All I can depend upon is his help, and we begin at sparrows, clearing old letters, dry-cleaning dockets, Pianello menus, anonymous keys that fit no known lock, football home-and-away dates, letters from Mother, old bus tickets, finger paintings from grand-children . . . all the junk that accumulates on dressers should they be within arm's reach of the front door.

Cobwebs! Why is it that negligence lurks unseen until someone important is coming? One never notices accumulated defects, and anyway, I contrive to assign lack of fastidiousness at home to my creativity. We dust and polish, wash and scrub and sweep out long-legged spiders and their webs. 'Look at the cushions! They are so dull and flat, they need new fillings. Luigi! Polish the picture glass, fly spots!' He shakes his head yet again. 'Amore, you are demented! I do not believe La Signora will be using the shower!' This man does not understand. 'What if she uses the bathroom to wash her hands and looks in? Can you please go downstairs and wash the front door?'

Rushing to the florist I return with outrageously costly blooms and half a kilo of tasty morsels from the pasticceria. I insist Luigi chill juice and white wine just in case, and prepare a bottle of . . . what shall we offer La Signora? Her own Brunello or that produced by someone else? Should we lead her to the salon, without a new sofa and with faded flat cushions? Would it be rude to lead her to our kitchen table? 'Let her decide,' counsels Luigi. A foolish male notion dismissed by my sullen glare. This is stressful; I would rather cook lunch for Lola!

'No! No! Signora, you have it wrong, after the fall of Siena the Colombini came to Montalcino on the lances of the Florentines. This is one of the absurd paradoxes of my family!' Oh, no, I am appalled, they are *not* reviled Florentines who took away the liberty of the Ilcinesi? 'Signora Colombini, then your family were Florentines?' I have it wrong once more, thankfully, although her assertion stands: the Colombini family fought on the side of Cosimo de' Medici and when the Grand Duke forced the capitulation of Montalcino after the four-year siege, on the bloodied steel heads of Florentine lances, they returned to Montalcino.

Gorgeous blooms are in the salon, but we are sitting in the kitchen. La Signora, of proud bearing, dignified and slightly aloof – understandable because she is in the home of strangers about whom she knows nothing – tugged the lead fastened to the neck of a fluffy white dog, a Maltese terrier, I think, and, with one stern glance, commanded the dog to lie beneath the kitchen table, which she could see from the door. I ignored Luigi's glare and the pretty dog obeyed and has not moved a paw; we followed La Signora, not demurring to her decision to sit at the kitchen table. Wine was unnecessary; La Signora explains that she drinks wine rarely, but a glass of water will be welcome. There is no bottled water in our refrigerator. Water from the tap in etched crystal is the best I can do.

'After the siege,' she clarifies, 'was the second time the Colombini came to Montalcino. I had better go back before I go forward. Our patrimony in Montalcino grew enormously after 1559, but there was a third coming, which enriched my family culturally and financially. But first, you must listen to this.' She is using the stern voice with which she ordered her obedient dog under the table. My initial impression seems correct. La Signora is the matriarch of the family. 'When you talk of ancient families and places and history you must allow for a margin of doubt. We have records, but many things become dispersed when handed through the generations. Magari! Things get left in drawers, or lost when a house is packed up. Scratchy records and scribbled lines are sometimes all we have.' This familiar picture of family domesticity relaxes my mind; a just comment, forcing me to remember the box of paraphernalia that contains everything from the top of our dresser.

La Signora is tall, facilitating her bristling straight-backed carriage. Guessing her age is impossible; as she talks perhaps it will become apparent. Greying hair is drawn severely to the nape of her neck, and she peers through oval glasses. Earrings and pearls adorn, but she is not formally dressed, wearing a floral suit with a collar and covered buttons down the front. An air of aloofness pervades, that inborn bearing of class and culture. Perhaps the Colombini really are Famiglia Nobile. She strikes me as a woman of strength, with perhaps a harsher than necessary external barrier, a form of self-protection. My thoughts make me smile for it is an image into which I moulded myself and hid behind for twenty years, before I came to live in Montalcino. An iron lady, impervious to hurt and repelling kindness, lest either creep beneath a shield and force the revelation of deep emotions and make her vulnerable. La Signora's story will be interesting. Up until now I have listened only to patrilineal descendants of ancient families; she is the first woman to tell me about her family. She skips briefly through the past.

By the 1300s the Colombini were already recognizable by their family crest: four doves on an ovoid azure background – colombo being Italian for dove. Like most Sienese nobles, they were wealthy merchants. A Colombini farmed enormous tracts of land around Montalcino, which he owned, as well as shops and palaces in Siena. But this was the era when men piously followed mystics like Saint Francis of Assisi – there was a lot of wandering about in the Middle Ages – and this man fell hopelessly under their spell, turned to preaching and, like Francis, gave his worldly possessions to the poor, to priests and convents. But his blessed generosity and benevolent outpouring to the poor multitudes saw the Colombini farmland around Montalcino, which included Castello della Mura, now Banfi headquarters, dissipate and disappear. Beatified by the Pope, and thereafter called Il Beato, he probably attained his place in heaven, but the patrimony was destroyed, and the Colombini were compelled to begin all over again. Returning to trade, at which they excelled, money went round and soon they were purchasing palaces and land in Sienese territory, including farmland around Montalcino once more. As family patrimony rose, so did trade wars between Siena and Florence. The

Colombini turned their eyes – in protection of trading routes and their merchandise, the reason for all the wars – towards Siena's rivals, the despised Florentines, and promptly got themselves exiled from Siena. Stripped of noble Sienese title, their palaces, shops and land were captured by the Sienese.

But victory, in the end, went to Florence and in 1559, when Montalcino capitulated, the last bastion of liberty in the dominion of Siena, everything fell under the grasp of the hated Florentines. To the victor goes the spoils . . . and the Colombini had their second coming, as the Signora poetically describes – on the bloodied lances of the Florentines they returned to Montalcino and took back their land.

'We do not know for what reason, perhaps better trading opportunities, but for a hundred years, between 1600 and 1700, the family patrimony transferred to Lucca. Then in the 1700s they began buying land around Siena, drifting back, and in the 1800s a religious Colombini left Lucca and arrived in Montalcino. His wife gave birth here to a son called Pio, and he was my grandfather and had in his care and control the farms around Montalcino. But when my grandfather married Elina Padelletti things changed, because he gave up a brilliant medical career and came to live permanently in Montalcino.'

Her grandmother was a Padelletti! Deciding only to listen, rather than interrupt, I do not tell her that I am friends with the Ingegnere. This could be leading somewhere interesting.

'Elina was the daughter of Raffaello Padelletti, an immensely wealthy man, and hardly had my grandparents been married than an enormous inheritance of houses and palaces and land became hers. Her father was passionate about viticulture, a member of the Society of Oenologists, and experimented with pure sangiovese along with Riccardo Paccagnini, a brilliant oenologist who obtained his laureate in Rome and wrote a technical thesis about making wine. His mother was also a Padelletti. I have a bottle of 1892 Brunello in my cellar, for which Raffaello won his first medal. Padelletti Brunello was exhibited between 1820 and 1850, although we have no documentary evidence.'

The large print of Riccardo Paccagnini at the museum has real family significance, after all. Pio Colombini married Elina Padelletti, whose father was Raffaello Padelletti, and the brilliant oenologist Riccardo Paccagnini's mother was also a Padelletti. Did Raffaello's name cross the lips of the Ingegnere when he referred to the wider patrimony of his family? I am not sure . . . but he did *not* say that an enormous part of the family patrimony was absorbed by marriage into the Colombini family. And the Brunello claims are astonishing. If Padelletti Brunello was exhibited between 1820 and 1850 it backs up the date of 1842, which I read in the newspaper article. But then, Tito Costanti was supposedly among the first of four families to use the name Brunello, as well as the families Tamanti, Anghirelli, and the fourth was Santi, who became double-barrelled Biondi Santi. But that was not until 1865. Many riddles are entwined here, but one thing is tantalizingly apparent: some incredibly wealthy and brilliant men of the Padelletti family are strongly linked to the Colombini.

'Allora, my grandfather Pio and grandmother Elina Padelletti had a son, my father, and he was named Giovanni Colombini. He inherited all the property and riches on his father's side, a Colombini, and the immense farmland and fortune on his mother's side, a Padelletti. In 1935 my grandfather died, and my father possessed this huge patrimony, which had to be looked after.' This tangled web connects and dissects the elite families of Montalcino. Until now I have seen no indication of huge wealth moving from one family to another. Something is unravelling, but claims and counterclaims confuse my mind.

'Giovanni, my father, a few years before he took over the family holdings, married a Montalcinese. Her name was Giuliana and she came from probably the most distinguished and ancient family in Montalcino. My mother was a Tamanti.'

I cannot believe my ears. The Tamanti family . . . is this story tangling or unravelling? I am not sure. Did she see my eyes flicker as these threads ran through my mind? I think she did. La Signora enlightens me about the Tamanti. 'My mother died young, she was only fifty-six, but she brought great riches into my family. I am sure you know about the Tamanti? They were fabulously wealthy, with an enormous patrimony – they owned the land south from Castello Romitorio, and east towards Torrenieri; it was a tremendous fortune and they were an ancient cultured family.'

Castello Romitorio? Yes, I am certain this is something I have heard before. When Antonio Padelletti was sent into spiralling bankruptcy and broke his neck riding his horse down the icy slope through the quarry to the Madonna, Castello Romitorio was lost to the Padelletti through his bankruptcy. So the castle went to the Tamanti! Now it is joining the bene, the matriarchal wealth of the Colombini by the marriage of a Tamanti to Giovanni Colombini.

'Do not make the mistake of thinking the Tamanti suddenly became Roman.' I nod dismissal of that idea, without knowing why, not understanding her need to negate such a thought as if it were ridiculous. La Signora is relaxing into her story. She bristles now and again, but talks with pride and now that she is talking about own parents, Giovanni and Giuliana, her tone is mellowing and her smile warmer as she recalls the extraordinary household in which she was raised. But she has not lifted the crystal glass, is uninterested in cookies, and the little dog moves not a paw.

'Two sons of the great Casa Tamanti, House of Tamanti, were sent to Rome to study at an elite university. They were rich, they had houses in Rome, and one son obtained his degree in engineering, the other in law. The Tamanti family belong to Montalcino, it was their seat of power and wealth, but the two sons fell in love with Roman women. One of the brothers was my grandfather, Gianni Tamanti, and he married a woman from a patrician Roman family, and brought her back to Montalcino. The brothers were educated in Rome, but how can you say the Tamanti were Romans?' I had not said so, and am still in the dark about why I should not think so, or why it is significant, but Luigi steals a glance at me and a silent message passes between us. Conspicuously, as La Signora rattled off her last sentence with a hint of absurdity in her voice, she drew the fingers of one hand into a point, raised them and, shaking them sharply, mouthed the exact exclamation that Luciano from Grappolo Blu, who is Roman, uses to emphasize a point: 'Eohh!' There, in a tribal trait, lingers a touch of Rome. 'Gianni Tamanti died, and his Roman wife was left with her family here in Montalcino. Her youngest child was Giuliana, who I have told you was my mother, and on marriage she brought into my family, through inheritance from her brothers, the fortune of the Tamanti.

'Can you see how deep, and rich, is the ancestral heritage of the Colombini? It is a union of direct male bloodline from the Colombini of the 1300s, of scientific study of winemaking passing through the female bloodline of the wealthy and intellectual Padelletti family, and through a female line of the fabulously rich and cultured Casa Tamanti. This is what my father and mother inherited; this is what I was born into, right when the world was about to turn upside down!'

La Signora tells me about her father, Giovanni. How many times have I heard that the landowners were torpid, slow and lazy, abandoned their land and left it to become desolate and barren, had no cash and turned to investing in steel mills and road building? This university-educated elite had never physically had their hands in the earth in their lives. Many had a privileged education, but did not ever practise as doctors, or lawyers, or engineers; they were fabulously rich and had no need to work. The contadini worked the farms and the padrone traded the goods, through foremen and merchants. But after the war the contadini wanted money, many went to work in factories, or emigrated, but the mezzadria, which had fettered the contadini in serfdom, under which the farms had been oppressively run for centuries, was rolling inexorably to an end.

For the first time I am hearing what faced the landowners, the padrone, who stayed when the mezzadria was dismantling. Giovanni Colombini understood the importance and potential of Brunello di Montalcino and knew the key to the future was on his land, but a social revolution was under way. With eyes wide open he drew the three branches of patrimony of the Colombini, Padelletti and Tamanti families under one name, calling it Fattoria dei Barbi. He believed he could create a radically new way of farming. 'Signora, you have to understand, this was revolutionary, it was like an earthquake! My father took on the battle and had to adapt his whole outlook to a new world, it was a staggering ambition and he needed capital – he had to sell many things, including our house in the piazza, which was a Padelletti palazzo. It required personal commitment; for the first time a padrone had physically to become part of the farm!

'Before he died, he said to me: Sai, Cara, you know my dear, you will not be directing a farm when I am gone, you will be directing and managing a huge agricultural enterprise with the responsibility of carrying it forward. How many women in Italy at that time do you think were steering agricultural enterprises? I was forty-six when my father died, he accomplished what he set out to do, and he guided me, taught me how to steer this enterprise. In the old days the farm kept pigs that were sold at the market, and we kept sheep but the milk went to the dairy. My father, thinking far into the future, began producing his own primary products: rather than sell the milk, he made cheese here, on the farm, and instead of selling the pigs, he cured his own prosciutto and salami. We have three thousand pigs and when he died I had to build a new slaughterhouse. Our Brunello went ahead, which he recognized and defended as singularly *the* most vital and important product. He was one of the pioneers who organized it commercially, the first to take it round the world, but he was also innovative with our other products: as well as two hundred and fifty kilograms of salami every year, Fattoria dei Barbi produces about seventy thousand kilograms of pecorino sheep milk cheese. He opened Taverna dei Barbi, which is still here; he cleverly realized a restaurant is a window into our farm.'

Her eyes take on a glazed look as she remembers the challenges she had to face. 'My father died in 1976; I had to run the farms, extend the cheese factory, buy new tractors, keep the slaughterhouse working, find markets for our products, fix broken machinery, keep the restaurant staffed and find women to roll the pasta by hand. It was exhausting . . . I had to be inventive . . . and don't forget, Italy was primarily masculine, women did not then hold managerial positions, there were so few of us! Brunello di Montalcino was exploding and at the Fattoria we produce around two hundred thousand bottles. I started to go round the world, to England and to America where I was invited to the first Wine Experience in New York. Out of one hundred international wine producers I was one among about four women.'

She is relaxed at last. Enjoying her memories and the thrill of adventure her eyes are happy and sparkling. I am fascinated to be listening to a super girl, super mum and super woman, which leads me to ask: 'Signora, in this masculine world, did you not feel the need to fight? I mean, it must have been difficult.' As I put the question, her back is instantly erect and she bristles: 'Do I look like a person who could not fight?' Fiery eyes bore into mine, intimidating, but not unkind. 'Yes, I had to fight. But I have always conducted myself in a feminine manner and do not believe in the masculinity of women. Being a woman is important. What a man can say with nonchalance, in a woman the same words can be in bad taste. Thumping a table is to renounce your femininity. You can have grinta, pluck and courage, defend your principles, without resorting to masculine behaviour.'

Our talk is drawing itself to a close. She tells me that her son and daughter, Stefano and Donatella, when they completed their studies, began to help her in the vineyard and farm. The Barbi holdings have been divided between them, and they now steer the Colombini enterprise in two halves. They too were born into it, and in her words, have chewed this bread since they were little.

'It was thrilling, all of it, and the house was filled with painters and literati, which is why I invented the Barbi Colombini Literary Prize. I was a great friend of Federico Fellini and had many contacts in the world of arts. I wanted to unite appreciation of this phenomenal Brunello with something elegant and cultural.'

Her story is told and she has decided to take her leave, tugging the lead which startles the invisible dog, who stretches and sniffs, then trots to her side. She leans down and picks her up, cuddling the silent bundle of white fluff into her arms. Luigi is curious, and asks if she misses the thrill of managing such a huge patrimony. 'Yes, I miss it, but now I have to be more courageous than ever. The farms and our Brunello are in the hands of my children and it would not be right for me to interfere with what Stefano and Donatella decide. They were born into this family and have intelligence, and when you reach a certain age, you need un pochino of intelligence too, to become an observer, and that takes tremendous courage.'

La Signora is a formidable woman. She makes me regret thumping boardroom tables and slamming down phones so often in my past unfeminine career. We shared a smile at her last sentence, after she had left, insisting that she did not require Luigi to escort her to her car, bristling as she said: 'Thank you, but I know the road well enough.' She used the words 'un pochino of intelligence', meaning, just a little intelligence. But she did not pronounce it as it is written, rather, she said 'un pohhino', dropping the harsh *c*, reverting to the dialect of a true Montalcinese.

CHAPTER THIRTEEN

A Cherry Red Coat and a Rainbow Shawl

Cradling bottles of Brunello, we wheel our suitcases to Bar Prato from where Luciano will collect them. Maria Pia and Luciano do not finish work until midnight at Taverna del Grappolo Blu so we are not planning a brisk departure; rather, we thought to have morning caffè in the piazza and from there we will walk down to Bar Prato and load the baggage. Maria Pia, under a smart hat with a jaunty feather poking from the side, jangling bracelets muffled by her gloves and burdened with a giant fluorescent hold-all, assembles herself in the piazza, but not Luciano, who, at eleven o'clock, is still at Grappolo, turning off gas heating at the main, pulling plugs from stoves and packing a whole carton of Brunello. The Brunello is not for us to drink; it is the most treasured of gifts, if blessed you are to hail from Montalcino. The bel vino is destined for friends we encounter along our way.

Outings with Maria Pia and Luciano, have hitherto been restricted to a hazardous walk to pick jonquils followed by a barbecue bigger than Ben Hur, a pizza-making afternoon at the farm of Maria's sister, a day at Saturnia, wallowing like whales in stinking sulphurous springs; and of the trip to Florence, the least said the better. Once we almost got to Sardinia: a three-day excursion was planned, but foul weather and rough seas called for the instigation of salvage plans. Luciano insisted, nevertheless, that we drive to Livorno perchance the ferry could plough through ten-metre seas. Thank God it could not. Instead, we drove a further two hundred kilometres and staggered around jazz-drunk Perugia in drizzle from one bandstand to another. Luciano and Maria Pia were truly in their element because music and dance are an irresistible lure to the wee small hours, by which small hours Luigi and I had taxied back and were tucked up in a castle-hotel. They were twinkling at breakfast. Every one of these pleasure pursuits offers happy memories and one or two best unspoken of recollections of looming disaster, somehow avoided at the ultimate second. Not once have my worst fears been realized beyond wilting with starvation and sitting down to dinner at midnight, or finding ourselves guests at someone's home, whom we do not know, and are not introduced to, and for whom we have no gift or wine in compensation for a bed overnight and copiously laden tables of food. Once, invited to join our Roman friends at dinner we arrived empty-handed but were cheered through the door to a birthday party for eighteen-year-old twins. Non preoccuparti, says Maria, with a wave of her arm. Don't worry about a thing . . . that danger-loaded phrase of Maria Pia's covers all, and when she throws it at me, my horizon blackens.

If only I were more like her; Maria lives in a baffling world of bohemian comings and goings. She does not care to arrive or depart at any stated hour, preferring to scatter her morning with planting tulip bulbs, dabbling in watercolours, or sewing sparkles on a costume for a drama in our theatre. Her daughter, Anna Vittoria, may drop in with her four-year-old son, and soon Eduardo is planting tulip bulbs, dabbling in watercolours and thrusting a huge needle through a sequin on to a velvet medieval costume, or together they will visit the neighbour's dog, because their own dog was exiled to Rome, or sit on the steps of the cappellone, licking gelato. That eleven o'clock may have come and gone is nothing to be lachrymose about . . . non preoccuparti, we can have caffè at twelve, just as easily!

I have resorted to not calling on Maria Pia at her home. One morning a pretty, sleepy signorina answered my buzz; white was her nightgown, and had it been fully on at least one shoulder, and not transparent, my shock would have been mollified. Next time I rang the bell to find myself face to face with a Nigerian brandishing a bread knife; he spoke no Italian, but had the most sparkling smile. These people are generally Grappolo staff, borrowed from Rome, or found by the side of the road, and it bothers Maria not a jot that they take up residence inside her house.

Maria Pia is a large woman, in every way, but especially in generosity of heart. She clothes her womanly curves in exactly whatever she pleases, adores outlandish colours and everything that sparkles. Sometimes patterned lime slip-ons encase her large feet, spreading dear little red cherries all over them, and, draped in Indian crimson, she glitters with sequins, and twenty bracelets jangle and pendants bounce around her cleavage. She is fabulous in the kitchen, her cooking and personality as vivacious as her appearance; a free spirit, she dives and darts in baffling pursuit of one undertaking after another. I am dull by comparison, organized, punctual and predictable. Maria Pia has room in her life for everybody. Her crazy world is adorable, enviable, and terrible to behold.

In striking opposition, exhibiting a crotchety façade, Luciano flakes with feigned exhaustion, vexing himself into melancholy at Grappolo Blu. Suffering the dilemma of a love-hate relationship with diners, he is at first fretful that no one is coming, then dissolves into quivering ambivalence about whether they come or not, and at the end panics, gnawed by anxiety that people will be queuing at the door. He is tall, by Italian measure, and maintains a fine Roman figure; olive-skinned, he dresses with exemplary chic and mesmerizes pale-skinned diners from other lands who seem to adore his suave Latin looks. While Maria Pia is humming away in the kitchen, decorating a terracotta bowl of ravioli with heart shaped angelica, or wrapping onion grass around five snake beans, or balancing three hazelnuts on the spine of a poached pear, Luciano will be hammering at the kitchen door, burying his head in his arms, moaning about where the zuppa for table six is.

'Stai calmo, Luciano,' she will sing, 'calm down, it will be ready the moment I put it in the bowl.' The season is long, commences with Easter and, barring a couple of dead weeks in late autumn, does not slow until invading Romans are fed on the eighth of December.

Luciano overslept this morning, our day of departure, because although Maria succeeded in swinging loose from Grappolo at midnight, Luciano was compelled to outlast two female diners – ringing justification for his on-going love-hate relationship with customers. Booked into one of Montalcino's hotels for the night, the two visitors drank, between them, a full bottle of Brunello, finished dinner with a grappa apiece, and then, giddy under the influence, ordered two glasses of Amaro liqueur, and two cups of boiling cappuccino, twice! Luciano fairly exploded when he woke Maria to tell her about the cappuccino. 'How can they,' he moaned loathingly, 'be so barbaric as to drink two cups of frothy cappuccino each, at one o'clock in the morning, on a stomach full of *our* food and a bottle of *Brunello*?' It was the double cappuccino that exhausted his patience and drove him demented. At two o'clock the two women staggered from the table. Luciano telephoned Emergency Services and had them carted back to the hotel in an ambulance. 'That's it! I cannot take these barbarians any longer,' he wept into the pillow, 'I need a holiday!'

Calling arrivederci to friends, Luigi and I exit the bar and walk through the piazza and down to Bar Prato with Maria Pia, rugged up like trussed chickens for our winter holiday in the north with two dear but oft exasperating friends. Luciano is here, loading bags into the station wagon. According to a law of questionable tradition that seems to apply in every society, Luigi will navigate in the front with Luciano and Maria and I cram into the cosy rear seat. Remembering that Luciano will talk with his hands and wrap them round the steering wheel only when they are inadvertently free, and that Luigi will deny that he is without dependable sense of direction, early omens are not encouraging. At last we are all aboard, cruising up the hill past the Madonna, around the walls, past the fortress and . . . 'Porca miseria!' It is Luciano. 'Damn, I have to go back, I forgot to turn off the generator. I do not want it coming on if there is a power surge.' Such a surge is a distinct possibility; querulous objection would be pointless. We have not driven past the main gate, Porta Cerbaia, so instead of leaving the walls and taking the road to the valley, we turn back into Montalcino, rattle up the cobbles, wave to our astonished friends as we sail through the piazza and Luciano draws the car to a halt at the steps that lead down to Grappolo Blu. Fortunately he has a permit allowing vehicle entry, and while he races inside to switch off the generator Luigi placates the driver behind who is seeking to drive to his home. Luciano hurtles up the steps, jumps in and off we go. Past Bar Prato, up the hill, round the wall, approaching the fortress and Maria's mobile phone rings. She responds, but Luciano curses: 'Merda! Shit! I have left my phone on the bench, above the generator!' Luigi and I sigh, dejected. This cannot be happening. Maria is talking with her grandson. Luciano swivels the steering wheel, once more, towards Porta Cerbaia. 'Luciano! What are you doing?' she screams. But it is too late, we are through the gate, bumping over the cobbles and, to open-mouthed amusement, sailing through the piazza. The air, by now, is frigid . . . Luciano is hopelessly self-infuriated, but Maria Pia, with laughing eyes, winds down the window and waves to everyone, drawing attention to our madness. Beetroot-faced Luciano unlocks the restaurant door, races in and races out, hurtles up the steps and with an apologetic wave to the driver behind, we screech away. Passing the fortress for the third time Luigi and I mentally prepare ourselves. Maria Pia claps her hands and gives a happy cheer as we turn to the valley – but Luciano is smouldering.

'Pia!' he growls. Maria is called Pia on its own when angst or anger justifies. 'Did you take my shirts from the wardrobe and put them in the bag?' He slams on the brakes in shock when we chorus deafening rejection of the very thought of a third journey through the piazza. 'Luciano! I am not responsible for your shirts. You are not going back – you can buy new ones.' Luciano, screwing himself round, weighing up visceral and conscious reasoning, has no alternative but to laugh or cry. After a moment's hesitation the four of us explode, our shoulders shuddering and heads shaking at the ridiculousness of our departure; he steers the car back on to the road, muttering about the cost of new shirts for a week. Maria's eyes shine like stars and she laughs with glee at his self-inflicted punishment.

At the bottom of the valley is a junction where we usually turn towards Buonconvento, which is within sight just a few hundred metres away, or where we can turn in the opposite direction towards Umbria. 'Non ci credo!' It is Luciano, again. 'I don't believe it.' Neither do we. A pair of carabinieri, one with a machine gun nozzle directed at the car, the other waving a red lollipop stick, signals for Luciano to pull to the roadside. 'Merda! Merda! Merda! This is not my car and I have not the vaguest idea if the ownership papers are even in it!'

Thus opens our holiday, filling me to the hilt with terrible foreboding of what trials we may pray to live through. We have been sat in the car for an hour and we are ten kilometres from Montalcino. A fifteen-minute search of the glove box, door pouches and even unpacking the wagon and removing the bags to expose the spare tyre, does not disclose the pink paper of ownership. Luigi, thinking to alight and assist Luciano, turned the door handle, but as the door opened a crack a gruff voice with a machine gun probing the air suggested that would be a mistake. Maria and I lower our eyes and remain cloistered during this belligerent right of search; smiling at carabinieri is like smiling at a crocodile. Unsmiling, they resentfully concede Luciano seven days to present ownership and insurance papers at Siena. He starts the engine, and then slumps back in his seat. 'I'm exhausted . . . I need a caffè, and I'm hungry, why don't we go to Buonconvento for lunch?' We turn in the direction opposite to our destination and I gaze longingly at beautiful, serene Montalcino, perched atop the hill directly above the roof of the car.

Hours of winter daylight are few and by five o'clock it is pitch dark. We bounce along a country byway for an hour with head-lights gleaming through descending blackness. Thunderous clouds threaten, but we outrun them, thankfully pulling up at the doors of our hotel in Città di Castello just as the first drops splatter on the windscreen. Città di Castello is in the upper valley of the River Tiber which has watered Umbria's farms for thousands of years, linking Umbrian villages that grew into trading settlements along its banks.

Our second day together is passing, comparatively, with barely a ruffle. Luciano and Maria left the hotel after caffè in search of new shirts for Luciano and Luigi and I spent an hour at the gallery refreshing memories of a processional standard painted by Raphael when he was just a boy, later meeting our friends in the piazza. Leaving Luigi and moaning Luciano – lamenting that he already has an identical pink shirt in his wardrobe – to ferret among the barmen and track down our Umbrian lunch, Maria and I scout the narrow lanes and find L'Antica Tessitura, a claustrophobic shop from which the weaving and selling of pure linens and flaxen byssus cloth has proceeded since 1842. The fibrous smell of flax and linen makes my nostrils tingle and there is hardly room for Maria and I to stand together at the counter but Maria chats fulsomely and fondles each cloth as the owner unravels bolt after bolt of jacquard weaves. He talks about the motifs, crooning over festoons and swags copied from Vasari frescoes, and wreath of fruit replicated from della Robbia ceramics. Without warning, the two of them disappear through an unseen door camouflaged by protruding bolts of cloth, so I follow into a workshop where weavers dressed in blue dustcoats, replacing black shawls and knotted head scarves worn in another epoch, stand at hand-drawn looms as old as the shop. The clackety clack of the wooden looms shuttling back and forth has not changed in a hundred years, nor have the swirls around which the women weave ghostly griffins, garlands of fruit and flowers and almond-eyed partridges. Less mesmerized than visitors by nostalgic romantic images, but instinctively at ease with quality, Italians claim their birthright to collective ownership of such treasures. We each make our first holiday purchase. It is one of the mysteries of Italy: spending an enormous sum on something pure, like a dozen squares of byssus so delicate that, holding one, the flimsy cloth seems not to be in my grasp; it caresses me, induces noble thoughts and I leave the shop magnanimous – grateful for the opportunity to spend so outrageous a pile of money on something so tiny and thin. It is, perhaps, a woman thing, like getting to sit in the rear seat of the car.

'Look!' gasps Maria, on our way back to the piazza. 'Pane dell'alta Umbria! Let's buy some.' So we purchase two vibrant orange-yellow loaves of bread kneaded with lard and impregnated with saffron. The smell from the ovens reminds us we are hungry, although when Maria is planning to eat two high-top loaves of bread I am not sure, as Luciano has booked a table for a banquet lunch.

The truffle season endures till December in the dark forests of Umbria and the pungent aroma of this underground symbiosis hangs in the air; Tuber Magnatum Pico, the white diamond of Umbria. Luigi and I knowingly accept that this holiday will be punctuated with feverish endeavours to search for and eat sublime food of mythical fame. Our Umbrian lunch, a degustazione menu approved by Luciano, accompanied by the fine red wine Sagrantino of Montefalco, takes our senses of aroma and flavour into the heavens. After terrine of truffle, tagliatelle with pigeon and truffle sauce, and homebred goose cooked in stone, brought in its granite cradle and carved before our eyes, and served with pebbly brown lentils, we can do no more than siesta for three hours before delivering ourselves to Borgo Sansepolcro, twelve kilometres away. Sansepolcro is the birthplace of Piero della Francesca. What peace and harmony I feel in this village museum, not roused by stirring air as someone grazes my shoulder constraining me to release my mind and coercing me to move on to another work of art. Cluttered museums in the cities make me cranky with their fullness, worrying me lest I neglect one of ten thousand works. Where *did* Piero find that jade pigment with which to paint the garments of the sleeping soldiers? To be the only one not sleeping, in Piero's Sansepolcro, waiting for the dawn to break behind a triumphant Christ. As He steps on to His own empty tomb, he did not disappoint my memory, filling me with joy at this day now ending.

A demented wind claws at the awning above the hotel door. It shudders on the hooks, billowing and snapping as the wind tosses it angrily here and there. We are under no illusion of finding fine weather, but this sullen morning blows dark clouds into the valley and fairly throws us to the car where Luigi and Luciano toss our bags into the wagon on top of cartons of wine, and we take our leave. Ruffling the Tiber into a frenzy at our side, the wind buffets the car until we begin to climb through stark black pines in the mountains of Umbria. Within half an hour pines are girdled by snow and we are driving through holes in a curtain of mist that hangs between the mountains. We smudge circles on fogged-up windows, watching icy particles scud across the glass as the mist unravels with every hill and valley we pass. Dancing snowflakes grow large and puffy, prowling round the forest floor and settling on trees, turning tall pines into glistening Christmas cards. The snow falls clean and the road is clear but we travel discreetly, not of a mind to stop until we are through the Alps of Serra and can turn east into gentle hills where our friend Pierluigi is preparing lunch, his sister is planning our late dinner, his uncle will be readying our rooms for the night and his father is probably already thinking about our lunch tomorrow at his farm.

Epicurus, the Greek philosopher, taught in 270 BC that the highest good is personal happiness, and his disciples who hold dear a vestige of refined taste from past eras, and from our own, know about Brisighella, a borgo in a perfumed paradise in undulating hills. It boasts four eating establishments, one of them an Osteria serving tasty local cuisine with flair, and three of a standard befitting gourmands who dine at the tables of great chefs. Applying the principles of the ancients, epicures from nearby Bologna and Ravenna, with religious fervour, must pilgrimage no further than Brisighella to devote mind and body to satisfying sensual desires. Without restraint we yield to thirty hours of flagrant sensual indulgence . . . at the table.

There is a sweet stillness, a fairytale sleepiness, to Brisighella, no more than a hamlet on a hillock. The Grand Lady of Time, a clock tower soaring on a cliff of rocky gypsum, tells not only the hour, but with astrological and prophetical exactness tells of celestial bodies moving in the night sky navigating human affairs and man's destiny. Midway through our midday feast, Maria is beyond joy, excited as a child as she analyses flavours, sniffs at subtle scents, and prods at unrecognized textures. Dainty parcels of wild grass dribbled with tepid rose sauce . . . of what? She summons the chef. On a yellow pond sail shaved curls of a hare, hunted this morning, he tells her. Definitely purée of corn, or farro, she pronounces. Fragrant tunnels inside miniature cannoli flare truffle into our nostrils, and we lean across our plates to study, to smell, and to prick at crustaceans criss-crossed with julienne of something apricot and green held tranquilly suspended in space with . . . is it a drawn and spun spidery web of sugar? Glasses are whisked away and into long-stemmed goblets Pietramora pours, rising dark in crystal, faultlessly matched with our sixth plate: scalded blue-purple beef, lifted from glowing coals and settled on porcelain inside a ring of blueberries. 'Pierluigi – what are you creating for dolce?' Luciano hankers for sweetness, he is a secret chocoholic and cannot wait for dessert.

Stirring from a cosy siesta after lunch we sense a deepening chill and add a layer beneath coats, double mittens and socks inside boots. We meander the pathways of Brisighella, walking along the arched road where panniered donkeys, saddled with sacks of gypsum, avoided rain or swirling mist when they plodded from a chalk quarry a kilometre away. 'Isabella, guarda, saldo! Andiamo!' In this fairytale, in a shifting mist that blots out whole buildings, on an evening threatening a blizzard, not a soul to be seen except we two donkeys plodding along a mule track, Maria spies the one and only clothing emporium in Brisighella; nothing escapes her gleaming eyes. Behind a narrow window a wan light casts more of a shadow than a glow on gold script announcing, as it did a century ago, that this establishment is a thriving hub of commerce importing merchandise from exotic places. Maria finds purple mohair jumpers with burgundy and orange circles on the sleeves, rummages through multi-coloured gloves and operatically wraps an outrageous shawl of every colour in the rainbow around her shoulders. Only she could wear that shawl; should I throw it nonchalantly round my shoulders I would look as beguiling as a multi-flavoured gelato. Swooping to unrobe a mannequin pinned against the wall, she denudes her with a flourish, then, at me: 'Isabella! This is your size – it is stupendous, put it on.' For a reason I will never understand, conservatively dun and beige from top to toe, I purchase a kite-like cherry red coat. 'Maria, how are we going to fit all this in the car?' While we are cleaning out the store, to the delight of a bespectacled little man who dives into glass cases and deep drawers and throws ever more gaily patterned articles from his exotic emporium on the counter, which vanish into Maria's carrier bags, Luigi and Luciano are purchasing Pietramora, the wine we drank with lunch. 'Non preoccuparti, Isabella,' those ominous words ring a warning, 'the wagon is not full yet.'

Dinner is delightful tasty morsels, spuntine, little snacks

prepared by Pierluigi's sister and piled in delicate shapes that tantalize the taste buds without challenging our digestion. On day four, the four Epicureans sleep late, tucked up in Hotel Gigolè, guarded by Pierluigi's uncle. Warming to our search for excellence, today we are lunching at the tower of Pierluigi's father. Even an austere stronghold of the sixteenth century mellows into homeliness when a log fire crackles and flames lick high, casting flickering shadows over our faces making us blush warm. At liberty to wander around the unfenced yard surrounding the old castle, the crowing of red-combed fowl confirms that the speciality of the house is cockerel. Italians adore to be so very close to the beginning of food, pragmatic and not a bit squeamish about the end of its life. Pierluigi's father integrates the fruits of his land with a humble medieval kitchen, but today there is naught but haute cuisine. At the end we are entranced by the vision and lingering perfume of fluffy layered nougat drizzled in liquorice floating along a river of green pistachio.

No chance for siesta today. The wagon is packed to the roof with Sagrantino, cellophane-wrapped high-top Umbrian bread, bolts of beribboned Vasari-like fabric, sacks of Umbrian lentils, jars of truffles and long stoppered bottles of Brisighella olive oil, a dozen bottles of Pietramora wine of Romagna, a distressingly cherry red coat and six shiny carrier bags concealing Maria's gay carnival. The gelato thing is wrapped nonchalantly around her shoulders. We have the rest of the day in which to reach our friends Marisa and Nelson, at Montagnana.

We would not have been fogbound had Luciano not been steering with his knees under the wheel while splaying his hands flat on the roof above his head; thus handicapped, he missed the turning. 'Luigi, dear,' I growl through clenched teeth, 'were you not following the map?' But Maria says it again, and I wince. 'Non preoccuparti! There is always another road.' And she is right, there is, but it swoops into the low plain of the River Po, ensnaring us in a dense motionless soup, a foggy curtain hanging across the river plains. On the edge of his seat, Luciano's nose is pressed into the windscreen while Luigi pushes his head out of the window into freezing air looking down and warning Luciano of his drift towards an algae-green canal. For three blind hours we dawdle roughly in the direction of Montagnana, reminding Luigi and I of the reason we settled in hilltop Montalcino, ten years ago, and not foggy here. 'Wait till you see it,' he enthuses to Maria when we cross over the River Po for the fourth time. The fog eddies as it passes and we at last rise above the plains.

A decade ago we loitered in Montagnana for thirty days. Luigi ventured into bars and shops without me, amiably seeking someone in whom to confide our desire to live in Montagnana. Being Italian by birth, less obviously a foreigner than I, we gauged his chance of striking a note of sympathy might heighten our chances. But it did not. In thirty days we did not inspect one apartment for rent inside the walls of Montagnana. Many were empty but not for rent, at least not for rent to strangers, whom they eyed warily, as if we brought with us the threat of death.

'Don't you remember, Luciano? I rang you when we left here, disappointed that we would need a year to infiltrate the minds of Montagnana – probably longer to find an apartment to rent, and we were almost out of money so we decided instead to drive to Montalcino.'

Marisa and Nelson are the proprietors of an olde worlde pensione. It is no longer easy to find traces of establishments like

Albergo Concordia, described so quaintly and seized upon by writers, poets and painters on the Grand Tour of Italy. It is the type of pensione where rooms meander along homely corridors, with attics wedged in the roof, where carpet runners lead to blanket chests from which you help yourself and the rooms bear trinkets and treasures harking to family taste, because always they are family owned. Concordia began life as an inn for travellers, on the way to somewhere else, but now it is an albergo for antique dealers and southerners, like us, who stumble upon it while on adventures of their own.

'Ciao, ciao Luigi!' Marisa bellows a greeting in the sing-song lilt of the Veneto, a song that reverberates in our ears, resonating louder the nearer she draws. She inspects me up and down and laughs, embracing me as she tells me how *well* I look. Which means I am padded with a kilo or two, which will probably be five by the end of this sumptuary law breaking week. Maria and Luciano visibly stagger backwards a pace. Hearing her booming voice and falling under Marisa's penetrating gaze is disarming. One senses she is cagey about whether you will be a friend until she has scrutinized you and measured your worth. Luigi handles introductions. Marisa is a curvaceous woman of voluptuous proportions; she is wrapped in a white cook's apron and, after courteous handshakes, she cosily tucks her hands behind the apron bib under her large bosom, which rests on her tummy, then she turns and bellows towards an open door. I watch Maria's face unfold into her most infectious laugh as Marisa's voice carries to the kitchen. 'Nelson! Nelson!' she commands. 'Come here!' Maria's eyebrows raise but I can tell she adores this spectacle; she shakes her arms from her coat, revealing her generous and colourful self, dashed and dotted with charms and chains and sashed with a rainbow shawl.

Marisa nods, as though approving kith and kin. 'Ey, ey, ey!' she clucks. Withdrawing her hands from behind the bib, she charges towards Luciano and cups her chubby fingers round his cheeks, squeezing his tanned face to distortion, as you would a baby, murmuring sensuously that he is veramente bello, really handsome. Whereupon she gathers him into her heaving bosom and plonks a smacking kiss on his astonished forehead. Maria's amused smile lights up her face and her green eyes gleam as she witnesses her sophisticated Roman husband writhing under voluptuous attack; there is no escape until Marisa recedes. 'Nelson!' she booms, but he is already here, wringing his hands on a tea towel. His black trousers and burgundy waistcoat are covered by a white bib apron too. 'Luigi, Isabella, buonasera,' he welcomes and we affectionately exchange kisses. Luigi introduces our friends, again, and hands lightly clasp because his are damp; he explains he was stirring risotto. Marisa is the cook at Concordia, but Nelson shares the kitchen. It is not that Nelson is obsequious, but that Marisa is abundantly high-spirited and overwhelming, that widens the impressionable gap. 'This is my husband,' she says, proudly claiming ownership of Nelson, and Maria Pia, gathering her jangling bracelets with aplomb, steps provocatively towards Nelson and noisily smacks a kiss on his cheek. Marisa roars, slapping Nelson so firmly on the back he jolts into Maria's arms. Synergy consolidated, Maria and Marisa are bosom pals. Sanctioning our tenancy, she bundles the four of us and our bags up the stairs, bellowing room numbers, instructing us the keys are hanging in the doors, and threatens us downstairs in five minutes or Nelson's risotto will be ruined. No menu is offered at Trattoria Concordia. You eat whatever Marisa cooks, and that depends on what she feels like cooking and when she feels like cooking it. 'Dai, dai!' Maria hurries

Luciano, speaking Roman dialect. 'Go, go, we have only five minutes!'

Marisa was born in the room where we are sitting at dinner, but Concordia was then rustic to the point where some of the floors were beaten earth. Under abundant curly hair, her full face is milky, skin velvety, showing only smile lines, although her life has not been one of ease. Nelson comes whistling to the table swinging a whole leg of prosciutto. He angles the bone on the table and shaves paper-thin slices on to our plates. A friend goes to Mantua and selects the legs direct from the piggery – while they are still on the wiggly pig, as you would expect – which are dressed, seasoned and aged just around the corner. It alone is almost the principal reason one needs to eat in Montagnana; sweet and soft, cured ham that melts in the mouth. Marisa bustles in with bowls of onions, artichokes, pepperoni, cauliflower and melanzane bathed in salty brine, biting against the sweet prosciutto. We launch into antipasto because the risotto will be arriving soon, but just as we thought we were done, Marisa is back, tea towel wrapped around the long handle of a round pan in which onion frittata sizzles. Resistance achieves nothing; she thrashes the yellow frittata into four and stabs a triangle with the knife, dropping one on to each of our plates. She gathered the eggs this morning from the chickens scrabbling outside the kitchen door and cooked this frittata for our personal happiness. A million miles from Pierluigi, his sister, uncle and father; light years away from tepid rose sauce, suspended spun sugar and that unforgettable liquorice flavoured nougat we may be, but Marisa's kitchen does not lack epicurean happiness nor evocative sensuousness, for Italian cuisine is not highborn. Nelson has stirred half a bottle of dark Barolo into the risotto.

He heaps mauve mountains on our plates and the aroma of vinous must rises.

Secondo piatto is delayed because Maria and Marisa, excluding the rest of us from a heart-to-heart cook-to-cook consultation, unite souls about when, how, and how much of this or that should be added to risotto. Marisa, I know from experience, will return to the kitchen exactly when she feels like it – to suggest otherwise is to be met with a volley of indecipherable Venetian rhetoric. Nelson slips away from the table; perhaps he knows what must be done. One of his ancestors was swept away and drowned in the River Po, and it occurred to generations that followed that Nelson, being an Admiral of the Fleet of Gran Bretagna, would fare better navigating the turbulent river, so the name was handed down to him.

Run by her father and grandparents before her, Marisa has worked at Concordia since she was twelve. In the ancient sense of the word, Concordia was an Osteria, an eating house serving great quantities of food and even more wine to workers in the cornfields or at the dairies. 'By the time I was twelve I was used to cooking up a big pentolone of pork, including all the bones. I put everything in – ears, tail, feet, snout – and while it stewed the men would get merry, then really happy. It was a kind of brotherhood.' Marisa booms with laughter and bellows out her story to Maria. 'I can remember when I was small these workers would arrive at five o'clock in the morning. They sat on a wooden bench outside my mother's window. Cough, cough, cough, they would clear their throats, and then start calling, Ti alzate? Are you getting up? They were waiting for a drink. One was called Gino Cheesemaker because he slept on the ground with the cows, and at five in the morning he would come here first to drink aniseed, then a small grappa and a glass of red wine.

But he was always back in the bar at eight-thirty with two raw eggs in the pocket of his jacket and a piece of bread. He would pierce a hole in the shell and suck out raw egg, then eat the bread and drink more red wine. That was his breakfast!'

They started off with one room for workers, then two or three, because men arrived from the south, without families, desperate for work after the war. Many nights Marisa was shaken awake by her mother because her bed needed to be remade for a worker who arrived in the night. Her father transferred the licence to Marisa after she married Nelson, who is from Parma. An uncle in Parma left Nelson a few antiques, which they sold because they needed the money to plumb the bathrooms and renovate the pensione. Over the decades antiques developed into a consuming passion; credenzas and candelabra, oil paintings and silver salvers lend the pensione an unexpectedly gracious air.

'Pronto!' Nelson calls that whatever it is, is ready, so Marisa heaves her various parts from the table, seizes the iron ladle hanging from the cauldron and heaps a dollop of yellow polenta on to our plates, then, from a second pot, she ladles sinewy aromatic meat stew. 'What is it?' Maria asks, but this is not the first time I have eaten musso and polenta, so I stay silent. Meat eaten on dinner tables around the world repeats pork, beef, and all kinds of fowl, but the addition of baby kid, rabbit and hare, or pigeon, and up here in the Veneto, frogs and snails, and the Veronese favourite, horse, causes many visitors to rear back in horror. This is not horse, although the equine butcher is twenty metres outside the door. Musso is donkey, making me doleful, picturing a thin little creature whose footsteps we followed along the donkey walk at Brisighella.

Our plates are empty. Maria has not guessed it was donkey

but we have discussed a spectrum of beasts I would not contemplate eating. 'I'll make dessert tomorrow,' promises Marisa, 'but I'll whip up a sorbet, if you like?' Into a shaker she dollops lemon gelato, pours in half a bottle of lemon vodka, a tumbler of grappa, and half a bottle of Spumante. It is an exquisite liquid bomb, making me less mournful about the thin little donkey.

We cannot find Marisa this morning, but three cakes, Torta Margherita, fifteen centimetres high, pale and fluffy, are cooling on the kitchen bench. The noise of a sputtering engine rushes in at the window, it fires and rumbles, then settles into a purr. Maria and I gulp our coffee and race to the door to find that Nelson has dragged the tarpaulin from his pride and joy. The weeniest Fiat, a Topolino, a little mouse, pants. He folds down the sunroof, and Maria, rainbow shawl flung over her shoulders, lowers herself in beside Nelson; the Topolino groans under their collective weight. The air is freezing, but if your first glimpse of the towers and walls of Montagnana, wreathed in mist as they will be this morning, is from the front seat of a tiny Topolino convertible it is as good a magic as you can weave. We wave Maria off and Marisa arrives, wobbling on her bicycle. Pedalling the countryside under a plastic cape from head to toe in winter, with a wicker basket on the handlebars, she cycles to the farms of her friends, gathering carrots, radicchio, a few lettuces and often a farm chicken or a rabbit crouches in the basket, unaware of its fate. In spring she gathers white asparagus. She told me once: 'I have never put a foot inside a supermarket because once I went to a shoe mart and got so confused I screamed for Nelson to find the way out.'

We pass a happy day in bleak weather. A Palladian villa, lost and lonely, is a fairytale temple dissolving in the mist and we rise from the fog that has Montagnana in a vice-like grip, into the hills where we visit the house of Petrarch at Arquà Petrarca, taking care to lunch lightly, for Marisa's basket was brimming. We visit a curing shed and Maria leaves with three legs of sweet prosciutto and a bundle of sticks of salami. The last hour of the day inside the walls of Montagnana is not long enough, but by five it is dark and the fog, which has not lifted all day, is thickening. This magic village girded by towers, blindingly cold, can be fogbound for eight months of the year. We decide a siesta before dinner would do well, but feel compelled to walk into Montagnana late tonight when the town is quiet and the fog down.

Our faces harden, stiffening with the dire cold – even smiling hurts as we blink away tears forced out by bitter air. Nocturnal acoustics, sharpened by the fog, echo the sound of our feet as we turn down stone-flagged lanes and walk beneath conical steeples and shuttered windows where strange images shift in the mist, turning over in my mind the story Luigi and I read, ten years ago, the one that first brought us here, when we thought to make Montagnana our home.

It would not be so tiresome, in Montagnana, to suffer from insomnia on a foggy winter's night. You find another dimension, nocturnally, escaping from the noise and bustle of every day orchestrated by shops and banks and business. At four in the morning, the most still and lonely hour of the night, you can see things that, in daylight, seem not to exist. A kind of magic, a dreamy childlike belief that after midnight inanimate objects come alive, as in a fairytale. On this December night ghostly swirls of fog confuse our path and in white gloom the milky moon is hazy, a smudge of light doing its utmost to show us the way. In wee silent hours we feel the walls like eyes following our feet, opening and closing at our backs so that whenever we peer down a lane, there it is, at the end or alongside us, consoling our hearts from whatever danger lies outside on the plains.

Last night's dinner, the sorbet bomb, and our nocturnal impressions on our midnight walk round the towers shrouded in fog are topmost in our minds as we repack the wagon this morning. We give two bottles of Brunello to our friends, but in return Marisa presses Maria and I with a porcelain plate from her collection. Maria packs our precious plates, three legs of prosciutto and numerous sticks of salami and a few recipes from Marisa in the wagon, shuffling a case of wine with pure spring water from Arquà Petrarca, putting the wine on the floor between our feet. 'Wait! Wait!' Marisa bellows, thundering back from the kitchen. A fifteen-centimetre Torta Margherita, for each of us; ideal for the sixth day of a car journey. Two puffy Margherita sponge cakes wobble on the centimetres of seat between us, and even Maria winces at the likelihood of an elbow punching them into a crumbly mess before we find our way through the fog and skirt the walls of Montagnana.

Today we travel on the autostrada, diverting to circle Verona, where Luigi has aunts, uncles and cousins, but we do not have time to enter the city. Instead, we divert to the vineyard of Pierangelo Tommasi – Luciano refuses to give up on his ambition to take a couple of cases of Amarone and Valpolicella back to Grappolo. Maria betrays no emotion whatsoever, lodging two cartons of wine on the floor at our feet, repositioning the one that *was* on the floor to the seat, between us, with fifteen centimetres of wobbling Torta Margherita quivering on top of the box. The other Margherita, which was hovering between her knees, is in a thousand pieces, so we are eating it. 'Oh! Pia, you are getting crumbs everywhere!' accuses Luciano, typical of the gender, as he pokes his hand between the seats demanding a slab. *This* is why women get to sit in the back. We navigate a horrendous traffic snarl round smoggy Milan, and turn towards beckoning Swiss Alps. The day is dull and dirty, sleet spreads an icy veil across the windscreen, but we do not care, confident it will be breathtaking. We are taking Maria and Luciano to divine Lake Orta. We have one more night and a gastronomic highlight for we must be home tomorrow night so that Luciano can present car ownership papers to the carabinieri in Siena the next day, and so that Grappolo can reopen for Christmas trading.

A Moorish minaret pierces clouds above our villa, the folly of a Milanese cotton magnate. Tessellated mosaics form stylized Islamic polygons across the floor and diamonds interlace on the walls, carved and embossed on gold-painted fretwork. Sumptuous four-poster beds canopied and floating in silk organza and lashed with tassled cords create exotic Bedouin bedrooms overlooking Lake Orta, crowned all round with mountains glistening white.

It is no longer little known, as it was ten years ago when Luigi and I half froze to death miserably camped under damp canvas on an exposed ridge overlooking the lake. In eighteen months we travelled Italy on an alarmingly short shoestring. We had no money, then, for an opulent sultan's tent like this crimson dream, but we indulged outrageously – rashly, considering our budget – and have never forgotten the utopia of dining, long and slow, seven plates fit for the gods, with Daniela at Ristoro Olina. This is our grand finale . . . she will not let us down.

We have been gourmandizing for a week. Travel conversation has pivoted around the pros and cons of finesse and simplicity, haute cuisine verses cucina povera, the poor kitchen;

fragrant wines, cloying and delicate, wafting perfumes compared with bold reds with pungent forest floor and farm aromas
that pucker the lips and tie up the mouth. Comparisons and
verdicts sway first one way, then another. To our joy, we are
about to add Alpine meadows and lake fish to academia.

'This is absolutely il migliore,' the best cervo I have ever eaten,
sings Maria. Paper-thin slivers of deer fillet lap a pink poached
pear and soft rounds of ewe's milk Robiola cheese. We are bound
to agree, but we have six more plates with which to be seduced.
Luigi pours perfumed Erbaluce to accompany the first fish
course – fleshy and white in a yellowish fuzz of curry sauce, and
timbale of Sant' Andrea rice, grown twenty kilometres away.
'Luciano, we must travel home via the rice plains and pick up a
sack.' How big a sack? I dismiss nervous thoughts. Daniela has
stacked three kinds of mushroom in trifoliate composition, each
clover divided with tepid Castelmagno mountain meadow
cheese. 'Daniela –' Maria is into top gear – 'can you sell me
Castelmagno . . . just a few rounds?' Unfortunately, or fortunately, Daniela is apologetic, she does not stock the cheese; it is
brought daily from the farm. 'Peccato,' a pity, says Maria,
momentarily disappointed. 'But, non preoccuparti, Daniela,
where is the farm?' She is sounding more like bellowing Marisa
by the moment. 'Luciano, when we go to the rice plains we are
almost at Alba. We can stop there too, and buy some cheese.'
Luciano gasps, torn between Castelmagno and the long road
south. I throw Luigi a withering look, much as to say, unfairly,
you led us into this terrible blunder. I will be sitting on a sack of
rice all the way to Montalcino. But I am torn asunder – rice is my
preferred way to eat and cook Italian at home. All thoughts of a
direct route home are expunged when Daniela sails to the table
bearing a platter of gleaming, jet-black riso nero tossed with lake

mollusc. Nothing has impressed me more. To the rice plains we must go.

Since we have three plates more Daniela sensibly paces our foray. Through a window we watch agnolotti pasta kneaded and rolled, then rapidly folded into pretty parcels hiding full cream cow's milk fontina, our fifth plate. The chef orders us back to the table; the agnolotti cooks in a minute. One bite and the half-melted flavour of alpine meadows explodes against our cheeks. We are blown away, reduced to gasps. Quail is delicate and sweet, at Olina, falling from fragile bones and served alone, save a green nest, and does not push us beyond our limit. Luigi selects Gattinara red and we revel in gluttonous personal happiness. 'Luciano!' we all hiss at him when he has the temerity to ask Daniela about dessert, but it is too late. Hot thick syrupy zabaglione with a sauce of Muscat grappa leads us to the sensual aroma of grinding beans. We reach caffè, and are done. Linking arms, four abreast, we brace ourselves for a blast of icy air and, winking back at blinking lights on bobbing boats, laugh our way round the lake and up the hill to our harem tent.

The bedroom is black as pitch. Why is the telephone ringing? 'Maria! What's the time? What's the matter?' She whispers into the phone: 'Seven o'clock . . . Open the curtains and look out your window!' A tinny dawn light filters pale into the sky, but the world is glowing white! Snow clings to the branches of larch and pine, has gathered on the window shutters hooked to the sill, and in the distance the lake shore gleams under a mantle pure and undisturbed. I grab the phone. 'Andiamo! Let's go, I'll beat you downstairs.'

Three cars, including ours, are joined in white drift. Our eyes meet, laughing: 'That is definitely a man thing! *They* can dig out the car . . . That's why *we* sit in the back!' We are avenged. The snow lies deep, to the top of our boots. Maria wraps her rainbow shawl around her head and I have my Fendi wrapped around my shoulders. We tramp through white loveliness to the road, then, holding each other by the hand, gambol through the drifts; there is something childlike about virgin snow. We frolic past the white rimmed villas, rippled roofs white and soft, and banks of camellia and rhododendron below larch and magnolia. Everything is heavy and low, decked in white, pearly crystals glistening and red robins, puff-breasted and chirruping, our only witnesses. Rounding a corner we suck in our breath and, holding the moment, stop to stare at a shimmering mirage, hesitant between water and heaven, where legends hover; it drifts like a ship lost at sea. 'Let's go to the island of San Giulio, Maria, if the boatman is awake.' We reach the village of Orta where horse chestnuts line the shore and boats, white-pointed prows fluffy and soft, are icily roped to moorings, plashing softly up and down against rubber buoys. We are too early even for caffè! From the island we hear the hollow tinkle of ringing bells from the monastery where wimpled nuns bake opus mannum, the bread of San Giulio. We listen keenly, realizing how much we have missed the bells of Montalcino. The bells tinkle prettily in crystalline air, bouncing across the lake and bidding us to the island; if only we could find the boatman. 'What's over there besides the nuns in the monastery?' asks Maria. I read the book over summer, so I tell her the story.

'Around three hundred and something after Christ was born, two Christian brothers, battling paganism lingering in the dying Roman Empire, came to this lake and one brother, Giulio, decided that he would build a temple and find a peaceful place in which to end his life. But the boatman – who we will have to find if we are to go across – refused this vagabond passage and threw stones at him, saying: Have you no fear of God that you would challenge the perils of fire-spitting dragons and snakes that roam around that cursed island? Laying his shabby mantle on the water, Giulio stepped lightly on to it, and defying the legendary monsters, rowed himself across to the island. He built a temple – his remains are sepulchred in the crypt, and there is a divine pathway with little signs written and posted by the cloistered nuns.' Maria is easily convinced, but I have not yet told her of the other reason for my desire to brave the water. 'Let's go up the motta, where the boatmen live, maybe someone is around.' The motta is a pebbly rise where, in hollowed-out arches, fishermen keep their boats below their houses. 'Signora!' this fisherman objects. 'Nothing is open over there except the basilica, it's too early . . . and it is winter!' But we plead and he relents, puts on his seafaring peaked cap, and we follow him to his boat, helping him shove armfuls of snow into the lake, freeing the engine box for our five-minute boat ride over the waters that were studded with legendary fire spitting dragons that roamed around the island a millennium and a half ago.

Our hands caress the columns of a black oira pulpit, rippling over entwined ribbons and curls spiralling upwards to a crocodile and a doe menaced by lions. 'Maria,' I whisper, overawed, 'come and look at this. In 590, a couple of hundred years after Brother Giulio rowed to the island and found his path to a heavenly mansion and sainthood, a duke of the Longobards came here; he massacred the poor boatman and rowed himself across to the sacred island of San Giulio.' I do not tell her the rest, but it ripples through my mind. Thirty-five years of Longobard mayhem is not yet up. Settling into a reign of terror he murders the priests, burns down the monastery and ransacks this very temple. He builds himself a castle on the island. Why is he here?

Hold back the Gallic invaders, commands the Longobard king, but the duke resisted the Francs not well enough. Cut off his treacherous head, ordered the king with the iron crown. *This* is what I came to see. How sweet it is to press my hands into the marble sarcofago in which the remains of the beheaded duke were laid. Fronds interlace and curl round flowers, perhaps they are vine leaves; the carving is sculpted with artistic grace in high relief. It is *not* barbaric.

The boatman signals with a whistle that our time is expired. Mooring at the landing under the horse chestnuts Maria sees the barman swishing snow from his doorway with a long-handled twig broom and offers our obliging boatman breakfast; we warm up with caffè and brioche. Maria's mobile phone rings. It is Luciano. Choosing the wiser option, she does not respond, switches off, and we plough up the hill through the snow, retracing our own footsteps, to meet our fate.

Is there a jumble sale under the covered veranda of the villa? No! But Luciano and Luigi are grumpily repacking the wagon. Snow chains are not easy to affix with frozen hands, having shovelled snow for half an hour to dig out the car. Livid Luciano utters only one word, in Roman dialect: 'Eohh!' which, accompanied with his hand movements, means: 'Merda! Thanks for nothing.' Ever the pacifist, Luigi announces, almost pleasantly: 'We have checked out.' Maria and I look at each other, horrified. 'Where are our clothes?' we wail in unison. They have packed our bags below prosciutto and sackcloth and lentils! We chorus objection, but are constrained to travel home to Montalcino with not a comb or cosmetics, wearing damp snow gear and sodden boots. Male revenge! Maria winks and whispers: 'Non preoccuparti, Isabella, I'll think of something.'

*

Fifty kilometres from Orta traction returns when the snowline finishes and chains are removed, but our hysterical screams are so fierce that Luigi dumps the wet filthy jangling things under his own feet, since we have locked our doors. 'It's a man thing,' I grin at Maria. We track down riso nero and Carnaroli and Sant' Andrea rices at the Abbey of Lucedio. Three five-kilogram sacks of rice are dumped beneath our feet, on top of the wine, and our knees rise higher. We are not yet forgiven our dawn escapade; Luigi and Luciano decide, without even referring to we females, suddenly invisible, to stop for a case of Erbaluce and one of Gattinara when we pass a sign to the vineyards. I have seen a car packed like this in a Chevy Chase movie; soon I will be sat on the roof.

Whizzing down an empty autostrada we reason that the provincial city of Casale Monferrato will have a cheesemaker and thus we may not need to go all the way to Alba. Casale is on a fertile plain, hemmed in by snow-capped French and Swiss Alps from which chips of ice are sent flying into town on a vicious mountain wind. Luigi and I hole up in a royal-looking bar in the piazza, ordering a light lunch for all of us, while Maria and Luciano find the cheesemaker. We stagger back to the car which rides low on its axles, and that is before the four of us are on board! Maria and I jeer mercilessly; we are wrapped and hooded in our snow gear, but Luciano and Luigi stamp their feet, shiver and gasp out frozen breath, backs to the blethering wind. Maria winks conspiratorially. The aroma in the car will be interesting in a few hours; packages of Robiola and Castelmagno cheeses are in the back with us. Reading my mind, Luciano's teeth chatter uncontrollably as he warns: 'We cannot even turn the heating on low, now, or the ch-ch-cheese will turn.'

At last, certain Maria has accumulated every farm, forest and mountain food possible to be gathered on a week's holiday, I relax. Luigi has the map and plans our homeward march. About six hours, I reckon, given the wicked weather and the weight of our swaying car. Autostrada all the way to Bologna, then through the Apennine mountain tunnels to Florence, super-strada to friendly territory, Siena, and we will be home around eight or nine o'clock tonight. Scattered and unconnected thoughts fill my mind flying at a hundred and sixty kilometres an hour along this rule-straight autostrada, thoughts as simple as red berries and green lettuces, broken only when we overtake lines of lorries spitting water from huge tyres on to the windscreen. Maria nudges me, and whispers: 'Stay with me, Isabella, back me up.' I have no idea why. She is silent for a full five minutes.

Shiny and green, the autostrada sign looms overhead and Maria shouts: 'Luciano, look, in ten kilometres we can turn off to Parma! We cannot go home without a round of Parmigiano Reggiano, not when we are this close!' She winks and nudges my shoulder, but I am torn between eight o'clock in Montalcino, or midnight, and utter not a word. 'Pia! No! Per favore!' Please! Luciano begs, but she has another bullet. 'Luigi, do you remember what Nelson said? He comes from Parma and he told us the name of the best place to eat chestnut pasta. Let's stay in Parma a couple of hours, find the restaurant, and drive home late when there are fewer trucks on the road.' She pushes her lips to my ear, elbowing me in the ribs, urging: 'The shops in Parma are *fabulous*! We'll buy an outfit . . . get out of these snow clothes.' Summoning courage from a doubting heart, wanting to demand where on earth in this wagon we are going to put our snow clothes, never mind a whole round of Parmigiano cheese, I stand by my friend.

For the umpteenth time I try to read my watch. Luigi snuffles, coughs and snores. Maria's head bobs up and down and side to side, and the feather on her hat, which she has on because of the dire cold inside this car, tickles my ear; her bobbing head drops on to the Parmigiano Reggiano, and her large body rolls towards me; a huge round of cheese slides across a collapsing cardboard wine case, drops off the edge at an angle, and painfully wedges into the side of my neck between my ear and shoulder. She cannot sway the other way because her snow gear and shopping bags are stuffed between her and the door. Ravaging and pillaging the big city shops like a barbarian, leaving in her wake a trail of settling credit card debris, she sprinted from shop to shop finding homecoming presents for the family, a sack of tights in wild sparkles and scrolls never witnessed in mild Montalcino, a hideous singing fish for her grandson, and a bag of gold tinsel and vibrant stars for her Christmas tree. I twist awkwardly and shove the cheese back on the case of wine; Maria jostles and her head falls forward on her chest. Like me, she cannot go further in that direction because our knees are as high as our noses.

'Luciano, what time is it?' I keep asking to make sure he is awake; he yawns and puffs out a garbled response as we rocket along the last dark stretch of superstrada before Siena. Bumps in the road shake six bottles of traditional balsamic vinegar which threaten to break in the bag under my elbow. (Maria could not pass Modena without the real thing.) Buried somewhere behind me are two loaves of week-old high-top yellow bread, and a Torta Margherita, reduced by now to birdfeed. And a blasted cherry red coat! A woman's thing, I smile to myself. This incorrigible woman would have half a donkey in this car, were that possible. Crinkling cellophane packets of chestnut pasta crackle under my chin as I turn, dropping my tired eyes to peer between the handles of shopping bags, looking into blackness through a tiny oval where my gloved finger rubbed the misted window. 'Luciano, what time is it? 'Quarto alle tre.' Quarter to three. Less than an hour to go.

'Luciano, what time . . . oh, Dio, no!' Flashing lights and red lollipops wave Luciano to the verge of the road. Luciano growls under his breath. 'What the . . . merda, not again!' Snoring Luigi and bobbing Maria, stirred from slumber, wake to find us stationary, ten kilometres from home at the junction with Buonconvento. Blue-white filaments flash and swirl in coruscating circles from the roofs of police cars and burrowing torches pierce the windows while the long thin barrels of machine guns menace us from a cadre of carabinieri. Ought we put our hands up, like they do in the movies? A machine gun signals for Luciano to lower his window while half a dozen unsmiling black balaclavas stare at the pillaged booty picked up by roaming torches from which we try to shield our eyes. Spooky eyes peering through slits glare into the car at what they righteously comment must be merchandise from a midnight raid on a supermarket. Luciano runs ever so politely through the story of why he has no papers for the car, and attempts to explain why this vehicle is loaded to the hilt with multiple prosciutto, cheeses, pasta, wines, balsamico, salami and other unrecalled merchandise, that we are not robbers on the run and that we all have lived almost for ever in the village twinkling behind him on the hill. There is no reply – but the computer in a police car whirs on and we sit and wait in terrified silence. This is too much for my pounding heart; any moment helicopters will swoop upon us, flames of light boring into the car and red berets will stream down ropes. 'Signor,' the machine gun addresses

Luciano, 'you are already registered for a misdemeanour last week. You will present your papers in Siena tomorrow, twice, is that clear?' Thank heavens they decide not to unload our car. We only look like robbers. It seems that at four o'clock on a freezing morning we blundered into a stake-out for some other vagabond bandits. 'Move it!' he growls. 'Get out of here before you are caught in the crossfire. You should be home in bed.' I could not have put it more succinctly. Luciano accelerates, but Maria's eyes are laughing as she whispers in my frozen ear: 'Isabella! Non preoccuparti, it's a man thing!'

Luigi and Maria are bright-eyed as we wind round familiar hills and climb through the vineyards up to dear little twinkling Montalcino, past Porta Cerbaia, under the fortress, round the wall, down the hill and creak to a halt in front of Bar Prato. Luigi and I will walk home from here and the bulging car we will unload later today, because it is already half past four. 'Grazie, ciao, ciao,' we yawn affectionate farewells, but I am shaken alert by the bitter chill. It is well below zero up here on the hill. 'Isabella!' calls Maria. 'Here, have my shawl!' A crumpled, wine-stained, cheesy-smelling rainbow rag flies from the window into my arms. 'Ciao! Si, tremendous fun, si, si, we'll never forget that sublime food, will we? Nor Marisa . . . and what about that donkey?' Laughing as my mind flits lightly over our sumptuous holiday, blanking out the bulging mess in the back of the car although I am not quite mentally ready to joke about the carabinieri, like Lot's wife I turn into a frozen lump, listening to Maria's parting salvo: 'Luciano! What do you think? Next year, let's close Grappolo for a month. Luigi and Isabella, why don't you take us to Australia?'

Old gate in the wall of the village of Montalcino

CHAPTER FOURTEEN

Black Rice in White Snow

Eyes closed, dragging myself from sleep, I count the gongs echoing from the bell tower; seven, eight . . . nine o'clock! I thought I would sleep for a week when I crashed between frozen sheets at half past four this morning. A whistling wind rushes at the window and screams away, dementing the shutters on their hooks, rattling them so that intermittent dim light pierces the

413

bedroom gloom. Dressing quickly and creeping from the bedroom, leaving Luigi to slumber, I grab my wet weather coat, unbecoming hat and – damn – my boots are still in the car!

Up at the Madonna the Siberian is cruel, tossing dirt and leaves into my eyes, forcing me to lower my face and stagger up the slope in the wind's eye, guided by the path edge. Slit eyes, watery and blinking in the biting chill, are all that I expose; gloved hands sink deep into pockets. My fur-lined waterproof flaps my ankles and a woolly hat scrunches over my ears, but nothing can hold back the bleakness of this blast of air funnelled by a desolate wind that brings a plaintiff Siberian howl baying at our walls. When Luciano drove around the walls and back into the village hours ago, I saw nothing more than dark haze through misty windows when we passed the depredation which was once a wilderness of brambles and olive trees. Cautiously raising my head at the top of the hill my face prickles under a stream of white crystals dancing on the wind. Shoulders of jagged earth hang where once boulders bound terraces tight. The wind searches the frozen landscape, rushing over stones and tugging at the earth. The yellow monster has vanished; workmen have gone home for the festive season. An open wound cuts brutally into the hill with not a hint of wild growth except a few gnarled olive trees swaying drearily along the topmost terrace, where runs the white stone path.

Putting my back to the howling wind I turn below the Madonna where sheets of ice confining puddles along the track crackle and splinter into transparent shards under my feet. The wall offers shelter and I huddle against it, staring out to the hunting woods. Inert along the valley floor, to my left, lies an emotionless stone graveyard where trucks have carted a mountain of hammered stones from the broken walls; stones are immune to the wind from Siberia.

A couple of days and Christmas will be here. Not a celebration of spectacular gaiety in Montalcino, with Babbo Natale, Father Christmas on every corner and reindeer sleighs piled high; it is more religious than pagan, but Christmas lights will be blinking by now, and a Christmas tree will be twinkling under the cappellone. I cannot remember if our fish dinner in Pianello is tonight or tomorrow. Someone in the piazza will tell me. Instead of walking all the way around the walls this freezing morning I will see how the village looks, dressed in Christmas baubles. Anyway, Ercole and Lola will be waiting to hear that we are safely back inside the walls, and on the way home I will ring Amelia's door bell. Perhaps Ofelia will be able to meet me for caffè this afternoon; I have so much to tell her – but if our fish dinner is tonight, then Massimo will be cooking, so we will sit together.

As I reach up to press Lola's buzzer a stable door on the roadway swings open and standing behind it is old Gina, whose light bulb I replaced not so long ago. She is holding a bottle of red wine by the neck, wearing her house slippers and a blue coat is thrown around her shoulders. 'Oh, Signora, buongiorno,' she says, her eyes wide with surprise, 'I was looking for someone passing . . . can you help me? I need half a glass of wine to warm me up – the Siberian is blowing – but I cannot get the cork out!' Through a bone-cold salon to the kitchen she leads the way by feel and habit, not by sight, for the place is shuttered and black and she will not switch on the fifteen watt light. Surely the bulb cannot have blown already? 'Gina! This is never going to pull out a cork. It has no arms to pull it with!' She fiddles in a drawer and looks up, displaying a less sophisticated but workable opener with which I draw the cork. She sets two glasses on the table and, sitting close by her kitchen stove which is barely warm enough to send more than a degree from the chill in this room, I tell her about the places we visited but it might just as well have been Siberia itself; old Gina has never been further than Siena.

'Cara! You are home! Come in, come in!' Ercole keeps the fire glowing all day in winter and through the night dying embers heap and smoulder so that in the morning he fans coals into flame with a twist of newspaper and feeds it two logs at a time, keeping their kitchen cosy and warm. 'What's been happening?' I am eager for news, both amused and astonished when Lola relates dramatically that on Tuesday the fire engine raced into the village to put out a fire in the fruit shop. A faulty cord from a refrigerator caught fire, smoke *poured* into the road. While I listen, commenting gleefully at the goings on, Ercole shrugs into a bulky coat and slips out to the balcony. 'Angelo in Bar Mariuccia was quick as a wink! He hooked up a hose from his cantina before the firemen came. Then,' she theatrically relates, 'on Wednesday, they had to come again! The pensioners were playing cards at the parish club, but someone smelled gas, so they called the fire station and the police. Everyone was evacuated on to the road . . . even before they had time to put on their coats! We had to take blankets and wrap them up or they would have died of cold; and we brought them into our houses. There really was gas leaking from a pipe – it could have exploded!' Ercole taps timidly on the glass door and purses his lips to warn me to be quiet and, stepping gingerly to the window, I watch him feed crumbs to a family of three robin redbreasts dancing and chirruping on the railing. It is comforting to be certain they are not destined for the spit roast in this household. Ercole has made friends with a family of red robins who scold him with declamatory titters until he goes out with a few crumbs. Next Lola tells me their daughter and granddaughter are coming on Christmas Eve for the family dinner, but will only stay a day or two, so we agree on a time when Luigi and I can call together. 'How did the holiday go?' asks Lola. 'Perfect! Wonderful!' I reply, running briefly through the less worrying aspects of our exploits.

Coloured lights strung across the narrow road blink on and off while 'O Come All Ye Faithful' tinkles from the opening door of the grocer. Christmas tunes are the same as English ones, but sometimes the words are Italian . . . but not jingle bells, Italian children jeengle happily. Most shops have fastened trailing holly or wreaths of ivy and red berries round the doors, but not excessively. Christmas trees and coloured lights are not even to be seen until five or six days before the twenty-fifth. At the end of the road I see a three-wheeler Ape; shovels and rakes poke from the tray. Good! That is Mario's Ape. He is setting up the nativity under the Cedar of Lebanon for the children; they will line up for presents from Befana under a starlit tree. Mario supervises a load of black soil sliding from a truck, dressed as always in his black suit and black tie and hat.

'Amelia!' There is no joy in my voice, only distress. 'Whatever have you done?' My dear friend tries to make light of ugly black and blue bruises down the side of her face. 'Isabella, amore! I am so glad you have come home! I am all right,' she promises, 'the Madonna saved me.' Confessing to a nasty fall when her legs slid from under her on icy stone slabs coming out of Mass at the Madonna, she pushes up her sleeve to the elbow, which is bruised black and yellow, and my eyes fill with tears of fear as she slides her skirt, revealing her blue-yellow hip. We hug tightly, holding on, and she, too, has tears in her eyes. 'Nothing is broken – the Madonna looked after me – but I am so depressed. I was worried you would not come home before I go. My daughter who lives past Milan is arriving today, she is taking me to the mountains to stay for a while.'

Amelia does not want to leave Montalcino. She has lived in this house for so many decades, but Bruno is not here to chop the wood and she has no other form of heating or cooking. When the fire is blazing her house is warm, but it is dangerous for her to go down the path to the cantina when cobbles are iced over, and that is where her wood and wash trough is, and she likes to fetch onions and garlic which are strung from a wooden coat hanger, dangling from the wood pile. 'I am afraid I will never see my little home again, but I could not leave without saying goodbye.'

Trying to cheer her up, I stay for an hour, chatting and letting her fuss. She makes caffè and forces a second slice of torta upon my bulging bottom. Soon we are laughing; she listens to my censored holiday news, and our conversation turns back to Christmas. We shed tears of togetherness, talking about Bruno. We have no walnut-stuffed figs, and no basilico liqueur which Bruno always made for Christmas. She makes me write down my phone number and slowly reads the numbers back to me. 'Amelia, don't worry – I have your daughter's number, she gave it to me at Bruno's funeral.' But she insists, determined, because she *knows* how to write the numbers and slowly, one after the other, each number appears with solemn deliberation. 'There!' She is triumphant, happy when we make a double solemn promise to ring each other every week. This is a hard parting for both of us; we have shared many intimate moments over a decade. Consoling her, I promise that I will keep Bruno clean and tidy, from time to time, up in the cemetery, and pledge on my heart to rub a cloth around the marble angel who guards Silena. Her daughter has promised to bring her home before Easter, as soon as winter passes. 'Ciao, ti voglio bene. Ciao, ciao, amore!' Ciao, my love, is the way Amelia always farewells me, even when I am taking six paces to cross the path to my doorstep. We hug tightly and cry easily, smiling bravely through our tears. I step from her door and look back, blowing kisses from the cobbled path, but welling tears splash freely on my cheeks.

The merry season takes hold. We join friends for our fish dinner in Pianello and Ofelia and I have been in a chatty huddle for half an hour; she has listened to my holiday tales, uncensored. One after the other prawns and then swordfish are grilled on a wire brazier by Massimo and Lorenzo, who stand in front of the fiery coals outside the door, and Cinquino and Gabriele hurry out and rush back in with filled iron trays. We are in our downstairs dining room and the children are here, too; young Leonardo is swung through the air by Gaetano and little Alice is dancing with her mother, Caterina, and Walter and his young friends are running round, excited to be on holiday from school. Everyone has been discussing, as all families do, who is going to which half of the family for Christmas Eve, the traditional family dinner, and Santo Stefano, Boxing Day, and what they will be cooking and eating. From memory they will be eating exactly the same as last year, and the year before that. Italians never tire of their own cuisine, seeking not to spring surprising alternatives upon each other, but only to exalt pasta and sauce, or to seek clues from grandmothers about when to add the wine, or a handful of herbs. Happily bantering across a table laden with delicious food about delicious food yet to be eaten, we pull prawns from skewers and lick our fingers and thumbs. Except for sensational fiddly bits on sticks last spring, this dinner is about as daringly alternative as Pianello members wish to venture, cuisine wise.

'Isabella, have you heard that Mayor Massimo has made another proclamation? Everyone held their breath,' Ofelia sighs, 'but it is good news.' Our mayor, in light of all the new babies born in Montalcino this year – a bumper crop of twenty-two births – has put in place a plan to add a room to the school so that, in four years, all these children will have a new classroom. One of my responsibilities as Secretary is to deliver a Pianello scarf to newborns in our quartiere, and we have our share – and Carlo and Costanza's baby will arrive next year, too. Mayor Massimo did not hesitate to point out: 'Young people are staying in our village, marrying and bringing up their children inside the walls.' Another iron tray, much longer than the first, is borne in with Cinquino at one end and Gabriele the other, and Lorenzo follows behind with tongs in his hand. This tray is brimming with charcoal orata, bream, and a whole fish is served on each plate. We have bowls of salad greens on the table, doused liberally with olive oil, and Luciana brings golden roasted rosemary potatoes straight from the oven. Ofelia, finishing her discourse, adds that work on the new post office has begun, but the big news is that the Comune has wrestled agreement from the state. It may take many months but everyone is jubilant because the Mayor has promised that our panoramic window under the cappellone are to be returned to us. 'He says he still plans to initiate work on the staircase in the tower at the end of winter.' In Montalcino, where every single thing that happens involves our lives so pertinently, a week away has put me way behind.

A white Christmas is not a certainty in Montalcino but often enough, like today, snowflakes flutter and settle on window ledges and although the village is not mantled in glistening white, half-open shutters push fallen snowflakes into little piles that gather on sills in miniature drifts. Christmas lunch with Maria and Luciano will mean we get to eat some of the food from other regions we brought back from our holiday, except the two high-top lard and saffron bread loaves, which were no longer yellow, nor high, and no longer a pair, having merged low, grey and hairy, more like a run-over rat when we peeled them from the floor of the wagon, along with Marisa's cake, also beyond recognition.

Maria's table is a picture, dressed in jade and gold, not yet definitively a table cloth, but we will hardly notice selvage threads tickling our knees. Vasari swirls and curlicues she has overlaid with pale biscuit organza on which she sprinkles red berries and ivy. Maria, a truly remarkable woman, tinsel threaded through her henna-red hair and sparkling sequins racing all over her legs, floats from kitchen to table swinging a leg of sweet prosciutto. Twenty new Christmas bangles jangle and eyes laugh as she mimics Marisa hugging Luciano to her voluptuous bosom, and she tells everyone about the donkey dinner, now that she knows what Marisa put in the stew, but her story becomes confused with the donkey walk at Brisighella, and they think we ate *those* donkeys. She is not bothered that her grandson, Eduardo, follows her in and out of the kitchen cradling that hideous singing fish which is singing 'Yankee Doodle Dandee'; surely the battery will run down any minute. She brings a porcelain platter to the table, the one which her soul mate Marisa gave her, on which is layered affettati, sliced meat, but I do not recognize it from our holiday. By the time she has recounted stories of missed turn-offs, river plains in a curtain of fog, midnight at misty Montagnana and leaving Luigi and

Luciano to dig the car from the dawn snow drift at Orta, Maria has laid the table for a merry feast for twenty and she calls us to be seated. She soon has everyone enraptured describing the divine food and splendid wine we savoured every single day, swooning dramatically over aromas and flavours, not necessarily in order . . . She carries us back and forth from Orta to Brisighella, Città di Castello to Montagnana via an impossible route, tumbling plates and places into mismatched sequences. My stories, weaving gloomily around her indefatigable happiness at whatever predicament we found ourselves in, revolve around my poor little crunched-up knees and creaking neck – and being mistaken for robbers and haring up the hill to Montalcino at four-thirty in the morning in a temperature of minus five degrees.

Luciano struggles from the kitchen – adding validity to my story about cheese and my pained neck – under the weight of a whole round of Parmigiano and everybody erupts into cheers and claps as if it is the very first time any of them have ever seen anything like it in their entire lives. The round is gently tapped, caressed and rubbed reverently all over, knowingly knocked lightly with knuckles, and held by one after each other, close to their ears, as if the cheese should speak! Luciano sets the trophy from Parma, like a Christmas cake, on the middle of the table and those nearest heap it with holly and berries. Maria promises: 'At the end of dinner, we'll break apart the Parmigiano and taste it with Brunello, and I'll sprinkle it with a few drops of fifty-year-old balsamic vinegar. Allora,' she adds, getting things underway, 'who is going to be first to try the donkey?' My eyes meet hers, stunned. Her eyes are gleaming: 'Non preoccuparti, Isabella, the affettati on the porcelain platter – Marisa gave me four sticks of donkey salami that Nelson makes himself.' Damn, she *did* have half a donkey in the car.

Maria's primo piatto is as unbelievable and unpredictable as her very self. In from the kitchen she waltzes carrying high above her head, by a handle on each end, a giant silver salver. We can see billowing clouds of steam rising . . . and the aroma . . . yes! Tartufo! Tuscans are never fooled by the scent of truffle . . . but when she lowers the tray to set it on the table, we are awed into silence. Heaped into a volcano in the middle of the tray is truffle risotto, shiny and black as midnight, made with riso nero from the Abbey of Lucedio. From its sunken heart rises the flame of a tiny candle, flickering, but all around the edge of the tray, circling the gleaming black beads, are glistening mountains of white. She has gathered snow from her window sills and formed it into peaks like a crown of white mountains around a flaming black volcano. I do not recall seeing anything on a table so beautiful – not even in Città di Castello, Brisighella, Montagnana or Lago di Orta. We are speechless, staring open-mouthed at gleaming black rice in glistening white snow. Maria sparkles like a star on the Christmas tree.

We spend Santo Stefano with Ofelia and Chiara who, without Massimo, on duty at the fire station, come to our home. I surprise Ofelia by cooking an oriental lunch with my wok and rice steamer. First frying poppadoms and stirring a green seafood soup, Ofelia helps me skewer saté chicken for the grill and mix spicy chilli sauce. The wok delivers crisply noodles, then beef, bamboo and cashew nuts with perfumed rice – again from the Abbey of Lucedio. A long slow lunch, cooking and then eating, and I am redeemed because Ofie adores my lime and poppy seed cake. 'Ganzo!' she says, when I promise that soon I'll go with her to Florence and search the shops for a wok for her. Ofelia is curious about the world outside the walls, but Massimo is Ilcinese to the bone, it is written in blood on his forehead. How he will react to poppadoms and saté is yet to be discovered.

The days between Santo Stefano and New Year pass with Armando's pizza night in Pianello, for which all the young are home to help. The boys wear Pianello aprons and roll the dough, pretending they are pizzaioli, pizza makers. Cinquino spins floppy dough on the end of his finger, and he succeeds . . . for a moment, but Armando boxes his ears when his fingers poke through, making an ugly hole. Whirling like Frisbees, saucers of dough wheel across the kitchen between Gabriele and Samuele and Tomaso. Armando has an assortment of jars on the bench and from these he pours tomato and basilico purée preserved last summer. The colour is vibrantly red, the texture lumpy and the aroma tantalizing as Davide spreads it across the dough with a flourish. Margherita, cheese and tomato, is the favourite. Tuscans eat pizza for the sake of the pizza, not confusing the savoury dough with mixed-up toppings and fussy ingredients. Three at a time the pizzas slide from the ovens and Fabio, singing like a Neapolitan, rolls the cutter theatrically. The steamy aroma reaches the tables – why does simple Margherita pizza taste so very delicious, in Italy?

One by one our festivities pass, keeping us in intimate contact with our extended family. The night before New Year's Eve we join our young in a darkened cavern smelling of incense and atmospherically veiled in black and red and yellow. Cecilia and Riccardo serve drinks from behind the bar, charging everyone, which is how the night is paid for, while a band taps on bongo drums and strums guitars. Seven-year-old Leonardo and little Alice, turning four, are the youngest bar-disco guests, wheeled into the air by Samanta and Filippo, with whom they dance.

Fabio grabs elegant Maria Rosa, who tries to shrink into the wall, but soon they are dancing along with Fiorella and Claudio, and many of the elders, to a rhythmic Jamaican beat. Young dance with old, the very young hang on to skirts and dive in and out of legs, some of us watch from the sidelines, but as ten o'clock strikes, the decibels rise, the lights go out and the music changes into unrecognizable thumping. Cecilia lights candles behind the bar, and ex-President Maurelia gasps, but they are safely encased and high on a shelf.

An unspoken reminder, politely given, means it is time for the very young and the older than young to go home. We begin our arrivedercis, calling to each other above the din, but President Maria-Teresa hushes the band, who put down their instruments, and she draws our attention to Francesco who holds up his mobile phone. 'Ragazzi! It's Michele!' and a rousing cheer and ciao and happy New Year rolls across the world to Michele and Alida in Canada. Michele misses Pianello; he knew we would be gathered in the sede tonight. The thumping begins again and, with this din spiralling into a frenetic beat, we charge away from the deafening racket and fathers lift their children on to shoulders and follow us out to the road, leaving the youngsters to their disco. Outside, leaning against walls and sitting on the steps of San Pietro, members of other quartieri are gathering, as well as friends from college in Siena. This disco will hum into the small hours.

An hour before midnight on New Year's Eve muffled, booted, gloved and carrying goblets, we brace ourselves for the sub-zero temperature and swirling night mist and draw up alongside friends in front of a bonfire blazing in the piazza. Some folk are dancing because Angelino is singing and his band is playing under the cappellone but many, like us, stand around the fire, letting the flames flicker close, warming faces. Just before twelve, our glasses are filled with Spumante and the countdown begins. Watching the tower we wait for the moment the bronze bell will begin to sway, gather momentum, and the clapper will sound the first stroke. The moment is here; rockets shoot from behind the tower and blaze away into the black night sky exploding balls of starry purple and green and gold above the tower. Our bell rings on, and once twelve strokes of midnight are done, the hundred celebratory bongs of mezzogiorno, which do not normally ring at mezzanotte, reverberate from the tower. The bonging bell is synchronized to the shooting rockets firing and exploding in elaborate symphony. Pigeons are unaccustomed to a hundred gongs at midnight, and even more alarmed by the rockets. Fiery confusion sends roosting birds scattering and a hundred of them shoot out from the bell tower. We hug and kiss, link arms and toast each other with Spumante. 'Auguri! Auguri!' sings Ofelia. Bringing the New Year in and ushering San Silvestro out, whose night it is, we forget, in our close embraces, the freezing air. Warmed by our festivities, our village friends, the Spumante and the fire, we sing 'Auld Lang Syne' and toast wedges of panettone on the embers, managing, for once, to stay in the piazza to the small hours. 'No!' I shout and cringe away from Maria when she pulls my arm and entreats that we go with them to the village of Camigliano. They will dance till dawn!

'Isabella, there's a message on the machine, come and listen, I cannot understand it.' Luigi rewinds the tape and the voice begins again. Some form of English. Was that Isola di Giglio? 'Luigi, it's the Ingegnere – he is wheezing, he suffers from bronchitis, that is why it is hard to understand.'

426

'Signora,' the message begins, 'I have eetchy feet, and want to let you know I am leaving the cold for a few weeks. I am going to Isola di Giglio.' The message is charming. Well-spoken English but occasionally accented; I decide never to erase. The learned savant speaks not only English, Italian and German, but also Spanish, Portuguese and French – and Greek and Latin. The message proceeds: 'If you would be kind enough not to forget to return to me the papers I lent you . . .' Oh, goodness. I do not want to be accused of squandering the Padelletti family archives. I will have to act pronto. When he offered me some documents to study I wrote the details on a piece of paper, one for him and one for me, signed and dated, so that he would not fret about where they were, nor who had them. I am relieved he has the written details in his memory, or his hand. He assures me, once again, that his part of the story will not take long, and then: 'I am leaving tomorrow, but the house is upside-down because my daughter has everything half packed . . . It may be better . . . would it be inconvenient for you and Signor Dusi to visit me at the villa at Isola di Giglio?' Thank goodness he is not going to the Island of Elba.

'Luigi, what's the weather forecast – is the Siberian going to blow for ever . . . is the sea rough – can we take the ferry to Giglio before the end of January?' I hassle Luigi to go on the web and search ferries operating to Giglio in the middle of winter, and add, as an afterthought: 'Why don't we plan an overnight? Let's book a hotel.' And in case he has forgotten my stoic suffering at Elba, I add cheerily: 'We can eat fish at a romantic waterside trattoria, just the two of us!' I wonder how the Ingegnere and his family get there? Perhaps by light plane. We have visited this island before; it is about an hour on the ferry from the Tuscan coast. I want to find out who is sepulchred in the Protestant chapel, and hear what the Ingegnere has to say about the Colombini, now that La Signora has told me her story and about the patrimony of Padelletti that united, by marriage, with her family. But also, some of his asides, when I dare not interrupt lest he stray too far, are curious. Once he confided to me that he had hatched a plan to leave it all behind, to run away, desert Montalcino; and I was saddened to learn that his Brunello holding is tiny. There was another intriguing comment: one thing they will never forgive us for, is our wives.

Perhaps the saga of the Padelletti dynasty is truth and half truth. Unintentionally, his memories may be illusion or dreams, or grossly embittered, his point of view clouded by personal sadness, exaggeration even. Family history and stories handed down through the generations have intertwined and in the passing of time perhaps they have become legends. But to him it is all true, and perhaps that is so . . . and perhaps I really am the only person to hear these things.

January is piercing cold. Ice diamonds, blue-white and sparkling, pile along tree branches, dripping into semi-frozen tears tugging at the underside of leaves, waiting out the day, freezing again in the night like stalactites. We are relieved not to be struggling against the wicked Siberian, which is not howling across the hills, not rifling through coats and hats, pushing us hither and thither into places we didn't intend to go. But the temperature, when lace curtains stick solid, frozen to the window pane, is eight or nine below zero. Drifting snowflakes sprinkled the village and gave us a white Christmas, but, predictably, a day or two before Epiphany, the village is blanketed in white. A tame snowstorm swims and swirls, drifting without violence, flicking white against our faces when we stand about the piazza, laughing with the children, catching sight of the mysterious witches of Befana skulking in shadows and behind walls. Steaming hot chocolate for everyone is poured into cups from an iron kettle to ward off the chill. The village band is here, hat rims trimmed in white, puffing into trumpets and trombones, and six pretty witches, without broomsticks, but made up garishly with painted faces, line the steps of the cappellone in choral evensong. The piazza changes clothes as snow drifts and crowns balconies and rails; we gather, letting the flakes pile up around our feet until our boots are reflected in snowblink. A white eve for Epiphany, perfect for the haggish black Befana vainly to seek forgiveness; she is doomed to fly on the back of her broomstick with a sack on her shoulder filled with presents, passing all the doors of the homes where good children live, giving them what she could not give Gesù Bambino. This evening, mysteriously, no bad children are penalized with dreaded lumps of black coal from the sack.

The nativity, under the Cedar of Lebanon, is magical on the morning of the sixth. Snow coats the pointy coned hats and wooden brooms of three hook-nosed black-frocked witches who sail into the branches while thirty children from the nursery school clasp hands and make a ring around the nativity, dancing first in one direction and then the other, singing carols. Befana is a marvellously ugly old hag, the most brutish I have ever seen; some of the smaller children look terrified, shunning the ugly one. A guttural rumble sends the fear of black coal into the hearts of all the boys and girls. Always-in-black Mario, whose beautiful nativity is set in mossy waterfalls, tries to reassure them, but not until stooped Adelmo pulls the ragged sack from his head and black rimmed glasses from his own bumpy hooked nose do the older children laugh. Luigi visited Adelmo in hospital last week; he quite enjoys it there. 'Plenty of food and warm and comfortable,' he told Luigi. Although Montalcino's restaurants provide lunch and dinner to old Adelmo each day, the doctor admits him into hospital for a week now and again. He is one of Montalcino's characters from the past, a real Ilcinese who was born on the hill and has rarely left it and who, in many cultures, would be shunned because he lives unto himself, apart from and not adhering to modern society's expectations. But Luigi says that the last hospital visit turned out disastrously for Adelmo, which is why he volunteered to dress up and play Befana . . . and signed himself out. 'You won't recognize him,' Luigi said to me, 'he doesn't recognize himself!' The nurses took to him with toothbrushes, they scrubbed his wrinkled skin as white as the driven snow! When the children have their gifts and Befana flies away on her broomstick, the festive season is done.

Before we walk to the car I telephone Amelia to remind her of our weekend with the Ingegnere on Giglio. We exchange calls twice a week, but sometimes she forgets we have already spoken and I suspect that if her daughter leaves the house to do some shopping, Amelia picks up the phone and chatters with me until she hears the car returning. I assure her that her azalea in pots are covered in white plastic, protected from the snow. When I walk past her little home, all shut up dark and empty, I rub my hand across the door and call out, ciao amore, which keeps us close. Once she spoke to our answering machine: 'Isabella, speak to me! Luigi is talking, I hear him, but he won't answer me! Ciao, amore!'

Mild under the leeside of a sparsely vegetated mountain, I had not imagined to be sitting on the Island of Giglio at such an abrupt height on a terrace where a bushy hedge of green hydrangea in pots grows thick against the rail. Spiky cacti behind me are fat and tall and palm fronds sway, lending a tropical air. A wrought-iron arch captures the descent between lemon trees on the hill opposite, dropping to a rocky inlet where boats bob in a turquoise sea. There is a savageness about Giglio; this island is not tame, a conclusion born out by wild mountain sheep and by the amber-hued Ansonaco wine that flowed from the bottle at dinner last night at eighteen per cent alcohol. It is as well the Ingegnere has begun his discourse by diverting to the mezzadria while I come back to the conscious world with caffè on the terrace, and adjust to the oddness of listening to the end of his story so far away from Montalcino.

'The hills are arid, Montalcino gets less than half the rainfall of Siena and the contadini alternated crops because they could not create fertilizer; they sowed grain only every third year and that is why chestnuts were substituted for grain. On arid, unforgiving land, a hectare of chestnut trees gives five times as much flour as a hectare of grain. Then the padrone fled, some were torpid, unable to confront the changes demanded of them when the mezzadria began to shatter. Donkeys and oxen were still pulling ploughs, just as they had in medieval times – there were hardly any tractors. The mezzadria was a battlefield for the padrone and the contadini were the enemy . . . but there was good and bad in the system. In the end it died, not just because of the government, nor even the war; it was really the fault of the women. The worst handicap of the contadino was his solitude. When it was dark he closed up and went to bed. But there was a rebellion and after the war, the women called their own strike. They refused to knead bread for the family and the baker in the village had to bake and deliver bread to the farms. The women had never seen money, they knew only how to barter with eggs and flour. I grew up when these things were happening – in the 1950s I was thirty years old and my father was a padrone. These were tragic years when the contadini walked off the farms because they wanted money in their hands and the women wanted more than merely to subsist, as their ancestors had, in dilapidated farmhouses with no electricity, running water or civilized hygiene. They wanted television, but most of all they wanted to gossip, they needed the company of other women. And that is why the mezzadria broke apart and the whole agricultural world was shattered. But there is not one contadino who farmed for my father who did not buy his own small farm at the end of it. They did not love him, they would not stay and work the land for him, but he made contracts and all of them ended up with a farm.'

I am interested in learning more about the mezzadria – and this is the first time I have heard the blame for its collapse lying squarely on the heads of gossiping women – but I need to draw him back to his own story, lest he tire before he tells me. His face is less gaunt, he is not wheezing so deeply, the sea air is mild and probably beneficial, but he is far from spry, his creaky knees moving with terrible effort, forcing his weak legs to support his body weight and hold him upright, leaning on his cane. The body clock is running down for the Ingegnere but there is nothing wrong with his diamond-sharp mind. We are well wrapped up and it is pleasant to be on the terrace with the smell of the sea in my nostrils. 'Ingegnere, when you left a message on my machine, you said you had itchy feet; have you always wanted to travel?'

'I'll tell it to you this way.' Pausing, he draws his cane between his knees and leans forward with his chin on the crook. 'When my father fled to Switzerland after the Montalcinesi burned down his factories and threatened to kill him, of course I went with my parents. But things settled down after the war, and we came back because my father, as I have told you, loved Montalcino so much he wanted to live here. But the Church made life hellish for Protestants, and my father was growing old. Everything was war damaged, our side of Montalcino came under cannon fire from the valley. I studied in Bologna, particularly interested in mineral engineering, but I did not finish the course – I never had time to finish anything because I always had to go somewhere else. So I dedicated myself to agriculture, and at the same time consulted as chief chemist in a sugar factory, and helped my father. The farms were slow to react to the changes because none of the padrone who held on to their land had any money, and the torpid ones had no interest – some had never done a day's work in their lives. Only one or maybe two, and my father was one of them, replanted vineyards with American root stock after the devastation of phylloxera. In fact, whether others choose to believe it or not, all the wine that Signor Biondi sold between 1925 and 1936 was vinified from grapes grown by my father. They were all Padelletti grapes from American root stock vineyards, grown on the land towards Canalicchio, because my father was the only one who still had a producing vineyard!'

That sounds highly controversial. He means Signor Biondi Santi, whom I will meet for the first time when I go with Ivo to see his artefacts at the villa. Wanting to be doubly sure of my ears, I ask him to clarify exactly what he means.

'Look, I have told you that my father was a saint, but an economic criminal – and this Biondi story is an example of his stupidity. Father was a friend of Ferruccio Biondi, who came to him asking for help because his two sons, he said, were lazy and did not want to do any work on the farm. They were comfortably idle and had never needed to work. At that time it was just Biondi, the Santi was covertly added later on – I'll tell you about that in a minute. More problems arose after Ferruccio Biondi died because his two sons did not get along at all well; one of them was Tancredi Biondi. After the war, when part of the Veneto had to be evacuated because of the dire desolation and death of so many men, some families were evacuated to Montalcino, and two evacuee girls married Ferruccio's sons, the two Biondi brothers. One was Signora Anna, she married the son called Tancredi. She had been married once before and had a son – probably her husband had died in the war – but things got to breaking point because the two women, both Veneto, got along worse than the two brothers, their husbands! The brothers Biondi divided and sold off a large part of the terrain, and it transpired that they sold it badly. Tancredi took on the debts and later tried to buy back part of the patrimony, but was not able to do it.

'My father, meantime, had founded the Cantina Sociale for Montalcino winemakers and, wanting as usual to help anyone in trouble, gave Tancredi a stipend of seven thousand lire a year to help him rise above his financial predicament. His wife, Signora Anna, was as busy as an ant, she was marvellous and helped him tremendously in every way to salvage the remaining family patrimony. It was abundantly clear that Tancredi knew how to make wine, splendid wine, but as an administrator he was a disaster and the Cantina Sociale went broke; it was forced to disband. That is another example of my father's insistence on frittering away money in Montalcino, burning it up, but at that time he was in the forefront because he was the only one with root stock vines.' He shakes his head, disbelieving his own predicament. 'From this heritage, so great a patrimony, when my father helped everyone and consumed his money for Montalcino, how is it possible that I can be left with nothing but six hectares of vine?' The Ingegnere's holding is not as large as that of Primo, at Canalicchio, once also a part of the Padelletti patrimony.

If I knew anything, other than what I have read in a multitude of press reports and journalistic praise in articles around the world, about Signor Franco Biondi Santi and his wine, I could ask questions to compel the Ingegnere to search and clarify his story, but I am completely in the dark and cannot comment or even draw conclusions.

'It annoys me when people create their own nobility.' Oh, he mentioned this many months ago, I wondered if we would ever get back to it. 'The Santi are a family from Pienza or San Quirico way, they owned land in Montalcino and Pienza, but that land known as Biondi Santi's, Il Greppo, came through the female line – it came from the mother, and she was a Canali, not a Santi, so why did the Biondi not call themselves, as anyone else would, remembering the origins of their family, Biondi Canali? It is a huge joke really, and I will tell you why. I am sure you realize already that everyone around here has a nickname? The Canali, from San Quirico, were known as the family of coloni – big buttocks. In the men it was not special, but in the women it was something grand! It was not until the 1960s that Biondi got permission, if you look in the registry, to add to their name, but they did not change their name to Biondi Canali, because they would have become Blonde Big Buttocks, so they added a male name, Santi, becoming the circumspect Biondi Santi.'

If this story is right, it rankles with people because of a name change adding a male line to an already existing male line when the very reason for the name change, namely property and vineyards, was inherited through a female line.

'Ingegnere, were there problems in the past, friction between families?' I am probing because he may shed light on other wine families. 'Politically, yes, because there has always been the old Guelf and Ghibbeline division. Some families were loyal to the pope and others to civil power, the emperors of old. This problem did not exist, for instance, in England, but in Italy there have always been two powers, and it obliges people to follow one or the other and has brought the greatest misfortune to Tuscany. In noble families it was shameful because they divided into white nobles, siding with the king or emperor, and black nobles who sided with the priests. The emperor was recognized as a descendant from the great Roman Empire, but he could not be emperor unless he was crowned by the pope. The emperor commanded the troops, but the pope could refuse him the crown. I will give you an example. The great Casa Tamanti, another of Montalcino's ancient families which in name is almost gone, married women from Rome who were black nobles, papists, which tainted the Tamanti family.' Intricate pieces of a complicated jigsaw are circling the board. My mind flashes back to La Signora Colombini who had me shaking my head, denying, without understanding why, any notion that the Tamanti were Romans. Is this why? I decide not to ask, I will let the Ingegnere talk on. 'The Tamanti originated from Greece and came to Italy when the eastern empire fell – as a matter of fact they married into the Colombini family among others. These aristocrats were forced, time after time, to renounce noble titles to avoid exile depending on who was in control, pope or emperor. And *that* is why we have no true nobles of imperial bloodlines in Montalcino. The only true noble we have is the

Count from the Veneto. Rich they may be, and questionably aristocratic, but they are *not* nobles!

'But I have digressed from my story, Signora, which you came to hear, so I will tell you the rest. Probably it is not as captivating as the history of my ancestors, but nobody would believe all the things I have done. In my life I either had the fortune or misfortune to find myself where things were happening. I was right on the spot, in Africa, consulting in the copper belt, when the aircraft carrying the UN secretary-general was shot down; I was called to Russia because of inefficiency in a machine weighing twenty metric tonnes, costing millions of dollars, because it was wearing away three hundred grams of metal and they called me in to minimize friction; and I was in the canal, in Suez, at the moment it was closed to shipping. You see, I was a kind of industrial tourist and spent my time inventing solutions to other people's problems. I worked with Ferrari engineers, and at Indianapolis, and then I specialized in a new industry – petroleum. I founded an oil corporation and travelled the world. Do you know about the product called Bardol?' I am compelled to shake my head, no. He shakes his head, as if to say he didn't think I would. 'I set up my companies in Brazil, Moscow, Africa, the east and even Mongolia! When rich industrialists wanted to enter those markets with their products they came to me.'

'But Ingegnere,' I object, 'that means you were not at Montalcino!' But in the end, the story comes back to Montalcino, when he says: 'The ship was anchored here, and I came and went, but I never went to bed with a Montalcino girl!' What am I getting into with this eighty-six-year-old intellectual? He sees the smile cross my face and his mouth turns up at the corners into an impish grin.

'From the window of my study in Bologna, when I was at

University, every day a girl came by on her bicycle, and every day, as soon as she tried to ride round my corner, she fell off. I watched for a while, but, inevitably, one day I went down and talked to her. Opportunity makes man a thief, they say, and she was an exceptional woman, but she was *not* cut out to be a wife, and definitely not cut out to be *my* wife! Marry someone else, I begged her, there are plenty of men who will marry you. Come to bed with me, but marry another . . . but she would not. I never dreamed of marrying and having a family, I wanted to be free. A lover is always welcome when he returns from travel, but a husband never – everything that happens when he is away is his fault, and I knew this. So we married, and to Montalcino I brought my Bolognese wife, Alba. When my father grew old, and we were surrounded by so much hate and inveterate bitterness I began dreaming of my freedom, I hatched a plan, set a few things up around the world thinking to vanish from the face of the earth – start again, incognito, in another corner of the world. But my father was old, and in the end I could not cut the cord. I stayed, and now I have grown old.'

He could not cut the cord with Alba and the children? Or his father? 'Do you love Montalcino the way your father did?' He does not hesitate. 'No,' he admits, 'but it is an attachment, I belong here and it belongs to me, and I have no wish to escape. They respect me, but they do not love me any more than they loved my father. You see, I have always done imported stuff.' Oops, there is still a twinkle in his eyes and we have reverted to women. 'The only way to be accepted here is to get into bed with the women. If you can do that, and marry a local girl, you will be accepted. The people here never accepted my family, and the Church was consumed by long-lasting rancour, and one of the reasons is that they will never forgive us for our wives! I cannot find a record of who Giovanni married in 1529, but think about it: Antonio married a woman from Rome, his son Pierfrancesco married a Florentine, Guido, my grandfather, married Hilda Zumpt, a Berliner and a Protestant, my father married Jane Grenier, a French Huguenot, and I married Alba, and she was from Bologna! It did not help that we are not communist, and waged a political and psychological war with the Catholic Church ... and as long as that Protestant chapel stands, they will maintain their hatred of the Padelletti.'

Extraordinary. I think I will not tell Luigi about the possible benefits of getting into bed with the local women! 'Was Alba happy here?' 'Aha!' he gives a little Homeric laugh. 'So long as there was something to buy, and someone to talk to, Alba would be happy in Timbuktu. She was the most incredible parlatrice, chatterbox. If she had gone to the Vatican, in an hour she would be arguing with the Pope!' His words are borne out by what I have heard about vivacious, bella Signora Alba, who sat at my table at Fiaschetteria, sipping macchiato, and who dressed in sumptuous gowns and wore dazzling jewels, throwing fabulous garden parties at Casa Padelletti. And I heard, too, that she was not only a parlatrice, but a spendatrice, spending money like water! Her purse was limitless and her tips to hairdressers and waiters became legendary. Perfume, clothes, shoes . . . she bought half the shop wherever she went. But behind this gay façade Alba concealed her sadness, often repeating sad words confided to me by an older Montalcinese, who told me: 'Sometimes she would be gaily flinging money around, or we would be drinking caffè in Fiaschetteria, planning a party. Suddenly she would become wistful, tears would well in her eyes, and she would turn and whisper in my ear: I *do* wish he would come back. Alba wept, silently.'

But the Ingegnere had itchy feet. Prompted by my own retrospection, I ask, 'Why do you stay?' 'Because I search for the details of many things, I want to know about my roots, and the decline of the Padelletti family began, and will end, in Montalcino. They were squanderers of wealth, and have frittered away a patrimony of riches and richness. The only hope for the future is my grandson, Silvano. It is my *disgrazia*, my misfortune, that I am the only one interested in the past. But there is a plague on my life; I cannot write because my hands are shaking; I cannot dictate because I am breathless and my voice deteriorates; I cannot walk because of the incompetence of doctors, and arthritis ... so I sit in my library, robbed of my third age, watching the wealth and patrimony of my family dissolve into nothing, like salt in water. All I have left is my eyes, so I read, and I search for clues and, like a good Protestant, I protest against everything!'

There is nothing for it but to ask, 'Ingegnere, what will happen to the chapel – one of your family is buried there – if things do not work out in the future?' He tosses back his head, and for the first time in our many hours together, laughs from the belly, and those hunted eyes glint at me, coercing me to join his laughter without knowing why. 'At great trouble and expense, years ago, I managed to have the chapel listed with the Belle Arte – much to the chagrin of the church in Montalcino. The Protestant chapel is a national monument of Italy! And my wife, Alba, will stay, too.' The great *parlatrice*, the amazing *spendatrice*, vivacious Alba is sepultured in cold silence, for the present in solitude, where no sadness can reach her ever again, in the Padelletti chapel.

CHAPTER FIFTEEN

Biancoverde! Biancoverde! Alè . . . Alè . . . Alè!

Icy days of January slip past and snowflakes fall softly in the night, but rarely settle and only once or twice is the village blanketed in white. Blustering up and swooping down, flakes patter, touch my face gently then melt away to nothing. It is not

441

unpleasant to be outdoors on days when the sky is shuffling flakes but today, within ten minutes, my face feels cold and wet and within twenty a stiff numbness in my cheeks forces me to seek shelter. Staying to the east, avoiding a piercing wind rushing from the west, the church of San Francesco comes into view, floating on a sea of swirling valley cloud and mist, sailing through the air, seeming not to be reachable from the hill of Montalcino. Chickens cackle, their ruminations reach me but they are invisible, cooped at a farm under the wall which I cannot see for it has disappeared in the mist. There are no mountains, no Alps to the north, no Apennines and no Gran Sasso hovering in the south. The horizon begins at the endless white mist swirling at my feet and the whole world is blotted into non-existence. Walking along the garden trail, where the old signora keeps her chickens and fattens rabbits, stone slabs have pushed from the wall and looking to the terrace above I see the upturned roots of a cherry tree. Lilac blue heads on rosemary bushes seem too cheerful for this blustery day, sprightly and upright when all else cringes low. Pulling a prickly tuft from a branch I carry it under my nose as I walk, inhaling the delicious scent of Tuscany.

Someone is approaching me along the path, a basket over her arm. Scarfed and with her head down, I am afraid she will be startled when she bumps blindly into me, so I call out buongiorno. She looks up: 'Ah, Signora, are you going to pick berries?' In the basket are green branches of tiny red berries, but I do not know what they are. I tell her, no, I was just walking. So she pulls out a branch. 'Here,' she offers, 'take this, the berries will quench your thirst when you get to the woods.' This signora is well on in years, and perhaps not firmly in command of all her faculties, but I have seen her often enough, wandering about with her basket – surely she has not been in the woods on a day like this? Thanking her, I take the branch of berries and we part. 'I'll see you in church,' she calls over her shoulder, making me smile, comforted that I will recognize thirst quenching berries, should I need them in the woods, but not at all certain that she will see me in church. I will not be visiting Bruno at the cemetery today; Amelia has ceased asking me every second day if I have been and the last time I went one of her other friends had tidied up, and left a few flowers. Roberto, nonsensical football supporting Roberto who syphons wine at Festa di Primavera, was there: 'Oh, Isabella,' he moaned, 'I *hate* February funerals, grazie Dio it will soon be spring. Look, the ground is as hard as ice, I cannot get my damn pick through it – there is a funeral tomorrow and Matilda's uncle will be barely below the ground!' Roberto works for the Comune. Blasting and cursing he tossed the pick behind his shoulder and thrashed it forward over his head as hard as he could, banging it to the ground, where it juddered and shuddered, sending a few pebbles flying, but not making more than a ripple in the granite ground. Despondent at his efforts, he muttered: 'I'll have to dig him up and rebury him when the ground softens.' A spectacle which fills me with horror! Would he really do that?

My cheeks feel frozen, and as I dab tears from my eyes weeping from cold, I decide to cut short my walk and reward myself, retreating inside Fiaschetteria, where others will be hibernating, sensibly sipping cappuccino and reading newspapers. Two tables nearest the espresso machine substitute for the old men's tables outside the door, where loud dissertations and debates hold sway in summer, and these indoor tables are where the playing cards come out every day in winter, morning and afternoon. With few customers and no tourists to fetch and carry for, the bored baristi join the card games. When I push open the door and stumble in, huffing white clouds of vapour, they all look up. Shuffling and dealing, slapping cards and grunting, I can barely see their heads through the clouds of smoke. Luca raises his cards, a questioning look on his face; he is halfway through a hand in which his father Gianfranco is also engaged. 'No hurry, Luca,' I assure him. He knows I will be here for an hour, so I ask him, when he wins or loses, to make me a steaming hot chocolate, thick and syrupy so the spoon stands unassisted like a flagpole in the centre. At the table near the door a young father and his daughter, around three years old, sit side by side discussing, with the studied seriousness only an Italian can devote, the appropriate way in which to roll the spoon and dissolve sugar in a cup of cappuccino. He delivers a fatherly lesson on the merits and common sense, because it is two hours from lunch and a freezing morning, of gently sipping, and he cautions her not to hurry, but to let the hot whipped milk first warm her mouth, then, he coaxes, 'drop the creamy liquid down your throat and . . . there, now can you feel it warming your cold tummy?' She giggles and nods her head, reaching over the table to clasp both hands around the cup. I am relieved I ordered uncomplicated hot chocolate.

Someone has rubbed a coat sleeve and cut a swathe of wetness across the glass on the fogged-up door. Hardly a soul passes, but one by one those who seek shelter, or an aperitivo before lunch, peer through the hole, then throw open the door and dive in, crashing the door closed behind them and calling out buongiorno, shaking frozen hands and stamping feet. Fiaschetteria is a warm smoky haven, becoming crowded and noisy, and both Luca and Gianfranco are compelled to forsake the card game. The rich aroma of grinding beans and the noise of the hissing espresso machine working overtime for new arrivals had changed the atmosphere from grunts and groans over cards to bustle and chatter as folk wander from table to table, lounging at one for a brief exchange, then moving to chat to someone else, or to read a football report. Caffè Fiaschetteria was here before any of them were born, an institution in Montalcino as familiar as our own living rooms. It is not as if we go *out* for caffè; Caffè Fiaschetteria is ours, they would say, like the roads, and the fortress, and the bell tower.

'Buongiorno, Isabella.' Courtesies are exchanged even though we may see each other two or three times a day, but I do not see Giancarlo, the barbecue king, every day, because he lives on the fringes of the village. He goes on: 'I saw you earlier this morning when I drove past the tower, what has old Baffi got growing in his garden that was so fascinating? Has he bedded onions already?' Looking up from their tables, people laugh and wait for my response. 'Buongiorno, Giancarlo, no, it was not onions I was looking at, it was brussels sprouts; he's already got plenty of purple onions strung up in the cantina, I've seen them.' I am not sure why everyone finds this so riotously funny, nor do I add the reason why I was staring so intently at the brussels sprouts. In truth, I was surprised. I adore this cabbagy vegetable, but all those round green balls clinging up and down the trunk astonished me. I cannot believe that I have eaten thousands of brussels, and did not know how they grew on a plant. It is infinitely wiser not to admit this lack of basic food knowledge, but I join in the laughter with which this talk of Baffi and onions is infecting everyone, volunteering to take onion talk further. 'Baffi has told me he eats lots of onions. Every morning at seven o'clock when the bells of the Madonna reverberate him out of bed, he tucks into a raw onion with a lump of bread and two

445

fingers of red wine in a bowl,' I pronounce, authoritatively. I have long since arrived at the conclusion that the Ilcinesi eat lots of onions, because they grow in every garden, but I had not imagined my story would engender such a wildly enthusiastic uproar among Giancarlo and friends, causing memories of onions to unite them in a tale of their own youth which, half addressed to me and half bouncing to and fro between each other, they cannot wait to relate.

'When we were kids –' Giancarlo waves his arm to include Piero and Ilio Raffaelli, who is reading in a corner – 'in the fifties, when the war finished, there were lots of kids but there wasn't much to do after school and we didn't have anything to play with so we made up our own games. In our group there were about fifty or sixty of us.' Ilio, always ready with authoritative-sounding statistics to back up any tale with fact, interjects: 'Every family had five or six children, they all wanted as many boys as possible so they could work for the benefit of the family in the future.' Giancarlo takes up the story, not wanting Ilio to steal his spotlight. 'We would divide our numbers into two squads and select a battleground. Sometimes it would be down near the church of San Francesco, another time it might be over at Porta Gattoli, but it had to be somewhere so that one team had high ground, and the other low ground. Our pockets were full of stones, and we walked to the battleground gathering more arms along the way.' Ilio is determined to cement into my mind vital strategy: 'You always fought with your brothers though, you couldn't break up kin, the eldest brother was in charge of the family, and you fought alongside other boys who were connected with your own family.' Once he was comfortable that I understood this crucial tactical allegiance, Giancarlo launched into a description of the battle. 'We would signal a start and be into it, pelting stones at each other, trying to duck behind fences if we were on low ground, sticking our heads above a wall if we were higher. Sometimes we had slingshots, which were deadly accurate, but mostly these were confiscated by Maestro Ercole at school. We ended up with swollen purple lumps on our faces, our hair matted from bleeding cuts on the back of the head, and bruises and welts on arms and legs. Thing is, we could go on for hours because we picked up the enemy's stones and hurled them back. None of us would admit that a swelling bruise or bulging eye was anything but a trifle. Sometimes a stray stone hit a window in the church so we had to scatter over walls before the priest came out.' Piero winced, pragmatically recalling, 'Getting caught by the priest was rotten because he would tell your father and you had to do Hail Mary penance.' I am wondering if this tale is going to end in throwing onions, but Giancarlo is not going to be put off the coup de grâce. 'We listened for the bell in the tower because that meant the day's battle was finished and we had to go home for dinner. Facing our mothers was the worst part of the whole battle because she would know straight away that we had been stone fighting. Our mothers terrified us, they controlled everything, including our fathers. I would pull my cap down over my face, pull my socks up to hide bruises, try to sneak in the door without limping and slide into my bench at the table, pretending nothing was hurting. But she always knew, she would drag me out and give me a good thrashing, boxing me round the ears, and then the words I dreaded most of all: No minestrone . . . you can go to bed . . . Here's an onion for your dinner, but *senza pane*, you're getting no bread! I don't know how many nights I went to bed with a purple onion senza pane!' Piero and Ilio shake their heads, remembering how barbaric it was to have to eat an onion without bread, pointing at scars on necks and recalling battle wounds.

Should the door of the cantina be ajar at Giancarlo's home, or Piero's, you would see rows of purple onions, ingeniously looped so that a dozen or more bulbs do not touch each other, hanging from stone walls, or dangling from ceiling hooks. Onions are a link with a rough and simple childhood that afforded no escape from punishment from a terrifying mother. In his garden behind the Madonna, Baffi probably believes he is extravagant, eating an onion *with* bread and two fingers of red wine in a bowl every morning for breakfast.

The reminiscences of breadless onion dinners are at complete odds with the whooping yells of delight and snatches of conversation springing from the other side of the bar. Mario is reading aloud a quotation from a New York press release. A hiatus of distance in time and space, it is incongruous that as we laugh about poverty and onions, the name of Montalcino and Brunello is beamed around the world and through space by satellite. Dramatically emphasizing his words, Mario, who is related to Primo's family, but I am not sure how – the same Mario who was a pallbearer for the Madonna at the Easter procession – reads the words: 'Eccezionalissimo! A sleek, harmonious, ethereal red from the majestic vineyards of Montalcino . . . rah rah rah!' He looks up and grins, and everyone hurries him back to the paper, so he buries his head and reads another line: 'Powerfully structured, opulently rich . . . this is the glory of sangiovese . . . This wine is stupendous!' Glowing reports drift from the other side of the world, written by international wine experts who have been given the privilege of analysing the 1997 Brunello di Montalcino on the eve of its official release at Benvenuto Brunello, next weekend. Bordering on awe, these gurus grovel, clutching reverently at the stem of a crystal glass, heaping acclaim on our territory and winemakers. 'The 1997,' concludes Mario, flipping the page, 'is sending the world into enrapture. This ruby wine is mythical! Signor dah dah dah, a foremost critic, after scrupulous chemical and organoleptic analysis, is awarding the 1997 Brunello ninety-nine points out of a hundred!' He slams down the paper and everyone cheers. Mario sardonically puts it into perspective. 'What would *they* know? Only *exactly* what we have been telling them for months!'

We have been bombarded by glowing reports for two weeks. Every time I read about the ninety-nine points I want to write to that high profile chemical and organoleptic analysing guru from America and ask for what reason, if everything was so brilliant, did he deduct one miserable point! Why not give us a hundred and be done with it? Perhaps he will come to Benvenuto Brunello and taste mythical ruby wine from another hundred growers. Wistfully, I remember that I am not on the international guru invitation list. This year my participation is restricted to peeling Pianello garlic and helping serve lunch to a couple of hundred guests and I will not even get to see the commemorative harvest tile cemented into the wall. Last year I was Primo's guest, but this year I must do my Pianello duty, along with Ofelia, and anyway, I know what happens at the lunch. Infinitely more mysterious is the official tasting – but without a badge or guru recognition and a Consorzio invitation, admittance to the hallowed hall of tasting is as tight as the doors to paradise.

I remember that Luigi will by now be waiting anxiously for my homecoming and I begin my departure, but just then the sound of voices raised in argument, carrying from the wine cantina at the rear of Fiaschetteria, stops me in the doorway. I try to recognize the orators in the back room, who began calmly enough discussing our mayor's next exciting initiative: our Città del Vino, Mons Ilcinus, famous all over the world, Mayor Massimo says, will soon be the seat of an international Master of Oenology through the University of Siena. But the discussion has suddenly degenerated into a volatile argument. Conflicting opinions cross back and forth until I hear an angry and emphatic voice: 'Well, I'll tell you this. I know who *didn't* create Brunello, because it was *not* who they say it was. The dates do not fit . . . it does not add up.'

Luigi gave me his solemn promise, after our spine-chilling return from the Island of Elba last year, that never again will he commit me to ride, sleep and eat with our football team. In return, I agreed not to desert our team just because of one night of terror in a hysterical pink bus, and I loyally take my place in the stand below the fortress at home games and, unless I have very good reason – and nothing good enough has yet impressed him – we drive together to faraway places to barrack for our green and whites, the biancoverde. Luigi, more so of late, is besotted by our football team. The black-and-white ball is taking control of his life, most definitely his brain. In the mountains and on the plains we barrack loud and long, tossed together in a grab bag of rabble supporters not all in accord with our ambitions. Fair to say we have participated in some thrilling wins, and suffered one or two devastating defeats, but, whether we win or lose, to Luigi our team is unequivocally the most talented, spirited, brilliant bunch of lads this side of the black stump, which is to say that anyone on the other side of the stump – his measuring device – is not worthy of a second thought.

Football began again in autumn and, halting only for Christmas festivities, the season is at an end today. Not to be with the lads at the bitter, or glorious, whichever end, would be tantamount to betrayal. I admit to a teeny flutter in my heart when our green and white boys run all clean and polished on to the field, chests broad and heads high, and, knowing them by name, like a true tifosa screaming caustic abuse at the common enemy. I own that a proprietorial relationship has developed. When the field is icy I worry less about the score and more about broken heads when Crazy Cristian crashes to the ice executing one of his spectacular ballerina toe twirls to steal the ball. But he bobs up grinning like a swivel-headed ball-gobbling clown in a sideshow every time. I think he is left-footed, mancino, as they say in Italian, but I cannot be sure; he doesn't always use his feet.

Today we play the final game away from home, which is a relief, because it means that Luigi has not been called upon to spend all Saturday and this morning shrouded in plastic, teeth chattering, grappling with an antique roller contraption which he hauls around our playing field painting perimeter lines, centre lines, goal lines and circles, and daubing, with finite accuracy, the penalty spot. In autumn the football committee engaged a groundsman, but his ability to walk a straight line mysteriously diminished as the weather deteriorated and Luigi, proud club secretary and ever willing to curb expenditure and present a bella figura for our squad, volunteered to take responsibility for the filthiest, coldest and loneliest winter job on the field. When he staggers up from the changing room and slumps next to me in the stand at home games, he implores, and receives, heartfelt pity when he bleats: 'Mia amore, look at the lines, are they straight? Look, aren't they white? Can you see the penalty spot?' I nod my head, positively amazed to be able to see the penalty spot, and raise my hand towards the nearest line marvelling at how straight and white it is. Nobody else notices. But his crinkled blue fingers and spattered face have forgotten themselves because, with only today's game to be played, we lead the table by one single point. If we win, reaching Eccellenza, it will be an historic achievement for Montalcino, the championship will be ours, and we reach for the first rung of *professional* Italian football!

'If shit were gold, la, la, la, at Torrenieri there'd be treasure!' This ditty, ever sweet from whence it came, is accompanied by taunting hand and arm movements. A second refrain (less pretty) is bellowed from the open windows of the bus as we drive through the heart of the village of Torrenieri. I do not know if football songs are the same all over the world; my father took me to watch civilized five-day cricket matches. We are on the way to the championship game in a bus, but fortuitously, not the hysterical pink wreckage which, with the exception of Pippo, departed with our team, coach, trainer and medico, a few hours ago. 'Mia amore!' pleaded Luigi. 'We *cannot* miss the atmosphere of travelling on the bus with the fans to the last game of the season. We are going to win the championship!'

I relented, and sitting directly behind the driver, among a group of happy, dedicated and sensible football followers who wear ties, as far away as possible from the declamatory circus in the back of the bus, I smile along with everyone else at their songs, glad that the majority of scarlet prose passes over my head. I do find myself spontaneously singing along with barracking fans when I am in our stand, at home games, especially our biancoverde song, but I am horrified when Luigi later translates a particularly devastating slander. I am forced to believe that, as football changes Luigi's personality, so too, it changes mine. Among our football followers is a group of boisterous young tifosi, among them Luca from Fiaschetteria, and Cinquino from Pianello, and Alessio from I don't know where. When we are at Pianello, Cinquino and I are quartiere friends, mutually respectable, obliging, polite – allowing for a flash of extrovert behaviour when we win archery tournaments and disco rumba – but at football matches Cinquino and I barely acknowledge one another. He becomes a fanatical tifoso, with a profane and scintillating wit, to be sure, dreaming up the most outrageous repartee to rain down on opposition fans. I often wonder what he must think of my personality change for I mutate into a shrill wench, wailing along with our screaming fans (even if I don't understand the precise words), and, jumping to my feet, I wave my arms and sing 'Biancoverde, Biancoverde, alè alè alè', as if it is my life's only worthwhile passion. There is some self-denial that allows each of us to navigate with mysterious ease around the image of our circumspect roles in Pianello; I ignore his cussing and cheer his vitality, and although I am not sure what he ignores in me, it works for both of us. With Luca, Cinquino and Alessio and other young and *vital* personalities at the back, on this bus I am mute. Pippo was not on the pink wreckage because this morning his father fell off his motor scooter and broke his arm – a hiccup which threw our football coach into spasms – but by now Pippo and his father are taxi-ing together to the match.

The bus rolls on and we approach the next village; windows slide open, sending a blast of freezing air chasing round my feet. I wait to hear what provocative refrain will sail into the piazza at quiet Sunday-afternoon-sleepy Lucignano where a tooting horn is enough to cause a sensation. 'Ladri! Tredici portafogli! Vergognosi! Briganti!' It is not a song, but a torrent of wicked invective about some wretched deed. 'But they are elderly pensioners!' I reason with Illiano, so he explains the motive behind this abusive indignation. Twenty-five years ago, when Montalcino played in a lowly league and ran on to the field against a team near here, unknown persons from Lucignano stole into the changing room and nicked thirteen wallets from the jackets of our players! 'Thieves! Thirteen wallet thieves! Shame on you!' Our jeering young men screech and blaspheme at old women in gardens and grey-haired men with walking sticks sitting along the wall. Twenty-five years ago, I am told, *they* are the ones who would have been at the game; or in the changing room, nicking our wallets!

We rattle along a rutted stretch of road by the side of a passeggiata walk, and the tifosi sing a wicked chorus several times. 'Vafancullo Sinalunga', bounces along to a rhythmic beat in Italian, meaning something along the lines of, but far more terrible than, Luigi assures me, 'up your arse, Sinalunga', and, after we are whistled and jeered and stones bounce off the side of our bus stuffed with football hooligans, things quieten down, temporarily, because the driver halts before our destination. Thirty chanting tifosi disembark and, standing with their backs to the bus, in unison, sing and pee into the field of some poor farmer trying to grow corn. *Why* can Italians not adopt cricket? I cannot bear to think what our return journey will entail should we, as they most definitely anticipate, win this match. Then again, I cannot bear to think what slothful behaviour we sensible tie-wearing fans might suffer should our team not bring home victory.

The Mister, Valerio, our calm coach, is on the bench, together with Lorenzo our assistant coach and Luca with the magic water that miraculously heals everything twisted or dented, and our spare players – fearless Lorenzo, young midfielder, another Alessandro, and Massimo, who has been injured all year, but if all goes well today our coach will give them a run, as this is the final game of the season. Disguised as an insignificant bystander, an afterthought slouched on the bench under camouflage, like a dying hope in a broken dream, we are relieved to see the Joker. Firecrackers and rockets explode and the fans rise up in a crescendo of chants for biancoverde, the green and whites, who charge all spit and polished on to the field to line up with the enemy. The whistle blows, and the game is under way.

Players from both teams race from attack to defence, but psychologically we have an advantage because today's opposition cannot win the championship. On the other hand at another game somewhere up a mountain in Tuscany the team that trails Montalcino by one point are playing for their lives to win their match because if we lose, or even draw, they will snatch the championship from our grasp. The green and whites *must* win. Confidence rises as we watch Sauro's ringlets fly; he presses and blocks and spiky-haired Nicolo dribbles first left and then right round a defender and swivels the ball elegantly to Crazy Cristian, ready for a blistering attack. Technically, we assure each other, we are superior; but a black-and-white ball does not know about such things. Alessandro, our aerobic Running Screamer, all pruned and pretty with curly locks on top, scorches up the field screaming to Crazy Cristian: Attaccolo! Attaccolo! We see Vito in position, calling for the ball. Cristian! . . . take it to Michele – we order him from the stand – and then . . . put it in the air Michele – we scream out the next obvious pass. Thank goodness sylph-like Michele hears us! We believe, as do all fans in the stand, that players do whatever we tell them even when we shriek from fifty metres away in a grandstand full of hysterical tifosi screaming opposing demands and odious abuse. Michele, our gorgeous hunk who flaunts his naked chest provocatively from time to time, gracefully swerves, obeys our command and turns the ball, sending it looping through the air, straight on to our super striker Bomber Vito's . . . where is Vito? His foot was there and then it wasn't! They have flattened him – in the penalty area! Ah! We can relax, a penalty in the first half will put us ahead one-nil. If it had been Yuri the Wardrobe taking the ball they would not have flattened him, but no matter, a penalty will do just fine. Luca our medico runs on to the field and sprays magic water on Vito's knee. We chant and shout, harrying glum opposition fans, and Luca and Cinquino and the others fire rockets and throw crackers on the iron roof of the stand, singing 'Biancoverde, Biancoverde', as Vito takes his kick from a not very white penalty spot and . . . goal! One-nil. And we sing our best song:

Lotteremo fino alla morte	We will fight to the death
Innalzando i nostri color	Raising high our colours
Che ci vien dal profondo	And it comes from the depth
del cuor	of our hearts
Alè . . . Alè . . . Alè!	Alè . . . Alè . . . Alè!

Smugly we rest feet on seats, arms crossed in told-you-so poses as if the whole thing is a bit of a yawn, really, and we smile benignly at opposition fans who make ugly gestures at us. A hundred mobile phones send the news back home, we shake hands and hug Beppe, and Alessio and Luca lead a chant to our Presidentissimo President. We munch pumpkin seeds and bask in our success, talking about a championship dinner . . . we've got it in the bag . . . we'll wrap this up in the second half.

Graziano commands the defence impeccably; cute Mirko, in perpetual slow motion, makes my nerves tingle but never misses, lolloping from ball to ball with nanosecond timing, and Vincenzo, our sober senior goalkeeper, has not been pressed beyond theatrically diving and punching away balls that did not even cause us to rise from our seats in fear. A scuffle on the side line sees the ball out of play and the linesman signals our throw in, whereupon Vincenzo retreats into the goal net, Graziano, Mirko and Nicolo turn away to take up a triple line of defence leaving the throw in to Michele, knowing that Crazy Cristian will come up to receive the ball taking us into attacking formation. Merda! The ball is spinning round in the net! *Our* net! What has happened? We are stunned, even *their* fanatical fans hold back, silent for a few seconds, waiting for the referee to whistle a stark mistake! He does not! They *stole* our throw in . . . but the linesman's flag is still up – *our* way! What crude effrontery is this? The referee is not interested – he overrules the linesman but nobody told our players. No whistle . . . nothing! The opposition took our throw-in and somehow it went into the net; they are celebrating an illegal, stolen, despicable not-fair goal!

Pandemonium breaks out. 'Imbecille! Cretino! Bastardo! Vergognosi Ladri,' the fans scream, and we repeat. Livid with the referee, we warn him he will need a police escort home . . . figura di merda! Who has paid him off? It's dirty politics, you criminal – how much did you get from Berlusconi? We know he despises Montalcino! Your mother is a puttana! Oh dear, we are at the mother-insulting stage – that means I move seats before the exchange becomes ugly. Insulting sisters, even fathers and sons is acceptable, but not mother! In the mêlée down on the field one of our players grabs the ball, I believe it is Bomber Vito, and angrily boots it as hard as he can. It sails clear out of the field over the stand and on to the road behind – crashing and tinkling and shrieking curses come from down there somewhere so we scramble up to the windows at the top of the stand. Ganzo! Good shot, Vito! Goal! You've bombed it right through someone's bedroom window! Down at the fence the fans are going ballistic but Vito's accidental vandalism sends us into spasms of justifying rage. Oh, Dio, the carabinieri are here!

Our more vital tifosi have reasoned that opposition fans ought to pay for this travesty. The referee flashes a yellow card to irascible Graziano for complaining, then one for uninvolved Mirko, but we don't know why. The cheek of him! He races over and warns our trainer, Mister Valerio, who is jumping on the spot, purple veins standing out on his neck, righteously vociferous! Things *are* hotting up; firecrackers are flying dangerously near the referee's head. He ignores a volley of life-threatening curses and allegations that his mother is a whore and takes the ball back to the centre. Mobile phones are drawn like weapons, numbers punched and news spreads. Play restarts and everyone calms down, but this is dangerous: somewhere up a mountain our rivals are winning two-nil. Bring out the Joker . . . we coach our coach. We want Pippo! We want Pippo! Grazie Dio, the Mister hears us, even above a cacophony of screeches and whistles, and from way over the other side of the field! Pippo is tummy twisting and leaping like a one-legged frog; ten minutes and he will be on, but there are only twenty minutes left!

The opposition, pride at stake, hassle Vito, fouling and tripping and blocking his path, impeding our attack, but the referee is inexplicably blind and the overruled linesman totally submissive. Crazy Cristian has reverted to his other self; a death-crazed warrior on a battlefield. He charges up the field and smacks chest to chest into a defender, the mid-air impact so agonizingly loud and solid that the referee raises his whistle, about to call a mercy halt. We watch the two players in slow motion between upstandingness and downfall – they untangle and gravity flails them to the ground . . . Cristian springs up like a jack-in-the-box, shakes his head, grins at the referee and runs away with the ball, calling on nifty Alessandro to take it forward, but the whistle blows – the opposition defender lies half comatose on the field and on comes his magic water carrier. And on comes Pippo!

Grinta! Grinta! We coach them, grit your teeth! Go, biancoverde . . . dai Cristian, don't stop now, take it to them Alessandro, you can do it, hassle them . . . take a run Pippo! But Pippo loiters behind the play, tying a bootlace, flicking a stone from the field. Cinquino and Luca turn to face us, screaming out, zitto! Quiet! We understand this brilliant strategy and stop calling Pippo's name; the opposition are torpid, we will fool them! Michele is the key to this brilliant move, or maybe the linchpin is Nicolo, who is racing to the right. Where is Cristian off to, powering up the middle? *He* must be the playmaker . . . how I am not sure . . . must be diversionary tactics. No, he turns and the ball has left Michele, brushes busy Alessandro's head and is on the end of Cristian's mancino foot (I think that's the one he uses sometimes) . . . What's happening over there? Here's the key! A hurricane is swooping down the left wing, his feet don't touch the ground; all the opposition can do is trail behind Pippo as he makes a scintillating run. We hold our breath, then find our voices all at once and scream out orders. The timing, Cristian, it's all in the timing! Wait! Wait! Hold on to it! Pippo cannot stop! And he doesn't, Pippo sails over the halfway line and charges down the wing. Now! we thunder at Cristian, he obeys, and the ball floats in like a wafting balloon and dances on to and away from Pippo's running toe and Vito receives this wicked cross and slides it on to Yuri's granite head who turns towards the net with the ball skewing . . . goal! Two-one. Biancoverde! Biancoverde! alè . . . alè . . . alè!

Where is our Joker? Has he run full pelt off the field? Pippo is on the ground – he smacked into two desperate defenders who thought he was the one taking a shot at goal! Why is he cradling his arm? Where are you Luca? Get on there with the magic water. Why is the ambulance driving through the gates? Cristian turns to us and grins, pointing at his chest and waving his finger to and fro. The ambulance is not for him. Pippo, face scraped pale, is carted from the field. Two broken arms in one family on the same day! But victory is ours and before the whistle blows Bomber Vito seals our triumph with a third goal and the Mister gives fearless Lorenzo, young Alessandro and Massimo-who'll-be-fit-for-next-season a few minutes on the field to share the victory with their team mates. Up a mountain somewhere in Tuscany the score is three-nil, but we do not give a . . . !

Tears run down our cheeks and we hug and kiss people we barely know, and all the ones we do. All the way home on the bus we raise our colours and chant and sing from the depth of our hearts, Vafancullo-ing through Sinalunga, hurling ditties about wretched deeds to those shamefaced old biddies still brazen enough to be outdoors at Lucignano – but we save up our worst and most melodious insult, and every one of us, ties and all, hangs out the coach yelling: 'If shit were gold . . . at Torrenieri there'd be treasure!' When at last we empty from the bus and race to our piazza there are heaps of people waiting to be hugged and kissed and slapped across the back. The bell in our tower is bonging a hundred bongs, just for us! Soon our heroes will be here. Presidentissimo Beppe glows like a firefly and Luca and Cinquino and Alessio plant crackers as big as bombs and position rockets behind walls and under arches, waiting for our bus full of boys to arrive.

With one fading headlight, horn blaring and weaving dangerously between overhead balconies, grazing shutters on either side of the road and sending villagers into palpitating panic, Maurizio has met the biggest challenge of his black-white seldom wrong life. He steers the bus along the narrow cobbled road straight into the piazza! Grinning heroes hang out the windows throwing filthy shorts, sweaty shirts, socks and odorous jockstraps to adoring fans! What are they wearing? The bus looks odd. Why is the glass smashed in the last three windows? Why are those faded pink seats piled haphazardly atop one another in the back? Why are ragged curtains waving about from wooden sticks above the roof? Maurizio creeps to a halt and bashes both fists up and down on the steering wheel in triumph. No! In despair! Our talented, spirited, brilliant bunch of heart-warming lads have wrecked the hysterical pink wreck!

Tooting draws our attention back to the roadway and from the door of a taxi, magic water carrier Luca helps Pippo out, plastered elbow to wrist, while from the other side of the taxi struggles his father. Same arm! Twin breaks! The bells bong, crackers bang and rockets shoot, and we launch into our football song: 'Biancoverde! Biancoverde! alè alè alè,' ending, as always, with '. . . and it comes from the depth of our hearts.' Bel vino tumbles into our glasses. Luigi is focused on next season, reciting for my approval a letter he has written in his head to Ferragamo,

Banfi Vintners and Michael Schumacher, all wealthy investors in Brunello vineyards. We are in Eccellenza, he recites, Montalcino is the centre of the universe – surely you will sponsor our professional football team next season? Dutifully I nod my head, staring at our pink wreck, and then he adds that he will set up a chatroom for fans. U.S. Montalcino will be as famous as Brunello!

Angelino is moving his mind into the future, closer to home. He hands me a torn sheet of paper. 'Isabella, put this in your bag so you don't make other arrangements.' Is this the date for our championship victory dinner? No, it is not. My knees buckle. How can a year go by so fast? He has scribbled: Eleven days this spring . . . we must raise money to field our team in Eccellenza. It is the dates for Festa di Primavera . . . and the goddess with the dreaded swinging ladle!

Scurrying along slippery wet roads, sober black suits scribble on clipboards and clutch leather briefcases and slinky city skirts swing handbags stuffed with documents. Inside Fiaschetteria, under the cappellone and on the steps of Consorzio headquarters microphones are thrust under chins and cameras roll and flash as television news crews capture the moment; journalists scribble when they bail up one of eighteen wise oenologists who scrupulously taste, analyse and pontificate on the glory of 1997 Brunello di Montalcino at Benvenuto Brunello. 'This wine is destined to pass into history,' they nod sagely. 'If you can get hold of any, buy now, tomorrow will be too late, because five million bottles will be gone!' Under a mop of unruly hair Belgium's Prime Minister justifies desertion of his country. 'I heard about the '97 and had to taste it for myself,' he says, then laments, 'but there is not even a plot the size of a handkerchief for sale.'

Spreading salsa verde on crostini in a communal kitchen with Ofelia by my side, under eagle-eyed Luciana, we are laughing at Onelia, who is peeling garlic at the speed of light. We do our duty and prepare our quartiere's share of lunch for a couple of hundred visitors who are cold and sodden from top to toe. It has not rained for weeks, but for several days before Benvenuto Brunello Montalcino has been wrapped in black clouds and a year's worth of rain has dumped in a week. Drooping suits and dripping noses find no shelter along our cobbled roads, much less inside the marquee; many hail from sunny wine countries across the globe but the tent is barely tepid. Forced to make a dash they scuttle from the rain and in for lunch, needing a hearty meal to drum up physical endurance for the afternoon tasting session.

Last night high-powered dignitaries banqueted at the table of Guido Havercock on terrine of duck, herb risotto and Brunello bistecca with liver and honey served with ruby wine, at Castello Banfi, but, alas, we humble crostini spreaders did not get a look in at the famous gala dinner at the castle. Half a bucket of garlic cloves are sizzling in the iron cauldron and Luciana tips in chopped tomato by the full bucket. After tagliatelle with tomato and garlic we are done and Ruga cooks will take over the kitchen for risotto.

Peeping through the door I enviously spy on familiar faces. Signor Campatelli, Director of the Consorzio, arrives and guides someone to a VIP table. That must be Signor Miuccia Prada, flown in from his America's Cup yachting obligations. He has unveiled the commemorative tile that, by now, will be cemented into the wall. Pianello cooking obligations have precluded me from witnessing the proclamation in the theatre and unveiling of the tile, but *we* already know the star rating of last autumn's once-in-twenty-year harvest. Enviously watching the black-suited officials, rubbing raindrops from spectacles and mopping wet brows, the prevailing confusion among these dripping dignitaries persuades me to believe that, perhaps, somehow, I might be able to wangle entry to the sacred tasting marquee in the fortress. Once the splendour of Benvenuto is over the tent is open to invited visitors, but experts have vanished by then, the tent holds no tension, no fragment of mystery; only weary growers and their families watching clocks until the swigging non-connoisseur classes stumble out the tent flap. I want to get in there when the air is electrified with point-scoring gurus sniffing and sipping hundreds of wines.

This year has brought me closer to the truth about the creation of Brunello di Montalcino. I have caught tantalizing snatches of accusations, unearthed smouldering resentment and am piecing together astonishing revelations about ancestral families, the so-called nobles, and my understanding of contadini like Primo and cittadini like Enzo has thrown up surprising truths. With one possibility remaining when I might unravel the final knot at the villa of Signor Biondi Santi, I am determined that I will sneak inside those fortress walls and see what goes on behind those tent flaps. What *are* these experts saying about technologically futuristic Banfi Brunello? And how do growers like Beppe fare? Do gurus pay as much attention to the wine of a contadino grower like Primo as they do to farms that developed under the hand of a padrone, like Colombini? Is Fattoria dei Barbi at a disadvantage because they breed pigs and milk sheep as well as grow wine? I read a report that Signor Franco Biondi Santi has just returned from a dinner in New York attended by one thousand eight hundred guests, a huge international Wine and Food Institute of which he is President, a receptive audience thrilled to be hearing about this mythical wine. I focused on one intriguing line in the report: '*Ferruccio Biondi Santi is generally considered by many to be the inventor of this wine.*' A sentence loaded with ambiguity! Can the Biondi Santi high public profile be justified? I wonder why I do not recall seeing photographs, or even a mention, of the Biondi Santi family at the new Museum of Brunello at Fattoria dei Barbi? With so many shrouded and stooped figures coming and going under black umbrellas, dashing and splashing from cars to the marquee in the fortress on this filthy day, surely the minders on the gates will not notice me?

I am wearing my best black Versace jacket and through-the-glass-ceiling straight skirt, and patent gold-trimmed Ferragamo heels, with an impressive bundle of importantly dishevelled documents tucked under one arm and six pens crammed into a breast pocket. At lunch, when I was working at the communal kitchen, a careless journalist rushed out, leaving on the window sill his rain-spotted Benvenuto Brunello folder . . . which sneakily finds its way on top of my pile of documents. I seal my camouflage, pinning to my lapel a plastic name tag, not altogether dissimilar to those appended to the dignitaries at lunch, and draw myself up to self-important iron lady height of one hundred and fifty-two centimetres. Once I am in that tent I will be safely among friends – getting past the door without an official invite is the reason for all this wicked deceit.

Seeing my moment, clutching my documents, I dive out from behind a car and hurtle up the ramp towards the fortress gates where two guards are examining papers belonging to a waiting guest, sheltering under an umbrella, waiting to be identified and ticked from a list. 'Giancarlo!' I call sweetly. 'Ciao! How are you? I *am* glad to catch up with you!' Giancarlo Gorelli is a grower who lives a few doors from me. Nonplussed, he stares, for he saw me not half an hour ago, but he comes straight towards the door and, as I draw level with the guards, ignoring them in my brash importance, he reaches out his hand and I prop and shake, straddling a high step. Nobody can get in or out and, having certified the man under the umbrella's papers, the guards are trying to admit him. Absently, a guard touches me on the back, a slight push that tips me over the step, closer to Giancarlo, so I take a step, then a sidestep, then two . . . and linking arms with Giancarlo, who by now is astonished at my familiarity, I enter the fortress and, trembling lest the guard demands non-existent papers, scoot inside the door of a tent.

I am over the first hurdle. Now I am faced with a desk behind which sit three suited people, each with a list. This is the official invitation list, on which my name is *not*. Not willing to suffer the embarrassment of admitting to Giancarlo that I used our friendship under false pretences, I explain that I am waiting for someone else. He, identified with a red sticker on his lapel, walks straight through a flap and into the marquee. Smiling at one of three handsome young men behind the desk, because he has known me for ten years, I implore authoritatively: 'Would you *please* find Signor Campatelli, the Director, and ask him to come and speak with me?' Bored sitting behind the desk all day he is more than willing and jumps up to obey, disappearing through the tent flap. Slinking into the back wall I rehearse my lines, but fortune shines upon me. Signor Campatelli is struggling towards the door, trying to respond to a journalist while a television camera swings side to side, capturing visuals of the Director at work. He does not come out of the marquee but absently smiles and waves his hand, more or less inviting me in! Sliding behind the Director, as the journalist inches up and thrusts a microphone under his chin waiting for him to answer a question, I vanish into a sea of black, grab an empty glass from a passing tray, and mingle.

One end of the marquee is lined with tables behind which stands the head of the family, or vineyard, and two helpers, ready to pour for whoever requests a taste of their Brunello. This is handy, they are alphabetically sequenced and, catching the eye of Carlo, Travaglio archer and Banfi employee, I step brazenly forward for my first official taste of 1997 Brunello di Montalcino. At the other end of the tent, at white-clothed tasting tables, sit thirty or forty VIP wine writers. Lined up on their tables a battalion of Brunello goblets, each one individually numbered and identified with a white slip of paper circling each stem. They are tasting, assessing and point-scoring Brunello, grower by grower. Around me, conversations drift: 'Absolutely power blasting! Incredible structure! Bracing tannins!' Hums and nods, then: 'But the length . . . it's phenomenal . . . I thought it would dry out, but there is so much internal energy in that wine, it's wound up like a ball of string and just goes on and on. And you can taste the polyphenolic ripeness.' What speak is this? It is way above my lowly wine appreciation; a sinking feeling overcomes me. Now that I am in the marquee, I haven't a clue what they are talking about.

Watching for an empty tasting table, I waltz across and lay down my pile of important documents and, resting my glass, sit down at the shoulder of someone bent on writing an epistle, enthralled to the point of exclusion of anything, or anyone, else. Fat black letters scrawl down the page and he slams each page on the edge of the table – right where I can see them. The first one reads: Plums and cherries, silky tannins, fresh cedar . . . aroma excellent. Ninety points. Enzo Tiezzi. This I understand. It is my science fiction friend Enzo! Plums and cherries? Of course, the trees he left in his eco vineyard. This journalist is reporting for a magazine in language wine lovers want to hear. Page number two slams down. I let it pass – not a grower I personally know. Page three, and I lean imperceptibly closer. This *does* interest me. It is Conte Andrea Costanti. Roses, long cherry, floral berry and fresh leather, tight and well structured, wonderfully perfumed. Brilliant work Andrea! Ninety-three points! This is incredibly exciting but, not wanting to push my luck, I pull back, walk away and bring back to my table a taste of ninety-three-point Conte Costanti Brunello. Holding the stem between finger and thumb I frown, seriously examining sparkling ruby wine, twisting and twirling and looking through and down, then I leaf through my papers and drag out a blank page, scribbling more or less what the guru next to me wrote.

'What do you think of it, Isabella?' It is Carlo from Banfi. He speaks in gruff guru tones, bending over my scratchy paperwork and tapping the glass of Banfi Brunello he poured for me when I snuck into the tent. 'Wow! You must be thrilled!' I bluff and bluster, keeping my voice subdued . . . and then a diversion. 'Are John and Pamela here?' Thank goodness, he tells me, they departed back to America this afternoon and left an hour ago. Then he spills the news: 'Ninety-four points isn't bad, eh! The American tasters adore it, a wine for Americans – red liquorice and strawberry . . . plenty of body and ready to drink, and they know it is going to get even better as it ages. It *is* a great Brunello, don't you think?' I shake my head disbelievingly, lifting the glass of Banfi Brunello and telling him it is truly fabulous. What did John Mariani tell me when he set up Banfi, when he thought winemakers here were still in the stone age? I have to make a wine millions of Americans want to drink. Well, John, it's a blockbuster!

Behind me someone is discussing the growing of the 1997. A growing year to be dreamed of, they say, flowering wasn't brilliant, but that gave us quality over quantity. Reasonable rain in June and it gradually warmed up. Not much rain in summer, but we had enough intermittent showers not to compromise the fruit – and then in September it rained for a week or two, but we ended up with clear sunny skies, not too hot, so the fruit came in abloom, flushed with health, skins thick and deeply purpled. That was five years ago; if you were to mention any year in the last twenty I am sure they remember the conditions precisely. A hubbub of excited chatter, clinking and laughter comes from the other end of the room, but at this end, at the tasting tables, it is all swilling work. I watch my unknowing partner-in-crime examine colour through and down, he swirls and allows the wine to rest, pokes his nose right inside the belly of the glass and rolls it around the rim, inhaling and scribbling. He takes the wine into his mouth and I can hear it swishing as he sucks and blows it in and out through his teeth, letting it coat his cheeks. His head is rigidly still as he records the sensation in his mouth, coated in dribbling wine. He has not identified the wine, but I watch the words run from his fingers, straight from his mouth and mind to the page. Blackberry, perfumed violets, chocolatey fruit, *full full full*, velvety tannins, loads of jammy fruit, too, and long. Really, really long. Lasts for *minutes* on the palate . . . glorious! Will age brilliantly. He rearranges his erratic notes and begins to rewrite on a clean page. I am on the edge of my chair, trying to see, goose bumps are prickling my neck – a sudden sensation makes me think someone has discovered my ruse and is piercing my back with their eyes. I turn quickly . . . but there is no one; I am safe. Whose wine *is* this?

I am supposed to be bristling with self-importance, an iron glass-ceiling lady, not teary eyed with a pounding heart. Forcing myself to raise a glass brusquely from the table, my face seriously expressionless, I nonchalantly stand up and move to where the crowd is thickest. I make myself weave around the marquee, blinking and taking deep breaths. Incredible! *Ninety-seven points* . . . La Contessa Ciacci Piccolomini d'Aragona. She is here, watching over Beppe – and me.

Wandering around, wood, leather and spice overlap with candied fruit, minty on the nose, wound up, and what was that? Arctic conditions? Oh, that's the tasting tent! Some folks chat about pH levels and colour molecules, but all admire the ruby jewel in their glasses. Walking back to my table of documents I pause, hearing: Lots going for it on the nose and palate, this style of wine is unfashionable, but it has a certain nobility in its own right. And a black suit responds: I agree, an old style of wine that has lost some of its quality . . . still interesting, but an under-achievement . . . better drink it now. My head is reeling, trying to imagine who among two hundred prestigious growers that could be. An unfashionable but noble wine that will not age. Back at the tables I see my mystery accomplice is packing up – no more secretive eavesdropping over his shoulder. He slaps the folder shut and I am overjoyed to read on the cover the initials WS: Wine Spectator is probably the most highly regarded reportage on wine in the world. These reports will appear in the morning paper, but watching and listening as gurus deliver verdicts is a joyous culmination to my investigative year, the more delicious because I am here under wicked false pretences. Tomorrow I will learn about Primo's Brunello, and the Colombini and my neighbour, Signor Gorelli, who unwittingly helped me weevil my way into this hallowed hall of wine. I wonder if the non-Catholic non-communist Gentlemen Padelletti Brunello is in this tent? And I wonder: whose wine has lots going for it in an unfashionably noble way?

look back to the flicking washing, and listen . . . the bell in the tower is pealing. I count eight strokes. The school bus to Castelnuovo del Abate will be stationary at Bar Prato; if I am quick, perhaps I can catch a ride when the driver takes the bus to pick up the students; he will be having breakfast in the bar for another ten minutes.

The driver tells me the times of returning buses, but I am unconcerned about how I will come back. Someone from Montalcino will see me – the butcher, or Maria's sister will be coming into the village – there is no danger of my being stranded, and I do not want to be constrained by time. I will visit the abbey, wander up to Castelnuovo del Abate for caffè, and walk back down to the road; someone will stop and offer me a ride.

The blue bus chugs up the hill towards the Madonna. It is irresistible; I glance towards Siena, across that dreamy panorama of rolling hills that fold and curl one into another like whipped cream. Wisps of white drift in the valley, more haze than mist; it is like looking at Tuscany through a scrim of soft organza. Turning the corner at the Madonna, I do not wish to see, but it is impossible not to be shocked by the enormity of the car park construction from this angle, sitting high in the bus. Why destroy ancient walls and then build more? But, I am smarting, having been cut to the quick as a consequence of my best intentions. Our fighting committee had grievances aired by a senator in Rome but politicians of various persuasions hedged, lamenting the grave consequences, but chose not to interfere. Headlines raged: This is worse than all the damage inflicted by despotic Florentines and siege-minded Spanish! And for our mayor was reserved an infamous accusation: the new Attila the Hun, intent on destruction. As the bus chugs along, yesterday's headline flashes into my mind; they *are* creating the Great Wall of China, swallowing up the hillside with concrete and stones. Having decided, with a sense of civic duty, to support the 'no car park inside the walls' campaign, I was crushed one day by a voice on the end of my telephone, barking at me: You strangers should walk on the points of your tippy toes. That was a turning point. My mind thrashed about, reprimanding me, trying to tell me I should have remained uncommitted, not smirched my reputation, opening myself up to his upbraiding. But with the passage of time I reconciled his words, and my future. That he was so offended by my interference perhaps meant that my words counted. Is that a clear measure of integration, or non-integration? I have chosen to cradle my ripest thoughts – I am where I belong, living in a closely knit community whose rituals I share, but it is a village that struggles to accommodate modern life. It is presumptuous of me to believe that I deserve a reward, just for having chosen to be here – they do not need me, after all. The Ingegnere's family have been here for a thousand years, and the Colombini came back on the lances of the despised Florentines. What can a stranger like me bring to this village in return for all the riches I receive just by living among them? I shall worry no more about, nor strive for, integration. I do not wish to be anywhere else, and I am fortunate to have Montalcino as my home and, as it *is* my home, I must accept my share of responsibility for *all* that happens.

The bus is no sooner past the Great Wall of China than it is manoeuvring around our latest symbol of potency. We need a roundabout to assist traffic flow, but do we need this ghastly dollop of concrete? Creation of the roundabout gave us palpitations, and then heartache when we witnessed what looks like Pharaoh's tomb rising, but in the same breath Mayor

Massimo calmed our palpitating hearts with news that the Bank of Monte dei Paschi di Siena has allocated funds for the salvage of the first cycle of Vincenzo Tamagni's deteriorating frescoes – and restoration has begun. It is as if each horrid proclamation is counterbalanced by two worthy ones. At the end of the week our citizens will gather in the piazza with our mayor and firemen, who will drive in the smart red fire engine with a telescopic ladder for the official ceremony to launch his project to install a staircase in our bell tower. How difficult it is, to be mayor of a divine medieval village in the hills of Tuscany when everybody wants to move forward at the expense of losing nothing from the past.

The roundabout is out of sight and the bus scoots along at a rush. When we turn towards the first valley I am surprised to see fields of vivid spring grass and hedgerows blanketed in white. Never have I seen spina bianca blossom in such riotous profusion. This thorny berry bush shedding white-petalled flowers flourishes along errant waterways and races up and over hills skirting gullies, even along the rims of vineyards, now coming into view. Berry flavours in the wine! How perfectly the earth interprets itself. Hair-like rootlets in the dark underground are busily wriggling and squirming, hunting out moisture and minerals in shelves of shale, wrapping around tree roots and energizing, sending messages of life back to the earth's surface.

Today, all I see is grey lifeless stumps. Oh! *These* grey stumps belong to Il Greppo! The bus is passing the vineyard of Signor Biondi Santi where I will be in a couple of days and hope to taste his wine. I am fortunate to have inadvertently gleaned familial stories about the Biondi-Santi-Canali families, but I need to talk to the man himself, otherwise I fear my jigsaw will not portray a balanced picture. We whiz past an avenue of cypress leading to the villa Il Greppo; and it dawns on me that this road to Castelnuovo del Abate is also taking me past Fattoria dei Barbi, which is coming into view, up on the hill. Stefano Colombini, responding with gnashing teeth to provocative rumours that the Consorzio might relax disciplines, has acted upon his threat and withdrawn membership from the Consorzio del Vino Brunello – a loss that shuddered like an earthquake through the Consorzio, and sent tremors through all of Montalcino. Ninety-two points for Stefano Colombini at Fattoria dei Barbi. His 1997 comes with high rankings; a big, ripe red, tar and raisins, full, powerful, silky tannins, long finish. Biondi Santi and Colombini vineyards are a stone's throw from each other yet the wines bear not a skerrick of resemblance – but that is the secret of Brunello. The curiosity I heard in the hallowed tasting tent, at Benvenuto Brunello, niggled at my mind for days. Whose was the wine described as unfashionable, with a certain nobility in its own right? Fuelling my curiosity, Stefano, a purist, made it excruciatingly plain that he would never be party to changing disciplines for producing Brunello. One would have thought, as I did, that if his winemaking is so enshrined in tradition with such confining insularity, might his wine be unfashionable? The Colombini do not lack noble lineage through ancestors. But I jumped to a wrong conclusion. Perhaps the comment was made by a giddy guru grasping for a headline . . . but it *was* repeated in the press.

The blue bus weaves around the last curves shut in close by hills and we enter the foothills of the Valley of Starcia. Castelnuovo del Abate, untidily straddling a hill, is bathed in morning light beaming from a bright ball low in a cloudless sky. The wooded hills thin out and at last the valley opens in front of the bus to reveal Sant' Antimo. Months have passed, taken up with life's busyness since my last visit, when Luigi and I visited Beppe at the Castle of the Abbot – and La Contessa. Blinking flashes of the abbey between trees gives me only a split second to look; already it has fallen out of sight, behind the bus. The driver stops at the junction, and I alight; he will drive up the hill to where the school children wait outside the arched portal. Walking down the gravel road between oaks a flicker of excitement lights up my eyes as I strain to see into the distance, to the bottom of the hill where this masterpiece rose a thousand years ago. Will they be here? Can I be certain that all will be as it was, one year ago? No cars are parked near the abbey. It stands solid and alone, as if, of itself, it chose this valley in which to set down foundations. I have missed the moment of spellbinding magic when the sun pushes above the hills and falls into the valley. The abbey is glowing brightly in a sparkling sun, warm and smiling.

Hastening my feet, momentarily disappointed because I see nothing stirring, I stare at a gate leading from the garden just as it swings out, and into the olive grove swirl four white-hooded monks. Lauds is finished; I will have to come earlier, next time, to fill myself to the brim with their melody. Hessian sacks, bulging with cuttings, lean around a trunk and dark bottles, perhaps filled with wine, support each other in a pyramid. Lifting a wooden ladder, thrusting it firmly into the branches, the first monk disappears in the foliage and a brother passes a saw up through the branches. It is not lingering angst, now that I know about the historic betrayal of monks, that brought me here this morning. I should love to have seen the sun rise, and to hear the stones in the abbey sing, but that will happen tomorrow, and the day after. This morning I wanted to be sure that white-hooded monks would be in the trees, chopping and hacking at the olive grove because I found it so moving, a year ago, to be a tiny part in the rhythm of the Abbey of Sant' Antimo going back a thousand years. Perhaps this uncomfortable spring pruning is a kind of once-a-year penance for what they did to Montalcino all those centuries ago. Closer now, my eyes light on one tree after another, watching them as I pass by, walking quietly over stony gravel to the abbey doors. My mind is focused on the relentless rhythm of the place . . . but something flashes into my thoughts. White gowns sweep and flap against their ankles and the monks, dropping heels and pushing forward, dig their toes into leather, trying to grip the ladder. Brown sandals creak and buckle and slide over the rungs, as they did a year ago, but – yes, that was it – olive trees and monks have been here for a thousand years, but, now that Luciano has closed his workshop, who will mend the monks' sandals?

Right where I stand, beside this magnificently carved portal, might have been a pen for squealing swine. The silence is so acute that it lowers the heavens. I tiptoe past the crouched lions and creep past the holy water stoup, shrinking on to the nearest pew, as if to break the air further on would be an intrusion into the peace. Morning sunlight streams through the arched window, beaming in long radiant shafts picking up specks of trembling dust, whirling it around in a silent mystic beauty. I sit and think about the stink and the desecration – which was not the fault of cows or roosting pigeons or rooting pigs. If it were not for Ilio and the good citizens of Castelnuovo del Abate, this House of God, overflowing with joy and peace and a place of uncommon beauty, would be nothing but a pile of rubble.

Legends cling to places of antiquity. Like the time the abbot demanded that one hundred plates, on which the monks could eat their dinner, be brought in payment of taxes. A humble peasant, groaning under the weight of a sack of plates on his shoulder, stood in front of the abbot. There are not a hundred pieces in that small sack, grumbled the greedy abbot. So the wily peasant unburdened the sack and let it crash to the floor. Now there are more than a hundred, your worship! he squeaked. And the wee bird I saw in the woods, walking with Ilio, Re di Macchia, the King of the Woods, was similarly demanded as payment of taxes. Show me my bird! demanded the worldly abbot, and a woodcutter untied a knotted rope and the sack fell open. But there was no cage. The King of the Woods darted into the abbey rafters, flying round and round, chirping at everyone, until it flew right out the door!

Sleepy Castelnuovo is all of a frenzy. Zigzagging through lanes and up alleys not wide enough even for a three-wheeler work truck I am met with a hail of buongiornos as aproned women step one after the other from doorways with buckets and twiggy brooms and brushes and cloths. Slurping suds from buckets, nimble troops wash steps and stoops, swishing a rag back and forth on the end of a brush, calling to one another as they sweep suds on to the cobbles, sending a trickle down the bumpy path which becomes a stream, gathering soapy foam as it races from door to door. When I ask if this path will take me to the bar, a chorus from six at once is so garbled that had they not all raised a hand to point, I could not have understood. Stepping over rivers of suds I thank them, we exchange our buongiornos in parting, and I turn the corner to see, a few paces away, the shape of a slight man with a hat pulled down over his ears, dressed in green hunting gear. In a cloth bag balanced on the palm of one hand and resting over a shoulder his rifle is probably smouldering still, for dangling from his belt, feet up, head down, is a pheasant. But not only the plumed pheasant dangles; from his pocket hangs a ring with the bulkiest collection of keys I have ever seen. How can he walk, let alone hunt pheasant, with that much jangling iron swaying on his hip? Following him, not because of the rifle, or the pheasant and dead weight of keys, but because it is the way to the bar, I am fixed on an incongruity. As if in contrast to all that dead severity, cradled over his other arm is a broad straw basket. Grasses and herbs poke from one end but the whole thing is overlaid by a mass of long-stemmed roses, deep crimson blooms, some so full blown that loose petals float on to the path and I grab them up, putting perfumed wild roses to my nose. Reaching the bar, I stop but he keeps going, stopping a little way on, and, setting down the basket, he drags the heavy keys to the front and, selecting an iron one so long that I can see it from here, rattles it into the lock of the door to Palazzo Ciacci Piccolomini d'Aragona. The dawn hunter is Beppe ... that is *her* chatelaine of keys ... the perfumed wild roses will sit on La Contessa's ebony piano.

The fish man, whose name I do not know, stops the truck and I jump out before we reach the fortress. He was packing up his trays of silvery bream and knotty octopus at the bottom of the hill outside the gate at Castelnuovo del Abate and, knowing that his next stop is Montalcino, I politely asked for a ride. His truck was cold, decidedly smelly, with ice blocks rattling around in the tray as we bumped along, but he has kindly brought me back and I have promised to go to the grey steel door in the wall and buy fresh fish later this morning. But it is too lovely to return home yet. My mind is so full – white spina bianca and hunters with roses and, as impetuous as spring, I tell myself that this may be the least painful morning for me to return to my sweet

Madonina, whom I have not visited for months, ever since a snarling bulldozer began tearing Her silent world apart, wrenching at my memories.

Passing through Porta Gattoli I am momentarily surprised to hear no birds, which normally chirrup and flutter at my approach, but dawn is long past; they have flown in search of breakfast. The morning sun is blindingly bright, reflecting warm on stone walls where blood-hot lizards in green coats sun themselves; hearing me, they wriggle and dart in and out of crevices, climbing ivy branches and raising heads towards the world. Ivy advances year by year, slowly strangling the stunted tower that once kept watch along the wall; thick as a man's arm it tangles and twists, imprisoning blocks of stone where lichen covers them grey. The wall of stone bulges towards the path, insidiously thrust apart by tree roots, resisting the day when weight and thrust will topple it on the track. Clumps of iris, not quite in flower, but revealing mauve tips, push up between the rocks and along the pathway I smell a honeyed perfume but cannot see over the wall to an almost blossoming almond tree. Aside from the rhythmic thump of a pick or perhaps an axe, away in the distance, the track is silent. Across on a hill slope there is shadowy movement as workers, with hand hoes, tickle the soil around vine trunks, preparing the way for the message of spring.

Through the passage, where the wall rises on both sides, and with the sky so blue and spring air so warm I gird myself for whatever mayhem I may find looming in the shadows, just ahead. Almost at Her shrine, my anxiety mounts; I glance over to where bulldozers tore at the earth, forcing me to jump for my life into brambles, then glance forward towards a row of cypress pines, which seem taller and darker than I recall. I am here. I sit on the step of Her wayside shrine, passive and contemplative, absorbing the recoil of worries unfounded, thanking God for a miracle. My eyes dwell where mother nature has propagated a wall of green, camouflaging the cliff and hill, now levelled, and although I see the tips of wooden stakes, the vines are invisible. Spring growth has been fast and luxuriant, perfumed branches and purple secrets of spring reach out towards Her shrine. In another week She will be hidden in Her magical world, smiling into eternal silence. Everything has changed, and yet it is the same, or even more lovely. I drop a few coins into the slot and listen to them rattling and rolling down the tube until they reach the tin with a thump and clang to the bottom. A thankyou. I should like to stay here for hours . . . but will come the oftener, now that I know my sweet Madonina is safe.

Will I be able to talk with Signor Biondi Santi? Eleven of us drive in several cars a couple of kilometres to Il Greppo, but when we are near, our number swells closer to twenty. Many members walked and wait for us, and Ivo, our President, is standing at the beginning of the avenue of cypress which leads to the villa. Animated and chirpy, several of our archaeology and history minded folk talk of family members who work here, or how many times they have visited, alerting me to the fact that many of them, too, have never seen Il Greppo, other than passing the estate from the road as I did a couple of days ago. One of our number cannot resist, as we gather the scent of cypress into our nostrils, recounting his visit decades ago.

'I was about fourteen. With friends I did the round of all the farms because back then they were not just vineyards, they had chickens and rabbits as well. Foxes were a real problem for the farmer, and valuable to us because we sold the skins, so if we caught a fox the idea was to boast about it to as many farmers as we could; they were always happy to see one less fox. They gave us something in reward, maybe an old boiler of a chicken, or some vegetables, which we could take home to mother. Well, this day we reached the farm of Biondi – there was no Santi then, just plain old ordinary Biondi. Look, I said to the Signora who came down the steps of the villa, I have caught this fox down by your boundary. She was so excited, really thrilled, and called to one of her workmen, telling him to go at once to the chicken shed and bring a basket of eggs. I was all smiles, thinking, she is going to give me a basket of eggs for frittata, my mother will be pleased. The basket arrived and she laid it on the ground, then, one by one she picked over every egg until she held the smallest tiniest palest one she could find, and this is the egg Signora Biondi gave to me!' We all laugh and heads nod in confirmation of foxes and frittata and tight-fisted farmers. I most definitely do not intend to pass on stories divulged to me by the Ingegnere about this family!

Ivo calls us to order, explains that we will proceed up the road through the cypress and, alluding to his first-name intimacy, tells us *Franco* will be waiting to walk us round the vineyard to the cantina, where we will taste his wine, and then we will be taken inside the villa and *Franco* will bring out his collection of Etruscan artefacts. When that is done we will probably be offered vin santo, and the whole thing will take around two hours. Ganzo! I *will* be tasting his wine, and seeing inside the villa will be fun . . . but a tightly structured visit does not fit my ambitions. Still, who knows what might happen.

There is something sacred about walking up this white road between stately cypress. To our left and right wooden stakes file across the vineyard but grey trunks, ranks closed, do not give away the secret of life underground. Signor Franco Biondi Santi, tallish, thin, elegant in a tasteful suit and with starched dignity, greets Ivo and one by one we are introduced and he serenely shakes each hand. He seems actually to be acquainted only with Ivo – and perhaps his eyes are just a tad vacant. His arm waves towards a vineyard and he comments in a precise, exacting tone, not inviting comment, about primatura vines, first root stock being the earliest ancestors of the type, with a kind of hallowed hush in his voice. We are glad of our jackets in the cantina, which is chilly and old, and it seems that squat cement tanks are still used for the fermentation of his wine, which must make pumping the must over the hard crackling pomace a very tricky business. There is less of the brand-spanking-newness of the equipment in most Brunello cantinas where the latest of everything shiny and technical lines the walls. But the heady perfume is unmistakable; delicious scents of ageing wine reposing for years, undisturbed, in silent darkness.

Our excitement heightens when a worker draws the corks from two bottles of 1997 Brunello but my head shakes in utter disbelief when I learn that this is the first time two of our members have tasted Brunello. His 1997 is already sold, Signor Biondi Santi tells us, but he keeps a few bottles back for his own use, and for his collection. An interesting comment, heightening my eagerness to taste his wine, because the Biondi Santi 1997, described as pretty, aroma of violets, light cream, full bodied, smooth, raspberry finish, turns out to be the much-criticized 'unfashionable wine with a certain nobility', described as an old style of wine. A debate is raging between wine pundits who, on the one hand, tell wine lovers that Biondi Santi Brunello is uncompromisingly hard and difficult when young, and meant to age for long periods – and therefore people who criticize the wine miss the whole point – while others proffer that it may be out of step with current taste, but it represents a style that has disappeared, hence it is old fashioned in a noble sort of way. Severe criticism has not ruffled a hair on the head of Signor Franco Biondi Santi. 'Our wine,' he said, 'has become a searched for symbol of quality of life, like a Valentino gown or a Ferrari car, in the image of Made in Italy. Perhaps it is not the easiest Brunello to drink, and I am not saying it is the best, but it is specifically different to Brunello produced in other zones. For years I have been requesting the Minister to concede Il Greppo as a sub-zone, giving us our own denomination, because of our peculiar microclimate and organoleptic qualities, in the same way that the great Châteaux of France exalt and value the terroir.'

Putting his wine to my eyes, nose and lips is a joy and my senses fill with the heady bouquet. Spina bianca, wild berry bushes growing along the hedgerows, rise into my nose and mouth. With appropriate awe, we listen to his earnest voice, which tells us about Biondi Santi wine. There is none of the usual chatter and giggles that our members usually cannot resist in our group gatherings. This man expects, commands and receives hushed attention when he speaks. With Ivo by his side, and the rest of us straggling in his wake, he slowly walks between tanks, vats and barrels, turns a few corners and stops in front of an iron gate, curlicued and padlocked. This is a spiritual journey, calling for hallowed silence; one by one we take a turn and peek inside the sancta sanctorum at the last two dust-coated, cobwebbed bottles of Brunello stamped with the year 1888, and half a dozen labelled 1891. Even to *see* these bottles, more than a hundred years old, sends a tingle through my bones. This is a myth staring me in the face. Only a handful of chosen connoisseurs have tasted one-hundred-year-old Brunello, a tasting that took on mythical dimensions and sent the name Biondi Santi and Montalcino whirling around the world in a blaze of glory. The 1888, they pronounced, is an enjoyable wine, the fruit is still there, and the colour is rose tinted and tawny. The 1891, only three years younger, astonished them with its tar and mushroom, caramel and spice aromas, sweet and youthful fruit on the palate, and long finish. One guru, claiming he was on his knees in front of a miracle, declared that at a hundred and ten years old the 1891 is impressive, convincing and delicious with no signs of ageing and will be good for probably another hundred years.

The villa is divine. One of those rambling, graceful, ivy-clad country homes, partly blocks of stone and partly fading terracotta wash mixed into plastered walls. From a wide stairway I look down to a triple arched loggia, and up to symmetrical arched windows behind a balcony. The whole blends asymmetrically, a harmonious coming together of hips and slopes of tile and stone. The doors and windows sink deep into the walls, allowing room for planter boxes of purple and yellow pansies, and my eye is led by terracotta pots in which tulips, bursting to bloom, lead to a fountain in a manicured lawn.

'This is Ferruccio Biondi Santi, my grandfather.' On a mahogany pedestal table by the door is a silver frame portraying a youth with fair wavy locks, surely not yet out of his teens. He could never have imagined so much glory would be built around his name. We pass through the faded loveliness of a family home, one decidedly blessed with sufficient wealth to gather an air of antiquity; the heirlooms are of a quality which do not wear out, never needing to be replaced by modernity. We shed our jackets, ushered into a room where a fire burns low in the grandest fireplace I have ever seen in a private house, big enough for ten people to sit in. At a long wooden table we sit for our meeting.

Many of the Etruscan artefacts were unearthed over the decades when Signor Biondi Santi cleared land for more vineyards. Black bucchero drinking cups, spinning whorls, flat plates and one large craterous bowl for mixing wine, with mythological black figures on the sides. Ivo explains the Greek myth, adopted by Etruscans but adjusted, drawn to portray their own religion. Patting it reverently, Signor Biondi Santi estimates its age at around two thousand five hundred years old. The vin santo is on the table and so are crunchy cantucci biscuits to dip in the wine, but our time is almost up and I am resigned to getting no closer to Signor Biondi Santi than three metres down the table. Ivo has a self-satisfied look on his face, proprietorialy he stands beside the man himself, benignly smiling at us plebeian devotees who are not *his* school friend. Never mind, I think to myself, I am glad to be here, just the same, and looking up I send back to Ivo my widest smile, acknowledging his right to superciliousness. 'Franco, you have met Signora Dusi, haven't you?' He cannot resist claiming the wideness of my grateful smile. Signor Biondi Santi is not quite certain whether to hedge his bets or make a faux pas by saying no, because he cannot remember if he met me at the end of the avenue of cypress. And then, bless him, Ivo comes to his rescue and walks me in. 'She has lived in Montalcino for many years – she researches and writes.' The man himself responds, eagerly: 'Ah! Signora, there are writers among my ancestors, would you like to come and see my library?'

I would. Our group visit is over. Folk are making their way out; I have no idea how I will return to Montalcino, but I will walk, in the dark, over hot coals if need be – it is only a few kilometres. Behind glass-fronted cases a vast collection of books and literature are lined up in orderly, segregated, tidy rows. It is so at odds with the Ingegnere's mouldy lair, the musty biblioteca, that I am disconcerted, hard pressed to maintain a bland smile.

I have heard tales from the Ingegnere, and have gathered snippets from wine folk in the village and in the press, which I hope will make piecing the fragments together less difficult than I had first feared. Signor Biondi Santi tells me that he frequently needs to talk to journalists about Il Greppo and his family, so he has ready to hand the background on the main players – his grandfather, Ferruccio Biondi, and his father, Tancredi Biondi. Does this mean I am about to receive a sanitized version of his story?

He confirms that the name Santi derives from Ferruccio's grandfather, Clemente Santi, whose mother was a Canali, and yes, *she* was the owner of Il Greppo estate. 'Why did the family become Biondi Santi?' The answer is straightforwardly given. A tribute to the family Santi, but he makes no mention of the unusualness of annexing a male name to an existing male name. Clemente Santi received his laureate in pharmacy at Pisa University; he specialized in botany and chemistry and wrote a treatise about winemaking. 'And did Jacapo Biondi marry Clemente's daughter who was called Caterina?' He did. Thus, any children from the marriage of Jacapo and Caterina were, naturally, Biondi children. Ferruccio Biondi was their son, and much hinges on Ferruccio – the young lad in the picture frame by the door. Signor Franco leaves me to leaf through the precisely typed papers and certificates neatly assembled into a folder on a writing table in the middle of the library.

It is unfortunate that from his grandfather, Clemente Santi,

Ferruccio inherited the passion for wine, but he did not inherit the passion for writing down words, even in his elderly years for he lived to be almost seventy. Ferruccio seems to have been the eccentric secretive type and chose not to put on paper a single word, nor any explanation about his experiments or details of how he was making wine, which in 1888 and 1891 was bottled and labelled Brunello Biondi Santi. Two things I capture immediately. First, nobody can be sure how Ferruccio ended up with Brunello in his bottles – how or when he carried out scientific experiments – because in almost seventy years he wrote nothing down. Thus, Brunello *creation* by him relies on conjecture. Secondly, way back then, in 1888 and 1891, the bottles, and I have seen them in the sancta sanctorum, were labelled Biondi *Santi* – even if, as the Ingegnere claims, the name Santi was not legally appended to Biondi until the 1960s, Ferruccio was labelling using the name Biondi Santi.

But there are one or two odd pieces in the puzzle that niggle at me as I leaf through screeds of notes. Where did Jacopo Biondi, the father of Ferruccio, come from, and why did Ferruccio feel the need to add a male ancestral name to the bottle, along with his own and his father's name of Biondi? I can find no mention of a university, or laureate, only that Jacopo Biondi was a Florentine medico, though I do not know how, or in what field. Perhaps I have stumbled upon the reason for the Ingegnere's undertone hinting at made-up nobility. I see the words that the *noble Biondi family* came from somewhere south of Pisa, but I can discover no authenticating reason *why* they are noble. Perhaps they, like many others, lost their nobility twixt pope and empire, or perhaps there is a blurred indistinction here between a noble family, and *Family Nobility*.

Scanning the notes about Ferruccio, there is no mention of his university studies either, or a laureate; nor is there a birth date, only that at seventeen years of age he fought under the patriot Garibaldi in a battle for the unification of Italy, which I know took place in 1866. A quick calculation tells me then, that Ferruccio was born around 1849. A few lines in a book claim that others in Montalcino tried to copy Ferruccio, but that he maintained the secret, and anyway, the book says, the technique and vinification to make Brunello were too complex and laborious for contadini who were used to antiquated ways. It pops into the back of my mind that it was not contadini, but brilliant intellectuals, like Raffaello Padelletti and Riccardo Paccagnini, who were known to be experimenting with sangiovese grosso. Claims and counterclaims cloud the issue. I scribble a few notes as I go, planning to unravel this complex history in the days to come. But, whatever he did or did not write down, and whatever he called himself, the Ingegnere confirmed, without hesitation, that in 1888 and 1891 Ferruccio bottled splendid wine – and *that* has been tested and proved one hundred years after he bottled Brunello and labelled it Biondi Santi.

Ferruccio also had a son, and he was Tancredi, born in 1893, about whom I learned a little from the Ingegnere. Whether the Ingegnere's tale of a father's frustration with lazy sons be true or not, it is true that Tancredi married Anna, a fine woman from the Veneto, and that he parted ways from his brother. Tancredi received his laureate in agronomy and oenology from the University of Pisa, and after dividing with his brother, kept Il Greppo and, with great foresight, did not drink the ageing bottles of Brunello reposing in the sancta sanctorum. Tancredi lived in hard times. He was wounded in the First World War, then followed the depression, and his vineyards were devastated by phylloxera. I pick up a black-and-white photo of Tancredi standing in a piazza in Montalcino supervising the loading on to a truck of a shipment of Brunello bound for America, and the date transfixes me. It was photographed in 1932. The Ingegnere claims that all the wine that was sold under the Biondi Santi label between 1925 and 1936 came from Padelletti grapes grown at Canalicchio; and in any case, weren't Tancredi's vines devastated by phylloxera?

Tancredi clashed with other grower families – or they clashed with him – differences of opinion about the right to call their wine Brunello, as well as claims to its creation, were at the crux of lingering bad feeling. But it is significant that nobody among the lot of them thought to, or were able to, take out a patent on the word Brunello. Tancredi went on to produce marvellous wines – there is no doubt about his winemaking skill when one glances through the prestigious success of Biondi Santi Brunello. The name Biondi Santi stands tall among Versace, Ferragamo, Alessi and Ferrari – symbols of Italian primacy in design and manufacture, whether it be a fancy dress, a fast car or a fabled wine. Wine Spectator, sending legendary fame Tancredi's way, has pronounced Brunello Reserve Il Greppo Biondi Santi, from the 1955 vintage, to be one of the twelve greatest wines of the last century. The choice dozen included sublime wines like Château Margaux and Château Rothschild, Romanèe Conti, Penfolds Grange Hermitage and Heitz Cabernet Napa Valley – a stunning international line-up, and the criteria was not price or star ratings, but rather, wines that have made a difference, stood the test of time and exemplify their type and country of origin. The Brunello was forty-four years old when they tasted an explosive, elegant and powerful wine with depth and complexity; eight hundred or so bottles of Tancredi's 1955 sit in the sancta sanctorum evolving into mythical greatness, because the gurus predict it will comfortably reach a hundred years of age.

Signor Franco, Tancredi's son, is a traditionalist and now dwells at Il Greppo and makes the wine along with his own son, Jacapo. In this age of mass media exposure and international travel he carries forward the Biondi Santi name, guarding his heritage, and that of Ferruccio and Tancredi, unquestionably exceptional winemakers. These days Signor Franco and his son are clashing with the Minister for Agriculture about a sub-zone denomination to differentiate their Brunello, a move which would, if successful, further alienate Biondi Santi.

The longevity of Biondi Santi Brunello *is* extraordinary. What is it that accounts for this wine's capacity to age for more than a hundred years? Is it Biondi Santi first root stock primatura vines, is it the terra at Il Greppo, or is it because they are the fortunate ones to have conserved so many ancient bottles? Perhaps future decades will tell us if other growers can imitate their success. Tucking my notes into my bag for further study, with a smile on my face I scan a recent newspaper report. When Stefano Colombini first threatened to withdraw from the Consorzio, several reports like this one scotched rumours, denying that Biondi Santi would now join. Tancredi's bitter words, spoken in the 1960s, have stood firm for nearly forty years. Tancredi said: I have no doubt that the Consorzio has more need of Biondi Santi than Biondi Santi has need of the Consorzio. A discreet number of months have passed. Are we witnessing a historic shuffle? The unraveling of a one-hundred-year-old power struggle between elite families? On the closing day of Benvenuto Brunello, nodding heads in the piazza confirmed tantalizing words in the morning paper: Tenuta il Greppo, symbol of Brunello around the world, has entered the Consorzio del Vino Brunello. Signor Biondi Santi has come into the fold.

The red fire engine will creep into the piazza at six o'clock this evening. Our mayor has invited all citizens to witness the ceremony to unveil the architect's plans for a staircase in the bell tower, and the bucket on the end of the telescopic ladder will carry two firemen, one of whom is Massimo, Pianello's archer, to the belfry. The bucket will then be lowered so that the mayor can be hoisted into the sky. He, being Citizen Number One, will be the first for many decades to look over the hills of Tuscany from the very top of our twelfth-century bell tower. No civic-minded citizen will want to miss this appointment.

Dressed for passeggiata, agreeing to meet Luigi in the piazza, I have three hours to search for the answer to the enigma that surrounds Brunello di Montalcino. For two afternoons I sat on a bench under the trees near the Madonna, looking over the hills where every sunny day the earth blushes greener and contours change infinitesimally. Hidden seeds have awakened in damp earth and, warmed by a gentle sun, shoot luscious emerald spires across a patchwork of diamonds and squares and triangles that grow taller and stronger. Soon the ranks will pack tightly, united in strength, and the slightest puff of wind will quiver the tips and a carpet will swish and sway in fluid symphony over the hills. It is the dance of another spring.

But today, needing time to be by myself, I have decided not to sit. I planned my route: from the lower track below the Madonna I will walk past the fortress and out of the village, visit the cemetery, walk on into the hills and take a fork along a gravel track among the vineyards. When, after a couple of kilometres, I emerge on the sealed road I will be close to the Etruscan dig, where I will sit among the stones and eat tangerines from my backpack, which also conceals a change of shoes. A thirty-minute walk will return me to the fortress so that, if my timing is right, I will be in the piazza at six o'clock. I am loath to miss the mayor's ceremony.

Plots are finely raked for the first planting, which, judging by the hilly ridges and gullies and grey ash spreading across the garden below the wall, will be beds of purple onions. A man tends a fire beside the last olive grove along the track sending smoke spiralling into a blue sky. The delicious scent of crackling wood drifts into my face. He is a village farmer who cannot forsake his contadino roots. The demarcation between cittadini and contadini is blurred, especially in spring, when there is a rush of activity in the gardens. Cittadini were identifiable by privileged education, and lived in grand houses, with their own well for washing whites. Independent artisans and merchants, too, lived in comfortable homes, often two storeys with a workshop or storefront opening to the roadway, from which they traded baskets, or shoes, or ropes. Employed workers and their families lived in just one or two rooms, a basic existence, but they had a wage. Over time, woodcutters and carbonai have risen into cittadini class and merged into the village; the misery of their lives has transmogrified into a symbol of endurance, bringing pride and honour to a life in the woods that was, in reality, one of dreadful hardship and social rejection.

Pulling a tissue from my pocket, I rub Silena's guardian angel, polishing the white marble, and bend to pull a tuft of grass from between the stones along the ground in front of Bruno. Someone is looking after the miniature roses; a trickle of water has left a line across the path. I do not know if dear Amelia will come back before Easter, although she sounds well enough when we talk.

One day she will be laid in the empty slot in the wall next to Bruno, but this prospect no longer fills me with dread. It is part of the relentless rhythm. There is nobody else lamenting the souls of the dead at this early afternoon hour. A smile to Bruno and I skip down the steps, content to have passed a few minutes with my old friend.

The gravel road forks between vines and woods, skirting olive groves and farmhouses and just in case I need to look menacing, I pick up a long stick. I have not forgotten the stand-off months ago when my approach maddened three dogs who came tearing through the trees barking at my bold intrusion. There are no grand villas out this way, but plenty of recently restored stone farmhouses that were left unplumbed and crumbling when the padrone abandoned the land and scuttled to the cities. The landowners, mostly title-less Sienese who owned vast tracts of land, seem to me to have been an elite in the sense that their ancestors were of noble lineage, but they were stripped of the status of Noble Sienese. They did not possess cash wealth, but they possessed the poor contadini, who were excluded from the village by closed doors – physically and socially. But then the women wanted to shop, to see each other every day and gossip! So says the Ingegnere, at any rate, and the contadini began the struggle for social acceptability. The landowning elite, not all of them, but for the most part, vanished. From vague points in the past I detect a blurring of noble lineage among elitist families that seems to take interesting diversions of convenience in the ebb and flow of generations. Once the last war was over some of the landowning families came back, but they never regained elite status because the scene had shifted, the boundaries of elitism among social classes changed, and a curious social game developed. There *is* uneasiness and enmity within a social structure that, as Montalcino flexed its economic muscles, reinvented itself and turned upside-down in a world of its own making, far removed from the passions and scandals of clashing aristocracy. Who would have had the perspicacity to imagine that a poor agricultural village in the hills of Tuscany was destined to produce a mythical wine and become a household name around the world?

Looking back from the top of a rise before I turn and descend into a valley, the rear of the church of the Madonna is just visible on the end of the ridge on which Montalcino sits. My footsteps crunch along the road, but tufts of weeds grow around the stones, cushioning my steps; walking in a trance, it is as well no yapping dogs charge from the farms – they would startle me before I had the chance to bluff them with my stick. The last downward slope brings me to the sealed road and, jumping across a ditch to safety when cars and trucks whiz by, in ten minutes I cover the distance to the dig. The excavation is not open, but when archaeological students come back in May, along with Professor Donati, the campaign for this year is to navigate a route through the brambly woods along which a walking trail can be built, and then the Etruscan fortress at Montalcino will be ready for visitors. Last year Professor Donati walked me through a rough circuit of his outlined trail. In that dense no man's land, pushing bodily through tangles of bramble and undergrowth with feet slipping to who knows where on mossy boulders and stumps, he was totally absorbed in his own enthusiasm; he was wearing mountain boots, but I was not. He dived under and jumped over and careered through everything in his path. Peeling tangerines among my friends the Etruscans reminds me of that fearful trek.

From what I can see, through a welter of inconsistencies, the earliest claim to do with identifying Brunello derives from the

Colombini, who believe that the Padelletti presented Brunello in wine exhibitions before 1850 – but I have seen no documentary evidence for this. A newspaper report alerted me to a date of 1842 for a Colombini family medal for Brunello, which, in the end, I must conclude turns out to be an editing error – La Signora Colombini alluded to no such medal, nor that date. The medal was for Raffaello Padelletti and was awarded in 1892, coming into the possession of the Colombini through matriarchal descent after Raffaello's daughter married into their family. On the other hand, hanging on the wall in Count Andrea Costanti's villa is a document naming four Montalcino families who entered a wine called Brunello in an exposition in Siena from the harvest of 1865: Costanti, Tamanti, Anghirelli (of whom I have discovered no trace) and Santi. In the back of my mind I sense an inconsistency here, one I cannot account for and which displeases me. Ferruccio Biondi was born around 1849 and that means that when Count Costanti and the others were exhibiting a wine they called Brunello, Ferruccio could not have been more than a sixteen-year-old boy. And if the notations I jotted down when I was at the villa are to be believed, Ferruccio experimented with clones of sangiovese around 1870, when he was barely twenty-one. I find it hard to reconcile Ferruccio carrying out scientific grafting experiments, identifying and selecting a clone of sangiovese grosso with which to create a wine, when he was but a lad and apparently, significantly, had no university or agricultural laureate behind him. Material evidence of existing bottles, labelled, in the sancta sanctorum of Biondi Santi dated 1888 when Ferruccio was around thirty-nine years old, is compelling, but that was twenty-three years after the identification of Brunello in the Costanti document and does not exclude the possibility that others were making Brunello in those intervening decades, for they cannot have been twiddling thumbs, and anyway, they were most definitely not contadini. Raffaello Padelletti's prize-winning bottle of 1892 is only a few years later.

Much hinges, for the Colombini family, on Raffaello Padelletti and Riccardo Paccagnini, who are not on the list hanging on Andrea Costanti's wall – but it would be perilous indeed to underestimate those brilliant men. Both of those ancient families united in marriage with the Colombini, bringing their brilliance as well as wealth and heritage in their baggage. A cloud confuses the sunbeams here and there; for instance, where would Ferruccio Biondi be without the Ingegnere's father, Carlo Padelletti, who responded to a father's plea for help? And later, Carlo paid Tancredi Biondi a stipend and helped him back on his feet financially. Even cittadino Enzo, below the wall, from whom I have learned much about this wine, is growing Brunello on land that he bought from descendants of the brilliant oenologist Riccardo Paccagnini, whose mother was a Padelletti, land on which the great oenologist himself grew wine. And the Castello, too, in the middle of a splendid international family vineyard owned by the Mariani brothers, Banfi, set in glorious hills with rows of vines, was in centuries past part of the wealth of the family Colombini.

Undoubtedly because of awesome material evidence in the sancta sanctorum, Franco Biondi Santi has had open to him the way to fame in a mass media world, but is that lofty view an overindulgence? A bottle speaks louder than words. It is no small thing to have Ferruccio's wine in the cantina, more than a hundred years old, and deliciously drinkable – and to have Tancredi's Brunello honoured as one of the twelve greatest wines of the last century. And whether Carlo Padelletti helped Ferruccio and got Tancredi back on his feet or not, and whether

Biondi Santi wine made between 1925 and 1936 was made from Padelletti grapes from Canalicchio or not, and whether nobility can be proven and whether the uniting of Biondi and Santi offends some or not, material evidence *is* undeniable. But it is not definitive; the time lapse from the undocumented experimentation and creation of Brunello, until 1888, is too great, and the span of years from 1888 to 1892 is too little. And the birth date of Ferruccio Biondi, as I overheard in the bar a few days ago, although he has been credited with so much for which he wrote not a word of explanation, does not add up.

Tamanti, Colombini, Padelletti, Biondi Santi, Costanti, Paccagnini; they *all* created Brunello, didn't they? That's the way I see it. Poking about in the muddle I am struggling to reconcile fact, fiction and fable. The creation and identity of Brunello is not wrapped up in one story. But there are some certainties. One is that the contadini are in every bottle that leaves this territory. When it all began nearly a hundred and fifty years ago, grindingly poor, they worked the land for elite families, and now they grow Brunello on land that is their own. And the cittadini, who never abandoned this hill to greedy Sienese or despotic Florentines, and whose footsteps clatter still along the cobbles; they hold tightly to an Ilcinese culture, a sensibility to the earth they love, spilling their blood on the fortress battlements in defence of their liberty – they, too, are in every bottle, whether or not they grow a row of vines, or an onion patch, or gather for a gossip below the bell tower in the piazza, where they will be this very afternoon. And invaders from afar, like Banfi, who brought technical expertise, came not as colonizers, nor is that how they were viewed. Flapping millions of dollars, it was never feared that they might change the historical identity of Montalcino, much less the wine . . .

Tuscan roots in this land are too deep. Their invasion was positive, and, technically, their presence pushed the whole thing forwards. So, the invaders, too, are in every bottle. The once ennobled families, the landowners, among whom some may justifiably claim, by virtue of lineage, to be today's elite, collectively must *share* a place in every bottle. They did not work alongside one another, it was not a joint effort, and they did not pool scientific information; hence a span of more than a hundred years of tension and disharmony has led to an unwillingness by some to share the glory – instead, some covet the creation. There are many half truths and ambiguities, but there is no *one* truth; it was a choral symphony, playing out of tune, but without each other it could not have happened.

The creation of Brunello di Montalcino, in my opinion, was like a rolling stone, harnessing greatness as it bounced from one family to another, and as it bounced it gathered nobility because each of those families are joined in an intricate web of noble lineage, aristocratic land holdings, privileged education, inheritances that brought fortune, oenological brilliance, of marriage and alliances. Whether they perhaps like it or not, Brunello di Montalcino, born of their own past noble greatness, needed each one of them. Perhaps I am biased because I have grown so fond of the Ingegnere, but it seems to me that the family story of every one of them is woven, to a greater or lesser degree, into the incredible story of the intellectually elite Padelletti family. I am saddened that I have not heard one word, nor seen one bottle, of 1997 Brunello di Montalcino, nor any other vintage, made by the Gentlemen Padelletti. I have asked for it in the village, but it is not there. The real truth is that Brunello di Montalcino is more noble than any of its growers.

*

Behind me a car horn toot-toot-toots a friendly greeting. My arm rises in salutation as a white blur flashes past, but I do not look up; in front of my eyes is an imaginary chalice of ruby wine. Raising the glass I am dazzled by prisms of light sparkling like a string of diamonds. Swirling a river of wine around the glass reminds me that it has reached me on the arms of centuries of hard-working Tuscans, labouring on arid hills. Peering into dark rubies I see within its clarity their sensibility, pride and above all a hundred warm smiles. This chalice of wine has arrived in my hand through an extraordinary desire to grow something stupendous in a place where small and shabby things are unknown, whether it be a bed of purple onions or a cluster of purple grapes. Putting the wine under my nose I smell fragrant fruit and perfumed flowers, and tilled earth, and when it is on my lips I feel the sunbeams dancing. As crimson velvet trickles down inside my cheeks, exploding a myth inside my mouth, sending a thousand messages to my heart, I think of the defiant love of the Montalcinesi for this hill. The secret of Brunello *is* Montalcino.

A crowd hovers on the steps of the cappellone while others mill outside Fiaschetteria and Caffè alle Logge, where Ofelia and I stand. Roberto is on the step outside the doors of the pharmacy with adjoining shop keepers and Maurelia leans over the balcony above, waving to us to come up, but I want to hear what the mayor has to say, so we decline, waving back to Fabio who pokes his head from a window. His is not the only poking head. Those citizens whose good fortune it is to live around the piazza have cast open green shutters and chat to each other sill to sill, watching from their privileged viewpoints. 'Isabella,' Ofelia wants to know, 'when are we going to Venice?' Our sojourns the length and breadth of Italy are taking on the sacredness of a pilgrimage! Spouses passeggiata arm in arm, greeting friends, watching children playing tag. At this hour, citizens with homes along the road are eligible to drive through the piazza, but out of respect for the evening ceremony the road and piazza is closed to all vehicles and village polizia guard the way. Ciao and buonasera pass freely in a courteous rhythm; an atmosphere of animated liveliness pervades as we participate in this entertaining evening. Luigi is inside one of the bars with Giancarlo and Angelino, plotting the next championship.

Most citizens have come to terms with the mayor's initiative for a tower staircase, and even those less enamoured with the inevitable intrusion of visitors in their tower are here because there is need for proprietorial watchfulness, and besides, Ofelia confirms that Massimo says it is many years, a couple of decades, since anyone climbed to the belfry, so there is a heady tingle of anticipation.

The fire brigade's smart red engine manoeuvres up the barely wide enough road, hindered by the bucket and telescopic ladder folded along the top. The driver hangs half out the window, carefully gauging the proximity of stone balconies adorned with red geranium and colourful pansies and wires and cables looped across the road. Massimo and another fireman, whose name is Andrea, uniforms spick and span and encumbered by thigh-high black boots, clamber from the fire engine and, with safety procedures in mind, drape red and white ribbons from the truck to the corners of Palazzo Comunale, cordoning to ensure no children scamper beneath the telescopic ladder and swinging bucket, and, as the bronze bell in the tower can be seen to be lifting and working its way into its laborious metre-and-a-half sway, readying itself to toll the sixth hour, excitement in the piazza heightens. The bell's clapper slides around, gaining its liberty to bong just as the mayor, regally sashed in the red, white and green of his office, emerges from Fiaschetteria along with an architect carrying a roll of drawings under one arm. A spontaneous but not very audible murmur flutters from group to group, and a few hands clap when the sixth bong bongs. Eyes roll and sardonic laughs ricochet around the piazza because we all know the bell never sounds the hour with precise punctuality. Often the timer becomes confused and within a minute of the first round of bongs, a second round begins – but we are accustomed to the idiosyncrasies of *our* bell and understand its moods. The most striking hour of the day is mezzogiorno when the bronze bell rises into a frenzy and rings one hundred times, swinging from side to side in the belfry, resonating all over the village. I have it on reliable oath that so attached are the villagers to this bell that if an Ilcinese is called to work in Rome or Milan, the bonging mezzogiorno bells go with him. Imprisoned in some dingy office in a fog-bound city where all he hears and sees is traffic and confusion, on the stroke of twelve, at the press of a button, a tape recording of a hundred bongs from our bell fills his ears, staving off nostalgic wistfulness for blue skies and the hills of Tuscany!

As is the way in Montalcino, no citizens feel the need to move from the cappellone, or the bars, closer to the mayor. We stand about, or sit or kneel, loosely grouped, half listening to him tell us that this initiative will provide us and visitors, for the first time in its eight-hundred-year history, the unique opportunity to ascend the forty-metre medieval tower to the belfry and look over our breathtaking valley of vines and olives and woods and hills in every direction, with a totally new perspective. He elaborates on the design of a spiral staircase because, as we all know, the tower has never been accessible, having only a dangerously dilapidated wooden ramp inside and, decades ago, when last it was necessary to ascend the tower, the Comune was compelled to engage climbers who brought mountaineering gear and hair-raisingly ascended the tower using pikes and ropes. The staircase project, he promises, will begin within a week, fifteen days at the most.

Pronouncing the ceremony over, a few half-hearted claps end formalities, and a hum of muttering and chattering rises while we watch the mayor turn to Massimo and Andrea, shaking their hands as if it is they who have instigated proceedings, and the mayor, offering his open hands, gestures to the firemen that it is time for them to ascend so that, when the mayor is lofted high, they will be in the belfry to assist him from bucket to bell chamber. Massimo and Andrea strap on their helmets and step into the bucket and the ladder unfolds towards the sky. Past the windows of Palazzo Comunale they rise, past the clock face – which has not shown the correct time, nor have the hands moved, since I have lived in Montalcino – then they pass two little windows, diminishing in scale until they become black uniforms sailing forty metres high, level with the belfry. We watch two black shapes hoist each other over the wall and into the belfry, and the telescopic ladder begins to fold, lowering the bucket towards our radiant Mayor. The black dots in the sky vanish, circling the bell in the belfry, terrifying pigeons who coo and flutter, rising from their hitherto isolated and undisturbed roost in the sky.

'That looks like Massimo's broad shoulders leaning right out over the parapet,' I comment to Ofelia, straining to see. 'What's going on?' She senses something amiss. 'He looks agitated.' Massimo's arms are waving frantically, first signalling an upward motion, as if calling for the mayor, who has stepped into the bucket, then wiping out that frantic instruction by pushing his hands flatly side to side. A second black shape crowds round his shoulders and the firemen lean together over the belfry, cupping hands around their mouths and screaming out: 'Stay there! Signor Mayor, get *out* of the bucket! Send it straight back up here, subito! Immediately!' Agitated and bewildered, the mayor obeys, but Massimo and Andrea continue to wave their arms, frantically trying to relay a message to him.

This melodramatic spectacle is more entertaining than we anticipated; capturing everyone in the theatricality, we are spellbound staring from mayor to tower to waving firemen until, when the firemen clamber back into the bucket and it descends halfway, Massimo screams: 'Get *everybody* out of the piazza! Get the bambini away from the fire engine! The belfry pillars are cracked . . . the tower may collapse and topple into the piazza at any moment!' Half laughing and half screeching from fear and astonishment, scattering faster than the pigeons, we dart to the walls of homes and dive into the caffè and shops, grabbing children whose petrified mothers shriek shrilly from the safety of the cappellone. In three seconds the only person standing in the piazza is the mayor, who is mute, anchored to the spot, staring upwards at the bell tower in utter disbelief. Bumping the bucket to the ground and jumping out, Massimo grabs his shoulder and leads him to safety, out of reach of the menacing tower. 'It is absolutely horrendous,' he states, his ominous words terrifying the mayor, 'two wide lesions have cracked the pillars that support the weight of the bell in the belfry, and the pillars are crumbling. The risk is grave – if that bronze bell topples it will bring half the tower down with it, smashing right into the piazza!'

Italians call word of mouth passing the word by tam tam, and this news washes down the line at the speed of thumping tom toms. From shop to shop and bar to bar someone repeats Massimo's dire warning. 'There is not a moment to lose,' he instructs. 'I need the key to the tower. The timer must be switched off before the bell begins to sway for the half-past-six bongs; the vibration of the swinging bell has aggravated catastrophic damage to our tower.' The key is produced and handed over, sending the firemen high tailing into Palazzo Comunale. The mayor is desolate, his face grey, and he knows not what to say. Ilcinesi, ever ready with a battuta, a verbal counterattack, are quick to sum up the consequences. 'Allora! The bell in our tower has spoken. In Montalcino time will pass no more. We are stuck in the past!'

The mayor, at last steadying his mind and resigning himself to the gravity of the situation, and a ceremony gone terribly wrong, adjusts his sash, and his stance, and with a harrumph, clears his throat to deliver the ultimate proclamation. 'We may not hear our bell for many months. It is a daily symbol of the rhythm of life in our village and will be dreadfully missed, but there is no time to lose and I have given the order, we must stop our bell from ringing. But we will gather all of our resources, we will unite our efforts to raise money for repairs because our defiance, the blood of our ancestors and our liberty to dwell on our hill are symbolized when that bell rings from our ancient tower. Somehow, no matter what it takes, I promise that we will save our bell and tower.'

Friends of San Pietro

Dear Reader,

We contemplate many years of work to restore the Church of San Pietro. Initially we are compelled to arrest damage and protect the structure, and our altar, from further deterioration.

Fundraising ideas are co-ordinated by our Pianello committee, Amici di San Pietro. If you would like to contribute we invite you to become a Friend of San Pietro, and we offer you the unique opportunity to take up Honorary Membership of Quartiere Pianello.

Your contribution, large or small, will be acknowledged in a special way, and your family name can be permanently recorded in San Pietro.

For more about Pianello visit: www.montalcino-tuscany.it
For more about Montalcino visit: www.montalcino-tuscany.com

You are invited to send your donation to:
Il Presidente
Quartiere Pianello
Via delle Scuole
53024 Montalcino (SI) Italia

To deposit into the fundraising account email: isabelladusi@tin.it

We thank you for your support and generosity.

Amici di San Pietro
Quartiere Pianello
Montalcino
Italia

Consorzio del Vino Brunello di Montalcino

Vintage Evaluation

Insufficient to evaluate	*
Fair vintage	**
Good vintage	***
Excellent vintage	****
Outstanding vintage	*****

Year	Rating	Year	Rating
1945	*****	1990	*****
1955	*****	1991	****
1961	*****	1992	**
1964	*****	1993	****
1970	*****	1994	****
1975	*****	1995	*****
1985	*****	1996	***
1988	*****	1997	*****
		1998	****
		1999	****
		2000	***
		2001	****
		2002	**

For more information, visit www.consorziobrunellodimontalcino.com

Glossary

About Montalcino

Comune	Town council
Ilcinese	Person born on the hill of Montalcino
Ilcinesi	Plural
Montalcinese	A citizen of Montalcino
Montalcinesi	Plural
Palazzo Comunale	Equivalent to Town Hall or Village Hall
Quartierante	A member of a quarter, a supporter
Quartieranti	Plural
Quartieri	One quarter, or neighbourhood, of Montalcino
Quartiere	Plural
Sagra	Festival
Sagre	Plural
Sagra del Tordo	Festival of the Thrush – the annual festival traditionally associated with hunting migratory thrushes
Travaglio, Borghetto, Pianello, Ruga	The names of the four quarters, or neighbourhoods

Italian Words and Phrases

Affettati	Sliced cold meats
Altrettanto	The same to you
Alimentari	Grocery shop
Ape	Three-wheeler motorized work vehicle with rear tray
Babbo	Dad, daddy
Banditore	Town crier
Bella figura	A good impression
Benessere	Well-being
Biblioteca	Library
Boscaiolo	Woodman
Boschettiere	Thrush hunter, using traps rather than guns
Brutta figura	A bad impression
Calzolaio	Shoemaker
Cameriere	Waiter
Campanile	Bell tower
Campo	Firing range for archery tournaments
Cantina	Ground or underground level of a house used for storage of wine, etc.
Capitano del Arcieri	Captain of an archery squad
Capocuoco	Head cook
Cara	Dear, feminine
Carbonaio	Charcoal burner
Carbonai	Plural
Carbonaia	Carbon burner's kiln
Caro	Dear, masculine
Cava	Quarry
Cinghiale	Wild boar

Cittadino	Village dweller and citizen
Cittadini	Plural
Contadino	A land worker in the countryside
Contadini	Plural
Dottore	Doctor, or learned person in general
Enoteca	Wine shop
Fornellino	Tiny burner for heating wax
Frantoio	Mill where olives are crushed
Ganzo	Expression of joy or surprise, e.g. Great!
Gentiluomini	Gentleman
Hectare (ettaro)	One hectare = approximately 2.2 acres
Ingegnere	Engineer – professional title
Intanto	In any event, anyhow
Lesina	Hooked tool for pulling bristles or thread through leather
Magari	Expression of agreement, e.g. You bet!
Mancino	Left handed or left footed
Merenda	Snack
Mezzadria	Medieval farming practice whereby the peasant was forced to give half the fruits of his labour to the landowner who provided whatever the peasant needed to make the land produce
Mezzanotte	Midnight
Mezzogiorno	Midday
Nobile Senese	Nobility living in Sienese territory
Nonna	Grandmother
Nonno	Grandfather
Padrone	Boss – landowner who controlled the farm and the contadini

Panini	Bread rolls
Passeggiata	Social ritual of strolling around greeting friends
Pentolone	A big pot or cauldron
Piazza	Communal square or gathering place
Piazzetta	Small square
Piccolo Maestro	Master painter, but not necessarily of the first rank
Pizzaioli	Pizza makers
Ponte	Bridge
Pranzo	Lunch
Quindicina	Period of fifteen days
Ragazzi	Young people – males, or males and females
Sede	Headquarters of a quartiere
Sotto fattore	Under foreman
Stranieri	Strangers, outsiders
Temporale	Thunder and lightning storm
Tifosi	Fans or supporters – e.g. at football games
Tordo	Thrush
Tutti	Everyone
Vecchietta	Old woman
Vecchietto	Old man
Venerdì Santo	Good Friday
Zitto	Quiet